ATLAS *of the* BRITISH EMPIRE

ATLAS
of the
BRITISH
EMPIRE

☑ Facts On File
New York • Oxford

DVISEVRGI CLIVORVM

ATLAS OF THE BRITISH EMPIRE

Copyright © 1989 The Hamlyn Publishing Group Ltd/Amazon Ltd

Facts On File, Inc.
460 Park Avenue South
New York NY 10016
USA

Facts On File books are available at special discounts when purchased in bulk quantities for businesses, associations, institutions or sales promotion. Please contact the Special Sales Department of our New York office at 212/683-2244 (dial 800/322-8755 except in NY, AK or HI).

Composition by Florencetype Ltd, Kewstoke, Avon, UK.
Manufactured by Graficas Reunidas, Madrid
Printed in Spain

10 9 8 7 6 5 4 3 2 1

This book is printed on acid-free paper.

Edited and designed by Toucan Books Limited, London
Publishing Director: Robert Sackville West
Art Editor: John Meek
Editorial Director: Adam Nicolson
Project Editor: Catherine Bradley
Picture Researchers: Christine Vincent, Diana Phillips

CONTRIBUTORS

EDITOR: **Dr C.A. Bayly**
Reader in Modern History, University of Cambridge and Fellow of St Catharine's College, Cambridge

CONTRIBUTORS:

Dr Alan Atkinson
Senior Lecturer in History, University of New England, New South Wales

Dr John Belshaw
Lecturer in Canadian History, Simon Fraser University, British Columbia

Dr Carl Bridge
Visiting Lecturer in Australian Studies, Institute of Commonwealth Studies, University of London, and Senior Lecturer in History, University of New England, New South Wales

Dr John Darwin
Beit Lecturer in the History of the British Commonwealth, Nuffield College, Oxford

Dr Robert Holland
Lecturer in Commonwealth History, Institute of Commonwealth Studies, University of London

Professor T.O. Lloyd
Professor of History, University of Toronto

Dr John Lonsdale
Lecturer in History, University of Cambridge, and Fellow of Trinity College, Cambridge

Dr Hiram Morgan
British Academy Post-Doctoral Research Fellow, Queen's University, Belfast

Dr Richard Rathbone
Lecturer in African History, School of Oriental and African Studies, University of London

Professor Michael Roe
Professor of History, University of Tasmania

Dr Anthony Stockwell
Senior Lecturer in British History, Royal Holloway and Bedford New College, University of London

Dr B.R. Tomlinson
Senior Lecturer in Economic History, University of Birmingham

Professor Glyndr Williams
Professor of Imperial and Maritime History, Queen Mary College, University of London

CONTENTS

————◇————

FOREWORD

———————◇———————

'REVOLUTIONS devour their children; Nationalism eats its parents'. This, a famous examination question of Cambridge History some years ago, was a remark made by one of our most distinguished imperial historians, Jack Gallagher, a Liverpudlian Irishman of magnificent colourfulness who held the Chair of Imperial History at Cambridge until his tragically early death in 1980. He, with Ronald Robinson (who held the equivalent Chair at Oxford) wrote a celebrated book, *Africa and the Victorians*, which annoyed all of the right people. To this day, three decades after the book's appearance, people solemnly sit down and say that it is *all wrong*. But there must be something right about a book which goes on stimulating arguments: and Jack Gallagher would have been very pleased by this outcome.

He would also have been pleased, and not surprised, that his influence lives on most splendidly among today's historians of the British Empire, of whom the editor of this present volume, Christopher Bayly, is a distinguished representative. I have read this encyclopaedic and excellently illustrated work with great pleasure and profit. It covers a huge subject. The British Empire, from its beginnings in the sixteenth century until its end in the middle of the twentieth, is a vast affair, covering one-quarter of the world's land surface, and occupying a central place in the history of the world. You do not even stop at those areas which the British formally annexed. As Jack Gallagher pointed out, 'informal empire' was, for much of the time, more important than 'formal empire': in other words, the dominance exercised by British trade and influence on areas not taken over by the British Crown (Latin America and China) was really as important, in the first half of the nineteenth century, as the formal empire imposed on Africa and India, or the self-governing Dominions. In fact, Gallagher himself did not have much regard for the formal empire established in Africa: in another characteristic phrase, he dismissed the European conquests there as 'gimcrack empires, spatch-cocked together', and he was not surprised that 'de-colonization' offered headaches all round.

From today's perspective, the British Empire is now, for the Euro-British, quite remote: or as Proust said of history, about as relevant as the bits of egg-shell which a chicken contemplates when it is hatched. Looking round today's Britain, you wonder how on earth we acquired our notion, current in 1900, that we were the successors of the Roman Empire. We are the last of the anciens régimes, in

the sense that we never had an Enlightenment in the eighteenth century, let alone a Napoleonic Revolution, which would have turfed ancient lawbooks into the Thames, disestablished the Church (using its head, as Napoleon did, as furniture for his fair-ground coronation) and divided the country into rectangular blocks, called departments. Richard Cobb, my predecessor in Oxford's Chair of Modern History, and also a close friend of Jack Gallagher's, has a fantasy as to what would have happened had we lost the Battle of Trafalgar: Oxfordshire would have become the *département de la Haute Tamise*, swaggering Gascons would have stabled their horses in the Colleges, and the last Hanoverian would have been strangled with the guts of the last bishop.

But the fact is: we won Trafalgar. The British ancien régime, in many ways still unreformed, proved more resilient than would-be rationalized Continental systems. Not only that: it proved to have a political skill which left an extraordinary mark on the world as a whole, and led to the worldwide (and often regrettable) domination of versions of the English language, once a far-flung Germanic creole. The influence of grammar-obsessed ecclesiastics upon the language was far weaker than that of simple traders and warriors, who reduced the linguistic complexities in order to make themselves understood by their counterparts from across the seas. Nowadays, distinguished English literature is written by authors who, in many cases, have seldom come to this country at all: one of the most distinguished books of this century, in my opinion, is Nirad C. Chaudhuri's *Thy Hand! Great Anarch* (1987) – the autobiography of a one-time Bengali nationalist, a love-hater of the British. At a great age, Chaudhuri records his lament at the decline, together, of the British Empire in India and the Bengal that was once its greatest challenge. The book is written with an outsider's perspective on the values and the power of the British presence. Its author understands that British rule depended not so much on machine-guns and policemen as upon a mystique, which had a subconscious, almost operatic appeal rather than a purely rational one.

Just the same, the government offered by the British abroad stood at some distance from the nature of the government offered at home. Overseas, it is almost as if the reforming energies of the British Isles were offered a compensation and field of action all the greater for their frustration at home. The philosophical radicals of the middle decades of the nineteenth century devised 'good government' for much of Australia (here splendidly described) and built nineteenth-century cities which stand (in my opinion, with Glasgow and Pest) as the best of the genre: planned, disease-free, and with magnificent buildings in which everyone, from developer to decorative-artisan, co-operated in an enterprise of great significance. Systems of education were devised, abroad, and usually by Scottish Protestants, which made up for the woeful inadequacies of the system at home. To this day, the role of the minority peoples of the British Empire – Australians, Scots, and, *mutatis mutandis*, Barbadians and New Zealanders – is quite disproportionate to their numbers. It is almost as if the non-conformist consciousness found a field-day for itself abroad, where at home it was sometimes oppressed and 'marginalized'.

In seventeenth-century Europe the north-western, Protestant countries 'took off' in the direction of 'capitalism' and empire whereas the once-proud southern, Mediterranean, Catholic element declined. What did this have to do with Protestantism? It is a good question, still not really answered. The non-conformist and specifically Calvinist element in the creation of capitalism and empire does deserve stress; it is notable in the history of the British Empire how, again and again, the Scots surface. They do so in Ireland, in India, in a variety of military, money-making, statistics-collecting, drain-making and railway-building roles. They make Canada and much of Australia, and virtually all of New Zealand. They are well to the fore in South Africa.

Here, they are in some contrast to other low-church Protestants. That set of values, often utterly admirable, was not usually very adaptable to overseas empires. The Dutch, for instance, had a moment of glory in the seventeenth century, as did the Swedes. But their kind of rigidity and devotion to rules, highly effective in the short run, tended towards lack of imagination and, ultimately, to self-destruction. Scottish energy and resilience needed to be associated with a particularly English, and perhaps even Anglican, concern for wider matters, and an appeal to the imagination.

Great Britain herself, in the eighteenth century, was a remarkable combination of different elements – brought together in that century, for the first time, in an astonishing and uneasy synthesis of elements. There *was* social mobility at home, and a rule of law which guaranteed property in a way that other European countries did not know. On the other hand, there was a class-structure which made life quite difficult at home if you wanted to climb up the ladder. Time and again, you find the brightest elements in the British Isles going abroad in order to achieve a proper status at home – from the Pilgrim Fathers who departed in the *Mayflower* in 1620, through the 'Nabobs' who amassed fortunes in India, to the 'colonials' whose return to Edwardian London made the running for Edwardian 'plutocracy'. There were some ugly moments in all of this; and, for generations in the nineteenth century, there was a nasty smugness and hypocrisy about Empire, to which Thomas Carlyle memorably called attention. British Liberalism at home was open to the reproach that it was financed by coolie labour; the great Gladstone himself, high-minded Anglican and doer of universal good, was the grandson of a rascally Lowland-Scottish slave trader. We have left some nasty legacies, particularly in Northern Ireland and South Africa, which remain to plague the world. Just the same, our manner of leaving the British Empire says much for our sense of fair play and humanity. My own generation in France faced endless, pointless wars, the outcome of which was always foreseeable. In this country, we were spared that nightmare even if, sadly, we passed it on to the successor-régimes.

In Oxford, we are still surrounded by the relics of empire. This university was built up, around the turn of the century, to be *the* imperial university; we still receive great numbers of people from all corners of the globe, and the very cosmopolitan society which results does work rather well. On the other hand, we should never forget, in this country, that many of our institutions were not 'modernized' precisely because their rickety wheels and cogs were turned by a great flow of money from abroad. Now, it is no longer the case. We are left with a still-functioning ancien-régime, onto which rather haphazard war-time socialist arrangements were tacked, and, because of imperial profits, we never really looked hard enough at the experience of less-fortunate European countries where, long before, intelligent people looked at the right ways for a European country to function. In this book, the British Empire has been magnificently recorded. Its message? In my opinion, that we should govern ourselves with the same intelligence that we once applied to the rest of the world. Let Great Britain become the last Dominion.

Norman Stone
Oxford, May 1989

ESKIMO

CREE

SIOUX

SHOSHONE

MICMAC

IROQUOIS

HURON

SUSQUEHANNOCK

POWHATAN

APACHE

Tenochtitlán

AZTEC
EMPIRE

MAYA

ISLAND
ARAWAK

CARIB

AMAZONIAN
INDIANS

INCA
EMPIRE

Cuzco

ARAUCANIAN

SWEDEN

SCOTLAND

IRELAND

ENGLAND

POLAND

GERMAN
STATES

FRANCE

HABSBURG
AUSTRIA

Venice

ITALIAN
STATES

HABSBURG
SPAIN

PORTUGAL

Tunis

TUNISIA

Marrakesh

ALGERIA
(OTTOMAN 1537)

Timbuktu

KANEM
BORNO

MALI EMPIRE

HAUSA
STATES

KONGO

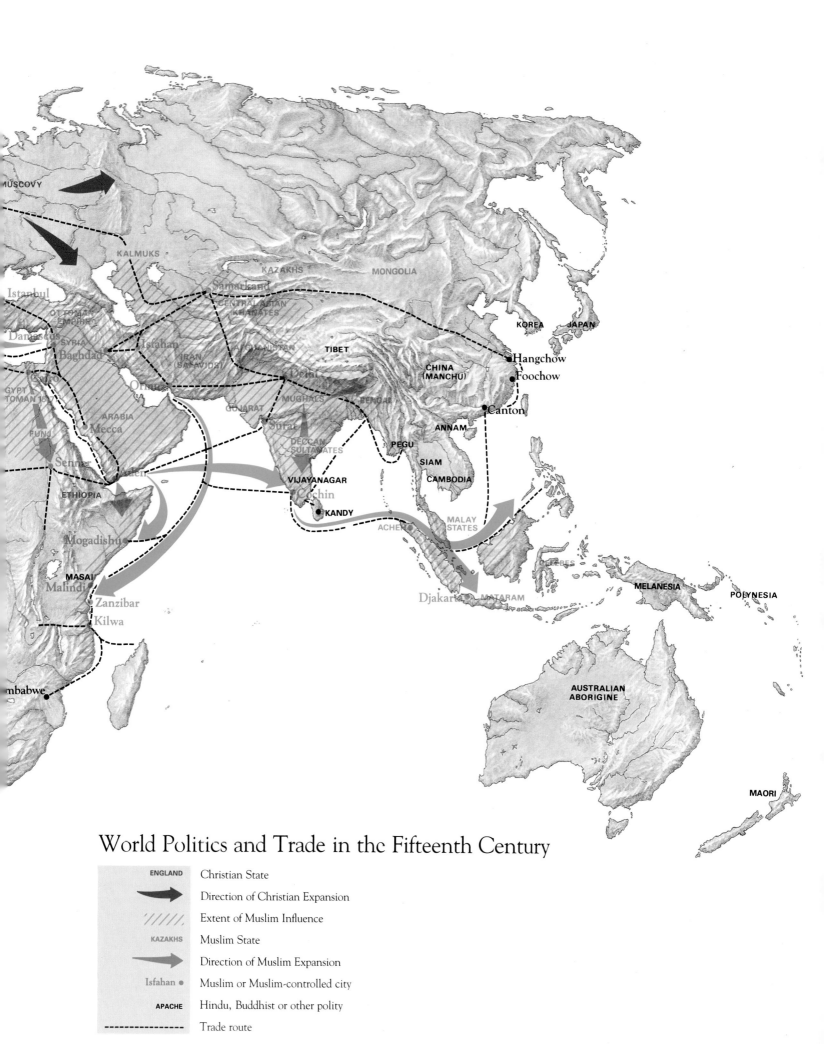

World Politics and Trade in the Fifteenth Century

ENGLAND	Christian State
➡	Direction of Christian Expansion
/////	Extent of Muslim Influence
KAZAKHS	Muslim State
➡	Direction of Muslim Expansion
Isfahan ●	Muslim or Muslim-controlled city
APACHE	Hindu, Buddhist or other polity
- - - - -	Trade route

MUSCOVY
Istanbul
OTTOMAN EMPIRE
Damascus
SYRIA
Baghdad
EGYPT
OTTOMAN 151?
ARABIA
Mecca
FUNJ
Senna
Aden
ETHIOPIA
Mogadishu
MASAI
Malindi
Zanzibar
Kilwa
mbabwe

KALMUKS
KAZAKHS
MONGOLIA
Samarkand
CENTRAL ASIAN KHANATES
Isfahan
IRAN (SAFAVIDS)
AFGHANISTAN
TIBET
Ormuz
Delhi
GUJARAT
MUGHALS
Surat
BENGAL
DECCAN SULTANATES
VIJAYANAGAR
Cochin
KANDY
PEGU
SIAM
CAMBODIA
ANNAM
CHINA (MANCHU)
KOREA
JAPAN
Hangchow
Foochow
Canton
MALAY STATES
ACHEH
CELEBES
Djakarta
MATARAM
MELANESIA
POLYNESIA
AUSTRALIAN ABORIGINE
MAORI

INTRODUCTION

◇

Among the many events designed to celebrate Queen Victoria's Jubilee in 1887, the Society for the Propagation of Christian Knowledge published *The Jubilee Atlas of the British Empire*. Its editors credited our precursor with grandiose aims: 'By thus diffusing a more general knowledge of the World's Greatest Empire, it will hasten in some degree the accomplishment of the one condition necessary to its stability and permanence – that is, the Union of the United Kingdom and its Colonies and Dependencies throughout the World into a Federated British Empire.' In short, the British Empire was to become mankind's first world-state, an aim that even the most idealistic of the founders of the future United Nations were to forswear.

A hundred years later, sentiments of this kind seem to hail from another millennium rather than from the last century. True, the Commonwealth continues to exist, shorn of its adjective 'British'; but the axis of world history has shifted so far that even the bonds of kin and sentiment between members of what used to be called the 'white Commonwealth' are increasingly frayed. India, the old centre of the Oriental British Empire, is now a massive, poor, but industrializing power centre within Asia: a leader of non-aligned opinion, she is now not only a major trading partner but is also often politically aligned with that ancient enemy of the British Asian Empire, the 'Russian Colossus' beyond the Hindu Kush.

In 1988 Australia celebrated the Bicentenary of its foundation as a British penal colony. During these celebrations, the British connection was often eclipsed by a new-found interest in the country's Irish, Asian and, not least, Aboriginal roots. Meanwhile, South Africa continues to play out the end-game of a fierce war of land and race. It is a drama which – although the British had once played a significant role – found its deeper origins as long as a hundred and fifty years before the Union Flag was first raised on the Cape, in the conflict between Dutch farmers and African pastoralists.

Most stiking of all has been Britain's own trajectory over this century. It is a country still littered with institutions and ideas which go back to the Empire. London today is perhaps more polyglot and multicultural than ever it was in its days as 'Capital of the Greatest Empire the World has ever known'. But the economic and political future of Britain lies in an association with Continental Europe as it waits for the completion of the single European market in 1992: an association that is closer than anything that has existed since the French wars of the Plantagenet kings. England now finds herself again in the position that she occupied in the early years of Queen Elizabeth's reign, before the great onrush of colonial expansion. Once again England is a struggling economy on the northern fringes of Europe, hoping to exploit divisions among her powerful neighbours on the Continent but saddled, as she was then, with a restive Scotland and conflict in Ireland.

What then is the merit of an *Atlas of the British Empire* in the late twentieth century? Is such a project not in danger of perpetuating a chauvinistic and sentimental view of British history? The answer is a resolute no. This atlas has been organized not only to show the rise and subsequent decline of British dominance but also to analyse and map the evolution of the states and peoples of the modern world as they interacted, traded and fought with the British over four hundred years.

A View from the Colonies

This shift in perspective is appropriate not only because it reinforces the relevance of the British Empire to the evolution of today's political and economic order; it also mirrors the point of view of professional historians who have increasingly considered the circumstances of the colonies themselves in explaining the evolution of Empire. Of course, the very word 'empire' still conjures up centralization, hierarchy and the rapid deployment of force against dissent. Yet the greater part of the history of the British Empire was forged by 'the man on the spot'. Indeed, the imperial centre – more often than not distracted by domestic and European events – usually came into the picture only to reconcile or rubber-stamp events which had already taken place on the periphery. Schemes of central imperial planning were not taken very seriously by the British Cabinet; they were hobbies for wet country-house weekends.

The hardy imperial pioneer, the missionary, the district officer and the entrepreneur imbued with 'Victorian values'; all of these have long been key figures in school books and in British national mythology. This atlas pays greater attention, however, to the less celebrated among them, to individuals of a more obscure pedigree. The Empire was created and ultimately upheld by force. But it was maintained, serviced and formed by a range of middlemen who mediated between tiny colonial garrisons or administrations and local society. The machinery of Empire was oiled by American Indian scouts, 'free blacks' who helped to run the plantations, Irish soldiers and railwaymen, and. Indian merchants and traders who moved the Queen's rupees around the subcontinent with their credit notes.

The form of this Empire was as often moulded by its foes as by its collaborators. At every period, the Empire was hamstrung and distorted by the costs and embarrassments of local revolt. It was, after all, the 1763 Indian revolt in Canada which brought about the introduction of imperial taxation, driving the American colonists into rebellion and latterly to independence. It was the cost of suppressing peasant uprisings, such as the Indian Mutiny of 1857, or the revolts in the Middle East after 1918, which kept the imperial budget teetering on the brink of collapse, delaying much needed investment, and threatening to drag the country into wars with other powers.

Empire: an Overrated Asset?

The importance of events on the periphery does not mean that the role of statesmen or domestic developments in Britain should be underestimated. The evolution of Empire was almost always driven by a coincidence of events at home and in the colonies. Reform and change were usually counselled by philosophers and

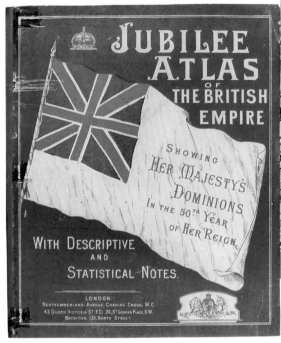

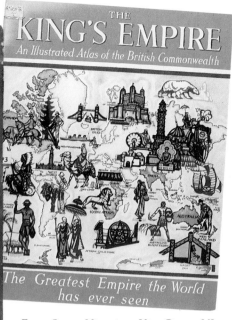

From Queen Victoria to King George VI,
atlases of the British Empire
glowed with imperial self-importance.

statesmen in Britain with as much urgency as they were demanded by revolt or ragged expansion in the farthest reaches of the Empire.

What is not often acknowledged is that British statesmen were, in the main, highly suspicious of extensions to the Empire. Pessimism and distrust were much more general responses than glorification of the latest conquest. Towards the end of the eighteenth century, for example, the Directors of the East India Company declared that 'schemes of conquest are prejudicial to the honour and good name of the British nation.' In the same vein, William Gladstone regarded his intervention in Egypt as 'an Egyptian bondage'. Hugh Dalton summed up the general mood of the British people when he declared in 1946 that 'People at home don't care a damn what is happening there (India) provided our people aren't being mauled about.' The imperial dreamers, such as Rhodes, Milner and Curzon, were always part of a small and embattled minority, regarded as slightly cranky by their colleagues and contemporaries.

The pessimism and mistrust were based on persuasive economic realities. The Empire was undoubtedly a huge bonus for some families of entrepreneurs (especially from the poorer parts of Scotland and Ireland). It also allowed the world to keep members of the British middle class and minor gentry in a style to which they quickly became accustomed. By shifting expenditure onto the shoulders of Indians or Africans, the Empire financed its further expansion for many decades. However, the doubts that even Victorian statesmen had about the ultimate economic value of direct imperial domination have been powerfully reinforced by the statistical research of modern economic historians. They argue that most of the benefits of empire – the cheap food and raw materials from the colonies, and the ready markets for the cotton mills of Lancashire – would have existed without benefit of district collectors and judges, viceroys and imperial armies. Trade would have been even brisker if the flag had never followed it. However adept Britain was at passing on the costs of Empire to her colonies, she still had to foot the bill for a vast imperial fleet and huge commitments to imperial wars, from the Indian Rebellion to the Anglo-Boer War. The imperial markets protected the inefficiency of British manufacturing as much as they did British profits. It has also been suggested that

the railways and canals and the technological and medical advances which we still see as heavyweights in the balance of historical judgement would have flowed abroad without imperial dominion.

There is much virtue in this analysis. It is true that many of the greatest advances in Britain's territorial empire took place when Britain was relatively weak; they were not necessarily a gauge of national strength. The great leap forward in territorial dominion at the end of the eighteenth century was a reflection of Britain's impotence in the face of French domination of the Continent. The partition of Africa and the surge of imperialism at the end of the nineteenth century were responses to the growing fear of competition from European countries and from the USA.

In the 1960s Dean Acheson said that Britain had lost an empire and failed to find another role. Painfully, pragmatically and reluctantly, Britain is now finding a new role within a European power bloc. National mythology will surely be rewritten as a result. The organization and concerns of this volume reflect how this greatest of all national myths – the myth of Empire – is slowly being rewritten.

Atlases and Heroes: The Phases of Empire

This 'myth of Empire' has changed over the centuries. Its evolution can be traced in two particularly striking representations: the 'imperial heroes' who were especially venerated at different periods; and the types of maps and atlases which were used to show the geographical extent and nature of Empire.

The Protestant Empire of the Tudors and Stuarts

The very word 'Empire' had a very different meaning at the dawn of Britain's overseas expansion. When King Henry VIII proclaimed 'this realm of England is an Empire', he meant that it was a sovereign state owing allegiance to no other power, and particularly not to the Pope. Together with his servant Thomas Cromwell, the King drew on a tradition established by medieval political philosophers, who upheld the power of the Holy Roman Emperors against that of the Church.

During the fifteenth and sixteenth centuries, men wrote of the 'Empire of the Bretaignes'; they were talking about the dynastic

Sir Walter Raleigh (1552–1618).
The Renaissance Man as coloniser,
North America.

Richard Wellesley, Lord Mornington
(1760–1842).
The imperial proconsul, India.

Sir Richard Burton (1821–90).
The savant, romantic and orientalist,
The Middle East.

conquests of both English lords and the English Crown in France and the British Isles. It was only after the English had been driven from France in the fifteenth century that the idea of the English Empire was applied more exclusively by the countries of Continental Europe, and Elizabethan maps began to adopt this idea.

But Elizabethan England had herself also begun to look outward. The Queen was represented as a conquering heroine and Empress of the seas and trade. And while the Crown was not concerned with territorial Empire, it did claim the lordship of these lands and of any profits from overseas enterprises. This was a right which had already been granted by the Pope to the kings of Spain and France. Elizabeth, however, claimed to be leader of a specifically Protestant Empire. The entrepreneurs and licensed pirates who served her, such as Martin Frobisher, Francis Drake and Walter Raleigh, became imperial heroes by association. The defence of England against both the Spanish Armada in 1588 and the Catholic Gunpowder Plot in 1605, and then the settlements in Ireland and North America, were all represented as incidents in the expansion of God's Protestant Empire. Historians today are more inclined to view the exploits of Queen

Elizabeth's 'sea dogs' as looting expeditions on the fringes of the much greater world empire of Spain.

An Empire of Trade and Embezzlement: the Eighteenth Century

Late seventeenth- and eighteenth-century maps of the British Empire reflect a shift of emphasis. Protestantism may often have been proclaimed and lauded as when, for instance, the Spanish cut off Captain Jenkins's ear (which he later displayed in Parliament). The maps and globes of the period, however, are intricate representations of an expanding world trade. This operated through thousands of small ports from America through to the Indies, channelling vast quantities of textiles, slaves and spices between Europe and Asia. The great London globe-maker John Senex, though, relied mainly on Dutch originals, since it was the Dutch who had pioneered the first capitalist empire.

A critical moment for the eighteenth-century British Empire was the beginning of territorial control in Bengal. Hitherto an empire of trade, Robert Clive's East India Company latched on to the territorial revenues of Bengal, mainly because its military costs were soaring ahead of its trading profits. Clive – the great

Imperial Airways in the 1930s were keen to advertise their close connections between the far-flung outposts of the Empire.

Sir George Goldie (1846–1925).
The entrepreneur as imperialist,
West Africa.

Robert Baden-Powell (1857–1941).
Empire builder and character builder,
Southern Africa.

Sir William Malcom Hailey (1872–1969).
The colonial expert,
India and Africa.

buccaneer who later became an imperial hero – was considered by many contemporaries as an embodiment of acquisitive vice. Just as Rome had once been corrupted by oriental treasure, so English civic virtue would succumb to Clive. By the turn of the century, however, there had been a shift. Clive was a hero by this time. His heroism was soon contrasted with the 'barbarity and ferocity' of the Indian, Chinese, Ceylonese and Burmese rulers who opposed the rise of British power. Tipu Sultan, ruler of Mysore, died defending his capital in 1799, true to his motto – 'Better to live a day like a tiger than a lifetime as a sheep.' Tipu, vilified by the nineteenth-century English, has now become a hero for the Indian state of Karnataka.

Domination and 'Responsibility': the Nineteenth Century

India's change in role from trade empire to territorial empire, and the expansion of that territorial empire to South-East Asia and Africa, called forth a new generation of maps and a new type of hero. The new icons were the great administrators who settled 'the races without the law' and brought the 'benefits' of civilization, Christianity and free trade to the outer world. Dr David Livingstone, Sir John Lawrence, Sir Frank Swettenham and Lord Lugard all found their pedestals as formal British dominion spread across the globe. Like Tipu Sultan, the parochial rebels and peasant dissidents who opposed the new systems of landholding and taxation are now seen as heroes and heroines by the schoolchildren of independent Asia and Africa.

Not surprisingly, nineteenth-century maps and atlases reflect the change. A huge survey, beginning in India and Ireland and spreading its one-inch maps to every part of the globe, was begun in the 1820s and 1830s: detailed statistical information was needed to assess taxation, build roads and railways, and save souls. Interestingly, one of the earliest atlases of the British Empire was the *Colonial Church Atlas* of 1845. It was contemporary with Robert Montgomery Martin's massive compilations of official statistics from the imperial blue books – the annual returns of facts and figures which flowed from the colonies and India to the Colonial Office and Indian Office in London. This new territorial British Empire needed to intervene more closely in local life to find money, crush enemies and initiate limited development schemes.

Empire as a Shelter from Competition

By the later nineteenth century, the 'white dominions of the British Empire' had already achieved a large measure of self-government. Their trusting farmers and industrialists were only prepared to work within the Empire on these terms. Nationalism was beginning to emerge in both India and Egypt. Meanwhile,

the Boer farmers of southern Africa were not to be reconciled. The French, Germans and even the Americans were developing into serious competitors for the British on the world stage. As a result, the atlases of this period became more strident. Customs unions and cultural similarity were to become the salvation of this increasingly embattled Empire. Indeed, the *Jubilee Atlas* of 1887 was hopeful when it declared: 'Wherever an Englishman may wander he is at home, almost as much as between the hedgerows of an English lane . . . The English Society is everywhere and nowhere can he feel himself an exile.'

By the turn of the century, the imperial heroes were overwhelmingly the military heroes once again: Gordon, Kitchener, the defenders of Ladysmith, even Winston Churchill in his early manifestation as enemy of the Mahdists at Omdurman. A huge outpouring of popular imperial literature and maps accompanied the Anglo-Boer War, Britain's first major campaign since the 1857 Indian Rebellion. The enemies of Empire were portrayed as religious fanatics and backwoodsmen. The Indian revolutionaries' religious revivalism was emphasized – 'froth tinged with blood' as a journalist expressed it – as was the Islamic purism of the Mahdi or even the Calvinist puritanism of the Boers.

Imperialism as Development: from the Thirties to the Present

The two world wars transformed the opponents of Empire and its mythology. The British were now faced with articulate nationalist opponents, many of whom, like Gandhi, were adept at using the colonial power's moral arguments against it.

From the 1930s onwards, Empire needed increasingly to be justified in terms of its mission of scientific improvement in the colonies. At the same time, the ethnic and religious divisions between different groups of imperial subjects were opened up by the rise of nationalism – and by British attempts to counter it. *The King's Empire. An Illustrated Atlas of the British Commonwealth*, designed to coincide with Edward VIII's coronation, summed up the mood. The rhetoric about Empire, however, was even more inflated than it had been in 1887. But there were some shifts of emphasis. Britain's role in giving religious freedom and upholding the ethnic balance was emphasized, as was her development and medical work in the colonies. The looming First World War was foreshadowed in the illustrations of 'our defenders' among the imperial troops. The true imperial heroes were now the medical and scientific experts who, following the Colonial Development and Welfare Act of 1940, justified British rule to an increasingly critical world. After 1950, even former enemies of Empire – Nehru, Nkrumah and Makarios – were enlisted to support its fading afterglow, the British Commonwealth.

SECOTAN

Dasamonguepeuc

Roanoac

Hatorasck

Pasquenoke

Voyages and Plantations
1500–1763

Trinety harbor

BER

FURS

WHEAT

Venice

Tobol'sk · Sibir · Narym
· Tomsk

Yakutsk
Okhotsk

Anadyr

Nizhni Kamchatka

Irkutsk

Nerchinsk

PORCELAIN

DRUGS
PERFUMES
SILK
PORCELAIN
TEA

Nagasaki
Deshima Island

Chandernagore
Calcutta

Macau

Diu
Daman
Bombay
SPICES
Goa
COTTON
Madras · Pulicat
Cochin · Pondicherry
Trincomalee
Colombo

COFFEE

Manila

Ternate & Tidor

Fernando Po
Principe
São Tomé

CLOVES
NUTMEG
MACE

Malacca

CAMPHOR

Macassar
Amboina

SLAVES

Luanda

PEPPER

Batavia
PEPPER

Benguela

IVORY

Moçambique

SLAVES

Sofala

Cape Town

The Expansion of European Trade c.1700

■   Major trading posts

→   (Portuguese Trade): Lisbon to Goa

⇉   (Netherlands' Trade): Amsterdam to Batavia

—   (English Trade) Africa, Jamaica, Britain

···   (Independent Contraband) N. Europe to River Plate

→   (Spanish Trade) Spring & summer fleets from Cadiz to Caribbean

···→   (Pacific Coastal Trade) Valparaiso to Acapulco

→   (Pacific Trade) Acapulco to Manila

-----   (American Coastal Trade) New England to Sugar Islands

17

CHAPTER ONE

THE WORLD ON THE EVE OF EUROPEAN EXPANSION

England was the magpie of early modern Europe; scavenging ideas and techniques from her continental competitors. Advances in cartography, boat building, exploration and business – all developed in the ancient heartland of the continent – were eventually picked up by this economically insignificant country on its northern fringes, and put to her own ends. Without these predecessors the British Empire could never have come into being.

In the fifteenth century Europe was not yet dominant on the world stage, but it differed from other great civilizations in one crucial respect: its focus was outwards, seawards. Other civilizations remained resolutely land-based and land-tied but, from the late fourteenth century onwards, Europe was increasingly intent on dominating the ocean and its commerce. Compare the opinions of a European empire-builder with those of an eastern potentate. Sir Walter Raleigh wrote: 'Whoever commands the sea commands the trade, whoever commands the trade commands the riches of the world, and consequently the world itself.' By contrast, Bahadur Shah, ruler of Gujarat, could only remark: 'Wars at sea are merchants' affairs and of no concern to the prestige of kings.' He was later drowned – accidentally – by the Portuguese.

City Rivalries and Nation-States

Unlike the huge empires of the east, Europe was an amalgam of vigorous and competitive Christian states. Their rivalries fuelled expansion on a continental scale. In the Middle Ages, it was the Italian city-states which attained the highest standard of living and culture. Their merchants – Marco Polo was the most famous – travelled as far as China in pursuit of profit. Florence became an industrial and banking centre; and as Venice and Genoa struggled for control of the Mediterranean, they pioneered trading posts, colonies, plantations and convoys – techniques invented close to home, which would later become the tools of empire-building beyond the confines of Europe.

Sir Thomas Cromwell, Henry VIII's Chancellor, (1485?–1540) declared 'this realm of England an Empire', an autonomous nation-state.

By 1500 the city-states were surrendering their leadership to burgeoning nation-states, such as France, Spain and England. These were much larger political units, which demanded religious conformity from their subjects and were controlled by an effective, uniform and centralized state apparatus. Their monarchs were personal rivals who vied as patrons of the arts and builders of palaces: the ostentation displayed by Henry VIII and Francis I at the Field of the Cloth of Gold was no more than a power-struggle in the most glamorous of forms. But this rivalry was expressed in one field above all other. According to Niccolo Machiavelli (1469–1527), the leading political thinker of the day, 'A wise prince has no other object and no other interest and takes as his profession nothing else than war and its laws and discipline.'

The influence of war permeated most aspects of government and society: its frequency encouraged technological innovation; its huge expense and the need for ready cash in wartime meant the establishment of close links between governments and financiers; and its escalating cost saw a search for new revenues with or without the consent of the nation represented in parliament.

It was gradually realized that the power to wage war depended on a country's economic strength. In the middle of the seventeenth century mercantilism (protectionist policies designed to nurture the developing domestic economy) was adopted in France by Colbert and in England by Oliver Cromwell. Only larger nation-states such as these had the potential for sustained economic growth, without which real political power was impossible.

Plague Victims and the Moneyed Survivors

The European economy had been expanding since the end of the first millennium. The growing population – it had reached eighty million by 1340 – meant an increasing demand for goods. Most of this population, however, could afford little more than their daily bread and this poverty restricted demand. By the early fourteenth century grain production had reached its limits and population growth began to outstrip food supply. There were famines in 1315–7 and 1346–7. The Mediterranean lands were no longer self-sufficient and imports had to be brought in from northern Europe.

This continent-wide food crisis led to malnutrition, weakness and a susceptibility to disease which culminated in the Black Death, a bubonic plague which swept Europe between 1348 and 1351. A third of the population died. Throughout the rest of the century the plague returned at intervals to decimate the population. This disaster had some beneficial side effects. The survivors – especially the middle classes – found themselves suddenly richer with the wealth of relatives who had died. Their purchasing power had also risen because the price of grain, now in surplus, had crashed. There was increased demand for Eastern luxuries, above all spices to enliven and preserve food and drugs to improve health and sex-life. In a paradoxical way, the Black

Elizabeth I encouraged her merchant adventurers to seek out new territories. In 'The Boyhood of Raleigh' (right), Sir John Millais depicted the Elizabethan sailors as idealistic explorers.

Death stimulated the European economy.

European centres of production adapted to the changed circumstances. Italy began to produce higher-quality cloth and switched to more lucrative cash crops as cheap grain flooded in from the Baltic. With less land required for wheat production, sheep farming became important in Spain and England. Their wool was exported to the mass textile industries in the Low Countries. England's own high-quality textiles were marketed in the Low Countries until the wars of the sixteenth century forced her to search for new outlets farther afield. The fishing industry developed as people could afford a more varied diet: 'Ten herrings a penny make many a full belly', ran the popular refrain. The Portuguese developed the Moroccan fishery and the Dutch the North Sea. Indeed, fishing was a primary industry from which much else sprang.

By the late sixteenth century the population of Europe had at last climbed back to pre-plague levels but, as a result of the strains and challenges brought about by the Black Death, the economy was now more diversified and trade much more international. The sheer volume of transactions meant that the precious metals needed for exchange were now in great demand.

Bankers and Businessmen

Commerce gradually became more sophisticated. In the Middle Ages the Italians devised contracts which permitted partnerships and investment in commercial ventures by land and sea. Their merchants developed double-entry book-keeping and employed commissioned agents in foreign ports to gather information and transact their business. Cheques and bills of exchange came into use. Merchant banks operated from Siena in the thirteenth century and from Florence in the fourteenth. Between 1310 and 1345, the Bardi Company of Florence employed 346 agents in 35 different branches throughout Europe. But these big banks were prone to collapse, especially when dealing with governments, from which it was always difficult to recover debts. After the Bardi Company collapsed in 1346, still owed one million florins by the Kings of England and Sicily, no comparable banks emerged until the Renaissance.

DISEASE AND EMPIRE

Spanish explorers brought syphilis back to Europe, and it soon spread across the Continent.

When explorers and colonists broke out of Europe's isolation, the 'disease pools' of the Americas and Eurasia were connected. Europeans had become inured to such infections as typhus, smallpox and measles, but the people of America had not. Vast numbers died of disease and stable societies were thrown into chaos by such random, large-scale losses. This was one reason why the great civilizations of the Aztecs and the Incas succumbed so easily to the relatively small Spanish armies that invaded their territories. A contemporary observer suggested that: 'The Indians die so easily that the bare look and smell of a Spaniard causes them to give up the ghost.' It is now thought that the population of the Americas declined by over three-quarters in some areas during the sixteenth century. Amerindians in the islands of the Caribbean were practically wiped out by disease: slaves and indentured workers had to be imported before economic development could begin. However, the flow was not entirely in one direction. Syphilis appears to have originated in South or Central America and been carried back to Europe by Spanish soldiers who had been enjoying the favours of the local women. While Europe was not thrown into chaos, changes in social behaviour did occur as this terrifying disease spread without respect for social distinction; Henry VIII of England was among the sufferers. The polygamous Maori culture in nineteenth-century New Zealand proved defenceless against venereal disease.

By the sixteenth century the banks had established a much more powerful position for themselves. Philip II, King of Spain between 1555 and 1598, was forced into bankruptcy on three occasions. Although two Spanish banks crashed on the second default, the banking system survived the crises largely intact and the King was able to re-negotiate his loans.

Northern Europeans were now the leaders of the business world. In England the Muscovy Company was chartered in 1555. This was a new type of commercial partnership, a joint-stock company, designed for long-term investment. The leading merchant bankers were no longer Italian but were the German Fuggers in Augsburg. After 1585, when Antwerp fell to the Spanish, Amsterdam became the nerve centre of commerce and finance. That city established public institutions such as the Chamber of Assurance (1598), the *Bourse* or stock exchange (1608), the Exchange Bank (1609) and the Lending Bank (1614), all of which effectively oiled the connections between capital, enterprise and profit. As late as 1728, Daniel Defoe could write that, 'the Dutch must be understood as they really are, the Middle Persons in trade, the Factors and Brokers of Europe.'

Invention and Expansion

Economic development was accompanied by technological change. Some innovations from outside were adapted and refined in Europe. Paper, for example, was a Chinese idea, but it was Europeans in the thirteenth century who built the first mass-production paper mills. Gutenberg printed text for the first time in 1452–3, using moveable type and a hand-press. This major breakthrough in information technology sped up the diffusion of knowledge and hence the rate of technological, economic and social change. The migration of skilled workers helped spread the new inventions. There were important advances in metallurgy: cannons could be cast in bronze and then iron; mercury was used in the refining of silver. New navigational aids – the quadrant, compass and astrolabe – came into use. The establishment of a permanent sea route between the Mediterranean and the Baltic allowed for the combination of the best features of northern and southern ships. By 1500 hybrid ships with one triangular lateen sail and two square sails had been designed to make best use of wind power. The Spaniards and Portuguese

An illustration from Daniel Defoe's celebrated novel 'Robinson Crusoe', depicts Crusoe's meeting with Man Friday.

created the galleon by adding broadsides of cannon just above the waterline. This method of mounting cannon in the hulls of their ships gave the Europeans worldwide naval superiority. Wang-Hong, a Chinese official, warned that 'the Fo-Lang-Ki [Europeans] are extremely dangerous because of their artillery and ships . . . No weapon ever made since memorable antiquity is superior to their cannon.' The Dutch developed the Fluyt, a highly economical freighter, through which they dominated the Baltic carrying trade. On land, watermills and windmills harnessed natural energy.

In Italy and then in northern Europe, the Renaissance revived the learning of Antiquity, but by the seventeenth century the pursuit of 'useful knowledge' – the beginnings of empirical science – had progressed far enough for the wisdom of the Ancients to be seriously questioned. England marched in the vanguard of the 'Scientific Revolution': her civil wars created an intellectual ferment; Dutch and Huguenot French refugees brought technical skills into the country; and young gentlemen, coming back from foreign travels, brought new ideas. This was the necessary background and stimulus to Empire.

Venturers and Financiers

Europe had long since burst its narrow confines when Dias rounded the Cape of Good Hope in 1488 and Columbus reached

SPECIES AND EMPIRE

As Europeans spread across the world, they took their own plants and domesticated animals with them, creating 'little Europes' in the Americas, Australasia and the Pacific. Horses and cattle interbred with native herds, often producing strains especially suitable for drier climates. The two bulls and six cows brought by the First Fleet to Australia in 1788 soon strayed from the settlers and, by 1804, had grown into a wild herd 4,000 strong. They numbered several million a couple of generations later. The introduction of sheep to Australia was so successful that the economy of the continent was transformed, as were similar regions of South Africa. Even honeybees were transported from Europe to thrive in Australia and the New World.

There were also many instances of ecological

The potato came from South America.

disaster. By the twentieth century, the rabbits that had been unknown in Australia just over a century earlier threatened to overrun the continent, and were controlled only by

introducing the infectious disease myxomatosis. The spread of rats, dogs and cats in many Pacific islands also devastated the local fauna, and in South America adaptable European rats bred in such numbers that it was said 'no cat dared look them in the face'.

The exchange of crops and commodities also stimulated trade and population growth: the potato made its celebrated progress from South America across the world, as did the turkey, guinea pig, tomato and tobacco plant. Maize or 'indian corn' became a valuable staple in Europe and in many Asian societies, which also assimilated South American chilis and manioc more enthusiastically than did the Europeans. Spices, narcotics and medicinal barks, including quinine, were to swell the coffers of merchants for generations to come.

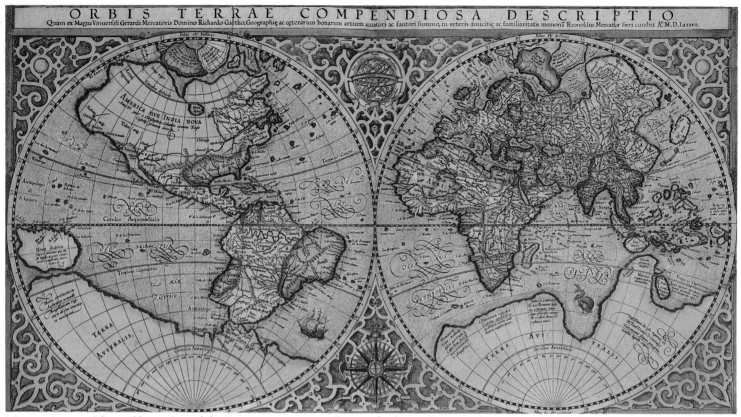

Mercator's map of the world transformed the European conception of geography during the sixteenth century.

America in 1492. Many of the continent's strengths and needs were reflected in this early phase of overseas expansion. The renewed Islamic threat – brought home by the fall of Constantinople to the Turks in 1453 – made Christian zealots anxious to outflank the infidels and find Christian allies in the East. The crusading fervour was still alive in the Iberian peninsula and it was Portugal – a small and impoverished nation-state – which led the way. Her kings, willing to finance voyages whose only reward might be prestige, sponsored various journeys south in the fifteenth century. The Portuguese voyages discovered Madeira and the Azores, explored the coast of Africa, and culminated in Vasco da Gama's pioneering voyage to India in 1497–9. The gamble of the Portuguese monarchy had paid off. Capitalists jumped on the band-wagon as soon as exploration and exploitation looked profitable. Genoese merchants poured money into sugar plantations on the islands of the Atlantic and in the Caribbean. A Spanish capitalist, Gaspar de Espinosa, invested 20,000 pesos in the conquest of Peru by Pizarro and Almagro.

The European demand for precious metals, made acute by an increasing volume of trade, drove the Portuguese down the African coast to tap the Saharan gold supply. In America, the Spaniards went on a crazed search for precious metals which they followed up by exploitation of vast silver mines at Zacatecas (Mexico) and Potosi (Peru).

Many of the factors that made up the explosive power behind the expansion of Europe can be seen in crystallised form in the voyages of Columbus: religious mysticism, an unshaken belief in the rightness of what he was doing and in the superiority of Europeans, a lust for gold, an exceptional knowledge of navigation, ships and ocean sailing, a blessing by the Spanish Crown, and finance from his fellow Genoese merchants.

Genocide and Money-Mines

The cataclysmic impact of this dynamic, expansionist culture was first felt most brutally in America. Conquest, forced labour, epidemics of Old World diseases and disrupted ecology consumed whole civilizations and devastated Amerindian populations. The Mexican population declined from an estimated

An idealized picture of foreigners' costume in the sixteenth century.

A view of Bombay from Edward Barlow's Journal. *Bombay offered the best harbour in India, and came to Charles II in 1661 as part of the dowry of his wife, Catherine of Braganza.*

10–15 million in 1519 to 1.5 million in 1650. The Spaniards overran the Caribbean islands and then, in two highly dramatic actions, they conquered the empires of the Aztecs (1519–21) and the Incas (1531–4). The small Spanish forces achieved success not by technical superiority but by exploiting the Amerindians' own internal divisions. In Mexico, Cortes won the support of local Indians against the Aztecs and in Peru, Pizarro took advantage of a struggle for succession to the Inca throne and then formed alliances with tribes whom the Incas had conquered.

From the outset the conquerors intended to exploit the indigenous peoples. Columbus reckoned: 'They are good to be ordered about, to be made to work, plant and do whatever is wanted, to build towns and be taught to go clothed and accept our customs.' In the islands, forced labour for the Europeans contributed to the elimination of the docile, loosely organized tribal societies. The empires on the mainland, however, had already organized labour systems which the Spaniards could make use of. Toledo, Viceroy of Peru between 1569 and 1581, consciously revived the Inca system of public works to increase gold production for the Spanish war effort in Europe. In the decade after 1585, an average of 7.5 million pesos was brought out of Potosi every year, and 10 million from Peru as a whole.

Not surprisingly, Spain's empire excited envy, imitation and attack. Sir Francis Drake's circumnavigation (1577–80) was less an exploring and trading mission than a long-distance plundering expedition against Spain. Likewise the abortive English attempt to establish a settlement in the mid-1580s at Roanoke, Virginia, was aimed less at colonization than at having a forward base from which to raid the Spanish Main. The Dutch achieved the greatest single success in 1628 when their Admiral, Piet Heyn, intercepted the returning Spanish treasure fleet off Cuba and captured four million ducats of gold and silver. That was the exception. On a more mundane level, the northern Europeans were happy to trade contraband with the Spanish colonists which Spain's own domestic industry was too weak to supply.

Luxuries and Rivalries
In Africa and Asia, Europeans had to settle for trade from coastal forts rather than extensive dominions. African societies were too

warlike and Asian armies too formidable. In Africa the main objects of trade were gold, slaves and ivory. In Asia they were spices and luxuries: from India and Indonesia pepper, cinnamon, cloves, mace, nutmeg and ginger; from China silk, porcelain and drugs. Even though Europeans usually had to pay for the goods in bullion, there were enormous profits to be made from the spice trade. As a result, there were extensive searches for the Northwest and Northeast passages, but it was the Cape of Good Hope route blazed by the Portuguese which proved the only alternative to the land route through the Middle East. In 1499 King Manuel of Portugal adopted the grandiose title of 'Lord of Guinea and of the Conquest of the Commerce of Ethiopia, Arabia, Persia and India'. This was more of a hope than a statement of fact and in the end the King had to settle for little barring a near-monopoly in pepper and, for the Portuguese nobility, the levying of tax on Indian Ocean trade.

Things began to go wrong for the Portuguese in 1580 when Philip II of Spain became their king. Within a decade the Portuguese Empire fell prey to Philip's rebellious Dutch subjects. In 1602 the *Vereenigde Oost-Indische Compagnie* was established with a board of directors and with shareholders investing 6.5 million florins. Technically private, this joint-stock company was in effect an organ of the Dutch Republic. The VOC established a more effective monopoly than the Portuguese by controlling the centres of spice production in the Molucca islands in what is now Indonesia and by manipulating the market in Europe. They pioneered the quicker 'Roaring Forties' route between the Cape of Good Hope and Australia, and closed down the Middle Eastern route which had been so profitable to the Venetians.

As rivals, the Portuguese and Dutch had much in common. Both the Portuguese colonists in Goa and the Dutch in Batavia (Jakarta) operated independently from their home countries. Their officials grew rich by exploiting the inter-Asian trade and both repelled other European interlopers: the Portuguese drove the Spanish out of the Moluccas to the Philippines and the Dutch forced the English East India Company merchants out of Indonesia, massacring the English factors at Amboina in 1623. The Company then removed to India. Here they were forced to develop a new trade in light cotton goods (calicoes) because they were denied access to the traditional exports of the East, but this was to be their making. First they were to benefit from India's sophisticated artisan production and then from its territorial revenues.

A World of Sea-borne Empires
For good or ill, a world economy had been founded by the Europeans; a Chinese chronicler wrote of the European traders: 'They will risk their lives in search of profit, and no place in the world is too remote for them.' The conquest of America, the extraction of its mineral wealth and its settlement by Europeans and Africans helped to create a buoyant Atlantic economy. Trade with Asia was in deficit, however, because Europe was forced to use so much American bullion in buying Eastern luxuries. Nevertheless, by the early seventeenth century, the world had undergone a radical change. The political and economic expansion of Europe – the idea of the sea-based empire – was there to stay. The countries that would win out in the great struggle to redivide the world's resources would need a strong and unified state and flexible financial institutions. By 1660 England, soon to bring Scotland into junior partnership, was such a nation.

CHAPTER TWO

THE EXPANSION OF ENGLAND

◇

The British Isles is a political, rather than geographical concept. At the end of the Middle Ages, these scattered islands off the north-west coast of mainland Europe had no common name, government or language. They were a chaotic mix of competing power groups and civil strife. However, in 1603, when Elizabeth I died and was succeeded by the Scottish King James VI (James I of England), England, Wales, Scotland and Ireland were united. In the century which followed, this union was consolidated – in spite of revolutionary wars – by strategic, social and economic policies that were often to reappear in the history of the British Empire. The united kingdom that James inherited in 1603 was as much the result of dynastic accident, marital misadventure and backfiring religious intrigue as of deliberate political manipulation.

England and the Islands at the Time of the Tudors

Two types of political system existed at the start of the Tudor period in 1485: monarchical states, operating from lowland Scotland and south-east England, and tribal lordships, which held sway in the western highlands and islands of Scotland and in the greater part of Ireland. Over the next 150 years, the monarchs gradually prevailed over the tribal lords, but not without a struggle and some major adaptations on the way.

The first attempt to integrate a Gaelic lordship had been made in 1493 when King James IV of Scotland annexed the 900-year-old Lordship of the Isles. His aims were to prevent its MacDonald lords intriguing with the English and to exploit the western fisheries. Royal justice and feudal land tenure were introduced, but the main results were resentment and civil disturbance. The only real beneficiaries were the royal lieutenants, the Earls of Huntly and Argyll.

To the south, the end of the Wars of the Roses saw a Welshman, Henry Tudor, ascend the English throne. His kingdom included the Principality of Wales, the Isle of Man, the Channel Islands, the Scilly Isles, the town and district of Calais and the Lordship of Ireland (effectively only about a third of the country). Although Henry VII did not add to these dependent territories, his administrative efficiency and sound business and political sense dramatically increased the Crown's control over them.

The Reign of Henry VIII

Henry VIII's reign began unpromisingly, with the glamorous young King frittering away much of his father's carefully accumulated wealth and failing to consolidate his achievements. However, it was through Henry's efforts that a national church was established in defiance of the Pope – although not quite in the manner that this Catholic monarch had intended. His first wife, Catherine of Aragon, failed to produce a male heir and so Henry decided to obtain a papal annulment of the marriage. He found his way blocked, however, by the Pope's fear of Catherine's nephew, the Emperor Charles V. The only practical way of divorcing Catherine was to take control of the ecclesiasti-

cal establishment in England, a move which had momentous consequences. The Act of Appeals of 1533 declared, 'This realm of England is an empire.' In other words, England was henceforth independent of all external authority. England was now a national sovereign state. The following year, the Act of Supremacy declared the king to be 'the only supreme head in earth of the Church of England'.

The Dissolution of the Monasteries (1536–40) followed the break with Rome. The Crown took possession of the wealth and estates of some 800 religious communities and pensioned off the nuns and monks. This act of nationalization was followed by the privatization of most of the land through grant and sale. In all, about a fifth of the cultivated land in England changed hands – with far-reaching consequences. Much of it was bought by the 'gentry' (i.e. the landowning class below the nobility or peerage) at a time when land prices were low and about to rise steeply. Agriculture too was becoming increasingly profitable, with a growing population and the extension of land under cultivation, as well as improved farming techniques. The gentry thus gained in wealth at the expense of the clergy and the Crown, and now constituted a powerful class with a vested interest in the new national ecclesiastical order. Much gentry wealth was later to flow into schemes of plunder and colonization overseas.

The subjection of the Church was only one instance of the new centralizing tendency of the Crown. Between 1533 and 1540 Thomas Cromwell, Henry VIII's most energetic minister, established a smaller, more effective Privy Council. In its role of assisting the king to govern, this body became the executive authority of the state. There were also great changes in regional government, the prime example being Wales, where the 1536 Act of Union established seven new counties on the English model. By 1543, Wales was fully integrated into the English

A 1521 pen-and-ink drawing by Albrecht Dürer showing the variety of weapons employed by Irish soldiers in the sixteenth century.

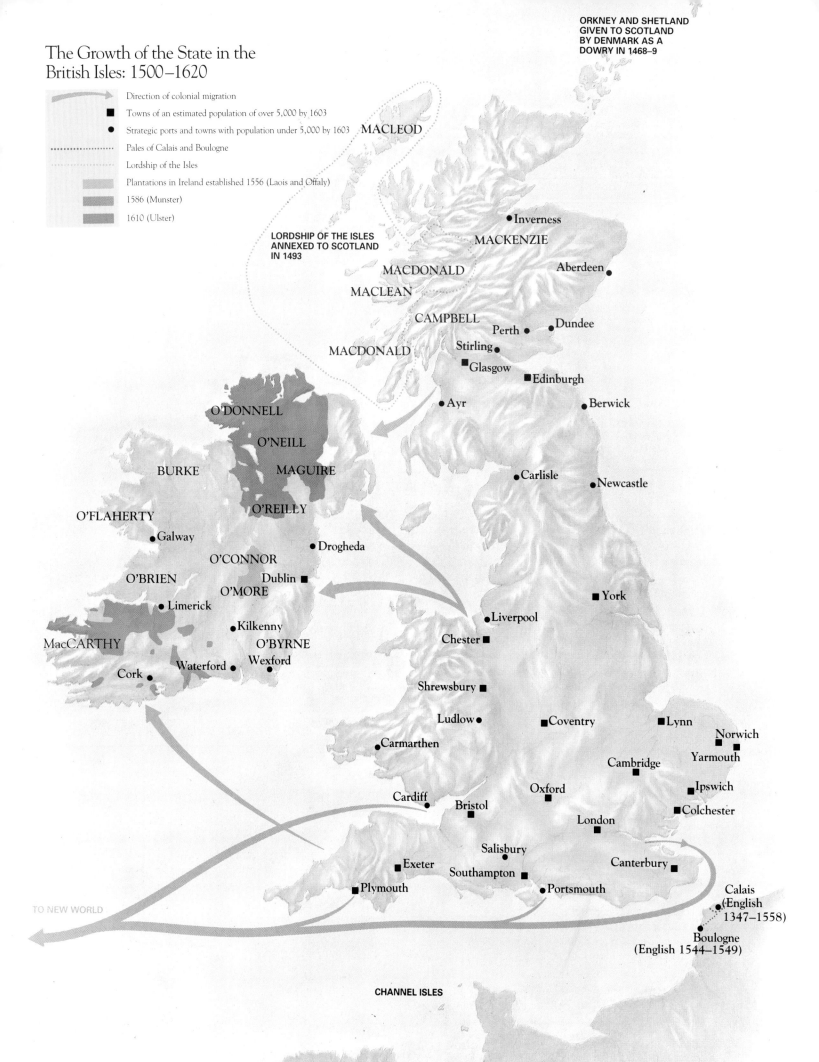

The Growth of the State in the British Isles: 1500–1620

ORKNEY AND SHETLAND GIVEN TO SCOTLAND BY DENMARK AS A DOWRY IN 1468–9

→ Direction of colonial migration

■ Towns of an estimated population of over 5,000 by 1603

● Strategic ports and towns with population under 5,000 by 1603

········· Pales of Calais and Boulogne

·········· Lordship of the Isles

Plantations in Ireland established 1556 (Laois and Offaly)

1586 (Munster)

1610 (Ulster)

MACLEOD

LORDSHIP OF THE ISLES ANNEXED TO SCOTLAND IN 1493

● Inverness

MACKENZIE

MACDONALD

● Aberdeen

MACLEAN

CAMPBELL

● Perth   ● Dundee

MACDONALD

● Stirling

■ Glasgow   ■ Edinburgh

● Ayr   ● Berwick

O'DONNELL

● Carlisle   ● Newcastle

O'NEILL

MAGUIRE

BURKE

O'REILLY

O'FLAHERTY

● Galway   ● Drogheda

O'CONNOR

O'BRIEN   Dublin ■

O'MORE

● Limerick

■ York

● Kilkenny

O'BYRNE

MacCARTHY

● Liverpool

Waterford ●   Wexford

Chester ■

● Cork

Shrewsbury ■

Ludlow ●   ■ Coventry   ■ Lynn

● Carmarthen

Norwich ■

Cambridge ■   Yarmouth ■

Cardiff ●   ● Oxford   Ipswich ■

Bristol ■   Colchester ■

London ■

Salisbury ●

Canterbury ■

● Exeter   Southampton ■

Plymouth ●   Portsmouth ●   Calais (English 1347–1558)

TO NEW WORLD

Boulogne (English 1544–1549)

CHANNEL ISLES

24

A drawing of Henry VIII, with his father Henry VII in the background, forms part of Holbein's original cartoon for his wall-painting in the Privy Chamber of Whitehall Palace.

monasteries. Those great families that did not acquiesce were then tempted with a share in the monastic lands or peerages in exchange for their renunciation of the Pope. In 1541 the Irish Parliament made Henry King of Ireland. None of this, however, secured Ireland's fundamental allegiance; the troubled entanglements of the English Crown were far from over.

Henry's plans for Scotland never went so far as dominion, but he was keen to involve his nephew, James V, in the quarrel with Rome. This he failed to do. When James died, leaving as his heir the one-week-old Princess Mary, there followed a period in Anglo-Scottish relations known as 'the Rough Wooing'. In 1543 an English army forced the Scots to accept the engagement of Mary to Prince Edward, thereby attempting to unite the two kingdoms. The Scots soon repudiated this agreement and Henry did not press the matter.

The rather haphazard and conciliatory policies of Henry's last years gave way to aggression under Edward VI. The Protestant regimes operating on behalf of the nine-year-old King felt beleaguered and hypersensitive to potential threats. A permanently garrisoned zone was established in southern Scotland and allies were sought among local Protestants. However, this policy only encouraged the Scots to accept French military assistance and to opt for the marriage of Mary to the Dauphin of France.

Conquest and Colonization under Elizabeth I

Irish policies under Edward VI and Elizabeth I had long-term consequences. To protect the Pale – Dublin and its home counties – garrisons were established in the O'More and O'Connor lordships of Laois and Offaly. This began a process of piece-meal conquest. Local English commanders used the pretext of a strategic threat to dabble in the politics of neighbouring lordships. Wars developed, requiring reinforcements from England, and so new territories were incorporated and the frontier extended. Once the Shannon was reached, it became necessary to pacify Connacht and Munster. In 1579 this policy provoked the Desmond War, which brought devastation to Munster. The poet Edmund Spenser was working in Ireland on behalf of the

judicial and administrative system, and the Welsh were given the right to parliamentary representation.

In Ireland, the essential problem for the English monarchy was to bring order and jurisdiction to a turbulent scenario of feuding local lords. Henry VII's temporary solution was to entrust the keeping of law and order to the most powerful of these lords, the Earl of Kildare. This policy was repeated (after various experiments with alternatives) by Henry VIII, but there was always an inherent danger that the favoured family would use its power to carry on its own feuds. When this turned out to be the case, Kildare was summoned to London and imprisoned in the Tower. A rumour spread that he had been executed and in June 1534 his deputy and eldest son, 'Silken Thomas', declared his allegiance to the Pope and appealed for help from abroad. His rebellion was initially successful but did not, in the event, last long. Fresh troops were sent from England and in the spring of 1535 he surrendered, later to be executed. Acts were then passed in the Irish Parliament, which repeated the bones of Henry's English Reformation: repudiating papal authority, placing the king at the head of the Irish Church and suppressing the

THE ULSTER PLANTATIONS: A PATTERN FOR THE FUTURE

Until the chieftain of Ulster, Hugh O'Neill, capitulated to English troops at Kinsale in 1603, Ulster had been the most rebellious of the Irish provinces. Relief armies from Ulster were sent so frequently to every corner of Ireland against the English that 'Out of the North comes forth help' became a famous adage.

After Kinsale, James I divided up the greater part of the six richest counties into 'plantations' of English and Scottish settlers – a system that was to be repeated in the plantations of the West Indies. The area was divided into 'lots' of varying sizes and given to 'undertakers' – usually merchant administrators financed from London – who were initially bound not to take Irish Catholic tenants. The dispossessed were ordered to 'depart with their goods and chattels at or before the first of May next (1609) into whatever other part of the realm they pleased.'

The colonists planted in Fermanagh and along the Lagan valley in North Down were mainly English, and elsewhere overwhelmingly

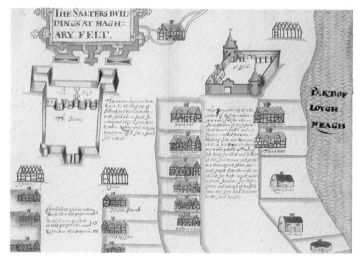

A seventeenth-century plan of Salters Town, built by the Salters Company as a plantation stronghold in 1619 on the west side of Lough Neagh.

Scottish. Religious differences, in an age of fierce religious strife, kept the Irish Gael apart from the newcomer. The insecurity of the settlers, terrified of being abandoned by the home country to the resentments of the

marauding Irish, was played upon by the King to ensure an absolute loyalty to the Crown. Eventually their descendants flourished and refused to accept the establishment of Home Rule for Ireland.

SIR THOMAS SMITH: COMMONWEALTH ECONOMIST

Sir Thomas Smith.

Sir Thomas Smith was the most important political thinker and economist in Tudor England. He was born in 1513, and published his first major book, *The Discourse of the Commonweal of this Realm of England*, when he was thirty-six. It was based on an examination of inflation in the mid-sixteenth century and advocated the creation of a market economy so that private enterprise could work unfettered for the common good. Smith was also an active imperialist, creating a joint-stock company to promote a plantation scheme in Ireland which he did not expect the government to finance. Instead he relied on his own prestige to attract private investors. Many younger sons of the nobility joined with him to seek their fortunes in Ireland. Sir Thomas Smith encouraged investment in his scheme by what was then a new concept in persuasion: an advertising campaign of printed leaflets distributed throughout the shires. It was a ploy often adopted later in colonization schemes for the New World. Almost 800 men assembled at Liverpool to embark for Ireland. Each horseman was provided with at least £20, each infantryman with £10, both to invest in land. The venture was then left in the incompetent hands of Smith's son and it soon fell apart. Only 100 men reached Ulster, where they met with strong opposition. The young Smith was killed in 1573 by his Irish servants and the expedition fizzled out.

Crown and witnessed the blood-chilling famine that resulted: 'Out of every corner of the woods and glens they came creeping forth upon their hands, for their legs would not bear them; they looked like anatomies of death; they spoke like ghosts crying out of their graves; they did eat the dead carrions, happy where they could find them; yea and one another soon after, insomuch as the very carcasses they spared not to scrape out of their graves.' English aggression was aimed at securing Ireland against its strategic use by enemy Catholic powers, yet such actions only encouraged the threats they were supposed to prevent. The Irish lords were soon seeking foreign assistance again.

A more effective tool in English hands was colonization. In 1565 Thomas Smith wrote that the conquest of Ireland 'needed nothing more than to have colonies, to augment our tongues, our laws, and our religion in that isle, which three be the true bands of commonwealth whereby the Romans conquered and kept long time a great part of the world.' Where possible, English colonies were settled on confiscated lands as models of civility for the natives and as more efficient exploiters of natural resources. The 'plantation' or colonization of Laois and Offaly was an expensive failure, but the larger scheme in Munster proved a success with three thousand settlers arriving in the first ten years. Military and colonial service in Ireland was attractive to the landless younger sons of the gentry, who were now more numerous because the closure of the monasteries had increased the number of marriages whilst simultaneously reducing job prospects. For them, Ireland became a frontier of opportunity.

In Scotland, Elizabeth I salvaged what she could from Edward's failed policies. In 1560 English intervention secured the triumph of Protestantism and the withdrawal of French troops. However, Mary Queen of Scots returned home in the following year. As the granddaughter of James IV and Margaret Tudor, she was considered in Catholic eyes to be a more legitimate claimant to the English throne than Elizabeth, daughter of Henry VIII and Anne Boleyn. Despite her political ineptitude, Mary's claim continued to be a cause for discontent against Elizabeth even after her imprisonment.

The real crisis for the Elizabethan state came when war broke out with Spain, the greatest military power of the age. Growing fears that the Spaniards would overrun the Netherlands led to the Treaty of Nonsuch in 1585, by which England committed herself financially and militarily to the cause of the Dutch

nationalist rebels. In 1588 Philip of Spain sent 'la armada invincible' to invade England. But the English fleet mauled the galleons in the Channel and the English weather did the rest: 'God breathed and they were scattered.'

In fact, the decisive engagement of the war came in Ireland thirteen years later, where an attempt to abolish Gaelic institutions only served to unify the lords of Ulster under Hugh O'Neill. He organized an effective army which brought the Crown to the negotiating table in 1596. However, Spanish agents arrived with a better offer and the Gaelic confederates decided to wait for the military assistance they promised. In 1599 Queen Elizabeth sent the Earl of Essex to Ireland with twelve thousand men but his disastrous campaign only exposed the inadequacies of her military machine. In 1601 a Spanish expedition finally disembarked at Kinsale. The Crown forces, who went to besiege the town, found themselves in turn besieged by a Gaelic army. However, O'Neill committed his army unnecessarily and was routed in a poorly executed dawn attack. The Spaniards were forced to withdraw. Kinsale was decisive not only because it was the final Spanish fling but

A contemporary portrait of Robert Deveraux, Earl of Essex (1566–1601) who led the second attempt on Ulster.

because it occurred at a crucial time: Spanish possession of Ireland would have threatened the union of England and Scotland, and their control of the western approaches would have prevented English expansion across the Atlantic (which was beginning to gather pace).

The United Kingdom of the Stuarts

King James, the Protestant son of the executed Mary, was a conscientious and independent-minded monarch – indeed, something of an intellectual when it came to politics and religion. His attitudes were more anti-Gaelic than those of former Scottish kings, perhaps because of his Calvinism. He wanted to civilize the highlands and islands and to extract Crown revenues from the region. He even contracted a group of speculators, known as 'the Fife adventurers', to colonize the island of Lewis with lowlanders. The adventurers gave up after three attempts. As King of England, James allowed his enthusiasm for colonization to extend to projects in Ireland and America. The largest of these was the plantation of Ulster. Six counties were forfeited to the Crown, and English and Scots settlers arrived to lay the foundations for a permanent British presence. James coaxed London companies to join together and to deploy their capital in the development of Derry. Paradoxically, colonization proved most successful outside the official plantations. Gaelic landowners, unable to cope with the increasingly market-oriented economy, ran into debt and sold up to a budding capitalist class. The greatest success story was that of Richard Boyle. Younger son of a Kentish yeoman family, he arrived in Ireland in 1588 and, by a mixture of legal chicanery, judicious marriages and land speculation, became one of the richest men in the three kingdoms and the first Earl of Cork, in 1620. In Scotland too, Gaelic lords found themselves falling more heavily into debt, but here clan solidarity and differences in the system of land tenure prevented such a large-scale transfer.

The multiple kingdom needed a capable king. However, James's successor, Charles I, was an insensitive politician who managed to antagonize interested groups in all three countries. His government became increasingly absolutist in matters of revenue and religion. European powers in the seventeenth century needed a wide taxation base. In this regard, Charles's most successful minister was Thomas Wentworth, whose policy of 'thorough' administration in Ireland produced a revenue

An equestrian portrait of a proud James I, with the Thames and old London Bridge in the background.

surplus for the first time in a century. It was a measure of Wentworth's success that by 1640 Ireland's various sectarian groups had united in opposition to him.

In England, Charles had stopped calling Parliament because it refused to grant adequate subsidies. He raised funds by various constitutional expedients, including the notorious nationwide application of 'ship money', a tax traditionally levied only in the coastal counties. The King's other principal supporter was the high-church, anti-Puritan Archbishop of Canterbury, William Laud. He was busy reforming the Church of England and alienating the gentry in the process. When Charles tried to impose Laud's views on the Scots by issuing a new Prayer Book

THE 1641 REBELLION

The conquest and colonization of Ireland was a great psychological shock for its Gaelic peoples. They had accommodated and absorbed such incursions in the past, but religious persecution was a new experience. In the late 1630s the constitutional crisis in England provoked an economic recession which fuelled sectarian tension in Ireland. In 1641 rebellion broke out. Although its original leaders were native Irish, the rebellion was initially an appeal to arms across the social spectrum. It was led by Rory O'More, a Catholic landowner with Old English family connections. He was disturbed by the social revolution in England which threatened to transfer the Catholic King's authority to

The crushing of the Irish revolt at Portadown.

Parliament. He and the 'rebels' were, in fact, royalists, defending themselves against the threat to their liberty and religion posed by Cromwell. When O'More met the Old English

army in the Pale of Dublin in 1641, he publicly declared his solidarity with them: 'We are of the same religion, and the same nation; our interest and sufferings are the same.' However, the nobles lost control of their followers, and a series of brutal, indiscriminate massacres resulted, especially in Ulster. Protestant opinion in England was so outraged that the cry for widespread retribution went up against nobles and peasants alike, those 'barbarous wretches who have imbued their hands in so much innocent blood'. In 1649 the Puritan army of Oliver Cromwell arrived on the scene to avenge 'the most barbarous massacre that ever sun beheld' in such bloody measure that the name of Cromwell was never forgotten.

A painting by Jan Wyck of the Battle of the Boyne, 1690 – a victory for the forces of King William III of England and the Protestant cause over the former King James II, who had been forced to abdicate in 1688.

in 1637, there were riots, and then armed resistance. This led to the Bishops' Wars. English taxpayers refused to foot the bill. The King was defeated by his Scottish subjects and thrown back into the arms of an English Parliament demanding constitutional safeguards against arbitrary government. Then, in 1641, a ferocious rebellion broke out in Ulster. An army was needed to suppress the Irish Catholics, but neither the King nor Parliament trusted one another to raise it. In the prevailing atmosphere of distrust, religious activists on both sides caused polarization into two armed camps.

A 16th century map of 'The Kingdome of Ireland' by the great Dutch cartographer, Jodicus Hondius, showing the social hierarchy.

Ireland and Scotland under Oliver Cromwell

The civil war in England renewed the whole question of constitutional relations between the three kingdoms, particularly when, in 1649, the English Parliament removed the unifying factor by executing the King and abolishing the monarchy. But the English revolutionaries soon found that they needed to extinguish royalist embers in Ireland and Scotland. Oliver Cromwell fought a brutal Irish campaign – most remembered for massacres at Drogheda and Wexford – which combined military efficiency with religious fanaticism. The poet Sean O'Connail saw this as the culmination to 'the war that finished Ireland'. Wholesale confiscations followed a national land survey by Sir William Petty. Millions of acres were distributed to those who had invested in the re-conquest under the 1642 Act of Adventurers and to those who had fought in the victorious army. The Cromwellian settlement of Ireland saw a major shift of land ownership away from the Catholics, and the establishment of the Protestant ascendancy.

English victories over the Scots were not accompanied by the establishment of plantations or by atrocities like those perpetrated on the Irish. Nevertheless, Scotland was a conquered territory and garrisons were built at strategic points to keep the native population in check. In addition, the Cromwellian régime pursued social reform in Ireland and Scotland and attempted a parliamentary union by giving each of the two countries thirty seats at Westminster. This experiment foreshadowed the more enduring unions with Scotland in 1707 and with Ireland in 1801.

When the monarchy was restored in 1660, the British state had emerged stronger than before from its worst internal crisis. Over the previous two centuries, the state-apparatus had become highly effective – developing in a way that was common to many other European countries during the Renaissance and the Reformation. As the state absorbed the Gaelic regions, its officials and soldiers had gained valuable experience in dealing with tribal societies. And, in the establishment of colonies in Ireland, a precedent had been set that would later be developed farther afield.

CHAPTER THREE

THE THIRTEEN COLONIES

◇

The English were late starters in the colonization of North America. It was the Spaniards who pioneered the exploitation of what is now the United States. They thrust northwards into California and New Mexico, fortified by the wealth of New Spain in silver and Indian tribute. If anything, the heady looting adventures of Sir Francis Drake, 'principal burglar of the Spanish Main', and the other licensed pirates who attacked Spanish shipping distracted attention from more durable plans of settlement. But England had a powerful state and, after the conquest of Ireland and the Union of the Crowns in 1603, she was less at risk from foreign invasion than her Continental neighbours. Her gentry had become prosperous on expropriated monastic lands and there were plenty of trained seamen in the ports of the west. In addition, Ireland had already proved a fertile field for colonial experiments.

Sir Walter Raleigh (1552–1618), the English adventurer and favourite of Queen Elizabeth I, as pictured by a woodcut from a news sheet of 1618, which describes one of his expeditions to the Guyana coast of South America in search of El Dorado.

From Privateering to Permanent Settlement

When peace was signed with Spain in 1604, there were large reserves of ambition, capital and enterprise ready to be unleashed on the American continent. In 1606 Virginia (which then meant the whole North American seaboard) was divided in two. North Virginia (soon to be known as New England) became the monopoly of merchants and fishermen from Plymouth; South Virginia the monopoly of investors and settlers from London. The London group established England's first permanent settlement at Jamestown in 1607. The colony on the west side of Chesapeake Bay went through some very hard years at first. During the 'starving time' of 1609–10, famine and disease reduced the population from five hundred to sixty, and it was even reported that one man was forced to eat his wife. Two things saved the colonies. Firstly, Sir Walter Raleigh himself had spread the American Indian habit of tobacco smoking in England (he even 'took a pipe of tobacco' before going to the scaffold on charges of high treason). Tobacco was a high-value, low-weight commodity which could balance the settlers' import bill for cloth and metalware. Secondly, artisans and agricultural labourers from England and Scotland were eager to do well in this huge empty continent. Land speculators and entrepreneurs supplied them with money and passage in return for their labour. The Virginia investors never got their money back, but settlers enjoyed a fair amount of prosperity from the 1620s onwards and attracted a stream of new immigrants. This, and the fact that tobacco exhausted the land, forced cultivators to move to fresh fields which, in turn, led to poor relations with the Indians for years to come.

The Plymouth group quietly caught cod in the summer and returned home in the winter. Continuous settlement did not begin until 1620. Resolute Protestants who went to the Netherlands to escape James I's Anglicanism found that their children were losing their English roots. So they sailed from Plymouth to a permanent home in New England. This was not a step into the unknown; both their banker and the captain of their ship, the *Mayflower*, knew to what they were going, although their preparations were far from adequate. The Pilgrims reached Cape Cod on 21 November 1620 (now celebrated as Thanksgiving Day) and went on to Plymouth, in present-day Massachusetts. Before disembarking, however, they produced the 'Mayflower Compact', which bound the signatories to form a 'civic body politic', the foundations of government for the colony.

During their first winter, half the little company of a hundred died. 'At times there were but six or seven strong enough to hunt, cook and care for the entire company who, to their great commendations', as William Bradford, leader of the colony, wrote, 'spared no pains, night or day, but with abundance of toyle, and hazard of their own health, fetched them wood, made their fires, drest them meat, made their beds, washed their loathsome clothes, cloathed and uncloathed them.' Nevertheless, the survivors could worship as they wished and, as time passed, they acquired a modest prosperity.

Religious Refugees in New England

James's son Charles was more intrusive in his Anglicanism and a much larger group made arrangements to escape it by emigration. They obtained a royal charter and in 1629 sailed to Massachusetts Bay. During the course of the 1630s, between fifteen and twenty thousand people crossed to this new colony, the largest exodus in seventeenth-century colonization.

The New England colonies of the 1630s grew into a dozen communities of mainly Protestant opinion, although in 1632 the Calvert family established a tolerant community at Maryland, which comprised Catholics and Church of England members.

Some New England colonies tried to keep trade down in order to avoid debt and religious contamination but, if it took place at all, it would be with England. There was little surprise when the English Republic, after overthrowing and executing Charles I, passed a Navigation Act in 1651 to say that trade, including colonial trade, should be in English ships.

The New England colonies preferred the Republic to Charles and his religious policy, which had looked very like Roman Catholicism. Virginia and Maryland, however, accepted the Republic mainly because it had a strong navy and welcomed the

Settled Region of New France

Unsettled Region of New France

Unsettled Region of New France

IROQUOIS

(1629) MASSACHUSETTS

(1691) NEW HAMP SHIRE

Saratoga

Salem
Boston

Plymouth
MAYFLOWER LANDED 1620
RHODE ISLAND (1636-44)

CONNECTICUT (1662)

NEW YORK (1664)

New York

Detroit

Fort Duquesne (Pittsburgh)

PENNSYLVANIA (1682)

NEW JERSEY (1664)

Philadelphia

DELAWARE (1701)

MARYLAND (1632)

VIRGINIA (1607)

Yorkton
Jamestown

CHESAPEAKE BAY

OHIO RIVER

N. CAROLINA (1674)
(Royal Colony in 1729)

MISSISSIPPI RIVER

S. CAROLINA (1713)
(Royal Colony in 1729)

Charleston
(Royal Colony in 1753)

GEORGIA (1732)

FLORIDA (Br. 1763-83)

New Orleans

The Settlement of North America: 1600–1763

- - - - - - - Boundaries of the 13 colonies

– · – · – · – Limits of French territory in 1763 controlled by settlements

– – – – – – Limits of British territory in 1763 controlled by settlements

GEORGIA (1732) Colony and date of foundation by charter or incorporation as a royal colony

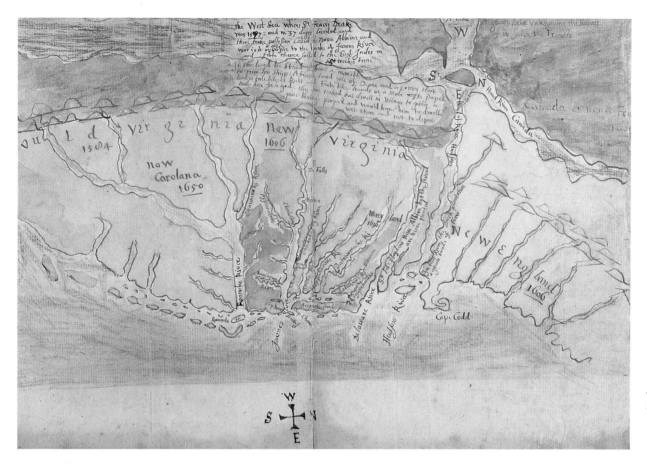

Various English explorers, including Sir Walter Raleigh, attempted to colonize the Americas on behalf of Queen Elizabeth I in the 1580s but failed. It was not until the 1650s, when this map was drawn by John Farrer, that farmers moved into 'Ould Virginia', which was renamed Carolina.

change when Charles II was crowned in 1660. Rhode Island and Connecticut adjusted prudently to the new situation; Massachusetts settled down to decades of discontent.

The Thirteen Colonies Take Shape

Charles's Government took more interest in colonial affairs than any of its predecessors. It renewed the Navigation Acts which gave the colonies a monopoly of the English market for their tobacco and other exports, and required them to buy their imports through England – with the advantage that 'Clothing new Nations cannot fail of encreasing the Demand for Goods.' This implied that the English government would provide military and naval support against other European powers, which it had not been willing to do earlier. The English government realized that while taxpayers might pay for a war against the French or the Dutch or the Spanish, they might feel that the colonists should pay for wars with the local population.

In 1664 the English captured the Dutch colony of New Amsterdam, at the mouth of the Hudson, with inland settlements running north up the river. By exchanging it for the Georgetown settlement in Guyana, the English kept New Amsterdam – and renamed most of it after James, Duke of York, Charles II's brother and heir. A slice of western New York was given to Cavaliers from Jersey and, in 1681, the King settled some of his debts by allotting an area still farther west to William Penn, a Quaker who wanted to found a new colony for religious toleration. Pennsylvania linked the New England and the Chesapeake Bay colonies. The Maryland–Pennsylvania boundary was not decided until the 1760s when Mason and Dixon surveyed a line – later famous as the northern limit of slavery – that divided the Penns and the Calverts. These two families had retained their proprietorial authority while the other colonies were ruled directly by the King. In 1702 three of Pennsylvania's counties merged to form Delaware, and the rest of Pennsylvania

THE ORIGINAL POPULATION

The relationship between the American colonists and the native population varied enormously. Its positive side is exemplified by the life of Pocahontas, the young Indian 'princess' who in 1608 saved Captain John Smith, the founder and leader of the colony at Jamestown, Virginia, from a sacrificial execution at the hands of her father's tribe. In the years that followed she continued to act as a benign mediator between her people and the settlers. Nevertheless, in 1612 she was seized and brought to Jamestown. There she was seen by John Rolfe who had just introduced an improved variety of tobacco plant into Virginia. Rolfe fell in love with her and they were married in April 1614. In 1616 the bride and groom sailed for England where Pocahontas was introduced at court by Lady Delaware. In the spring of 1617 Rolfe and his

The Indian princess, Pocahontas.

wife were preparing to return to Virginia when she fell ill. She died at Gravesend in Kent on 21 March 1617.

There was a dark side to the relationship between the colonists and the Indians. Land-grabbing by the Virginians led to a well-organized attack on them by the local Indians in 1622. Yet land could be acquired for settlement by agreement. William Penn was able to buy considerable areas of eastern Pennsylvania in 1682–4 and neither side reneged on the agreement, remaining true to the original spirit in which purchase had been made. As Penn remembered: 'When the Purchase was agreed, great Promises past between us of Kindness and Good Neighbourhood, and the Indians and the English must live in Love as long as the Sun gave light.'

William Penn (1644–1718) tried to put his religious principles into practice when the new colony of Pennsylvania was founded. During his visit of 1682, he negotiated a treaty with the Indians in which they sold him their land. When Penn returned to England two years later, the Quaker colony was firmly established on the basis of religious tolerance, government by popular will and an amicable relationship with the Indians.

became the only American colony to have no direct contact with the sea. Even so, the capital Philadelphia, a river port for sea-going ships, developed into the richest of America's eighteenth-century cities.

In 1663 Charles II granted several hundred miles of the coastline south of Virginia to eight Cavalier landowners. The Carolina land grant was anchored at its southern end by the charming port of Charlestown. People drifted south from Virginia, and these two centres of population, with a few hundred miles of empty coastline between them, led to the eventual subdivision of the original grant into North and South Carolina.

When James II succeeded Charles II in 1685, he started to combine the New England colonies (together with New Jersey and his own New York) into a Dominion of New England. This made sense militarily, as it was becoming clear that the St Lawrence colonies of New France might be a source of danger to the New England colonies, but James's Dominion of New England was never likely to be popular. Following the lead of Virginia in 1619, all the English colonies had introduced elected assemblies, whose approval was needed for the taxes and new laws. The Dominion, which had no assembly, looked much more like the French or Spanish colonies in which the authority of the monarch was supreme. James began to attack old-established charters, following the policy of his brother, who had won a court judgement nullifying the Massachusetts Bay Charter. However, James's attitude to the Constitution and his support for Roman Catholicism upset people in England as well; in 1688 he was driven into exile and his policy was reversed.

The Dominion of New England was broken up. The charters of New York, Rhode Island and Connecticut were all restored. Massachusetts Bay not only got its charter back; it also absorbed the Mayflower settlement of Plymouth, which had never had a charter. A little later, New Hampshire emerged as a separate colony and New Jersey was reformed as the single colony that Charles had originally created.

Virtually all today's seaboard states had been defined by the beginning of the 1690s – just as wars to control eastern North America were beginning between England and France. The French advanced down the Mississippi, but could not reach the English southern coastal settlements easily. Even when the British established Georgia in the 1730s, which had a common frontier with the Florida colony of France's ally Spain, no conflict followed. This new colony was intended to enable people who had been imprisoned for debt to make a fresh start in the New World. General James Oglethorpe, the founder, took the ideals of humanity so far that he wanted slavery to be forbidden in Georgia.

The thirteen colonies of the mid-eighteenth century stretched about twelve hundred miles from north to south but rarely penetrated more than two hundred miles inland. Like their relations and ancestors in Britain, they were loyal to the King but were always ready to disagree with his policies and his ministers. Their local assemblies had very little to do with each other and Benjamin Franklin's attempt to bring them together at the Albany conference in 1754 on Indian policy had very little effect.

The American colonies probably enjoyed the highest standard of living in the world and attracted a steady stream of immigrants from Britain and from Protestant Europe. In addition, there were the unwilling immigrants from Africa – the slaves, who at least lived better and survived longer than slaves farther to the south in the West Indian islands.

The colonies felt little need to trade amongst themselves. As a result, the early differences between the colonies were not blurred by contact with each other. Massachusetts remained less tolerant than the others, as can be seen in the persecution of 'witches' in Salem in the 1690s; over the course of four and a half months, almost two hundred people were imprisoned and twenty were put to death. Pennsylvania, on the other hand, attracted a wide range of immigrants with its policy of religious toleration. The Virginians also saw themselves as more gentlemanly and less troubled about religion than their neighbours. An American of the time might have felt that he lived in a geographically distinct part of the world and that he could run his own affairs very well. But it did not follow that he felt much in common with other Americans.

Most colonies considered trouble with the Indians as one of the difficulties of American life. Although tensions along the frontier between the colonists and the Indians were not as great as those in the sixteenth century along the English border with Scotland and Wales, there were some serious struggles, particularly in Virginia and Massachusetts in the 1670s. These conflicts could generally be resolved by prudent negotiation, but it was still easy enough for England or France to mobilize the Indians and to bring them into the European wars in upstate New York, western Pennsylvania and New Hampshire. The Five Nations of the Iroquois leaned towards the British while most of the other Indian groups were sympathetic to the French. No frontier settlement could be really safe while this continued.

The two imperial wars between 1690 and 1713 did little damage to the American colonies, but the colonies of England and France came face to face in the later imperial wars between 1739 and 1763. These were the wars the historian Macaulay had in mind when he wrote that 'red men scalped each other by the Great Lakes' as an unexpected consequence of the ambitions of Frederick of Prussia.

In the 1740s, American militias joined the British to march north and capture the French fort of Louisbourg on Cape Breton Island (although, at the end of the war, it was exchanged for Madras which the French had captured from the British). It was the Seven Years War from 1756 to 1763 that decided the fate of the French colonies. An overland march towards the Great Lakes by British troops, supported by militiamen under George Washington, ended in defeat near Fort Duquesne (later Pittsburgh) in the Ohio valley. But once Quebec had been captured in 1759, the whole of the French colony was at Britain's feet. Britain gained all of New France along the St Lawrence and the Great Lakes and the east side of the Mississippi down to New Orleans.

The Indians of the region realized that they would no longer be protected by the balance of power between France and Britain, and they organized themselves into what became known

as 'Pontiac's conspiracy'. Their attack was repulsed by the British army, but it did indicate the dangers of uncontrolled expansion. To avoid alarming the Indians, the British government drew a Proclamation Line in 1763, beyond which settlement was prohibited. The colonists, however, felt that this robbed them of the fruits of victory, first over the French and then over the Indians; as a result, relations between Britain and America began to break down.

The Road to Revolt

Two years later, the British government imposed a stamp duty on all official documents in the colonies to help pay for defence costs. Lieutenant Governor Hutchinson of Massachusetts might still write 'I know of no two colonies which think alike', but violent resistance to the Stamp Act united Americans. Almost all of them agreed that they were not liable to direct taxes from Westminster because they paid for defence by accepting the limitations on trade imposed by the Navigation Acts. But they were not yet sure whether or not their assemblies were subordinate to the British Parliament. They were placated briefly by the withdrawal of the stamp duties, but the question re-emerged in 1768 when Westminster imposed indirect taxes that were clearly intended to raise revenue. Resistance broke out once again and the Government removed most of the duties.

However, the financial problems of the East India Company brought the issue back to its previous level of intensity. In order to help the East India Company meet its debts, the Government allowed the company to ship its tea direct to America. This would have made tea attractively cheap in America, even though the colonists would have to pay a small duty there. The British Prime Minister, Lord North, believed that the Americans would not object to the tax, calling it a 'peppercorn of principle', but he was wrong. Determined opponents of the tax boarded the three ships and threw 342 chests of tea into Boston Harbour at the end of 1773.

Parliament imposed heavy penalties on Boston, including closing the port until the tea had been paid for. When John Adams, a future President of the United States, said that 'the revolution was complete in the hearts and minds of men before a shot was fired', he was talking about Massachusetts. But the penalties imposed on Boston convinced many Americans that their liberties were not safe until they had made it clear that Westminster could not legislate for them. By 1774 Britain was involved in a war three thousand miles from home against a rich and well-equipped people of whom about one-third were deeply committed to resistance; by 1776 the Americans had declared themselves independent.

At first, the British advanced from New York to Philadelphia and tried to regain the most densely populated regions. But, in 1777, an army marching south to the Hudson valley was surrounded in the woods and forced to surrender at Saratoga. France became convinced that Britain could be beaten and so the Americans gained a powerful ally. The British then marched through the less populated areas in the south, with considerable success in 1779 and 1780. By 1781 Lord Cornwallis had got as far as Chesapeake Bay, but the French navy commanded the entrance to the bay and the American armies combined to surround him. In October he surrendered at Yorktown, about a dozen miles from Jamestown, where the story had all begun: British rule in the American colonies was at an end. The British, however, were left with growing empires both in Canada and in India. A new era of the British Empire was about to begin.

History's most famous 'tea party', at Boston, in 1773.

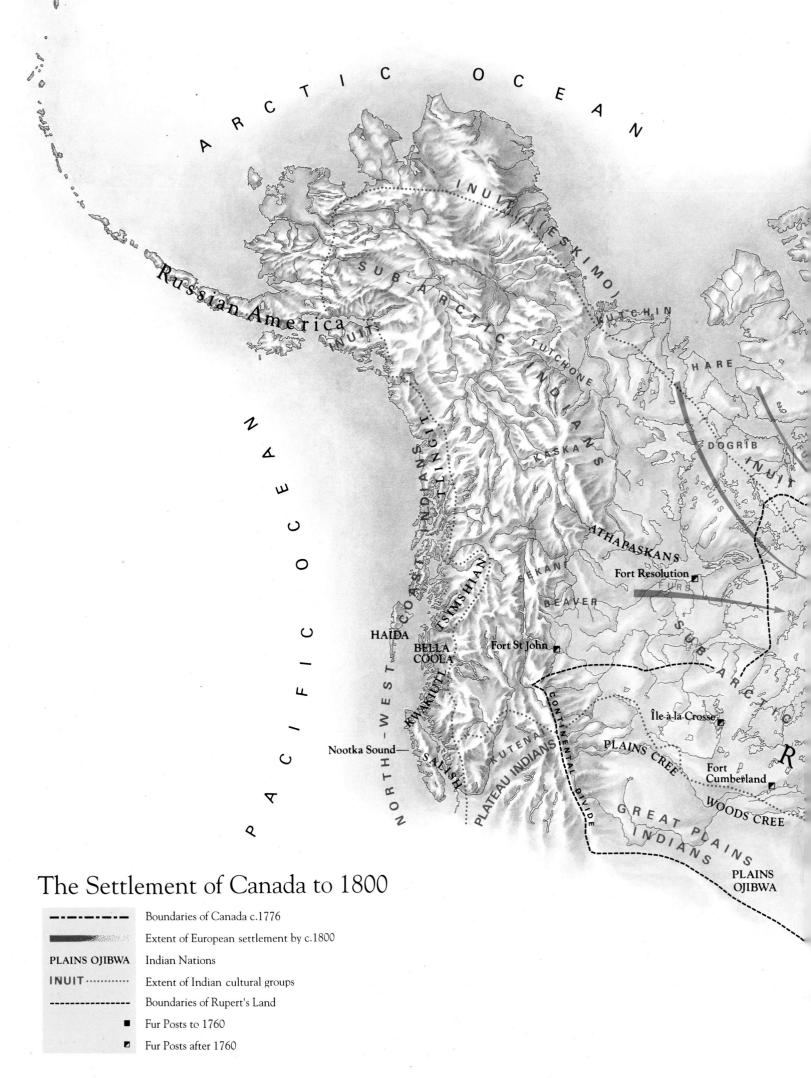

ARCTIC OCEAN

Russian America

INUIT (ESKIMO)

SUB-ARCTIC INDIANS

KUTCHIN

TUTCHONE

HARE

DOGRIB

INUIT

KASKAS

TLINGIT INDIANS

FURS

ATHABASKANS

COAST INDIANS

SEKANI

Fort Resolution ■

FURS

BEAVER

TSIMSHIAN

SUB-ARCTIC

PACIFIC OCEAN

HAIDA

BELLA
COOLA

Fort St John ■

KWAKIUTL

R

Île-à-la-Crosse ■

NORTH-WEST

CONTINENTAL DIVIDE

PLAINS CREE

Fort
Cumberland ■

Nootka Sound—

SALISH

KUTENAI

PLATEAU INDIANS

WOODS CREE

GREAT PLAINS

INDIANS

PLAINS
OJIBWA

The Settlement of Canada to 1800

—·—·—·—	Boundaries of Canada c.1776
▬▬▬▬	Extent of European settlement by c.1800
PLAINS OJIBWA	Indian Nations
INUIT ·········	Extent of Indian cultural groups
— — — — —	Boundaries of Rupert's Land
■	Fur Posts to 1760
◪	Fur Posts after 1760

INUIT

(ESKIMO)

Chesterfield Inlet

Prince of
Wales Fort
Churchill

York Factory

Severn

NDIANS

HUDSON
BAY

INUIT

VOYAGES OF
MARTIN FROBISHER 1570s

FUR TRADE TO BRITAIN

MANUFACTURED TRADE GOODS
(GUNS, BLANKETS, IRON TOOLS, TRAPS)

WHALING FLEETS

Labrador

BASQUE FISHERIES
(1525 - c.1625)

ert's Land

BEOTHUKS

ENGLISH FISHERIES

COD TO EUROPE

JAMES
BAY

Fort Albany

Eastmain

SUB-ARCTIC INDIANS

Moose Factory
CREE

CREE

MONTAGNAIS

GULF OF ST LAWRENCE

TIMBER TO BRITAIN

GRAND
BANKS
FISHERY

t Frances

Grand
Portage

OJIBWA

LAKE SUPERIOR

Sault Sainte Marie

Michilimackinad

NIPISSING

ALGONQUIN

HURON
PETUN
NEUTRALS

LAKE HURON

LAKE MICHIGAN

Montréal

Québec

Canada

FURS TO EUROPE

FRENCH
FISHERIES

Louisbourg

CAPE BRETON
ISLAND (1784)

NEW
BRUNSWICK
(1784)

NOVA SCOTIA
(ACADIA)

MICMAC

PRINCE EDWARD
ISLAND (1769)

Fort Frontenac

Albany

L. ONTARIO

Fort Detroit

LAKE ERIE

35

CHAPTER FOUR

CANADA: CONQUEST AND COLONISATION

◇

Although Norse explorers established a tenuous foothold on the inhospitable coast of Vinland (later Newfoundland) in the ninth century, it was not until the late fifteenth century that explorers from northern Europe were drawn once again to the vast wilderness of Canada. They were searching for the North-West Passage, an elusive second route to the spice lands of the East. What they found, according to a report by the explorer John Cabot in 1497, was a 'sea swarming with fish', especially cod, 'the beef of the ocean'.

French Initiatives in the Land God Gave to Cain

Despite the fact that Cabot's voyage had been authorized by King Henry VII of England, it was the French who took the lead in exploring and settling Canada. In 1534–5 Jacques Cartier made three voyages there. His first impressions of the coast were bleak: 'being composed of stones and horrible rugged rocks . . . I did not see one cartload of earth, though I landed in many places. In fine I am rather inclined to believe that this is the land God gave to Cain.' He reached as far as present-day Montreal where he found a well-fortified Iroquoian village, Hochelaga.

The first permanent French settlements were established during the expeditions of Samuel de Champlain in 1605–8. The early settlers refined the art of salting cod and exported it back to France, whose Roman Catholic population generated a huge demand for fish on Fridays and feast days. They also discovered an even more valuable commodity – beaver fur. Fur hats, gloves and coats, in a profusion of different shapes and styles, became the height of fashion during the cold European winters: a sure marker of gentry status. They were also light and easy to ship.

The early settlers encountered two main groups of indigenous peoples in Canada. The Iroquoians and the Algonquians spoke different languages and differed in their economic and social structures. The Iroquoian peoples included the Huron and Petun around Georgian Bay, the Erie to the south, and the Five Nations to the south-east of Lake Ontario. They lived in large, pallisaded villages which comprised as many as 3,000 people. As Marc Lescarbot observed, when he visited the infant French colony of the New World in 1605, 'They sleep on strips of bark laid on the ground, covered with wretched skins, whereof they also make their garments, such as otters, beavers, martens, foxes, wild cats, roes, stags and other wild beasts, though indeed the greater part of them go practically stark naked.' The Iroquoians cultivated vegetables and fruits in the fields, and smoked fish and meat as winter provisions.

In contrast to the Iroquoians, the Algonquians were semi-nomadic people consisting of small clans. The main Algonquian nations were the Nipissing to the north of Georgian Bay, the Algonquin in the Ottawa valley, the Montagnais in the Saguenay valley, the Micmacs in the Maritime region and the Beothuck of Newfoundland. When the Europeans arrived, the Indians were quick to recognize foreign demand for their resources. Not only did they supply the furs and fish which were exported back to Europe; they also introduced the French to the rich corn harvests of Huronia, to native medicines and to birch-bark canoes.

The voyages of exploration by Cartier and his followers were mapped by Desceliers on this sixteenth-century map.

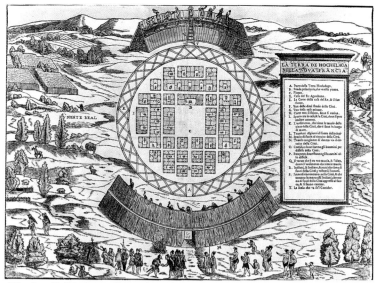

The fortified Indian village of Hochelaga stood on the site of present-day Montreal when Cartier arrived in 1535.

New France was a lanky colony stretching along the banks of the St Lawrence from the farming communities in the tidal marshland of Acadia to the fortress town of Quebec, which was founded in 1608, and Montreal, which was founded in 1648. By 1730 French influence, manifested in a fragile chain of trading posts and Jesuit missions, stretched south along the Ohio and Mississippi rivers to the Gulf of Mexico and west as far as the Saskatchewan River on the prairies. Most of the settlers traded in beaver pelts or scratched a living from farms that stretched in long, narrow strips back from the river. Life for the *habitants* (tenant farmers) in these.*seigneuries* (feudally run farms) was hard – given the poverty of the land and the burdens of their feudal obligations.

The English Gain a Foothold

The rich fishing off Newfoundland had attracted the English, Spanish and Portuguese fleets as well as the French. King James I even granted Nova Scotia to his Scots kinsman, the Earl of Stirling, over the heads of the French, who had already laid claim to it. Although the English had a powerful navy, they did little more than pick away at the edges of the French enterprise in the first half of the seventeenth century. In the meantime the fishing in the region was abundant enough to sustain a level of peaceful coexistence between the European powers. Each year the fleets would set out from their European ports in a race to secure the best harbours along the rugged Newfoundland coast.

During the fishing season, temporary harbour townships were established to wash, salt, dry and pack the cod. England was initially at a disadvantage since her Catholic competitors had superior natural salt resources and a readier home market for fish for fasts and feast days. However, to compensate, English Newfoundland soon developed characteristics that were unique in North America: 'The island of Newfoundland had been considered . . . a great English ship moored near the banks during the fishing season for the convenience of English fishermen. The governor was considered the ship's captain, and all those who were concerned in the fishery business as his crew, and subject to naval discipline while there, and expected to return to England when the season was over.'

By the mid-seventeenth century, the strength of England's interlocking trade between the West Indies and her North Atlantic colonies, combined with the defeat of the Spanish Armada, ensured her control of one of Newfoundland's most lucrative fishing regions: the Avalon Peninsula. This became a vital cornerstone for England, a focus for trade and shipping, and for financial and territorial interests.

However, the English soon turned their attention from fish to

From catching to curing, the cod-fishing industry of Newfoundland became highly organized during the seventeenth century.

THE VANISHING NORTH AMERICAN POPULATION

When the French returned to Hochelaga in the early seventeenth century they found the site deserted. The once-formidable Indian town had probably been a casualty of Amerindian wars and the debilitating effects of European diseases. Similar crises afflicted other native Canadians. Huronia was weakened by smallpox, then destroyed by the Five Nations Iroquois; and Newfoundland was invaded by a lethal combination of bacteria and indigenous rivals (the Micmacs).

For many tribes, trade with the Europeans quickly became an unequal partnership. The introduction of iron tools and weapons revolutionized the economies of these groups. During the seventeenth and eighteenth centuries competition intensified between the

Hurons and Algonquins, allied to the French, and the Five Nations Iroquois, affiliated with New Amsterdam. In 1649–50 the Five Nations gained the upper hand and destroyed Huronia.

Inter-tribal warfare only affected a certain number of Amerindian societies but all were highly vulnerable to the microbial baggage brought across the Atlantic by the new trading partners. With limited natural resistance to block the progress of diseases such as smallpox and measles, European-sponsored epidemics cut a swathe through the native Canadian population. As early as 1634 it would seem that half of the Huron and Petun populations had succumbed. European demand for furs stimulated the native trading network and

thereby accelerated the dissemination of fatal germs.

The severity of the plagues could also be explained by Amerindian child-rearing practices: in the absence of milk from dairy animals, the very young were breast-fed until they were as much as four years old. Coupled with this, the widespread Amerindian custom of sexual abstinence during nursing (to avoid sibling competition for food) would have ensured a small number of births per woman. These biological and cultural adaptations hindered any possibility of rapid repopulation. And, as a result, any acquired immunities could not be passed on from one generation to the next with sufficient speed to avert demographic catastrophe.

fur, which was by now very fashionable in Europe. In an attempt to control the fur trade, they seized Quebec in 1628. Although the trading post was returned to France four years later, the action initiated 150 years of sporadic fighting between them.

In 1668, two English trading vessels sailed into Hudson Bay and claimed the whole region in the name of King Charles II. One of the great strengths of British imperialism was the way in which Crown patronage and private enterprise were combined profitably. In 1670 the 'Company of Adventurers of England trading into Hudson's Bay' obtained a royal charter, which gave them a monopoly of trade all around the bay. Financed by many of the British nobility, the Hudson's Bay Company quickly became an effective and influential tool of English and later British imperial policy in the region. Charles's cousin, Prince Rupert, became the first Governor, and permanent trading posts were established in 'Rupert's Land'.

England and France at War

Enmity between the English and the French grew as rivalry for the fur trade intensified. In general, there were two factors which determined the relative success of the two nations: relations with the indigenous Indian peoples and the course of war in Europe. In addition, the English had, until 1776, the support of their powerful American colonies to the south.

In 1690 the English made second attempts to capture Montreal and Quebec; these failed, but a New England fleet did capture Acadia. At the same time the French under d'Iberville seized all but one of the Hudson's Bay Company outposts and terrorized English settlements from New England to Newfoundland. The Treaty of Ryswick in 1697 restored the status quo, but hostilities hardly ceased. During the War of the Spanish Succession in Europe (1702–13) England won possession of Newfoundland – which her Board of Trade considered was worth more than Canada and Louisiana put together – and all of Acadia apart from Prince Edward Island and Cape Breton Island. Fortress settlements bristled up, the French at Louisbourg on Cape Breton Island and the English with over 2,000 settlers at Halifax in Nova Scotia.

In coping with the belligerence of the English, the French were continually distracted by the ever-present danger of Indian attack. The Iroquois had wiped out several Jesuit missions and, in 1660, Montreal itself had been in grave danger of falling. Regular French punitive expeditions against the Iroquois allowed the English to consolidate their presence in the north. By 1756, there were about two million English settlers in the colonies, compared with around seventy thousand French.

As the Seven Years War broke out in Europe in 1756, the Marquis of Montcalm was sent to Quebec to coordinate the French colonial war effort. After some French success, the tide of war turned to Britain. In 1758 Louisbourg fell to the British, as did Fort Frontenac on Lake Ontario. At last, the gateways to the St Lawrence were in British hands.

In June 1759 British naval and land forces under General James Wolfe worked their way up the St Lawrence. At dawn on 13 September 1759, Wolfe's troops assembled on the Plains of Abraham outside the city. Both Montcalm and Wolfe were mortally wounded in the following battle. Quebec fell four days later and Montreal the following year. In 1763, the Treaty of Paris formalized Britain's annexation of New France and the islands off Nova Scotia. However, the harsh winters, the poor soil, the hotchpotch of indigenous cultures and the large French population that still remained made this victory over New France a mixed blessing.

British Canada: A Colony Built on Compromise

After so much effort, the British government was less than delighted with its latest acquisition and tried to swap it for the sugar island of Guadeloupe. With a certain degree of relish, perhaps, the French refused. British options for dealing with the new territory were limited.

In 1764 James Murray became the first governor of the new colony and adopted a 'softly-softly' approach. He was unwilling to be swayed by the fiercely anti-Catholic English-speaking merchants, who resented his policies and his 'rage and rudeness of language and demenour', and petitioned the king to have him removed. Murray was even less impressed with these 'licentious fanatics' than they were with him, informing the king in turn that nothing would satisfy them save 'the expulsion of the Canadians who are perhaps the best and bravest race upon the globe.' Murray's successor, Guy Carleton, fully supported his ideals and faith in the French-speaking Canadian people.

The Quebec Act of 1774 provided a compromise. It gave the colony a council of English and French nominees working under an appointed governor. English criminal law was introduced but French civil law was retained as well. Bars against Catholics entering office or enjoying the other benefits of citizenship were lifted, and the Church was permitted to collect its tithes. Edmund Burke thundered against this mingling of concessions: 'What can compensate an Englishman for the loss of his laws? Do you propose to take away liberty from the Englishman,

---

THE HUDSON'S BAY COMPANY

The prime mover behind the attempt to wrest the North American fur trade from the French was Prince Rupert, ex-Royalist cavalier and naval leader. It was he who introduced the two French adventurers, Radisson and Groseilliers, who had proposed the venture, to Charles II and he who organized the syndicate that backed their first exploration of the Bay. The Royal Charter was signed on 2 May 1670. The territory granted, known as Rupert's Land, comprised 40 per cent of what is now modern Canada from beyond the Arctic circle in the north to the Great Lakes in the south. Four weeks later, two vessels set sail from London.

The first Governor of the territory was Charles Bayley, a wild Quaker who was taken straight from his cell in the Tower to the ships. His jailer was also a member of the Company's governing council.

During the next nine years Bayley ran the Canadian end of the business with skill and discrimination, setting up posts at the mouths of the rivers that ran into the Bay. He maintained good relations with the Indians who supplied the beaver fur.

From the first, the Company had decided that useful goods, such as needles, muskets and hatchets rather than worthless trinkets, should be traded. The process became highly structured with ritualized trading ceremonies, in which the mutual respect of both parties was emphasized, before business began. The Indians bargained through their trading captain, while the Company worked through the local factor. Each post had a separate trading room in which negotiations were conducted. Because of the enormous distances involved and the difficulty of the terrain, tribes such as the Cree, whose territory adjoined the posts, assumed the role of commercial middlemen, evolving a system of trade with tribes living hundreds of miles from the Bay.

'The Death of General Wolfe' by Benjamin West. General James Wolfe (1727–59) was commander of the British army at the capture of Quebec from the French in 1759, a victory which led to British supremacy in Canada. Wolfe died of wounds received during the battle after hearing of his success.

because you will not give it to the French? I would give it to the Englishman, though ten thousand Frenchmen should take it against their will!' As an olive branch to the English-speaking merchants, however, the northern frontiers of Canada were extended to improve the viability of the fur trade.

This liberal and tolerant document was received coolly. The French peasantry faced the reimposition of tithes and seigneurial dues after an interruption of fifteen years while, in New England and New York, it was condemned as a reimposition of the old 'French threat' on the northern frontier.

Canada during the American War of Independence

Given the general dissatisfaction, it is perhaps surprising that the majority of French Canadians remained neutral during the American War of Independence. American hopes of Canadian support were soon dashed. Despite the appearance of hundreds of French-Canadian volunteers when the Americans marched almost unhindered into Montreal in November 1775, Benjamin Franklin wrote home gloomily that without help the American troops would need 'to starve, plunder or surrender'. Local dislike of the régime at Quebec did not amount to a desire to submerge Canada's identity in a union with America. The merchants would not endanger their own profitability by joining the trade embargo against Britain.

Nova Scotia, the '14th colony', was equally equivocal in its response to the American war. Although an extension of New England, with strong religious and commercial connections with Massachusetts and her neighbours, she had profited greatly from British trade and military investment in Halifax and the outposts. The fact that, during the war, New England privateers pillaged the small coastal towns of Nova Scotia failed to excite

any revolutionary instincts. Torn 'betwixt natural affection to our nearest relations and good Faith and Friendship to our King and Country', the 'neutral Yankees' of Nova Scotia took no decisive action and remained within the British fold.

After American independence had been declared, a band of dispossessed loyalists flocked into Nova Scotia and Canada from America, claiming political representation and compensation for their confiscated properties. New Brunswick was carved out of Nova Scotia as a loyalist colony, and the Constitutional Act of 1791 recognized the co-existence of French and British descendants in Canada and divided the country into Upper and Lower Canada, each with its own legislative Assembly. By 1800, the bi-cultural character of the country was established.

New Horizons

In the following years, British explorers reached the westernmost limits of North America. Attempting to substantiate claims of a North-West Passage, Captain James Cook made a preliminary survey of the coastline in 1778. He failed to find the mythical river which might open up new trade routes from Britain to the Pacific, but he did map the coast of what is now British Columbia and laid down the foundations for trade with the indigenous Indians. In 1793 Alexander Mackenzie explored overland from Rupert's Land to the Rocky Mountains and the coast. The Union Jack was raised at Nootka Sound on 23 March 1795, and a transcontinental Empire was officially established.

The nineteenth century would witness the modification of these frontiers and the consolidation of British claims to the vast central plain between the Great Lakes and the Rockies. For the time being, however, Britain seemed more perfectly placed than any other empire or nation to dominate North America.

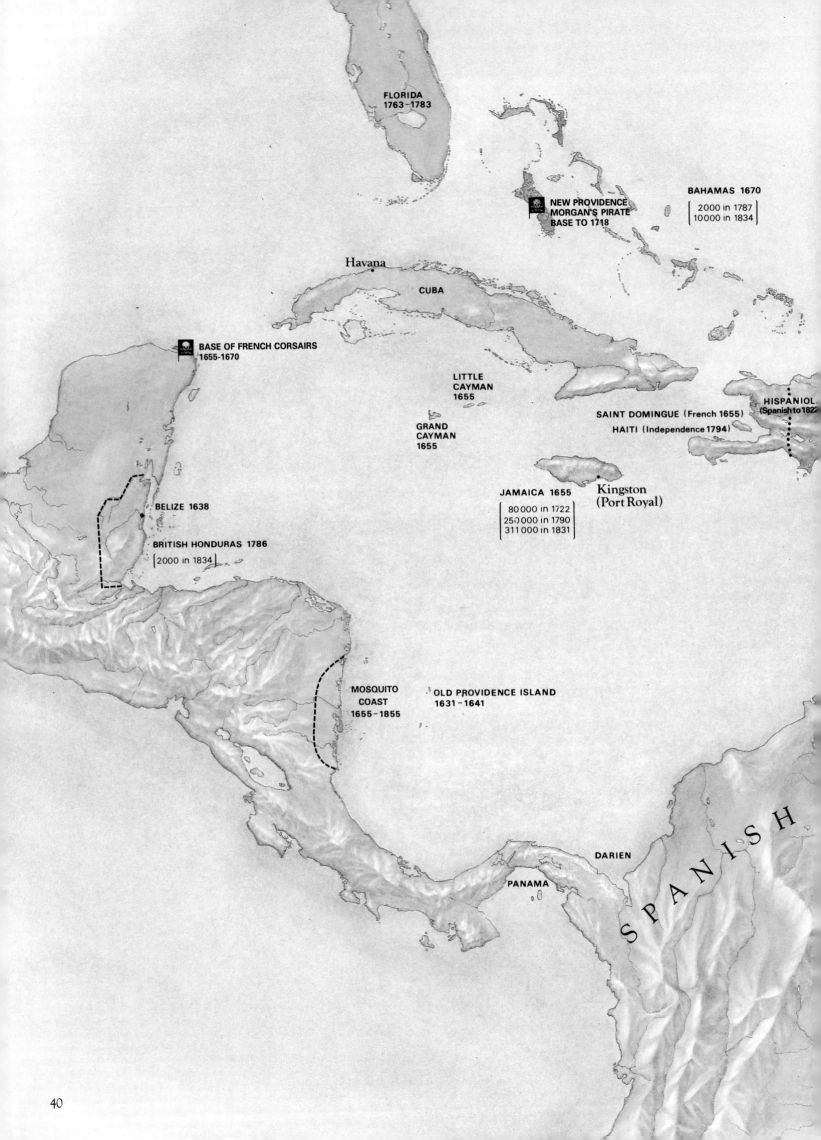

FLORIDA
1763–1783

BAHAMAS 1670

2000 in 1787
10000 in 1834

NEW PROVIDENCE
MORGAN'S PIRATE
BASE TO 1718

Havana

CUBA

BASE OF FRENCH CORSAIRS
1655–1670

LITTLE
CAYMAN
1655

HISPANIOL
(Spanish to 1822

SAINT DOMINGUE (French 1655)

HAITI (Independence 1794)

GRAND
CAYMAN
1655

JAMAICA 1655

Kingston
(Port Royal)

BELIZE 1638

80000 in 1722
250000 in 1790
311000 in 1831

BRITISH HONDURAS 1786

2000 in 1834

MOSQUITO
COAST
1655–1855

OLD PROVIDENCE ISLAND
1631–1641

DARIEN

PANAMA

S P A N I S H

The Scramble for the Caribbean: 1600–1800

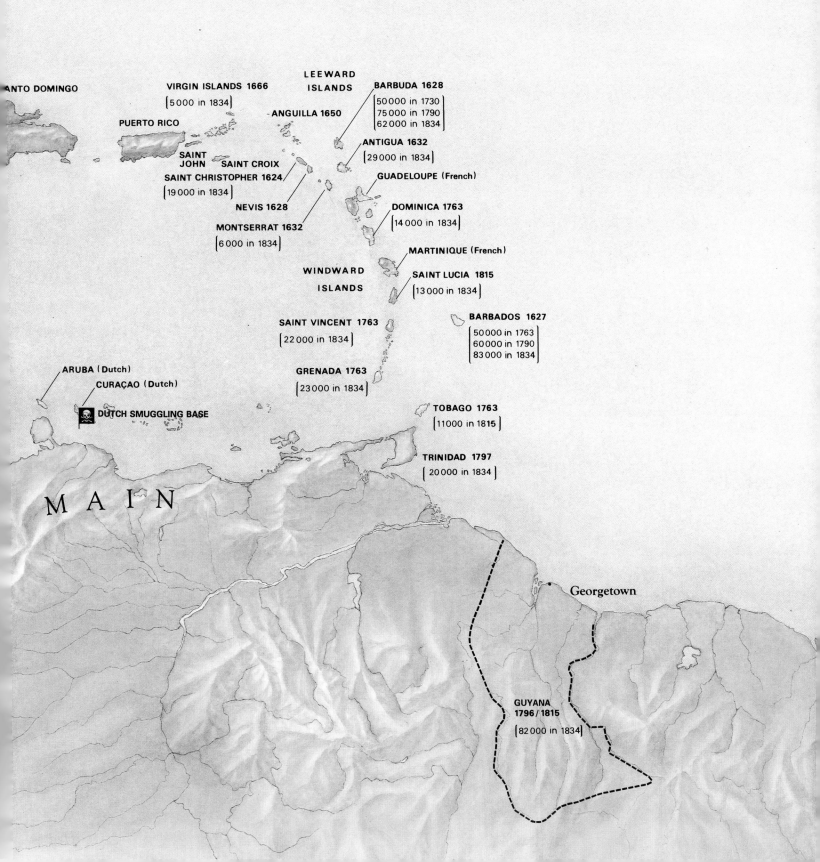

ANTO DOMINGO

PUERTO RICO

LEEWARD
ISLANDS

VIRGIN ISLANDS 1666
[5000 in 1834]

- ANGUILLA 1650

BARBUDA 1628
50000 in 1730
75000 in 1790
62000 in 1834

ANTIGUA 1632
[29000 in 1834]

SAINT
JOHN   SAINT CROIX
SAINT CHRISTOPHER 1624
[19000 in 1834]

GUADELOUPE (French)

NEVIS 1628

DOMINICA 1763
[14000 in 1834]

MONTSERRAT 1632
[6000 in 1834]

MARTINIQUE (French)

WINDWARD
ISLANDS

SAINT LUCIA 1815
[13000 in 1834]

SAINT VINCENT 1763
[22000 in 1834]

BARBADOS 1627
50000 in 1763
60000 in 1790
83000 in 1834

ARUBA (Dutch)
CURAÇAO (Dutch)

GRENADA 1763
[23000 in 1834]

☠ DUTCH SMUGGLING BASE

TOBAGO 1763
[11000 in 1815]

TRINIDAD 1797
[20000 in 1834]

M A I N

Georgetown

GUYANA
1796/1815
[82000 in 1834]

CHAPTER FIVE

PROFIT AND PLUNDER IN THE CARIBBEAN

◇

The economic importance of Canada as the heart of the British Empire in the Americas lay well in the future. To the men of the eighteenth century, the real prize of colonial wars was the sugar islands of the Caribbean. In 1763 the single French island of Guadeloupe was considered more important than Canada which was ceded to the British in exchange. Why was the Caribbean so crucial to eighteenth-century empires?

The West Indian islands of the Caribbean had enticed the Europeans ever since their discovery by Columbus in 1492. 'In all Castile there is no land which can be compared with this for beauty and fertility', he wrote of Hispaniola.

Never did a seeming paradise lead to such widespread exploitation and misery. Millions of slaves and indentured workers laboured and died to create fortunes for those colonists lucky enough to have established themselves early on the islands. The plantation owners were terrorized by marauding Spanish, French, Dutch and English privateers who were often beyond the control of their governments. Merchant ships were in constant danger of being looted and burned. Fortunes were made and many more were lost: the whole economy of the islands was built on a system of brutal suppression and corruption.

Although the Spanish had arrived first in the Caribbean, they were more interested in the gold and silver of their mainland settlements. By the mid-seventeenth century, relatively little attention was paid by the Spanish to the region, although her bullion-laden ships were to attract pirates and buccaneers for a century to come. The thin chain of islands falling away to the south of the Bahamas and the Greater Antilles remained unsettled by European colonists throughout the sixteenth century. Although the English had learnt about their existence through their early Caribbean trade, the only visitors to these shores were French buccaneers setting up temporary bases for their raids against the Spanish.

Early English Settlement
After the great success of Virginian tobacco the English looked for new lands on which the luxury product could be grown.

In 1623 the first English settlement was established on St Kitts and, four years later, on Barbados. The early years consisted of backbreaking work in an exhausting climate. According to Sir Josiah Child, a London merchant, the work was performed by: 'loose, vagrant people, vicious and destitute of means to live at home, being either unfit for labour or such as . . . had so misbehaved themselves by whoring, thieving or other debauchery that none would set them on work.'

Even at this early stage, it was obvious that, without slave labour, the whole of the contested Caribbean area would be unworkable. Apart from the South American Indians imported by the Dutch and Spanish, the major workforce at the time were white 'slaves or indentured labourers, who were imported and bound to their plantation masters for a period of around seven years, after which they could buy a small plot and set up in business for themselves.' Their lot was pitiful: 'being bought and

sold . . . or attached as horses and beasts for the debts of their masters, being whipt for their masters' pleasure, and sleeping in sties worse than hogs in England'. There were many appeals to the English Parliament for greater clemency which, for the most part, were ignored.

War at Sea
Over the next two centuries, the Caribbean was to become a major battlefield for European powers. The Spanish, not unnaturally, resented the intrusion of other Europeans into their 'Spanish Lake'. In 1494 Pope Alexander VI had divided the New World between the Spanish and the Portuguese; any interlopers in the region were therefore regarded as pirates by the Spanish and attacked accordingly. English settlers were not intimidated by this papal division. Some settled down to growing tobacco, while others turned into pirates, profiting from the colonies' proximity to the rich Spanish Main and plundering ships regardless of nationality. Between these two groups lay the buccaneers (named after the Brazilian cured meat that they ate on long voyages) who were fighting a private war against Spain. This war was approved as a holy war against European Catholicism by the English Protestants.

The whole region might have slipped into total anarchy had it not been for the collapse of tobacco prices in Europe during the 1630s, due to over-production and consequent market saturation. The English were forced, therefore, to diversify into other crops. At the time, the Dutch had lost control of their Brazilian sugar plantations – which supplied the great re-export market of Amsterdam – and hoped that English settlements might be able to fill this role. They turned to the English islands, beginning with Barbados, and introduced the sugar-growing and production techniques there. It was a complicated process and not one that the English could have developed by themselves at that time. It was capital-intensive, but it also needed a large and docile labour force, which the Dutch transported from the South American mainland.

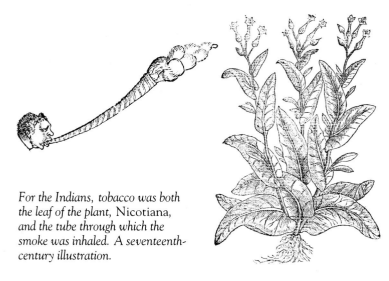

For the Indians, tobacco was both the leaf of the plant, Nicotiana, and the tube through which the smoke was inhaled. A seventeenth-century illustration.

The most infamous of all the pirates was Captain Henry Morgan, who plundered the Spanish Caribbean colonies in the seventeenth century with the unofficial support of the British Government.

Since England was paralysed by civil war at the time, there was little that the English government could do to prevent her settlements from becoming sugar suppliers for the Dutch re-export market. However, after the execution of King Charles I in 1649, the new government concentrated on bringing the former King's subjects firmly to heel and sent a navy to the Caribbean. The presence of ships from the home country, sent to restore discipline rather than to share in the spoils of private enterprise in the Caribbean, was unprecedented; as was the economic policy which followed, binding the settlers to trading through English ports. The first of the Navigation Acts provoked the Dutch into war, but increasing sugar consumption in England encouraged the colonists to maintain sugar production.

In 1653 Oliver Cromwell, the new English head of state, embarked upon his 'Western Design' in the Caribbean. He ended the Dutch war and launched England once again into the familiar anti-Spanish, anti-Catholic antagonism. A naval force was sent to rouse the colonies into attacking the large Spanish island of Hispaniola. This was too ambitious a task for the untrained troops, who were routed. The parliamentary commissioners were shaken by the Spanish resistance and blamed the rout on the lack of cooperation from colonists who had been picked up from Barbados to swell the fighting force. They complained to the Governor of Barbados that 'your men and the men of St Christopher's lead all the disorder and confusion . . . being the most prophane debauch'd persons that we ever saw, scorners of Religion, and indeed men kept so loose as not to be kept under discipline, and so cowardly as not to be made to fight.'

To raise morale, the thinly garrisoned Spanish island of Jamaica was captured. It was ten times the size of England's other West Indian holdings put together but was certainly not worth ten times as much. Whereas the little islands of St Kitts, Montserrat, Nevis and Antigua had followed Barbados in sugar cultivation, most of Jamaica was too high or too far from the sea for intensive cultivation. With her myriad coves and inlets, she was to remain for a long time the pit-stop of buccaneers.

England had little more control over the islands in the latter half of the seventeenth century than in the first half. Although the position of governor was a royal appointment, each island elected its own assembly. A travelling governor of the Leeward Islands found it hard to impose his authority on each of his islands except when he was there in person. When the governor was away – especially from Jamaica – restoring order was almost impossible. This independent spirit was largely due to the colonies having to defend themselves during the wars with France, the Netherlands and Spain in the 1660s and 1670s. These wars were ended with the Treaty of Madrid in 1670 with Spain, which gave the English the right to remain in the islands they had acquired.

The Last of the Pirates

News of the treaty was slow in reaching Captain Henry Morgan, the most notorious of the buccaneers. He was to continue operating as a pirate under the pious flag of patriotism until his death in 1688. Morgan had begun his career as an indentured labourer to a planter in Barbados. He escaped to learn his raiding skills from French buccaneers based in Tortuga, near Hispaniola. The French had perfected looting and cattle-raiding techniques, which were performed with such gusto that a French observer described a boatload of buccaneers returning from one expedition as looking like 'the butcher's vilest servants, who have been eight days in the slaughterhouse without washing themselves'.

Kingston, Jamaica: an early nineteenth-century view of the capital, then known as Port Royal.

Morgan was a natural leader and soon commanded a troop of desperadoes at Port Royal in Jamaica, with the tacit approval of the Jamaican Governor, Sir Thomas Modyford. Despite the Treaty of Madrid, Morgan led an invasion into Panama whose brutality could not be ignored. Morgan and Modyford were summoned to England for an explanation. Much to the indignation of the Spanish, the silver-tongued Morgan was treated to a hero's welcome in London, knighted by Charles II and sent back to Jamaica as Lieutenant Governor, in return for a promise of good behaviour. (The less persuasive Modyford was sent to the Tower of London for a while.) A new régime was instigated by which buccaneers could choose between enrolling in the Royal Navy or being harried as pirates across the Caribbean by an increasingly hostile English government. Under the charismatic Morgan, enough buccaneers chose the latter option for Port Royal to become immensely wealthy, despite its incorrigible Governor being stripped of all government offices in 1683. Morgan lived only five years more, his reputation blackened by drunken rages and brutalities. In 1692 an earthquake swallowed up Port Royal in what was judged as a divine response to the city's wickedness. A contemporary account published in the *Gentleman's Magazine* described the horrifying scene: 'In many places the earth crack'd, opened and shut, with a motion quick and fast, in some of these people were swallowed up, in others they were caught by the middle and pressed to death, and in others only heads appeared, in which condition dogs came and ate them . . . scarce a planter's house or sugar-work was left standing in all Jamaica.'

Port Royal never recovered its prosperity, divine retribution leaving nothing to chance as another earthquake destroyed the rebuilt town in 1703, followed by hurricanes in 1722 and 1744. The former pirate capital was, by the mid-eighteenth century, reduced to nothing more than a suburb of the new capital, Kingston. The cause of the pirates never quite recovered either. After the first destruction of Port Royal, the pirates withdrew to the Bahamas, pursued by a pack of English naval ships which captured their base on New Providence Island in 1718. By the 1730s, their trade was virtually eliminated.

One venture that ended in disaster was an attempt by the Scots to establish a Scottish trading company at Darien on the isthmus of Panama. Believing that it would become the cross-roads for world trade, a great proportion of Scotland's liquid capital was sunk into the scheme. The Spaniards, however, had been there for two centuries and had not overlooked the potential of the region: it was a malarial swamp. The dream of building a canal across the isthmus was not to be realized until the twentieth century; in the late seventeenth century the struggle to cross it was almost impossible. If there had been any danger of the colony at Darien succeeding, the Spanish would have attacked it. As it was, they were content to let it collapse by itself. Disease and lack of trade took their toll and, only ten years later, the colony surrendered to the Spanish. This failure deepened Scotland's poverty and forced the issue of a commercial and political union with England, which was finally achieved by the Act of Union in 1707.

The Success of Sugar

Union encouraged Scottish prosperity and the growth of Glasgow as a port. In England, Bristol and Liverpool in particular benefited greatly from the thriving Caribbean trade, although they resented the monopoly of the London merchants through whom all the Caribbean goods were re-exported. 'Almost every man in Liverpool is a merchant,' wrote a contemporary observer, 'and he who cannot send a bale will send a bandbox . . .'

Sugar came to be seen as the 'silver mine' of the Caribbean. One by one, the islands established huge cane plantations. At first planters had complained that the Navigation Acts forced them to send their sugar to London for re-export, and had evaded the laws by smuggling. However, English consumption of sugar shot up during the eighteenth century, making the planters devoted defenders of the Acts. In 1727 the price of brown sugar at the London Customs House was 24s. 10¼d. per cwt; by 1757 it was 42s. 5d. The new 'Sugar Kings' were planters who had made such fortunes in the islands that they returned to buy seats in Parliament, leaving overseers to manage the estates. The Sugar Kings formed a powerful clique, defending their interests in Parliament and opposing the call for the abolition of the slave trade. The French plantations, especially on the island of Saint-Domingue, also expanded rapidly in the early eighteenth century, although French domestic sugar consumption was less than half that of Britain.

THE LUXURY GOODS OF IMPERIAL LIFE

Admiral 'Old Grog' Vernon, painted by Thomas Gainsborough about 1753.

The seventeenth century saw a great wave of novel and highly enjoyable commodities flood into Britain: opium from Bengal; tea from China; coffee from Arabia; tobacco from America and sugar from the West Indies. These luxuries were originally intended for the rich but they soon appealed to all levels of society. Sugar became the most valuable of these novelties because it could be used for so many things.

Rum, which is produced from sugar, was fast becoming a staple drink in the West Indies in the first half of the eighteenth century. According to Captain Jackson, a newcomer to Barbados, 'the chief fudling they make in this land is Rumbullion, alias Kill divill, and this is made of sugar canes distilled, a hot hellish and terrible liquor'. The Royal Navy had originally drunk beer like other northern European navies. However, as long voyages increasingly became the norm, the Admiralty decided that beer did not keep and that it took up too much space. The planters had already been shipping rum to England at high proofs in order to keep costs down. This system was quickly adopted on British warships, and mixed with a ration of lemon juice to combat scurvy; 151 per cent proof Lamb's Navy Rum (75 per cent pure alcohol) has kept its traditional name to this day. The eighteenth-century sailor shared his taste for potent rum with the planters; when Admiral Vernon, known as 'Old Grog' because of his grogram coat, ordered that the rum ration be diluted in order to introduce some measure of sobriety amongst his men, the resulting 'grog' was stronger than the grog we know today.

Coffee-drinking was introduced to Europe during the sixteenth and seventeenth centuries, but it gained real popularity with the opening of the London coffee houses, the first of which was established about 1652. These houses gradually became centres for business and for political, religious and literary discussion.

The eighteenth-century diet was changing and the demand for sugar escalating. Tea was still a luxury enjoyed mainly by the upper classes but, as it arrived in greater quantities through the East India Company, it became cheaper and more popular. Cordials, jams and confectionery were becoming more popular, too, so that sugar consumption trebled in fifty years.

By the second half of the century, the British dominated the sugar trade. It was of such importance that William Pitt the Elder once reduced a wrangling House of Commons to silence by shouting 'Sugar!' several times, when he thought its members were lacking in respect for the noble commodity. During the Seven Years War (1756–63), the British captured almost every French or Spanish sugar-producing island: Dominica, Tobago, St Vincent, Grenada and the Windward Islands were all ceded to Britain as part of the Treaty of Paris in 1763. Britain even argued with France over swapping the tiny sugar island of Guadeloupe for the whole of Canada. The French, however, held fast to the riches of Guadeloupe, leaving Britain rather discontented with her frozen Canadian asset.

The sugar economy was built on an appalling wastage of human life. Thousands of Negro slaves perished either on the slave ships or through starvation and ill-treatment in the West Indies. In addition, the white population was gripped by the constant fear of Negro revolts. The black population outnumbered the whites by as many as ten to one on islands such as Antigua. It was not an imbalance that appeared to worry its Governor, Lord Lavington, overmuch. According to a contemporary observer, 'He was attended by an army of black servants, but he would not allow any of the black servitors about him to wear shoes or stockings, their legs being rubbed daily with butter so that they shone like jet; and he would not, if he could avoid it, handle a letter or parcel from their fingers. To escape the indignity he designed a golden instrument, like a tongs, with which he held any article given him. . . .'

The Age of Revolution

The American War of Independence interrupted this leisured opulence and disturbed Caribbean trade with the Thirteen Colonies. British naval supremacy in the region was stretched to the limit as France attacked and plundered the colonies. Tobago was ceded to France at the Treaty of Versailles after twenty years of British rule; over the next thirty years it shuttled back and forth before ending up in Britain's possession in 1814.

William Pitt the Younger followed his father's strategy in the French revolutionary wars of the 1790s. Realizing that Britain's

army was too small to do much in Europe, Pitt relied on his allies to fight there, while he concentrated his naval forces on attacking French colonies in the Caribbean. There were terrible losses through yellow fever and malaria, but the French sugar islands were successfully attacked, and French sugar production declined sharply.

Increasing the general atmosphere of tension, the French Revolution had reverberated around the colonies, to the anxious disapproval of many. Baron de Wimpffen wrote home in 1790: 'The French planters even at table, surrounded by mulattoes and negroes, indulge themselves in the most imprudent discussions on liberty, etc. To discuss 'The Rights of Man' before such people – what is it but to teach them that power dwells with strength, and strength with numbers?'

In the same way, George Washington seemed to consider revolution a white prerogative. 'Lamentable!', he sniffed, 'to see such a spirit of revolt among the Blacks. . . .' Indeed, the slaves of the French island of Saint-Domingue (later Haiti) adopted the principles of revolution themselves and revolted against the white population in 1791, massacring all those who stayed behind. Sugar production was never revived there, and Britain was left with a greater share of the market than before.

The British army historian Fortescue wrote that, although Britain had gained Martinique, Tobago and St Lucia, Pitt's campaigns had cost his country 'in army and navy little fewer than a hundred thousand men, about one-half of them dead, the remainder permanently unfit for service'. Because of Britain's greed for sugar, he concluded, 'England's soldiers had been sacrificed, her treasure squandered, her influence in Europe weakened, her arm for six fateful years fettered, numbed and paralysed.'

By the time of Pitt's death in 1806, Britain's position in the sugar market was so strong that Napoleon was forced to employ different tactics. He tried to destroy the trade monopoly by imposing a land-based blockade, forcing European countries to refuse British cotton and sugar. But Europe had become dependent on these imports and widespread smuggling was used to evade the continental system.

In the end, the sugar trade was to be fatally weakened from another quarter, although the West Indian planters had ominously watched the storm gathering for decades. During the Napoleonic Wars, the anti-slavery crusade had finally persuaded Parliament to end the slave trade to British plantations. The next generation had to find a new way of running the sugar estates – or face ruin.

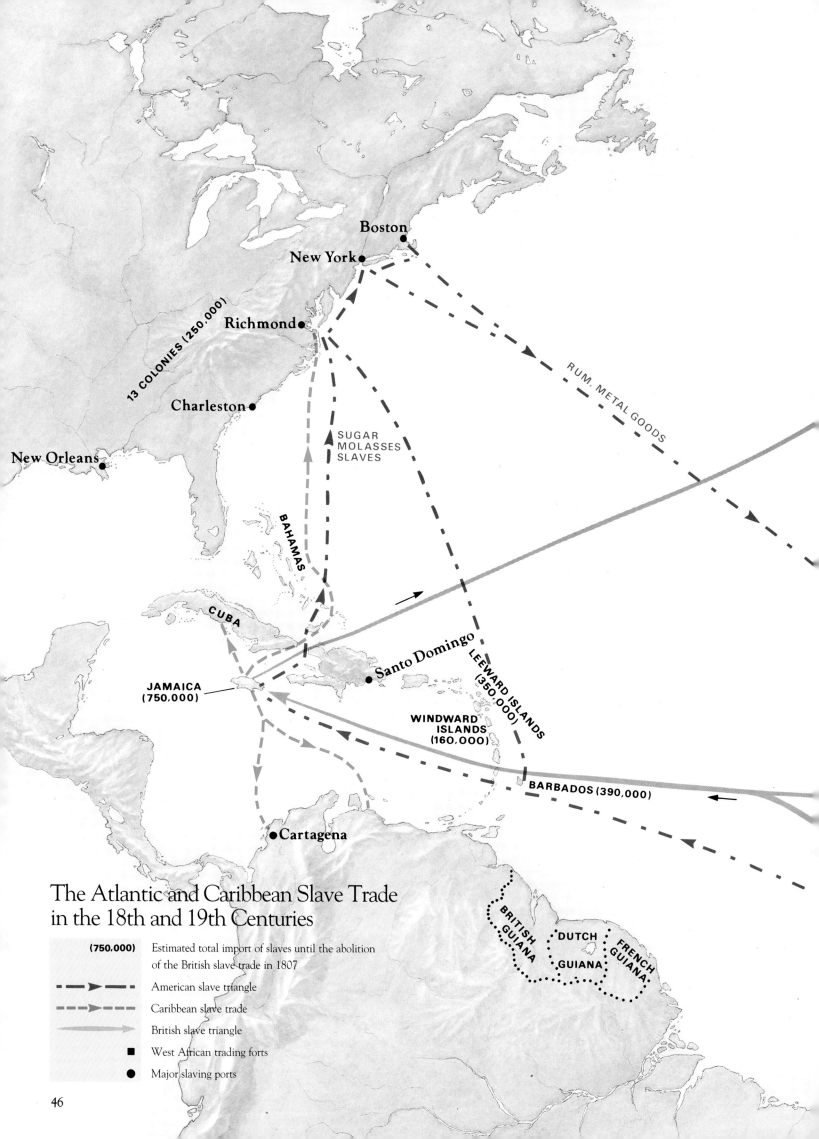

Boston

New York

Richmond

13 COLONIES (250,000)

Charleston

New Orleans

RUM, METAL GOODS

SUGAR
MOLASSES
SLAVES

BAHAMAS

CUBA

JAMAICA
(750,000)

Santo Domingo

LEEWARD ISLANDS
(350,000)

WINDWARD
ISLANDS
(160,000)

BARBADOS (390,000)

Cartagena

BRITISH
GUIANA

DUTCH
GUIANA

FRENCH
GUIANA

The Atlantic and Caribbean Slave Trade
in the 18th and 19th Centuries

(750,000)   Estimated total import of slaves until the abolition
              of the British slave trade in 1807

────▶─·─   American slave triangle

────▶──   Caribbean slave trade

─────▶   British slave triangle

■   West African trading forts

●   Major slaving ports

Liverpool

London
Bristol

SUGAR AND SUGAR PRODUCTS, COTTON AND GINGER

METAL GOODS

TEXTILES. ARMS

'THE MIDDLE PASSAGE' SLAVES

GAMBIA

■ **Fort James**

**SIERRA
LEONE**

LIBERIA

ASHANTE

GOLD COAST

Christianbourg

■ **Lagos**

Accra

SLAVE COAST

**BIGHT
OF BENIN**

NIGER RIVER

● **Calabar**

Elmina

Cape
Coast
Castle

Fernando
Po

CHAPTER SIX

THE PEOPLE BUSINESS

—————————◇—————————

For centuries before the beginning of the great age of European expansion, slavery had been regarded as part of the natural order. From the days of the Greek and Roman empires, there had always been an intellectual acceptance of slavery; indeed, up to the late eighteenth century, men such as Boswell would claim for slavery a Divine seal of approval: 'To abolish a status which in all ages GOD has sanctioned, and man has continued, would not only be ROBBERY to an innumerable class of our fellow subjects; but it would be extreme cruelty to the African Savages, a portion of whom it . . . introduced into a much happier state of life.'

The first instinct of the Renaissance European was to exploit the New World's vast potential for riches by using slave labour. The natural source of labour was South America, where Aztec Mexico and Inca Peru were based on slavery. The Spanish *conquistadores* needed a form of slavery in order to run the silver mines. The European settlers evaded the royal decree against slavery, and imported slaves to keep up the stream of bullion which, by the second half of the sixteenth century, seemed to guarantee the prosperity of Spain for ever.

The west coast of Africa below the Sahara soon became an attractive source of slaves and, by the 1550s, the Spanish, French and Portuguese were all involved. English traders, led by John Hawkins, tried to get into the business a decade later but the Spanish pushed them firmly out of the market. While Hawkins busied himself instead with building up the Queen's Navy, his cousin Francis Drake began a long private war against Spain. Both launched themselves into profitable plunder and privateering every now and then but, for the time being, slave-trading had been ruled out.

The Beginnings of Caribbean Slavery

Little use was made of slaves in the first years of the English colonies in North America and the West Indies. If slaves were offered for sale, however, they were not always turned away,

Sir John Hawkins (left) and Sir Francis Drake (right), the 'sea-dogs' of whom Queen Elizabeth I was so proud.

despite the declaration of an English trader to a Muslim merchant on the Gambia that 'we were a people who did not buy or sell one another or any that had our own shapes; he seemed much to marvel at it . . .'.

Nevertheless, the basic principle of slavery was established quite early in the West Indian colonies. Barbados Law in 1636 stated that 'Negroes and Indians that come here to be sold, should serve for life.' But the great bulk of plantation work was done by indentured labourers from the British Isles in climates that were deemed dangerous for white men.

In the early English settlements there was no simple distinction between slaves and freemen. Slaves were not the only unfree workers; they were merely on the lowest rung of an ugly ladder of unfreedom. At the top end of the ladder were the immigrants who had paid for their Atlantic passage by signing indentures to work for an employer for three to seven years. Until the indenture period came to an end, they could be treated very much like slaves. The 'Barbadosed' Royalists captured in the Civil War or the Protestants captured at the Battle of Sedgemore in 1685 who were sent to the West Indies as forced labourers could always hope that a turn of the political wheel might release them but, in the meantime, they did not even have those dim prospects of freedom enjoyed by the penniless immigrants. Below them on the ladder were the criminals who had chosen forced labour in the colonies as an alternative to the

THE SLAVE SHIPS

Loading a slave ship was a masterpiece of pitiless ingenuity. A ship of about 100 tons – the size of a modern ocean-going tug – could be packed with over 200 slaves and the supplies for a five-week journey. A third of the slaves were restricted to the open deck where sails or tarpaulins protected them from the weather; a third were confined to the hold; and the remaining third were consigned to an additional deck or shelf, about six feet wide, fixed to the ship's side between the other two, where they lay side by side. Male slaves were chained to prevent them attacking the crew. Little movement was possible and most had to lie in their own filth for the entire journey.

Human cargo on the slave deck of the Albaroz, *taken prize in the Congo by HMS Albatross.*

An average of ten per cent of the slaves died on the voyage, although illness among the human cargo would inflate this figure.

An unfavourable wind could double the length of the journey and lead to a shortage of food and water. In the case of the *Zong*, the captain excused the drowning of the slaves by claiming a lack of water. Naturally, the slaves that survived were not healthy when they arrived. As a result, they were polished with oil and made as presentable as possible before the 'scramble', in which the buyers rushed forward to grab slaves before their competitors did. Any slaves who remained unclaimed were left to die.

Henrietta of Lorraine painted by Van Dyck, with the fashionable seventeenth-century court accessory of a petted black page.

death sentence in England. After 1718 judges could impose a sentence of transportation and forced labour 'for the term of his natural life'. The only difference between this criminal and a slave was that the criminal's children were born free, while those of a slave would be born to slavery.

The Introduction of Sugar Cane

During the 1640s the Dutch were forced out of their Brazilian plantations. Far more interested in trade than in owning colonies, they persuaded Barbados and the neighbouring islands to produce sugar for the Dutch re-export trade. Whereas the existing tobacco crop on the islands was grown mainly by smallholders needing neither close attention nor high investment, the more profitable sugar was more demanding. The cane had to be cut and gathered at great speed, and crushed by expensive machines to extract the juice. The resulting liquid needed to be kept close to boiling point while it was skimmed for impurities; if the liquid solidified, as it would if there were any delay, it was almost useless. This required the planter to have high initial capital investment and a docile labour force. The Bristol merchant John Pinney wrote: 'Negroes are the sinews of a nation, and it is as impossible for a man to make sugar without the assistance of the Negroes, as to make bricks without straw.'

The West African Trade

During the 1650s and 1660s the Government in London pushed the Dutch out of the English sugar trade; the English planters did not know how to replace the Dutch as slave suppliers. Importing slaves from West Africa was a trade with its own peculiar skills. The most successful slave-traders were the Portuguese. They operated from Angola, while most other traders were lured to the Guinea coast, an unhealthy region as the sea-shanty warned:

> Beware and take care of the Bight of Benin
> Few come out though many go in.

Traders established good relations with the African states of the region, supplying them with arms so that they could fight their neighbours and afterwards sell the captives to the traders. Indeed, it was an established custom in the Muslim states that prisoners should be sold into slavery. Politically, the coastal states became stronger with their access to arms than their neighbours in the interior. Nevertheless, they continued to be monarchies in which a weak or unsuccessful ruler was likely to be replaced.

The Royal Africa Company

When English adventurers formed a company of merchants to trade with the Guinea coast in the 1660s, they concentrated first on gold dust and ivory – described as 'elephant's teeth'. 'Guinea' gold coins were of such high quality that they were actually worth more than the pound they represented; it was not until Sir Isaac Newton applied his mind to the problem that the value of a guinea was established at twenty-one shillings. The original traders made no profit either from the high-quality gold or from their tentative dealings in slaves, but they did acquire useful connections with African rulers, and set up the sprinkling of little forts which was needed to assert their presence. After a financial reconstruction, some of them re-emerged in 1672 as the Royal Africa Company, with a monopoly to supply slaves to the English colonies.

The Royal Africa Company faced serious difficulties on both sides of the Atlantic. The forts that bolstered the English presence on the Guinea coast were very expensive. Traders were often able to generate a profit from ignoring the Company's right of monopoly, while the Company's own resources went on defence. The Company itself was never able to sell enough slaves to the planters to cover their costs; at the same time, the planters were constantly complaining that the Company was not bringing them as many slaves as they needed. This was not as paradoxical as it first sounds. The planters were eager for slaves but were much less anxious to pay for them; they wanted the Company to become a banker who would finance the expansion of the Caribbean slave stock. As a result, the Company was soon forced to choose between doing too little trade to cover the fixed costs of their forts, and being submerged by bad debts. By the early eighteenth century the Company was doomed, and it became clear that monopolies were no longer the universally accepted way of doing business. The slave trade expanded greatly in the hands of smaller merchants, and the ports of Liverpool and Bristol thrived so as to rival London.

By the early eighteenth century, English traders no longer had to rely on other countries to provide the necessary slave labour; they could meet the needs of English colonies, and supply other countries as well. This change was recognized in 1713 in the Treaty of Utrecht, by which Britain gained the right (known as the *Asiento*) to supply 4,800 slaves a year to the Spanish colonies which had always depended on outside suppliers of slaves. The South Sea Bubble crisis of 1720 was caused mainly by financial manipulations surrounding an overvaluation of this right to supply slaves. However, the Asiento did provide a legal screen behind which a good deal of illegal trading with the Spanish colonies could flourish.

The Growth of the British Slave Trade

The demand for slaves in the West Indies continued to grow at an insatiable rate, and the Atlantic trade was dominated by Britain's maritime strength. By the middle of the eighteenth century over sixty thousand slaves were crossing the Atlantic each year; at least half of them were carried in British ships, destined mainly for British colonies. Jamaica became the main centre for re-exporting slaves to other countries.

In addition to her maritime strength, Britain's developing industries equipped her well for trading on the west coast of Africa. The main commodity bartered for slaves was weapons. This exchange was summarized by an African ruler: 'You have three things we want: powder, musket and shot; and we have three things you want: men, women and children.' In fact, the transfer was not quite that simple. Firstly, other metal goods, cloth and distilled spirits were also traded. Secondly, few dealers were interested in women and children – the Asiento provided for twice as many men as women to be sold in South America. Because planters were more concerned with harvesting the next crop than with maintaining their labour force, they were more interested in buying men than women as slaves. Many more men than women worked in the plantations, a fact which further heightened tensions in the volatile island societies.

The Slave Ships

Transporting the slaves across the Atlantic Ocean was the most brutal aspect of the whole process. Indeed, it was quite common for traders and sailors to become staunch abolitionists after their sickening experiences in the trade. Ships of about one hundred tons (little larger than Columbus's *Santa Maria*) were loaded with over two hundred slaves on the 'middle passage' of the journey from the African coast to the West Indies. The slaves were packed in airless holds with only two or three square feet per person. It has been estimated that, during the three centuries of the slave trade, well over a million slaves died at sea on their journey to the Americas, a loss of over ten per cent of the total cargo of ten million.

Conditions improved somewhat during the eighteenth century, due as much to a new awareness of this senseless waste of human life as to any emerging humanitarian protest. For a long time to come, however, economics would dictate the fortunes of the anti-slavery forces. Temple Luttrell declared in the House of Commons: 'Some gentlemen may, indeed, object to the slave trade as inhuman and impious; let us consider that if our colonies are to be maintained and cultivated, which can only be done by African negroes, it is surely better to supply ourselves with those labourers in British bottoms (ships) than purchase them through the medium of French, Dutch or Danish factors.'

The Plantation System

Conditions were not much better once the ships had arrived in the West Indies. The climate of the sugar colonies was, according to Captain Beckford, 'so inconvenient for an English

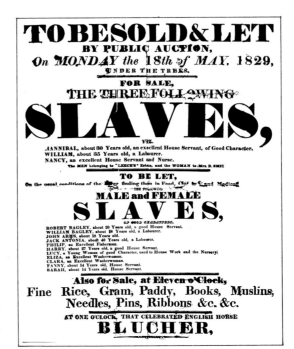

Slaves could be bought, sold and let at public auctions, irrespective of their age or family ties.

constitution that no man will choose to live there, much less will any man choose to settle there.' Most planters returned to England as soon as they could. The Caribbean estates meanwhile were left in the hands of tenants or agents, who were under great pressure to send substantial profits back to London, profits big enough to maintain the 'sugar king' lifestyle.

Under this system there was little incentive for the tenants to concern themselves with the long-term development of the estates or the long-term health and wellbeing of the slaves. Because far fewer women than men were transported, it was impossible for each shipment of slaves to replace itself fully. The rapid turnover, added to the fact that the slaves came from many different parts of West Africa and rarely had a common mother tongue, made it hard for African culture to survive. This helps explain why the descendants of the slaves saw themselves as either British or American subjects and why proposals for their repatriation to Africa were never very popular.

SLAVE LIFE ON THE PLANTATIONS

Even the most heartless sugar plantation owner could not keep his slaves in the fields for 365 days a year. At harvest-time a twelve-hour day was imposed, but 'crop' lasted for only a short period out of the fifteen-month growing cycle. Although the ground had to be cleared, and new canes planted and then weeded, the slaves were not driven without respite. Frequently they were given small plots of land on which to grow food for themselves. This was much cheaper than importing food for them, and their own produce would usually be fresher and more nutritious. Once they had land of their own many of them grew food to sell in local markets. Consequently, some slaves saved enough cash to buy their freedom, joining those who had been emancipated by the owners out of guilt or goodwill. Thus, by the late eighteenth century, the West Indies were inhabited by a mixture of slaves, free blacks,

Cutting cane on a sugar plantation: a romanticized view of 1823 which did not find it necessary to portray the whips and dogs of the overseers.

poor whites and rich plantation owners. After emancipation in 1834, the former owners continued to dominate the islands both socially and politically. However, by the late 1860s the white minority became anxious that the former

slaves might gain political power; as a result, the majority of the island assemblies voted themselves out of power, investing authority to govern the West Indies in Parliament at Westminster.

A boiling house on the island of Antigua in the early nineteenth century, where cane juice was stirred and heated to 220° F.

Slavery in the American Colonies

These developments in the sugar industry were in sharp contrast to the American tobacco and rice plantations, where slaves were a luxurious alternative to hard work, found in every colony, but not indispensable to the economy. Women and children formed a greater part of the work force, and a slave society and culture developed in a way that was not possible in the West Indies.

Virginia had grown its tobacco with white labour for some generations, while in Georgia slavery was even forbidden by law for the first twenty years of the new colony's existence. Enough white colonists immigrated freely to maintain economic expansion although, by the time of the War of Independence, the economies of the five southern colonies were firmly geared to the slavery system.

America exported rum and metal goods to the African slave coast as her part in the slave-trade triangle. The cargoes were exchanged for slaves who were then taken to the West Indies; there the slaves were exchanged, in turn, for sugar and molasses, which were taken back to the American ports to renew the cycle. A few slaves were taken back to the American colonies on the last leg of the journey, but there was never any mass slave importation. This pattern continued throughout the early nineteenth century, when the development of cotton-growing meant that parts of the South became entirely dependent on a slave labour that was mainly 'homegrown'. American social tolerance for the 'peculiar institution' of slavery continued into the 1860s; at a time when the British Navy was zealously hunting down any European slavers still plying their trade in the Atlantic, the American 'slave-runners' continued to trickle African slaves into the West Indies.

White Minorities and Slave Rebellions

On some British islands, slaves made up over ninety per cent of the total population. This was worrying for the small white colonies, who were meant to keep their numbers up and act as informal garrisons. The position of the poor whites was unpleasant: they tended to drift away to North America because no employer in the West Indies wished to pay for work that a slave could do. This left the white planters with a shrinking group of white assistants, isolated in a sea of disaffected slaves.

The precariousness of the planters' position was not lost on them. Attempts at rebellion or escape were crushed with extreme cruelty. On most islands runaways had nowhere to go, but on troublesome Jamaica the uncultivated hills became a refuge for the maroons, who had been runaway slaves under the Spanish. The British were no more successful in suppressing the maroons than the Spanish had been, mainly because no planter could envisage expanding cultivation inland. By the 1740s the maroons had made peace with the British; the understanding was that they could live undisturbed in the hills so long as they returned future runaways to the planters for punishment.

Punishments were savage, slaves often being beaten to death as a warning to others. All planters were united in their need for such severity. It was despairingly remarked by Methodist missionaries that: 'The whip has been used with an unsparing hand. However intelligent a negro might be, still he must be ruled by terror instead of reason.' To make sure that owners were not betrayed into mercy by the thought that a dead slave was a profitless one, local assemblies provided compensation for planters whose punishment damaged or destroyed their property. By the late eighteenth century, however, such solidarity was not enough. The local assemblies realized that they would scarcely be able to put down a revolt if it occurred, a fact relished by the irrepressible Dr Johnson who proposed a toast to a grave assembly of Oxford dons in 1777: 'Here's to the next insurrection of the negroes in the West Indies!'

At the same time, there was a move in England against the whole institution of slavery. London-based planters organized themselves into a parliamentary block of resistance, arguing with undeniable truth that an end to slavery would ruin them. Decade after decade – through the Seven Years War, the American War of Independence and the Napoleonic Wars – the two Pitts had driven Britain's armies into exhaustion to defend and add to her sugar heritage. Could a handful of Quaker idealists really topple such a century of achievements? Throughout the eighteenth century, the triangular trade in slaves and sugar had formed the core of the British Empire. But, at the same time that slavery was beginning to face a wave of moral indignation, the economies of the sugar islands were slowing down and a new empire was emerging in the east.

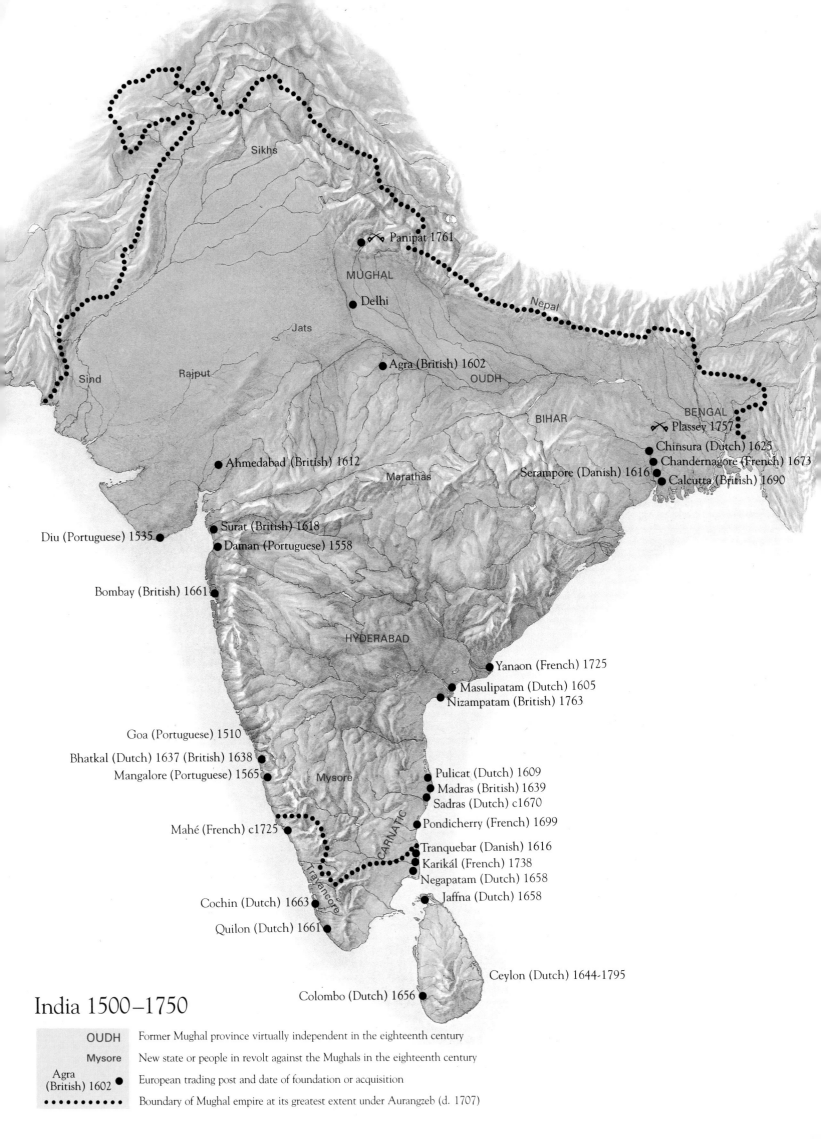

Panipat 1761

MUGHAL

Delhi

Jats

Sikhs

Nepal

Agra (British) 1602

OUDH

Sind

Rajput

BIHAR

BENGAL

Plassey 1757

Ahmedabad (British) 1612

Marathas

Chinsura (Dutch) 1625
Chandernagore (French) 1673
Serampore (Danish) 1616
Calcutta (British) 1690

Diu (Portuguese) 1535

Surat (British) 1618
Daman (Portuguese) 1558

Bombay (British) 1661

HYDERABAD

Yanaon (French) 1725

Masulipatam (Dutch) 1605
Nizampatam (British) 1763

Goa (Portuguese) 1510

Bhatkal (Dutch) 1637 (British) 1638
Mangalore (Portuguese) 1565

Mysore

Pulicat (Dutch) 1609
Madras (British) 1639
Sadras (Dutch) c1670

Mahé (French) c1725

CARNATIC

Pondicherry (French) 1699

Tranquebar (Danish) 1616
Karikál (French) 1738
Negapatam (Dutch) 1658
Jaffna (Dutch) 1658

Travancore

Cochin (Dutch) 1663

Quilon (Dutch) 1661

Ceylon (Dutch) 1644-1795

Colombo (Dutch) 1656

India 1500–1750

OUDH	Former Mughal province virtually independent in the eighteenth century
Mysore	New state or people in revolt against the Mughals in the eighteenth century
Agra (British) 1602 ●	European trading post and date of foundation or acquisition
●●●●●●●●●	Boundary of Mughal empire at its greatest extent under Aurangzeb (d. 1707)

CHAPTER SEVEN

INDIA: RICHES TO RAJ

◇

India had a long history of links with Europe. In classical times there was considerable contact between India and the West, most significantly during the brief occupation of the Indus valley by Alexander the Great and his successors in around 320 BC, and in the 'Greco-Buddhist' artistic style of the Gandhara empire founded in north-western India during the second century AD. Trade with India was also important to Greece and Rome – mostly imports of pearls, gems and spices – while in return, imperial Rome exported treasure to the East – so much so that in parts of India, gold coins circulated as currency. With the Arab conquests of Egypt and Persia in the seventh century, the direct routes for trade with Europe from South and East Asia were broken. The spice and silk trades continued but Muslim merchants, and later the Venetians, monopolized the import of goods from the East into Europe. A determination to break this monopoly caused Portuguese explorers of the late fifteenth century to search for another spice route to the East. Finally Vasco da Gama reached Calicut in South-West India via the African Cape of Good Hope in 1498.

In the sixteenth century, Portugal became the dominant power in the Indian Ocean, breaking the established Arab and Venetian trade networks. Sea power was the key to this success. After the 1507 victory over the Egyptian and Gujarati navies off Diu, Dom Francisco de Almeida observed: 'As long as you are powerful at sea you will hold India as yours; and if you do not possess this power, little will avail you a fortress on shore.'

With the Portuguese in command of the high seas, Arab traders could operate only under license. No local vessels could compete with the speed and power of the 'Atlantic ships', eight hundred of which crossed the seas that century. Next the Portuguese became involved in carrying trade between East Africa, the Persian Gulf, India and the south Pacific, which brought quicker and safer returns than the dangerous spice route via the African Cape.

The Coming of the Companies

The Portuguese had gained a head start over the other European sea powers in the sixteenth century, but they could not maintain their dominance for long: by 1600 their position in Asia was being challenged by both the Dutch and the English – the two powers most opposed to the Spanish Empire in Europe. The Dutch moved by force into Indonesia's spice and pepper trade, and established settlements in India, amalgamating their trading companies in 1602 into one United East India Company of the Netherlands. The English East India Company had been founded two years earlier by Elizabeth I, who granted it a charter giving exclusive trading rights to 'the Governor and Company of Merchants of London trading into the East Indies.' The English East India Company also concentrated on the spice trade, and only sent ships to India eight years later. It began to export the fine cloth manufactures of India's skilled artisans. In 1613, after the Portuguese had been defeated at sea, the Mughal emperor granted trading rights in India at Surat, to the English company, and in the next decade several other 'factories' (trading stations) were set up around the south-western and south-eastern coasts. Other European nations followed suit thereafter – the Danish East India Company being founded in 1616 and the French *Compagnie des Indes Orientales* in 1664.

The English slowly expanded their Indian operations throughout the seventeenth century. A fortified settlement – Fort St George – was established at Madras in 1640; the island of Bombay passed to Charles II in 1661 as part of the dowry of his Portuguese queen, Catherine of Braganza; and Calcutta was founded as Fort William on the mud flats of the Hooghly Delta in 1696. Each of these sites became the centre of a Presidency – of Madras, Bombay and Bengal – and these remained the chief administrative divisions of India under British rule until the late nineteenth century.

At this time, however, the East India Company had little

SIR THOMAS ROE AND THE MUGHAL COURT

When the first English traders reached India in 1608, Captain William Hawkins was sent to petition the Emperor Jahangir for trading rights at Surat. Hawkins, who could speak to Jahangir in *Turki* without the need for an interpreter, was welcomed at the Mughul court, granted a state title and given a Christian wife. Trading facilities at Surat were made available to the English, but were withdrawn shortly afterwards after opposition from the Portuguese. In 1613 Surat was opened again, and in 1615 James I despatched Sir Thomas Roe as a formal ambassador to the Mughal court to negotiate a treaty to guarantee the East India Company's trading position.

Roe spent four years in India and, although

Sir Thomas Roe, Ambassador to the Mughal court of Jahangir (1581–1644)

he was unsuccessful in securing a treaty with Jahangir, he did much to establish English influence and to research commercial possibilities. Both Roe and Edward Terry, a ship's chaplain from Surat who accompanied him, left accounts of their Indian travels which provide interesting glimpses of life at Jahangir's court. Terry thought Jahangir himself to be 'composed of extremes: for sometimes he was barbarously cruel, and at other times . . . exceedingly fair and gentle'; Prince Khurram, who succeeded his father as the Emperor Shah Jahan, Roe judged unsympathetic: 'he is most earnest in his superstition, a hater of all Christians, proud, subtile [sic.], false and barbarously tyrannous.'

From its modest seventeenth-century beginnings as Fort William on the humid Hoogly riverbank, Calcutta grew to become the capital of British India in 1772. By that time, the opulence of the architecture had given rise to the nickname 'the city of palaces'.

desire for rule or domination, and far less capacity. European merchants could only survive in India under the protection of Indian rulers. At sea the British could exert considerable power; challenged only by the Dutch, they were able to blockade ports, close sea lanes and force local shipping to purchase safe conducts. On land, however, their position was never secure. As the Directors in London reminded Fort St George in the 1670s, friendly relations with Indian rulers were all-important: 'We are not only in their country upon terms by which we *possess* what we have there, but also under their protection.' This was demonstrated decisively ten years later when the Company was temporarily expelled from its factories in Surat, Bombay and Bengal after a quarrel with the Mughal emperor Aurangzeb over customs duties.

By the 1720s a solid if unspectacular business had been established, sending up to £1 million worth of goods to London each year, almost fifteen per cent of Britain's total imports. Despite its need to maintain a large fleet of expensive and highly specialized ships, the famous 'East Indiamen', the Company enjoyed steady profits. It traded now primarily in cotton 'piece goods', many of which were re-exported from Britain to the Continent; other imports such as saltpetre, sugar, indigo and pepper faced stiff competition and were much less profitable. European traders did not organize the production of Indian cottons directly, but bought them from Indian middlemen and agents who were better able to deal with the complexities of the various Indian weaving trades.

The 'Company' also enjoyed a monopoly of China's trade,

importing tea for the English market in increasingly large quantities. Chinese goods made up a third of the value of the company's shipments by the 1750s. Exports from Britain to Asia were harder to find; China took some woollen cloth and India some metals, but most of the trade had to be balanced by bullion. Company servants also had the right to engage in private trade on their own account, provided that it did not infringe on the terms of the charter; this led to an expansion of their activities in the 'country trade' – buying, selling and transporting goods both within India and around the Gulf and South-East Asia. As late as 1750 only about a third of the cloth exports of Dacca – the leading textile-producing region of Bengal – was handled by European traders, and then often simply as a front for Indian interests.

The Decline of the Mughal Empire

It was these activities which had brought European merchants into contact with the Mughal empire, one of the great territorial powers of Asia. The first Mughal emperor, Babur, had invaded India in 1525 from Afghanistan; he had quickly conquered the Punjab and the Jumuna valley, and occupied both Delhi and Agra before his death five years later. The new empire was not fully established, however, until the military campaigns undertaken by his grandson Akbar, who came to the throne in 1556. In fifty years of warfare Akbar secured the north-western base that his grandfather had won and then went on to conquer large territories in western, eastern and central India, bringing Rajputana, Gujarat, Bengal and the Deccan under Mughal rule. By the time of his death in 1605, he had further consolidated his power by setting up an administrative system based on taxes raised by regular assessments of land revenue. The emperor appointed salaried *mansabdars* to maintain the system.

This empire reached its furthest extent in the second half of the seventeenth century under the rule of Aurangzeb (1658–1707). At his death the empire comprised around 180 million subjects, about 20 per cent of the world's population. Yet this powerful empire was never a centralized autocracy. The emperor was the 'king of kings', and his power depended on precisely that: the ability to manipulate the petty kings and magnates who exercised authority in the cities and provinces of the empire. The emperor was never an absolute despot, and could be better described as an 'entrepreneur in power', able to buy obedience by royal honours and to enforce it occasionally by military might.

Aurangzeb stretched his resources to breaking point by his constant wars in southern and western India. Even at the height of his power, his control was not always effective, and his strict Muslim faith made compromise with Sikh and Hindu leaders

The loss of the Halsewell, *one of the prized East Indiamen, off the Isle of Purbeck in 1786.*

LADY IMPEY AND THE FLORA AND FAUNA OF INDIA

Some eighteenth-century colonialists embraced the exoticism of India with an enthusiasm that may have been considered unwarranted a century later. In 1774 Sir Elijah and Lady Mary Impey arrived in Calcutta, where Sir Elijah had been appointed as Chief Justice of the Court. He spent much of his time learning Persian and Bengali in order to understand the new culture which he would help to rule, while his wife became fascinated by Indian natural history.

From childhood onwards, Lady Impey had only known the chilly drizzle of Shipton, North Yorkshire. The brilliance and diversity of India excited her so much that for five years she employed three native artists to paint and draw the Indian flora and fauna: the Muslim Sheikh Zain al Din, and the Hindu Ram Das and Bhawani Dan. Between 1777 and 1782, while her husband became entangled in legal scandals, she explored the forests, mountains and rivers of the subcontinent with her artists, recording all she saw. Purple-shrouded pigeons,

Lady Impey, the wife of the Chief of Justice of Bengal, in her boudoir about 1782.

blossom-headed parakeets and spotted cuckoos, as well as forest animals and flowers, crowd the canvases now in the possession of the Linnean Society. Her enormous collection of paintings was soon to become a cornerstone of British knowledge of Indian natural history.

(both inside and outside his empire) difficult. His bitterest quarrel was with the Maratha kingdom in south-western India, created by the military prowess of Sivaji, a Hindu warrior chief. Aurangzeb captured and executed Sivaji's successor, Shambaji, in 1689, and then captured the Maratha capital of Satara. Although these military successes temporarily asserted Mughal paramountcy, central control weakened after Aurangzeb's death and old rivals broke free once again from the restraints of imperial rule.

This period of Indian history is often portrayed as a black period of destructive anarchy rescued only by the imposition of British rule. Mughal power did indeed decline markedly, and the power vacuum was filled partially by reviving Maratha military expansion, co-ordinated from their new base at Poona. These forces ranged over central India in the 1740s and 1750s in pursuit of *chauth* (protection money) and plunder, reaching the Punjab in the late 1750s. They were checked here at Panipat by Afghan invaders in 1761. Thereafter, individual Maratha chiefs set up as territorial magnates in their own right. The English historian Thomas Macaulay exaggerated the melancholy confusion of India at the time: 'A succession of ferocious invaders descended through the western passes to prey on the defenceless wealth of Hindustan . . . and every corner of the wide Empire learned to tremble at the mighty name of the Marathas.'

This military insecurity certainly had destructive effects in certain areas, especially in the 'shatter zone' of north-western India, where the rival successors marched and looted. Elsewhere, new regional states emerged: some were created by Sikh and Maratha leaders, heirs to the long tradition of rebellion against the Mughals; others, such as Bengal, Hyderabad and Awadh, were created by Mughal courtiers and governors who had built personal power bases through their positions in imperial office. If they were to survive, these states had to maximize their military and fiscal strength. Severe tensions were generated inside the new states between military leaders, tax farmers and merchants, who were all intricately bound up in trade, usury and military finance, and who competed for the surplus production of town and countryside. All these internal tensions were to help destroy the political independence of India in the years to come.

The European Intervention

The trading companies had played little direct part in the political and military realignments following the implosion of the Mughal empire, but they enjoyed important privileges which gave them an interest in Indian affairs: their settlements were rich, but they were not liable for taxation; they had also negotiated agreements by which they paid low customs duties on their huge trade. The fiscal needs of the new Indian states made it likely that these privileges would be challenged sooner or later, and yet it was from Europe that the immediate cause of foreign intervention came in the 1750s.

In 1742 Britain and France went to war, and the conflict was transported into southern India. The Governor of the French trading settlement at Pondicherry, Joseph-Francois Dupleix, called in a French fleet from Mauritius: it captured the British settlement of Madras in 1746. Madras was restored to Britain by the Treaty of Aix-la-Chapelle in 1748, but Dupleix backed a puppet contender to be the next Governor of the Carnatic, who would be based at Arcot, from where the territories surrounding the French and British settlements were controlled. The British had their own candidate for the post and resolved the problem

Sepoys from the Bombay, Bengal and Madras armies. These Indian troops were welded into a powerful mercenary army by the English East India Company's financial power.

The British slipped into their role as nabobs (princes) of India, enjoying the pleasures and privileges that were formerly the prerogative of Indian overlords.

by capturing Arcot with five hundred men under the leadership of a young captain in the East India Company's army – Robert Clive. When war broke out again in Europe in 1756, the French besieged Madras once more, but this time British sea power proved decisive and Pondicherry surrendered in 1761. Two years later French power in the region was at an end, and the British installed Mahomed Ali Wallajah as Nawab at Arcot. By supplying him with troops for his defence in exchange for a 'subsidy' payment, the British bound him to them. During the following years, the Nawab proved unable or unwilling to pay the subsidy, and as a result the territories were annexed piecemeal, until his title was abolished at the end of the century.

The Politics of Bengal

In 1756 European rivalry surfaced in Bengal, where the situation was more complex and the consequences far more momentous. When war broke out in Europe, the English East India Company began to fortify Calcutta. This proved to be the final straw for the new Nawab of Bengal, Siraj-ud-Daulah. He was determined to reassert the authority of the Nawab against the established privileges of foreign merchants, Hindu financiers, court officials and landed magnates alike; he demanded money from the French and Dutch settlements and laid siege to Calcutta, which fell to him in June. The British reacted swiftly and in December recaptured Calcutta with professional troops who had been shipped up from Madras and who were led by Clive. Siraj-ud-Daulah was forced to restore the Company's privileges in February 1757. By now, however, the extent of internal opposition to the Nawab was clear. Clive joined a conspiracy to overthrow him in which the Company's armies were to supply the muscle and the government's banker, Jagat Seth, the money. After the Battle of Plassey, Mir Jafar was set on the throne, thereby ensuring extensive privileges for the Company, including a grant of territory to raise revenue for troops, and over £1.5 million from the state treasury to the Company men. Clive himself received a lump sum of £234,000 and land worth

£30,000 a year. These were the sums that led Clive later to declare himself 'astonished at my own moderation'.

The new strength of the East India Company made Mir Jafar's position almost untenable. The British soon fell out with their new ally when new territory was ceded to meet Company costs. Mir Jafar was deposed in favour of his son-in-law, Mir Kasim, in 1760. A desire to build up power brought the new Nawab into conflict with the Company just as inevitably as it had done for his predecessor.

Internal tolls were levied on the Company's private trade, which had been exempted by Mir Jafar. This internal trading was an important privilege for the Company, giving it the edge over its Indian rivals, and enabling it to penetrate the inland economy for the first time – to trade in salt and other goods that had previously been government monopolies. Mir Kasim decided to do away with this unfair advantage, protesting to the Company in 1762: 'This is the way your Gentlemen behave; they make a disturbance all over my country, plunder the people, injure and disgrace my servants. . . . They forcibly take away the goods and commodities of the peasants, merchants, etc, for the fourth part of their value, and by way of violence and oppressions they oblige peasants to give five rupees for goods which are worth but one. . . .'

The British Empire in Asia

The Company was determined to 'do themselves justice' and maintain the privilege. War broke out and Mir Jafar was brought back to the throne briefly until his death in 1765. Clive, returning to Calcutta as Governor, stepped in again. Declaring that 'we must indeed become the Nabobs ourselves', he signed the famous Treaty of Allahabad with the Mughal emperor. This stated that in return for a fixed tribute payment to Delhi, the Company accepted the *diwani* of Bengal – the right to impose and collect the revenue of the province for itself. This momentous agreement marked the arrival of the British as a territorial power in Asia.

ISLANDS AND CONTINENTS

◇

Since Magellan's great voyage of 1519–22 Europeans of several nations – Spaniards, Dutch, French and English – had ventured into the Pacific. But their explorations were mostly inconclusive and sometimes confusing. The immensity of the ocean, inadequate navigational instruments, the threat of scurvy and the straitjacket of wind and current had all hindered attempts at methodical exploration. By the end of the seventeenth century Europe's knowledge of the Pacific and its lands was still peripheral. Some of the island groups lying on the diagonal sailing track between the tip of South America and New Guinea had been discovered, but their position on the map shifted from voyage to voyage. 'There are in the South Sea many Islands, which may be called Wandering Islands', one geographer complained. The western bulge of New Holland (Australia) and stretches of the coastline of Van Diemen's Land (Tasmania) and New Zealand were known from the Dutch explorations of the first half of the seventeenth century, but the relation between these lands was far from clear. In particular, it was not known whether any of them formed part of that southern continent, *Terra Australis Incognita*, which had haunted pictures of the world since Ptolemy's speculations in the 2nd century AD.

British Buccaneers

Early English interest in the Pacific was chauvinistic and materialistic. In the pages of Hakluyt and Purchas it was the circumnavigations of Sir Francis Drake (1577–80) and Thomas Cavendish (1586–8), spectacular in intention but meagre in geographical information, which took pride of place. When English attention revived in the later seventeenth century the motives were those that had prompted the Elizabethans: trade and plunder. The Pacific caught the Elizabethan imagination, not as a vast, trackless ocean, but as the western rim of Spain's rich American empire. The 'South Seas' which now began to weave their spell over distant enterprises were confined, in English eyes, to the waters which lapped the shores of Chile, Peru and Mexico.

Among the buccaneers who pillaged and burnt along these

A famous world map of 1570 by Ortelius, showing the western coast of the New World.

coasts was William Dampier, a gifted observer whose books became classics of travel and adventure. Although Spanish America and the Dutch East Indies saw most of him, he also ventured into areas on the very margins of Europe's knowledge. On two separate voyages, in 1688 and 1699, he touched the western coasts of Australia. His account of these arid shores seemed only to confirm the dismal impression of New Holland given by his Dutch predecessors, nor was his description of the human inhabitants any more prepossessing. Naked, black, without covering, habitations or cultivation, they were the 'miserablest People in the world . . . setting aside their Human Shape, they differ but little from Brutes.' The seas beyond Cape Horn were not only the haunts of buccaneers and adventurers; they also provided the setting for two of the most popular fictional characters of the period. Of the identifiable persons named in *Gulliver's Travels*, 'My cousin Dampier' was the first, and Gulliver's brief and bruising encounter with the inhabitants of New Holland in 1715 was based on Dampier's experiences some years earlier. In the same period, Defoe's *Robinson Crusoe* owed much to the story related by the privateer Woodes Rogers of the marooning of Alexander Selkirk on Juan Fernandez.

From Privateering to Public Policy

A more purposeful surge of activity came in the mid-eighteenth century, as considerations of geographical science, government policy and mercantile acquisitiveness pointed to the exploration of the Pacific as one of the most important global objectives left to Europe. Above all, there was the lure of the unknown southern continent, perhaps five thousand miles across and with fifty million inhabitants, according to the theories of the geographer Alexander Dalrymple. The first Pacific expedition in this new era of oceanic exploration was that of Commodore John Byron in 1764 – a false start for, despite his assurance to the Admiralty that he intended to cross the Pacific 'by a new track', Byron followed the customary route heading west-north-west from the Strait of Magellan, and made no discoveries of note. In 1766 two further naval vessels were sent out under Captain Wallis and Lieutenant Carteret. After being separated in the Strait of Magellan, these vessels made individual voyages. Carteret crossed the Pacific farther south than any explorer had done before and made considerable inroads into the conjectural southern continent. Wallis, by contrast, showed little boldness in his western track across the ocean, but his voyage was marked by a chance discovery, the impact of which was out of all proportion to its geographical significance: in June 1767 his expedition reached Tahiti. Accounts of the landing – palm-fringed beaches, balmy weather, garlanded women – stamped an erotic imprint on Europe's image of the South Seas.

The Voyages of Captain Cook

Despite these additions by British (and French explorers such as Bougainville) to knowledge of the South Pacific, little progress had been made towards solving the central mystery of *Terra*

The Opening of the Pacific: 1600–1800

VOYAGES OF EXPLORATION

——————— Abel Tasman (Dutch) 1642–1644

—·—·—·—·— James Cook 1768–1771

— — — — — James Cook 1772–1775

· · · · · · · · · James Cook 1776–1780

COOK AND SCURVY

Captain Cook is still famous for the health of his crews, who were particularly free from scurvy, which we now know to be caused by vitamin C deficiency. As recently as the 1740s, Admiral Anson had lost around three quarters of his crew to disease when he circumnavigated the globe – mainly from scurvy. Not one of Cook's crews fell prey to the disease, which causes swollen gums, stiff joints and loose teeth in its sufferers. In the time between voyages of the two navigators, the Scottish physician James Lind had demonstrated the antiscorbutic properties of the juice from lemons, oranges or limes. Ironically, Cook's achievement delayed the adoption of this remedy. In defiance or ignorance of Lind's research, Cook preferred sauerkraut and malt wort but used a variety of foods and beverages. His success derived from the way in which he ruthlessly enforced his nutritional régime and

Admiral George Anson's (1697–1762) watering place at Tenian in the mid-eighteenth century, showing his ship, the Centurion, *and his men collecting breadfruit and other fruits to counteract the effects of scurvy, which, as Anson recalled in his log, 'had so terribly reduced us' in earlier expeditions.*

men were flogged for disobeying his instructions. He also enforced rigorous standards of cleanliness, provided dry clothes and bedding and used stoves to dry the lower decks. Uncertain of the causes of scurvy, Cook combined all the suggested remedies, traditional or otherwise, indiscriminately. With Cook's example before them, it was not until 1795 that the Royal Navy made the issue of lemon juice standard practice.

Australis Incognita. The lands east of New Holland remained marked on the maps as they had appeared after the Dutch discoveries of the previous century – in effect, swirling question marks in the ocean. Yet within a few years the Pacific took shape on the maps in much the same outline as it does today.

The explorer responsible for this leap in knowledge was James Cook. His three voyages revealed the Pacific to Europeans in a way no previous explorations had done, and the man himself became a figure of European renown. Other explorers were in the Pacific during the years that Cook's ships were out, but attention was focused on the discoveries of this remarkable Yorkshireman. On his first voyage (1768–71), accompanied by the naturalist Joseph Banks, Cook turned south from Tahiti to that area where, his instructions told him, 'there is reason to imagine that a Continent or Land of great extent may be found.' He reached latitude 40°S without sighting land, and so he headed west to New Zealand. There he mapped the coasts to show beyond any doubt that the two islands were not part of a continent. Cook then went beyond his instructions as he took the *Endeavour* towards that region of mystery, the eastern part of New Holland. He reached Australian shores just north of Van Diemen's Land, and coasted northwards, halting at Botany Bay and at the Endeavour River – mapping as he went. He was the first European known to have seen the east coast of Australia. As he sailed away through the Torres Strait, he settled the dispute as to whether New Holland and New Guinea were joined. With only one ship, and without losing a single man from scurvy, Cook had put more than 5,000 miles of coastline on the map:

Search-parties of sailors often encountered hostile receptions from Aborigines when they explored the Australian shores.

The manufacture of an accurate timepiece was essential to precise global navigation. In 1759 John Harrison made his Timekeeper No. 4 (left). Captain James Cook (1728–79) used Larcum Kendall's duplicate chronometer (right) on his second voyage to the Pacific.

the twin islands of New Zealand, the whole of the east coast of Australia and the Torres Strait had emerged from the mists of uncertainty.

Pressure mounted in Britain for another voyage as reports came in that the French were again sending expeditions to the Pacific: four, in fact, between 1770 and 1773. So, in 1772, Cook left England to search once more for the great southern continent, carrying on board chronometers, one of which was Kendall's copy of John Harrison's masterpiece, his fourth marine time-keeper. The instrument proved itself by keeping accurate time throughout the buffeting of the long voyage; one of the most persistent problems of oceanic navigation had been overcome. Equipped with chronometers and improved sextants, navigators would be able to determine longitude and latitude with an accuracy sufficient for all practical purposes.

Cook's second expedition (1772–5) ranks among the greatest seaborne voyages of discovery. In his three years away he disposed of the conjectural southern continent, went closer to the South Pole than any man before him and touched on a multitude of lands – New Zealand and Tahiti again and, for the first time, the Marquesas, Tonga, New Caledonia, the New Hebrides, Easter Island and South Georgia. He located and connected many of the half-known, half-remembered discoveries of earlier expeditions which had brought so much confusion to the map of the Pacific. At his farthest south he reached latitude 71°S, before being halted by the ice barrier which encircles the great continent of the south. This was not the fertile land of the theorists' dreams, but the frozen Antarctic – in Cook's words, 'a Country doomed by Nature never once to feel the warmth of the Sun's rays, but to lie for ever buried under everlasting snow and ice'.

With, as Cook put it, 'the Southern Hemisphere sufficiently explored', his third and final voyage (1776–80) took him to the north Pacific in an effort to solve that other major mystery – the existence of a North-West Passage – by searching for its western outlet. In taking the unfrequented route from Tahiti to the north-west coast of America, Cook discovered the Sandwich (Hawaiian) Islands before turning to his main task. He spent the summer of 1778 on the Alaskan coast, probing in vain for a passage to the Atlantic. He failed but, once again, the results of this single season of exploration were impressive. Cook had outlined the American coast from Vancouver Island to the Bering Strait and had done much to link the Spanish explorations from the south with those of the Russians from the north.

For the first time the shape and position of the north-west coast of America took recognizable form on the maps.

On his three voyages Cook had established the salient features of the Pacific. There were further voyages of exploration to the Pacific before the end of the century but the tasks and achievements of Cook's successors appeared more mundane and their voyages were rivalled by the activity of trading, missionary and settlement enterprises. Above all, English settlers arrived in New South Wales, perhaps the most portentous of all the consequences of Cook's voyages.

Convict Colony

Interest in the settlement possibilities of the east coast of Australia came in the unpropitious form of discussions in the mid-1780s about the choice of a new place of transportation for convicts, who would previously have been sent to the American colonies. Gradually, New South Wales worked its way to the top of the list. With Cook dead, it was Joseph Banks who was looked to for an authoritative recollection of the region. The land, he told the Beauchamp Committee in 1785, 'is sufficiently fertile to support a Considerable Number of Europeans.' The 'very few' natives – a wandering people with no fixed habitations – would, he thought, 'speedily abandon the Country'. New South Wales, as reported by Banks, was *terra nullius*, belonging to no one, ready for occupation and exploitation. In 1786 the Pitt Government chose New South Wales as the site for a new penal settlement.

In January 1788 the First Fleet comprising eleven ships and carrying more than thirteen hundred people – convicts, marines and crews – under the command of Governor Arthur Phillip, drew into Botany Bay. After a few days it sailed some miles north along the coast to the more secure anchorage of Sydney Cove inside the magnificent harbour of Port Jackson. The early years of the new settlement were precarious and hard. Attempts at cultivation were slow and interrupted by crop failures, as the settlers strove to come to grips with the unfamiliar cycle of reversed seasons, drought and floods. The lack of livestock for food, breeding and manuring was a particular handicap. Before the colony was a year old, an outlying settlement was established on the better soil of Rose Hill (Parramatta) at the head of the

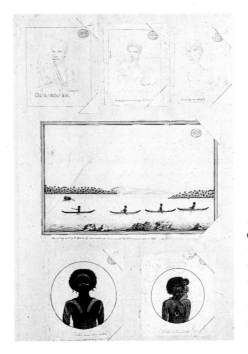

During the early days of Port Jackson, an unknown painter made a record of the local Aborigines. Governor Phillip, in the centre, meets a deputation after one of them had been wounded.

harbour. A riskier venture altogether was the sending of a detachment to exploit the reported timber and flax of Norfolk Island, a thousand miles out in the ocean – 'a second transportation', as one witness wrote. To keep discipline, and instil a sense of common purpose among the mixed company of officers, marines and convicts, proved difficult. If there was a bond, then it was the chilling sense of isolation and disorientation. Feelings of abandonment were sharpened by increasing food shortages after the loss of a supply ship at the Cape of Good Hope.

The appearance of the second fleet in 1790, and of the third fleet in 1791, together with supplies brought from Batavia and India, transformed the situation of the little colony. The human cargoes of the second and third fleets were in a desperate condition but, by the time Phillip left for home at the end of 1792, there were four thousand settlers at Sydney, Parramatta and Norfolk Island. Thirteen hundred government acres were under crops (plus a number of private farms), and there were cattle, sheep, pigs and horses. A new officer arriving in 1792 wrote that, 'to my great astonishment, instead of the rock I expected to see, I find myself surrounded with gardens.'

Culture Clash

The establishment of the colony was at the expense of the native inhabitants. Early contacts with the Aborigines were tentative, broken by violence and some killings (on both sides). Not until 1790 did Phillip's efforts at reconciliation succeed in bringing Aborigines into the settlement in any numbers. The Governor's acknowledgment that the arrival of the First Fleet meant the dispersal of the Aborigines of that area, the loss of their fishing grounds, and the spread among them of disease (especially smallpox) was an indication of the clash of material interests that followed the European intrusion. In turn, the unpredictable fluctuations of Aboriginal reaction to their dispossession incensed the settlers. Soon the pattern of misunderstanding, theft and killing bore the depressing stamp of frontier violence. But the matter cut deeper than this, for two incompatible cultures had been thrust against each other. On the one hand, there was an Aboriginal lifestyle based on family groups whose close knowledge of the land – its plants, animals and water – allowed them to exist in an environment where strangers would have perished without imported supplies. On the other hand, there were the incessant digging, enclosing and building activities of the English, determined to master their environment, and using military discipline and concepts of individual ownership as the means to that end.

After the five years of Phillip's governorship, Sydney was still the merest fingerhold on the edge of the Australian continent. But it gave Britain a lead in the exploitation of that continent which it was never to lose. In 1770 Cook had taken possession of the east coast of Australia in the name of King George III; in 1788 Phillip brought a royal commission giving him authority over a region extending from South Cape to Cape York, and inland as far as longitude 135°E (in effect, the eastern half of Australia). The gulf between these grandiose declarations and the sparse reality of the First Fleet was an enormous one. It was the achievement of the early settlers, some willing, most not, that by 1792 the intention of establishing an English presence in Australia had been carried out.

THE DEATH OF COOK

The death of Captain Cook in Hawaii in 1779 marked a change in eighteenth-century attitudes towards the Pacific Islands. No longer did they reflect a golden age of man's innocence. Later scholarship on Cook has stripped away the romanticism and shown him more erratic in judgement than on his first two voyages, and a different, Hawaiian dimension has been introduced.

When the *Resolution* and the *Discovery* first reached the Sandwich Islands in January 1778, the reverence shown to Cook was a puzzling development. When the ships returned at the end of the year, this respect had turned into something more significant. On the largest island, Hawaii, Cook was now regarded as a god – Lono, the bringer of peace and plenty. His escort of priests, the abasement before him of the populace and the offerings of food were all evidence of this. Less than a week after its departure from Hawaii in February 1779, the expedition turned back for repairs to the *Discovery*. By then, however, the islanders' attitude had changed dramatically.

The reasons for this are a source of contention. Hawaiian sources point to the similarity between the sails of Cook's ships and Lono's emblem of white bark-cloth. The season sacred to Lono was *makahiki* (October to January), when the banners were processed clockwise around the island, and tributes were

'The Death of Captain Cook', painted by John Cleveley.

collected for the god. Both Cook's visits at the beginning and end of 1778 fell within the *makahiki* season, as his white banner-like sails appeared off the coast, moving in a clockwise direction. It was the return of Cook in a crippled vessel, out of season and out of character, which in this interpretation explains the changed mood of restlessness which led to the fatal fracas at Kealakekua Bay. Cook had sailed from the island on 4 February 1779, the last day of *makahiki*; he was killed on 14 February, in the season of Ku, the god of war.

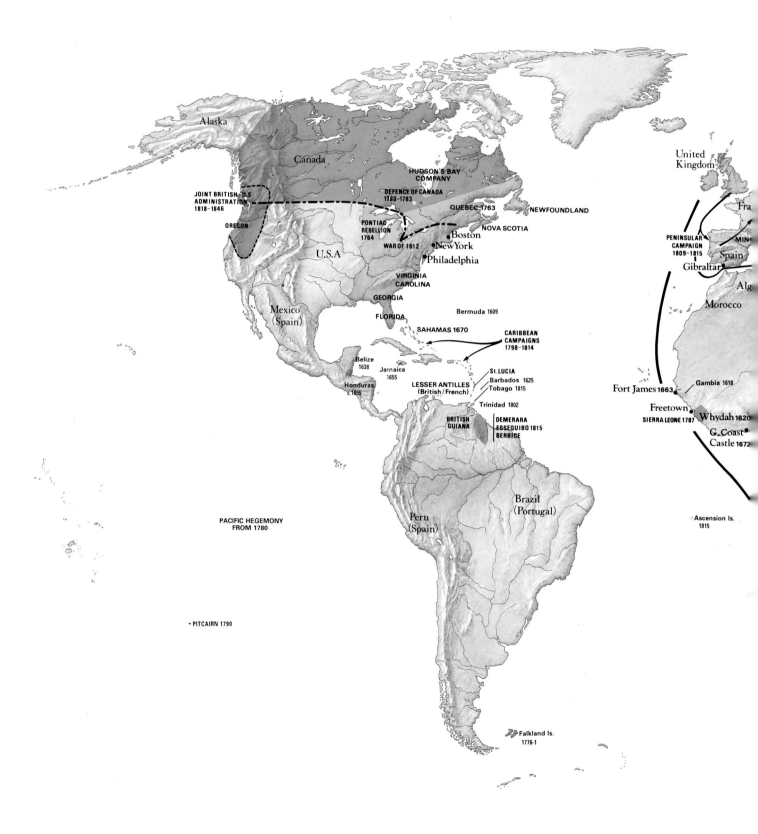

Alaska

Canada

HUDSON'S BAY
COMPANY

JOINT BRITISH/U.S
ADMINISTRATION
1818-1846

DEFENCE OF CANADA
1780-1783

QUEBEC 1763

NEWFOUNDLAND

OREGON

PONTIAC
REBELLION
1764

NOVA SCOTIA

WAR OF 1812

Boston
New York
Philadelphia

U.S.A

VIRGINIA
CAROLINA

GEORGIA

FLORIDA

Bermuda 1609

Mexico
(Spain)

BAHAMAS 1670

CARIBBEAN
CAMPAIGNS
1798-1814

Belize
1638

Jamaica
1655

St.LUCIA
Barbados 1625
Tobago 1815

Honduras
c.1655

LESSER ANTILLES
(British/French)

Trinidad 1802

BRITISH
GUIANA

DEMERARA
ESSEQUIBO 1815
BERBICE

United
Kingdom

Fra

PENINSULAR
CAMPAIGN
1809-1815

MIN

Spain

Gibraltar

Alg

Morocco

Gambia 1618

Fort James 1663

Freetown

Whydah 1620

SIERRA LEONE 1787

G.Coast
Castle 1672

PACIFIC HEGEMONY
FROM 1780

Peru
(Spain)

Brazil
(Portugal)

Ascension Is.
1815

• PITCAIRN 1790

Falkland Is.
1776-1

Russian Empire

Japan

Ottoman
Empire

Ionian Is.
1809-1814
PIED
1816

MALTA 1800

1798

Egypt
OCCUPIED 1801
ATTACKED 1807

rman
ates

Persia
TREATY 1809

Tibet

Chinese
Empire

Sind

INDIAN PARAMOUNTCY
1798-1818

PUNITIVE
EXPEDITION 1808

BENGAL 1757-1765

Calcutta
1696

Burma
1824-1826

Bombay 1661

ADEN

Madras 1639

TENASSERIM 1826

Manila

PHILIPPINES

CAPTURED
1762

COLOMBO

TRINCOMALEE

PENANG 1786

Ceylon 1796-1818

MALACCA 1824

Maldives 1802

SINGAPORE 1819

Bencoolen 1685

Seychelles
1794

Chagos 1784

Batavia
OCCUPIED 1811-1816
JAVA (Dutch)

Mauritius 1810

Norfolk Is.
1774

SWAN R.1825

N.S.Wales 1788

Natal 1824

PERTH

SYDNEY

CAPETOWN

CAPE
ROUTE
SECURED
1785

Cape Colony 1795/1806

Tasmania 1825

New Zealand
1787- 1840

The Expansion of the British Empire 1763–1830

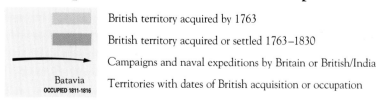

British territory acquired by 1763

British territory acquired or settled 1763–1830

Campaigns and naval expeditions by Britain or British/India

Batavia
OCCUPIED 1811-1816

Territories with dates of British acquisition or occupation

63

CHAPTER NINE

THE FALL AND RISE OF THE BRITISH EMPIRE

◇

In 1763, after seven years of war, Britain stood triumphant. For a time at least, the nation's prowess could be celebrated to the refrain of new patriotic songs, such as Thomas Arne's 'Rule, Britannia!' The administration of William Pitt the Elder had subsidized the emerging might of Prussia in her war with France and other Continental powers. His policy of short thrusts against the French in Europe and the colonies – once denounced by his enemies as 'breaking windows with guineas' – had paid handsome dividends. The French and their allies had virtually been driven off the colonial map.

Britain's relative power in 1763 was far greater than it had been during Queen Elizabeth's reign, when England was a small economy on the fringes of European civilization. In large part this transformation had been achieved by elbowing the Dutch out of their mercantile pre-eminence. London was now the world's greatest capital market; even the Dutch invested there. Rising agricultural incomes at home and burgeoning foreign trade had left the country awash with capital. The Royal Navy and merchant marine were much greater than Holland's; the sheer scale of their operations brought benefits of cost. With the foundation of institutions such as the Royal Society, Britain was now in the forefront of the 'scientific revolution', even if Oxford and Cambridge still resembled finishing schools for rural clergymen. Above all, Britain had a strong state, supported by the gentry and merchant classes of both England and Scotland. Fierce rebellions of the impoverished of the periphery would still take place, notably in Ireland, but the Protestant realm was largely spared the revolts, invasions and counter-invasions which plagued her Continental competitors.

Rule, Britannia!

The greatest successes came in North America. The restive Thirteen Colonies still regarded the French and their Indian clients as a more serious menace than the distant London government. They had cooperated in the conquest of the French peasant colony of Quebec, and now its vast hinterland of beavers, timber and Indian tribes lay at their mercy. In the Caribbean too, the British had been successful. Here, Admiral Rodney drove the French squadrons back onto Martinique, conquering all the French islands except Saint-Domingue. The sugar planters and slave owners of the British islands looked on with glee. At the very least, they could restrict the sugar production of their dangerous French rivals. At best, they would be able to colonize the islands themselves. This would supplement the profits from Jamaica and Barbados which were now beginning to decline as the land became exhausted and the price of slaves rose.

Britain had been almost as successful in the East, where a prize fell almost fortuitously into the East India Company's lap. Because the British had more troops than usual in Madras, in order to confront the French, they were able to respond vigorously when relations with the ruler of the much richer province of Bengal broke down in 1756. Siraj-ud Daulah,

Sir Joshua Reynolds' portrait of Warren Hastings (1732–1818), whose term as first Governor-General of Bengal established the pattern of British administration in India.

Nawab (Mughal Viceroy) of Bengal, a young ruler trying to establish himself, had grown weary of the demands of the British for tax exemptions and chafed at the power that their allies, the Hindu bankers, held within his state. In 1756 he attacked Calcutta. Robert Clive counter-attacked swiftly. He recaptured Calcutta and, in 1757, he defeated the Nawab at the Battle of Plassey. By 1765, the British were in complete control of the lucrative land revenues of Bengal. Hereafter, they were able to subsidize the failing profits of the company's trade and to support their military activities in India and in other parts of Asia from the vast wealth acquired in this way. Private citizens did well too. Clive accumulated a fortune of three million pounds sterling but declared himself 'astonished at his own moderation'.

For the time being, Ministers in Britain could congratulate themselves on their successes. They had acquired huge 'treasure' and, because most theorists and men of letters still thought that the world contained a finite quantity of trade and bullion, anything taken from the French was considered an absolute bonus for the British. The domestic economy seemed to be doing well, as productivity in agriculture increased rapidly and as Britain's flexible financial institutions – the Bank of England, the Stock Exchange and the new insurance markets – allocated resources efficiently. Population grew by twenty-five per cent between 1740 and 1770.

More subtly, the country's attitude to Empire was changing. The men of the early eighteenth century had been suspicious of overseas possessions. Brought up on the Latin classics, they believed that the 'civic virtue' of the Roman Republic had been corrupted by 'luxury and empire' – particularly, the Oriental empire. Might not Britain go the same way? These doubts can be glimpsed in the work of the great historian, Edward Gibbon, and also in the speeches of the parliamentary orator, Edmund Burke, who denounced the East India Company and its Governor Warren Hastings (in office, 1773–84) for corruption and tyranny in India. However, other voices were already saying that Britons could be both a 'free and a conquering people' and that, provided agencies such as the East India Company or people such as the Caribbean planters could be controlled, Empire

Robert Clive (1725–74), conqueror of Bengal, receiving a grant from the Nawab of Bengal.

could be a prop to domestic wealth and not a threat to domestic freedoms.

The Fall of the First British Empire

In the short run at least, the new proponents of Empire were over-optimistic. The vast expansion of British control brought its own ineluctable problems. How could this huge area be controlled? And, above all, who could possibly be made to pay for its defence? In America, the Government's attempts to raise more money for the policing of the new conquests, particularly the hated Stamp Act and Tea Duties, brought an already tense situation to the boil. Americans, convinced that they were the victims of royal tyranny, flooded by the 'baubles of Britain' (British manufactures) and fired by their non-conformist religious beliefs, rose in revolt.

While the British loss of the Thirteen Colonies was a closer run thing than many American historians admit, a majority of the population wished for independence and the Continental Congress quickly developed a form of guerilla warfare which was very well adapted to its surroundings. For a time, Canada seemed

to be going the same way, since the French settlers of Quebec were largely indifferent to whichever group of English-speaking heretics ruled them. It was only the logistical problem of fighting in the cold north which stopped the Americans. Even the Caribbean islands, treasure-houses of the eighteenth-century British Empire, seemed in danger. Here, the French were only narrowly defeated once again by Admirals Howe and Rodney. In the final analysis, however, the planters who dominated the colonial assemblies of Jamaica and Barbados realized that they needed the Royal Navy and the British Crown to protect them as much from slave revolt as from the revived French menace.

For a time, the picture looked no better in India. Here, the problem of paying for the great expansion of British territory acquired during the Seven Years War was foisted onto Indian rulers. These were bound to the British rule by a form of protection racket known as the 'subsidiary alliance system'. The Indian princes were 'protected' from their enemies by East India Company armies which were stationed on their territory and paid for at the rulers' own expense. This was a most unsatisfactory system, however. The Indian rulers struggled under the strain of paying the huge subsidies demanded by the East India Company for its military services. Some revolted against the British demands, the Raja of Benares in 1781, for example. Others, such as the Nawabs of Awadh and Arcot, had to cede large chunks of their territory to the company in lieu of payments of the subsidy. In either case, the frontier of British power rolled inexorably forward and the costs of protecting it soared upward, embarrassing the Court of Directors in London. Independent Indian powers, such as the Marathas in the west and the Sultans of Mysore to the south, were frightened into opposition by the expansion of the company, and the way in which its servants were eating away at the fabric of the Indian economy and society in pursuit of their private fortunes.

As a result, between 1779 and 1783, Warren Hastings faced a coalition of hostile Indian states which might easily have overwhelmed British power had the French naval presence in the East been stronger. Madras was nearly captured and the British in Bombay were emphatically defeated by the Marathas. 'His Majesty's Oriental dominions appear likely to melt away as surely as did the American ones', wrote one gloomy observer.

In 1782 Lord North's ministry tottered and fell, battered by a series of military failures. Even the Irish now began to take a leaf from the Americans' book. The Protestant magnates and professional people, joined by a fringe of more radical Catholics,

ADAM SMITH

In 1776 Adam Smith, Professor of Political Economy at the University of Glasgow, published his *Wealth of Nations*. Although the work was very critical of Britain's eighteenth-century Empire, it was to become – ironically – a bible for generations of colonial officials and statesmen who wished to bring prosperity to subject races. Smith welded together the pragmatic traditions of the 'Scottish Enlightenment' and the contemporary French *philosophes* in a way that virtually founded the science of economics. He argued that a free division of labour, unfettered by monopolies and state intervention, would bring the greatest wealth and the greatest 'moral

Adam Smith (1723–90), philosopher and political economist.

independence' to the greatest number.

Smith and his followers were fiercely critical of the monopoly of the East India Company and also of the restrictive English Corn Laws. From the 1780s statesmen and colonial officials experimented with freeing trade, freeing the market in land and withdrawing the state from the economy. By the 1830s, free trade was a convenient slogan with which the British could bludgeon their way into markets in Asia, Africa and Latin America. It was a philosopher's stone for Britain, the most competitive nation in the world. But it was disastrous for societies which wished to protect infant industries or agricultural producers.

Fort Cornwallis, captured by the British in 1786, occupied a strategic location on the Straits of Malacca.

formed the Volunteering Movement. These militia bands demanded the legislative independence of the Irish Parliament and trade concessions from Britain. Radicals in the streets of English, Welsh and Scottish towns insisted on the reform of Parliament and the purging of what they saw as a corrupt Establishment. England's empire seemed about to vanish, as the Portuguese Empire had done before. Colonialism had never been more unpopular. Publicists argued for the investment of labour and capital in Britain rather than in far-away places. What was the point of holding territories, such as America, inhabited by nothing but the 'Felons, Fanaticks and Madmen of His Majesty's Domains'? Why waste the lives of British seamen on the triangular slave routes to the Caribbean which (it was claimed) were neither profitable nor morally righteous?

The Rise of the Second Empire

Actually, the Empire was never in quite as much danger as many thought during the disastrous autumn of 1782. For a start, Britain was experiencing a massive increase of wealth and productivity which meant that the losses of war could easily be absorbed. Overseas traders prospered as Britain quickly re-established and then greatly increased her share of world trade. New areas were pioneered. The British acquired a foothold in the rich, Dutch-dominated East Indies with their taking of

Penang in 1786. In 1788, the foundation of a penal colony in New South Wales complemented the exploration of the Pacific coast of North America and mapped out the Pacific Ocean as a new area of British enterprise. More surprisingly, Britain's old trading partners, the Thirteen Colonies – now the independent United States of America – proved that they were even more valuable as a free society than as a recalcitrant dependency. Americans imported enormous quantities of British linens, ironware and other manufactures.

The value of colonies which many doubted in 1783 was forcefully reasserted when, a mere ten years later, Britain found herself at war with her old enemy France. However, this time, France was not merely Catholic but revolutionary as well, bent on sweeping away all that the British constitution and British aristocracy were supposed to stand for. Faced with the levelling zeal of the French armies and the military brilliance of Napoleon, the British were expelled from continental Europe. Catholic rebellion in Ireland was suppressed in 1798–9 as a French invasion force approached. The Act of Union of 1801 submerged Irish representatives in the British Parliament, ending the short-lived independence of the Irish Assembly.

Ireland was now as firmly shackled to London as was Scotland. But still the British could make little headway in continental Europe. Instead, she resorted to the time-worn strategy of seizing the colonies of her French, Spanish and Dutch enemies as compensation. During the course of the Napoleonic Wars, the British consolidated a new Empire which was to provide the foundations of her world dominance in the Victorian age.

In a series of malaria-plagued campaigns which cost the lives of more than fifty thousand soldiers and sailors, the British regained their dominance in the Caribbean. The job was made easier, but also more urgent, by the revolt in 1792 of the 'Black Jacobins' and slave populations of the French island of Saint-Domingue – a contagion that threatened to spread to the British slave islands. By the end of the war, the British had captured Trinidad and Tobago from France's Spanish allies; what was to become British Guiana from the Dutch and the French; and half a dozen French sugar islands. These all became Crown colonies. They were ruled with a rod of iron, partly from fear of slave revolt, and partly because the anti-slavery lobby in

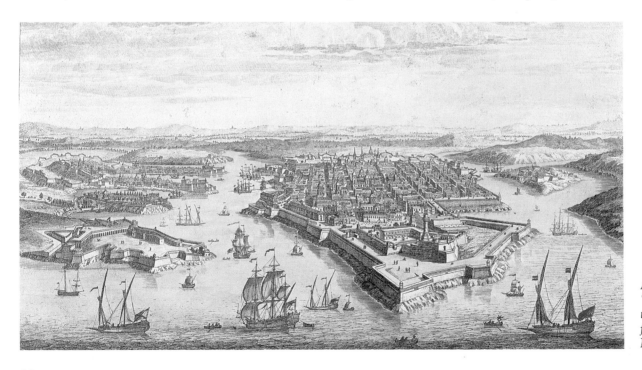

An eighteenth-century 'Perspective view of the town and fortifications of Malta'.

Following Napoleon's invasion of Egypt in 1798, British and French interests turned Egypt and the Ottoman Empire into a battleground. The two countries engaged in a war of diplomacy and cultural influence which lasted beyond the construction of the Suez Canal to the British occupation of Egypt in 1882. France saw Egypt as a land which had been wakened from a sleep of centuries by French enlightenment. The matter was more mundane for the British: Egypt was a listening post and a trans-shipment point on the route to India. For their part, the French attempted to map and describe Egyptian archaeological sites in the multi-volume *Description de l'Egypte* produced by the French Academy under Napoleon's direction. Following the precedent of the Roman emperors, Napoleon had large numbers of Egyptian carvings and obelisks carted back to beautify the museums and squares of Paris. The British, no laggards in the art of cultural looting, as the case of the Elgin marbles demonstrates, soon followed suit. In the 1810s and 1820s, Henry Salt, the British consul-general in Alexandria and a man of wide travel and artistic experience, began to ship back equally large numbers of antiquities.

A colossal head of Memnon on its way to the British Museum.

Many went to the new imperial halls of the British Museum, while others like the obelisk known as 'Cleopatra's Needle' were to find resting places in the open air during the coming decades. Appropriately, Salt employed a former circus artiste from Italy, Giovanni Belzoni, as his agent among the tombs and temples of Upper Egypt.

Britain and the new Board of War and Colonies were suspicious of the white planters.

The longer-term future of the Caribbean sugar economy, however, was precarious. It was protected by unrealistic tariff barriers and dependent on a dwindling supply of slave labour, which had been threatened by the abolition of the slave trade in 1807. Other fields for British enterprise appeared much more promising. The Royal Navy established its long-lived dominance in the Mediterranean when it took Malta in 1799; thereafter, the island became 'an outwork for India', as Admiral Lord Nelson described it. The British briefly occupied the islands of Sicily and Sardinia, but they made a deeper impact on the Ionian islands off the western coast of Greece which they held until 1864. Ginger beer and cricket were among the English trappings introduced to this unlikely corner of Empire.

In the East, the British Empire in India stamped its dominance on the subcontinent as a huge counterweight to France in Europe. Richard Wellesley, Lord Mornington, brother of the future Duke of Wellington, rolled forward the boundaries in a series of wars between 1798 and 1805. He also allowed the debts of the East India Company in London to escalate until halted in his tracks by an embarrassed Ministry. Wellesley defeated the most dangerous Indian enemies of Britain, Tipu Sultan of Mysore in the south and the Marathas in the west. He also took over large chunks of territory in Awadh and Arcot which were still nominally under Indian control. His successor, Lord Minto (Governor-General 1807–12), briefly extended British rule to Dutch Java, marking out Iran in the west and the Malay Peninsula in the east as the boundaries of British India's informal influence. The battle lines for the 'great game' – the diplomatic struggle between Russia and Britain in Central Asia – were already forming.

In southern Africa, the British pegged out a final enclave of Empire. They took Cape Colony from the Dutch in 1795 and secured it permanently in 1806, re-organizing and invigorating the ramshackle government of the Dutch East India Company.

The African opponents of European expansion, such as the hunter-gatherer bushmen and the pastoralist Xhosa people, were corralled behind firmer boundaries. Early British governors also moved swiftly against the republican recalcitrance of the Boer farmers. In this way, the three-way struggle between the Boers, the British and the Africans in southern Africa began almost as soon as the Union flag was hoisted in Cape Town.

Much territory had been won from Napoleon's allies during the fierce conflicts of the world crisis. Britain's conservative administration, led by Lord Liverpool (Prime Minister, 1812–27), consisted of cautious men not given to imperial sentiment. After the Congress of Vienna in 1815, the Dutch East Indies were returned to their former owners as part of a package which reconstituted Holland as a north European buffer against a future French revival. Lord Canning, the Foreign Secretary, was prepared to allow Greek and Latin-American nationalists to dismember the Ottoman Empire in Europe and the Spanish Empire in South America. But he was not keen to take on new territories. The scars of the loss of America and the millstone of Wellesley's Indian debts were an ever-present warning.

Rolling Back the Informal Frontiers

Ministers in London, however, were rarely in control of events. On its periphery, the Empire rolled forward under its own momentum. The merchant adventurers of the Hudson's Bay Company and the Quebec Chamber of Commerce chased the Indians and the beaver back into their north-western fastnesses. Demand for timber during the wars also pulled the informal boundaries outward. In Australia and the Pacific, the small penal colonies were already dispossessing the Aborigines, while missionaries and whalers were tearing apart the fragile societies of Melanesia and Polynesia. In southern Africa, Boers and English pressed into the vast 'empty country', defying the governors in Cape Town as well as the new Colonial Office. The 'turbulent frontier' of Empire was to be a glorious headache for most nineteenth-century politicians.

The Age of Free Enterprise
1763–1860

BRITISH
COLUMBIA

NORTH-WESTERN
TERRITORY

HUDSON BAY

New Westminster

FURS
WHEAT

RUPERT'S LAND

QUEBEC

TIMBER
FISH

ONTARIO

FRENCH REBELLION
1837-1838

NEWFOUNDLAND

Montreal

Saint Johns

U.S.A

Ottawa

Halifax

Toronto

NOVA SCOTIA

Washington

Boston

New York

San Francisco

RAW COTTON

Mexico

BRITISH
HONDURAS

JAMAICA
REBELLION 1865

CARIBBEAN
ISLANDS

HARDWOOD

United
Kingdom

Ireland
AGRARIAN
VIOLENCE 1881-2

Prussia

COTTONS
MACHINERY
CAPITAL
LABOUR

France

IONIAN
ISLANDS

Spain

DISTURBAN
1839-184

Gibraltar

Algeria

MALTA
1814

Bathurst

GAMBIA

Freetown

SIERRA LEONE

Accra

Lagos

VEGETABLE OILS
COCOA

St Helena

Rio de Janeiro

CAPE CO

BEEF
HIDES
WHEAT

KAFFIR WARS 177

Capetow

Buenos Aires

W
FR
W

FALKLAND
ISLANDS

CRIMEA 1853-56
URRANTS
Ottoman Empire
RAW COTTON
Alexandria
airo • Suez
Egypt
Russian Empire
Afghanistan
PUNJAB 1839
RAJPUTANA
INDIAN MUTINY
1857-58
OUDH 1856
TEA
SIND 1838
Delhi
Indian Empire
JUTE
OPIUM
SUGAR
RAW COTTON
Bombay
Calcutta
BURMA 1852
Rangoon
HARDWOOD
Siam
MYSORE
1831
Trincomalee
Colombo • Ceylon
TEA
PEASANT REBELLION 1836
Chinese Empire
Korea   Japan
OPIUM WAR 1839-1842
ARROW WAR 1856
Canton
TEA
SILK
HONG KONG 1842
LABUAN 1846
HARDWOOD
MALAY
STATES 1874
Singapore

ADEN 1839

ZANZIBAR

Mauritius

ORANGE FREE
STATE 1848
GREAT TREK 1836
Durban
NATAL 1845

Dominion of Australia
GOLD   SUGAR
NORTHERN
TERRITORY   MINERALS
WESTERN
AUSTRALIA   QUEENSLAND
WHEAT
BEEF
WOOL
Perth
SOUTH
AUSTRALIA
Adelaide
NEW SOUTH WALES
Melbourne
TASMANIA
Brisbane
Sydney
MAORI WARS
WOOL
NEW ZEALAND
1841

The Expansion of the British Empire 1815-75

COPRA	Major colonial exports
✕	Uprisings
PUNJAB 1839 ●●●●●	Territory acquired 1815-75
- - - - - - -	Boundaries of British colonies
Buenos Aires •	Major cities trading with Great Britain

CHAPTER TEN

THE AGE OF FREE ENTERPRISE

◇

The years between the Battle of Waterloo and the opening of the Suez Canal in 1869 saw Great Britain at her zenith – as the dominant military and economic power in the world. Although there was the constant rumble of war on the borders of her colonial possessions, this was not a period when vast new conquests were made. British statesmen certainly wanted to push the nation's moral and economic frontiers ever wider; they longed to inoculate the world with what later came to be seen as 'Victorian values'. But as far as possible, they wished this to be done by the operations of the 'free market' and not by costly colonial administrations. Where new territories were annexed, it was usually because of the zeal, or greed, of Britain's agents in the periphery. When, in 1843, Sir Charles Napier, the conqueror of the Indian province of Sind, telegraphed home his famous Latin tag 'PECCAVI' – 'I have sinned (i.e. Sind)' – most policy-makers would have approved of the conquest as well as of his pun.

A World Free of Competitors

Britain's power in the first half of the nineteenth century was due in part to her own strengths and in part to the weaknesses of others. On the one hand, she had no true competitors. France, which had looked set to catch up with Britain economically at the end of the eighteenth century, had set herself back a generation by the huge efforts of the Napoleonic Wars. Although she took Algeria in 1830, France had lost naval dominion to Britain even in the Mediterranean which had once been Louis XIV's own lake. Not until the reign of Napoleon III (1852–71) did France once again embark gingerly on colonial designs and even these were only in areas such as Indochina and Syria – the odd bones and haunches left from the earlier meal of the British lion. Meanwhile, Germany was still a mass of contentious princelings and Austria a land empire rent by ethnic tensions, which rose to a furious pitch during the revolutionary year of 1848.

Russia, of course, faced Britain across the chessboard of the 'Great game' in Central Asia. She even took a few pawns, following British India's humiliation by the fierce Afghan tribesmen in 1842. But Russia was still a backward economy; she expanded on her land frontiers and had little purchase at sea. The British countered the attempts of the Tsars to secure warm-water ports in the Mediterranean and the Far East by bolstering up the Ottoman Empire and, later, Japan as clients and friends. Most adventitious of all, the United States of America, the rebellious western arm of the old British Empire, proved a marvellous trading partner, while her jealous neutralism ensured that none of Britain's rivals could make much headway in the western hemisphere. Despite the Anglo-American war of 1812, the two nations found that they had much in common: both benefited from the expansion of free world trade; neither relished the prospect of another European war; and both affected to dislike the great European autocracies.

Institutions of Empire: the Navy, Industry and the City

On the other hand, the remarkable dominance achieved by Great Britain during these years was due first and foremost to the unchallenged pre-eminence of the Royal Navy and the British Merchant Marine. By 1815 all competitors had been swept from the sea. The Navy had access to huge stocks of timber in Canada, India, Burma and the north coast of Australia. It had created a new command structure during the great sea struggle with Napoleon. It had pioneered a powerful intelligence tool in naval charts, which had been mapped out by the great eighteenth-century explorers and were now ordered and processed with the efficiency of the early Victorians: every coast and every inlet and every source of food and water worldwide was pinpointed and recorded. This was a military and scientific project comparable with the exploration of space in the twentieth century. Charles Darwin's theories on the origin of species were nurtured aboard a naval survey ship, *HMS Beagle*.

RACE AND EMPIRE

In the eighteenth century, Britons regarded the great civilizations of India and China almost with awe. Sir William Jones, the great translator of Indian classics, compared these civilizations to ancient Rome and Greece. Philosophers too admired their stability.

But, by the early nineteenth century, evangelical Christians and colonial administrators denounced 'native' cultures for their barbarity and for customs such as infanticide, the ritual self-burning of widows (*suttee*) and foot-binding. The great British historian, Macaulay thought that 'one shelf-ful' of European books was worth all the literature of the Orient.

The court of the Asante king swears fealty to the British government in 1817.

After events such as the Indian Mutiny of 1857 and the Jamaican insurrection of 1865, non-European peoples were now regarded simply as savages, but pseudoscientific theories were enlisted to justify their subordination. As one American writer representing the new racism wrote, in 1855, 'There are no greater differences between the lion, tiger and panther, or the dog, fox, wolf and jackal than between the White Man, Negro and Mongol.' As larger European settlements grew up in the colonies, segregation grew more intense and the hatred more fierce. Murderous, but often unpunished, assaults were meted out by whites to their defenceless labourers or servants.

The P & O paddle steamship, Delta, carried British guests to the opening of the Suez Canal in 1869. The new breed of mid-nineteenth-century steamships transformed sea travel.

The Royal Navy's ability to roam the oceans unchallenged was an important prerequisite for the expansion of the Merchant Marine and Britain's world trade. 'Pirates' – often no more than local seaborne traders who wished to protect their own commerce – were swept from the oceans. In the 1810s and 1820s, the 'pirates' of north Africa, the Red Sea and the Persian Gulf were chastised; in the 1830s and 1840s, the seas of the Far East and South-East Asia were 'made safe for the intercourse of nations'. The Navy was also a crucial tool in breaking open new markets in the Ottoman Empire, China and South-East Asia during the great age of 'gun-boat diplomacy' when Lord Palmerston was Foreign Secretary (1830–41 and 1846–51).

Economic power and naval power reinforced each other. The development of the iron ship, the steam engine and the electric telegraph all helped to keep Britain ahead of her competitors. For instance, American wooden shipping accounted for much of the trade across the Atlantic in the 1830s. But the introduction of iron hulls, with their greater speed and safety, had increased Britain's lead once again by the 1860s. As a result, in 1870, the mercantile tonnage of the British Empire almost equalled that of all the other countries in the world and, in 1880, at 2,950,000 tons, actually exceeded it.

By 1830 Great Britain accounted for roughly forty-five per cent of world trade. This was not simply because she could transport her goods more cheaply and use her naval guns to break into other countries' markets. Increasingly, it was because the sophistication of her industrial production enabled her to undercut her competitors. In the eighteenth century British agriculture had been highly productive, but her flexible financial institutions had already ensured that trade, moveable property and financial instruments made up more than half her total wealth. After 1780 capital, accumulated through successful foreign trading – especially in the West Indies – and through the booming domestic economy, was rapidly being invested in manufacturing production.

The wars with France gave an added fillip to innovation and also forced British merchants to look to the wider world to sell their goods. Continental Europe was closed until 1815 and remained a slack market for some years after the end of the war. Therefore, the cotton magnates of Lancashire looked for new

markets to Latin America, where the Spanish Empire was dissolving, to India and to the Ottoman Empire. They exported not only Lancashire cotton goods but also huge quantities of twist and yarn. Exports of cotton manufactured goods increased from 253 million yards in 1815 to 3,562 million yards in 1875. By this later date, for instance, it was calculated that nearly thirty per cent of the medium-quality and higher-quality cloth worn in eastern India was of British manufacture. The local cloth producers in India, South-East Asia and the Middle East saw their markets melt away. Lancashire clothed the globe. During periods such as the later 1830s when the home market was quite slack, the pressure to find overseas markets grew even stronger. Merchants and publicists in towns such as Manchester and Birmingham vociferously demanded the support of the state in pushing aside competition and in forcing what they saw as corrupt foreign despotisms to lower their tariff barriers and to let more British goods in.

The textile industry was the leading sector of Britain's industrial revolution but, by mid-century, the 'workshop of the world' was producing a wide range of manufactured goods. Steam engines, iron ships, military hardware and, above all, railway engines poured from her factories. By 1840 the British Isles were criss-crossed by railway lines, and the nearer part of the Continent had also been linked with the help of British expertise. Now, entrepreneurs and capitalists began to look outside Europe, to the broad plains of Canada, Australia and India, and to engineering projects in Egypt and other parts of the Ottoman Empire.

It was not only machinery and manufactures that Britain exported at the height of her economic strength; she also exported money and manpower. From the end of the seventeenth century, England had taken over from the Netherlands as the greatest financial market in the world. Fortunes made in overseas trade and, later, the profits of industrialization were channelled through county banks supervised by the Bank of England. The French Revolution encouraged the concentration of even greater financial power within the 'square mile' of the City of London. The world's greatest Jewish banking house, the Rothschilds', came to rest here in 1797. The Rothschilds not only helped Great Britain to finance her allies during the

Napoleonic Wars but they also established one of the most effective intelligence systems ever devised. Baring Brothers, another great merchant bank, emerged later to orchestrate the financing of Latin America's push for industrial growth. The bank was soon known as 'the sixth great power', standing on a par with empires such as Austria and France. Even at the peak of her industrial productivity Britain was a great exporter of capital and of what we would now call financial services. 'Gentlemanly capitalism', as it has been called, was to be Britain's forte even after the hard graft of industry, which supported it, had contracted and withered.

British Citizens Abroad

There was also the export of people. In the years after 1780 the attitude of Britons to emigration had changed dramatically. In the eighteenth century, publicists bemoaned the draining away of skilled manpower from 'the British Empire in Europe'. But slowly the popular perception changed. Perhaps, after all, emigration was a good thing. It would spread the 'English language and British name' to the great open spaces of the globe. For instance, the emigration of sturdy yeomen to Australasia would turn that rather dubious penal continent into a great granary and ranch which could feed the Mother Country. More to the point, emigration might relieve the distress which was already apparent in the great English and Scottish cities when trade went through its regular cyclical slumps. In the same way, the fractious and impoverished Irish peasantry – now suffering from hectic population growth and flawed government policies – could be exported overseas. The ecological and economic theories of Thomas Malthus, an Anglican prelate, popularized the notion of exporting people. He argued that the 'natural propensity of mankind to progenitate without cease' would ultimately outstrip food supply and end in famine.

Between 1815 and 1912, almost twenty-two million citizens of the British Isles were shipped abroad. Many went to the United States or even to South America, but nearly forty-five per cent of them went to the British Dominions – especially after the discovery of gold in Australia in the early 1850s. Emigration from Ireland turned into mass exodus in 1848. During this year millions perished in a terrible famine which had begun with the blighting of the potato crop, but which was

LORD JOHN TAKING THE MEASURE OF THE COLONIES.

A satirical cartoon of the 1840's measuring emigrants for size, with the tallest going to Australia.

John Stuart Mill (1806–73), philosopher and political economist, entered the East India Company in 1822, and remained in its service until he retired over 30 years later.

perpetuated by the doctrinaire rigidity of contemporary British economic thinking.

Reform and Revolt

So great was the speed of change in ideas and in the economic fundamentals of Empire that, by the third decade of the century, substantial new thinking was forced upon policy-makers in London and in the colonies. In the first generation after the great conquests of the Napoleonic era, the Empire had tended to be run as a loose confederacy of proconsular fiefdoms. Some of the great characters of imperial history flourished at this time. Lachlan Macquarie, a farmer's son from the Isle of Mull, ran New South Wales as a Scottish lairdship, planting tenant farmers, educational institutions and the Anglican Church. In the Cape Colony, Lord Charles Somerset established a kind of personal monarchy which would have appealed to his ancestors among the Plantagenet kings of medieval England. Most flamboyant of all was 'King' Tom Maitland, another Scotsman, who established a benevolent despotism in Malta and the Ionian Islands. But times were changing. In London, the Board of War and Colonies had transformed itself into the fledgling bureaucracy of the Colonial Office. The need to make the colonies pay for themselves and the battle to suppress the slave trade forced 'Mr Mothercountry' to intervene more and more in the operation of these bailiwicks.

The tide of new ideas and institutional change became faster in the 1830s and 1840s. Free trade triumphed and the creed of 'utilitarianism' propagated by thinkers such as Jeremy Bentham and John Stuart Mill encouraged a practical and unsentimental notion of government. 'The greatest good to the greatest number' was the new watchword although, in imperial matters, this usually meant 'the greatest good to the greatest number of Britons'. In England, Parliament was reformed and the Corn Laws, which had restricted free trade in grain, were swept away. Abroad, the monopoly of the East India Company was abolished in 1833 and private merchants flooded in to make profits in the tea and opium trades. The institution of slavery was abolished throughout the Empire in 1833, although 'new forms of slavery' in the form of indentured labour were soon enlisted to fill the gap. Gradually, the problems of government became more complex.

One thing had become very clear by the middle of the century. A centralized Empire without representative institutions could not possibly be maintained where large numbers of free white settlers were gathered. In 1837 the French Canadians revolted against the corruption and despotism of the English Establishment which had ruled Canada since 1791. On the

THAT CURSED WIRE

As the last shots of the Indian Mutiny rang out, a rebellious sepoy was heard to say that the uprising had been defeated not by blood and iron but by 'that cursed wire'. He was referring to the electric telegraph that brought the intelligence of the imperial army from Calcutta to the front line in Agra. The rapid development of the telegraph was indeed a crucial feature in the unification of Empire. Telegraphic money orders and a public service were established by 1851 in Britain and Ireland; within ten years, cables were laid in Canada, southern Africa and India; in 1865 Europe was linked to Canada and the United States by undersea cable; by the end of the century, the telegraph allowed the Colonial Office and the India Office to communicate

General Charles George Gordon (1833–85), kept regular checks on his men by telegraph.

directly with the Empire within minutes when, previously, it had taken months. The men on the spot could be rapidly whipped into line. While General Gordon was Egyptian Viceroy in the Sudan in the 1870s, he is reputed to have routinely wired the message 'Release that man! Do not take that bribe!', believing that this would be bound to apply to the immediate predicament of one or other of his subordinates. The telegraph also gave great advantages to British merchants exporting cotton from India or Alexandria to England. They could discover the spot prices on the Liverpool market in seconds and so beat their 'native' competitors who were already suffering from poorer shipping and punitive insurance premiums.

---

frontier of the Cape Colony, the Dutch Boers grew resentful of the intervention of the British government. After 1836, these hardy farmers began to trek out of British territory like some modern tribe of Israel quitting the land of the Pharaohs. Even the new colonies of Australia and New Zealand caught the fever for representation and 'responsible government' within the Empire. More by chance than design, the British hit upon a system which conceded virtual local self-government to these fractious new nations, thereby avoiding perhaps a new rash of declarations of independence. Lord Durham, who was appointed Governor of Canada in 1838, urged the introduction of representative government and a continental federation within the Empire to quiet both the French and the British settlers. Over the next generation, this scheme was applied not only in Canada but also, by a process of trial and error, in Australia, New Zealand and, in a more limited way, in southern Africa. The Empire of self-governing dominions had been born – in the nick of time.

Blacks, Indians and Chinese, however, were not to share in this grudging expansion of English liberties. Even after the abolition of slavery, the continuing brutality of the planters' rule in the Caribbean led to a bloody rebellion in 1865, which was suppressed by British forces with even greater brutality. The Colonial Office stepped in, abolishing the 'liberties' of the local whites, as well as disciplining the blacks, and introducing Crown Government in a territory which was already fast becoming 'the slum of Empire'.

In India, Lord William Bentinck (Governor General, 1828–35) had tried to deflate the swollen finances of the East India Company and to halt its reckless expansion on the fringes, notably during the invasion of Burma in 1824–6. The 'Clipping Dutchman' – as he was known by the enraged Anglo-Indians – was better at grand statements than at practical remedies. After he left, the civil and military Establishment of British India quietly resumed its policy of squeezing the peasantry and conquering the fringes. The East India debt escalated again and even the 'signal catastrophe' of the war against the tribesmen of Afghanistan in 1842 caused little reflection. The sclerotic government of the East India Company managed to alienate the long-suffering peasantry, princes, landowners and, worst of all, its own army. On the very day in 1857 when *The Times* wrote of the 'perfect tranquillity pervading the whole of India', the illusion of the 'loyal native' was shattered with murderous terror. On 10 May 1857, 'in that brief hour before darkness, when the descending fireball of the sun ignites the Indian sky', the sepoys

– Indian troops in the East India Company's army – mutinied at the great military station of Meerut, near Delhi. British India teetered on the brink of collapse and the East India Company was finally blown away by the guns of the rebellious sepoys.

One reason why the British quickly regained control of the subcontinent was that, luckily for them, a fleet and army were close by on their way to China. The British had recently been at war with China in an attempt to open up her ports and to promote that most noxious of all forms of imperial profiteering, the opium trade. In 1842 they had forced the Chinese to open 'treaty ports' along the coast. They secured the cession of Hong Kong as a base but, punitive expeditions apart, their desire for further territorial expansion was limited; this was, after all, the age of the 'imperialism of free trade'. The aim was to secure the advantages of economic and political pre-eminence in a foreign territory without the bother and cost of administering it. Events such as the Indian Mutiny of 1857 simply reinforced the view that 'informal empire' was superior to 'formal empire'.

The problem was, however, that involvement in the complex politics of indigenous societies could easily lead to territorial empire. This was to become the story of the later part of the nineteenth century, supposedly the heyday of Empire. But it is important to remember that, in many ways, Britain's greatest imperial acquisitions – both in the late eighteenth and in the late nineteenth centuries – were reflections of weakness rather than strength. At the height of British world power between 1815 and 1855, British ministers tried to avoid territorial entanglements, however brutal their foreign policy. They remained secure in their belief that an aggressive policy of free trade, reinforced with a whiff of grapeshot from the gunboats, was a better way to manage the globe than a proliferation of district collectors, judges and fixed garrisons. The imperial durbars, the *Boy's Own Paper*, the bugles and the tiger shoots were all in the future. But, even as the first statues of Queen Victoria were being chiselled in workshops from Canada to New Zealand, signs of doubt were beginning to set in. As early as 1888 Meredith Townsend wrote: 'For whether for good or evil, a great change is passing over Englishmen. They have become uncertain of themselves, afraid of their old opinions, doubtful of the true teachings of their conscience. They doubt if they have any longer any moral right to rule anyone, themselves almost included.'

Economic decline and the rising spectre of colonial nationalism were to blight the hopes of the early Victorians for an 'earthly paradise' almost as soon as they were voiced.

Alaska
(Transferred from Russia
to U.S.A 1867)

B E A U F O R T
S E A

SEA OTTER TRADE TO CANTON 1790s ON

EASTERN LIMIT OF RUSSIAN AMERICA SET 1825

MACKENZIE

RIVER

Fort Good Hope ■

Fort Norman ■

GREAT BEAR
LAKE

SOUTHERN LIMIT
OF RUSSIAN CLAIMS

54° 40' N

NORTHERN LIMIT
OF USA CLAIMS

ALASKA PANHANDLE
(DISPUTED TO 1903)

Fort Simpson ■

Fort
Liard ■

Fort Providence ■

GREAT SLAVE
LAKE

British
Columbia

Fort
Simpson ■

Fort Smith ■

LAKE ATHABASCA

PEACE RIVER

THE CARIBOO
(NEW CALEDONIA)

BISON ROAD MID 19TH CENTURY

R

Fort Rupert ■

VANCOUVER
ISLAND

Fort
Kamloops ■

SASKATCHEWAN RIVER

CRE

Fort Edmonton ■

PEMMICAN

New
Westminster ●

Rocky
Mountain
House ■

Nanaimo ●

Fort Yale ●

Fort Victoria ●

Fort Langley ●

INTERNATIONAL BOUNDARY
(SETTLED 1846)

BNA
USA

Chesterfield
House ■

Red
Rive

INTERNATIONAL BOUNDARY
(SETTLED 1818)

Colon
(Establish
181

PEMMICAN SUPPLY TRADE

Canada: 1800–1870

- – – – – – – Extent of Rupert's Land
- · · · · · · · International boundaries
- - - - - - - Colonial borders (c.1876)
- ■ Hudson Bay Company trading posts
- ✦ Area of rebellion
- CHIPENYAN Indian nations
- ⚔ Sites of battle
- BNA British North America
- → Trade routes

INUIT

INUIT

NEWFOUNDLAND
St John's

orway
House
LAKE WINNIPEG

R p e r t ' s L a n d

(to Canada 1870)

ST PIERRE & MIQUELON (Fr.)

COAL (19TH CENTURY)

CAPE BRETON ISLAND

Fort
Garry

LAKE OF
THE WOODS

Charlottetown

NEW
BRUNSWICK

Fredericton

NOVA SCOTIA

Halifax

Abitibi House

Quebec
City

Fort William

L
o
w
e
r

C
a
n
a
d
a

BNA
USA

Saint
John

Montreal

Sherbrooke

Grand Trunk Railway

Upper
Canada

Ottawa

1812 (BRITISH CONTROL MAINE COASTLINE)

Portland

1812 York
(Renamed
Toronto, 1834)

Kingston

ATTACK ROUTE OF US TROOPS 1812

ED RIVER REBELLION 1869-70

Goderich

AREA CEDED
BY BRITAIN 1783

Guelph

Sarnia

1812

Sandwich

Grand

Niagara

1812 (US NAVY BURNS YORK)

1812
(US INVASION REPELLED)

BRITISH BURN WASHINGTON

CHAPTER ELEVEN

CANADA: BUILDING A NATION

◇

After the American War of Independence Canada was bisected, in an attempt to accommodate the different traditions of the British and French colonies. The Constitutional Act of 1791 divided the region along the line of the Ottawa River into two parts: Upper and Lower Canada.

Upper Canada, to the west of the Ottawa River, became the preserve mainly of British and Empire descendants: an exotic mixture of pro-British Iroquois, black ex-slaves, and merchants and farmers from the old American colonies. British influence in the region was consolidated by huge 'Clergy Reserves' of land held by the Anglican Church and by the lands claimed by the Hudson Bay Company. The government was dominated by a quasi-aristocratic network of anglophile Tories, described as the 'Family Compact'. In contrast with the feudal, or seigneurial, system of land tenure in Lower Canada, land in Upper Canada was designated as freehold.

Lower Canada, to the east of the Ottawa River, contained the old heartland of New France: Quebec and the St Lawrence River up to Montreal. Here, the population was overwhelmingly of French descent. The power of the Catholic Church was entrenched and the feudal privileges of the seigneurial class remained unchallenged. The merchant classes, however, became increasingly British as the Scots filled an important economic and political niche in Montreal.

The Growth of the Canadian Economy

At the beginning of the century, the economy of both Upper and Lower Canada relied primarily on staple goods; of these, furs accounted for two-thirds of the export value of goods leaving Quebec. However, as quick-ripening Red Fife wheat was developed in the 1840s, the agricultural potential of Upper Canada became steadily more important, making the region the breadbasket for British North America. The British Corn Laws – a system of tariffs passed between 1815 and 1846 – protected the production of wheat and other goods from foreign competition. They also encouraged the milling of grain and its transshipment to Britain and to other British colonies. The growing prosperity of Upper Canada was reflected in her growing population, which rose from 15,000 in 1825 to 950,000 in 1851.

In the Atlantic colonies, especially Newfoundland, the fisheries retained something of their former international character, although British sovereignty was never challenged. The salt-cod trade remained dominant, although the timber industry here and along the Ottawa River in Upper Canada was to become central to the region's economy in the years to come. New Brunswick in particular benefited from the fact that, during the Napoleonic Wars in Europe, Britain could no longer obtain supplies of timber from Scandinavia. The St John, Restigouche and Miramichi river valleys were famed for the mast timbers they provided for the British navy and merchant marine. Shipbuilding soon became a logical extension of the timber trade in this new world of 'wood, wind and water'. And by 1828 coal mining, under the General Mining Association, had been established on Cape Breton Island and in Nova Scotia.

Even the diminutive Prince Edward Island experienced a modest prosperity during the nineteenth century, despite its problems with absentee landlords. The island was a backwater, geographically and developmentally. There were no carriages on the island before 1820, because the roads were so bad, and only one Methodist chapel, a barracks and a courthouse. These modest amenities serviced a population of 10,000, most of whom supported themselves by fairly primitive farming methods.

Most of the problems experienced by the Maritime colonies, and by Prince Edward Island in particular, stemmed from difficult access to the North American interior. Unlike Quebec and Montreal, which dominated trade along the St Lawrence, these colonies were unable to rival New York and Boston. As the rest of Canada launched itself into a period of agricultural and industrial expansion, the Maritimes were left behind.

However, in 1850, work was begun on Canada's first railway system – the immensely ambitious Canadian Pacific Railway. The Grand Trunk system quickly became the longest in the world. Gradual settlement of the western prairies followed in the wake of the railways and this led inevitably to an encroachment on the Indian way of life. Tribes who, three centuries before, had never seen a European and had roamed over a whole continent, were allotted one square mile per family of five on the Indian Reservations; it was even proposed that each chief be given a medal by Her Majesty's Government for the privilege of acceding to the arrangement. Another casualty of the railways was the buffalo. Despite edicts that tried to preserve the animal from indiscriminate slaughter, the buffalo was hunted into oblivion by the end of the nineteenth century.

The railways rapidly accelerated the process of urbanization in Canada. Montreal outstripped Quebec in size and grew steadily through the successes of the North-West Company and through the handling of freight on the St Lawrence. The town of York (originally named after the 'Grand Old Duke of York and his Ten Thousand Men', who had fought the invading American armies) had been torched by retreating American soldiers straggling back to the border: in 1813 it was renamed Toronto, as a gesture of defiance towards the old British ruling class. By 1870 there were almost 70,000 inhabitants in the city, which had become the capital of Upper Canada. In 1855 a river and canal village midway between the two cities, called 'Bytown', was renamed Ottawa and was designated the administrative capital of Canada.

Relations with America

The first threat to Canada's new Constitution of 1791 came from her southern neighbours. The American War of Independence had left a legacy of tensions, which were fuelled by conflicting maritime interests in the Atlantic. In addition, many Americans believed that Canada was there for the taking – 'a mere matter of marching' as Thomas Jefferson put it. A simple desire for more territory was dressed up in the rhetoric of a great and free nation

CZAR OF ALL THE CANADAS

Lord Durham (1792–1840).

'Radical Jack' – John George Lambton, the First Earl of Durham – left a controversial legacy after his term of office as High Commissioner and Governor of Canada. His qualifications for the post rested on two missions to St. Petersburg during the 1830s, where he had been fêted by the Tsar. Once he was on his way to sort out the aftermath of the 1837 rebellions, he was dubbed 'the Czar of all the Canadas' by *The Times*.

His arrival in Quebec did nothing to dispel the impression created by this journalistic taunt, for he disembarked from his ship in full dress uniform riding a white horse. His enormous personal cargo of silver plate and racehorses followed. Durham was undeniably grand, even for an aristocrat and certainly for a 'Radical'. Not surprisingly, he lasted only five months in Canada. Early on, he blundered into exiling a handful of rebels to the West Indies, an action which was clearly beyond his jurisdiction, and he was forced to resign. On his return to England, he completed his 'Report on the Affairs of British North America' which was sharply critical of some key Canadian political institutions and concluded that there were 'two nations warring in the bosom of a single state'. Ironically, this foolish and vain individual has traditionally been regarded as the midwife of responsible government in Canada and a key figure in the evolution of an imperial Commonwealth.

---

extending the arm of liberty to an oppressed neighbour.

When General Hull led his American army across the river from Detroit into Canada in 1812, he distributed a broadsheet which explained the magnanimity of his actions: 'If the barbarous and savage policy of Great Britain be pursued, and the savages are let loose to murder our citizens, and butcher our women and children, this will be a war of extermination. . . . The United States offers you peace, liberty and security. Your chance lies between these and war, slavery and destruction . . .' French Canadians in Lower Canada remained unimpressed by General Hull's overtures, however, knowing that America's political suppression of French Catholics in Louisiana compared unfavourably with their own situation. Although General Hull's army vastly outnumbered its opponents, it ran into several difficulties. Tecumsah, the Shawnee war chief, led his Indian troops against the Americans and prevented them from attacking Montreal. Instead, General Hull attacked Upper Canada and the Great Lakes became the scene of naval battles. The towns of Newark and York on Lake Ontario were torched by retreating American forces in 1813. Meanwhile, British regulars, Canadian militias and Amerindian guerillas overran American frontier posts and took their revenge on Buffalo which lay just over the border in America.

In 1818 the British and American governments finally came to an agreement over the boundary between their territories. This was to be the 49th parallel of latitude which runs from Lake Superior to the Rockies; in 1846 this line was extended west as far as the Pacific Ocean.

Internal Divisions

The other major threat to imperial government came from within. In Lower Canada the elected Assembly, which had been established in 1791, became dominated by French Canadians. Led by Louis Joseph Papineau, it attempted to resist the power of the imperially appointed Executive Council of Upper Canada in exactly the same way as the American colonies had done – by withholding taxes. Papineau demanded an independent government in Lower Canada but still within the Empire, similar to that of Upper Canada. Sporadic local uprisings did break out in 1837, but these were easily suppressed.

At the same time, unrest was also brewing in Upper Canada over the excessive power wielded by the old Tory élite. Demands for reform were discouraged by being identified with French nationalism or with seditious American liberalism. What the radicals demanded, led by William Lyon Mackenzie, was an American-type constitution. Mackenzie published his famous

The American buffalo, depicted here in a seventeenth-century engraving, was virtually extinct two centuries later.

Bitter rivalry over the fur trade was an important cause of the Anglo-American War of 1812. The Battle of Lake Erie (left) was one of the war's late skirmishes.

Draft Constitution based heavily on its American counterpart. However, the rebellions of 1837 that followed in Upper Canada were put down with the same ease as those in Lower Canada, and both Papineau and Mackenzie fled to America.

Radical Jack

In an attempt to defuse the situation, Lord Russell, or 'Radical Jack' as he was known, was appointed Governor in 1838. Although Durham was in the province for only five months, his impact was tremendous. With the help of his advisers, among them Thomas Turton, who was author of the English Reform Bill of 1832, he wrote one of the most important documents in Canadian constitutional history, the Durham Report. This recommended the establishment of 'Responsible Government' and a partial political autonomy. The government of Canada was to be in the hands of an Executive, or cabinet (composed of members of the Assembly), who had to defer to the judgement of the Assembly. Questions of imperial significance, however, were to remain the prerogative of Westminster. As to the conflict between the French and British Canadians, he wrote: 'I found two Nations warring in the bosom of a single state: I found a struggle, not of principles, but of races . . .' He therefore recommended that the two Canadas be made into a British whole, assimilating the French Canadians. Their inferiority in numbers, he felt, would eventually oblige them to accept: 'the hopelessness of success would gradually subdue the existing animosities . . .'

In 1840, the Act of Union gave Canada West and Canada East equal numbers of seats in a single legislature. The widespread depression of the 1840s followed almost immediately. Montreal was no longer able to consider herself the gateway to the continent as the heart of the continent was mainly American and the Erie Canal siphoned off trade to New York rather than via Montreal. Once the rival North-West and Hudson Bay trading companies had been united in 1821, furs were shipped out through Hudson Bay rather than up the St Lawrence. To make matters worse, the Corn Laws were replaced by the introduction of free trade, ending the protected market for Canada's grain. It was hardly surprising that Montreal merchants began to see the only solution for Canada's economic problems as lying in annexation with the United States. In this

they were supported by a new reformist party, called 'the Grits', who demanded a Canadian-elected Governor and Parliament. Although they were at first dismissed as 'office seeking, bunkum-talking cormorants', it soon became clear that a new legislative procedure was desperately needed to revitalize the Canadian economy. Trade was moribund and the great railway system almost bankrupt, overtaken by cheaper American freight rates and the more rapid American pioneering drive to the West.

In addition to these economic difficulties, the population of Canada West (Ontario) had outgrown that of Canada East (Quebec) within a decade of the Act of Union, although the constitutional deal of 1840 denied the English Canadians the extra political voice to which they now felt entitled. The French Canadians, on the other hand, had won the right of equal status for the French language and had resisted constitutional attempts to submerge their national identity.

By 1867 a definite watershed in Canadian history had been reached. The British North America Act re-divided the Canadas and united them into a larger unit consisting of provinces. The Dominion of Canada was born.

Although they were initially indifferent towards the proposed Confederation, the Maritime colonies were drawn into the negotiations. Fenian supporters of independence for Ireland invaded New Brunswick from America in 1866 and helped to persuade the recalcitrant Maritimers to throw in their lot with the Confederation. London supported the Confederation proposals from an early stage and, by 1867, Nova Scotia and New Brunswick had agreed to colonial union with Canada. Prince Edward Island drifted in six years later.

Manitoba and the North-West Frontier

The Western provinces were to join the Confederation by quite a different route. At the turn of the century, the Scottish merchants in Montreal had established the North-West Company which was to rival the Hudson Bay Company in exploiting the fur resources of Canada – particularly in the regions beyond the Great Lakes towards the Rockies and the Pacific Ocean. Canada's greatest explorers set out on behalf of the North-West Company to open up the continent for trade. Alexander Mackenzie was the first white man to make the vast journey west across the mountains to the sea, although he and his party

The Governor of Red River on Hudson Bay, being conveyed round his domain by canoe in 1824.

almost perished among the jagged inlets of British Columbia. In 1804 Simon Fraser opened up the new Pacific territory by establishing posts among the Carrier Indians. He also explored the Fraser River as it twisted through the gorges and waterfalls of the Rockies: 'I have been for a long period in the Rocky Mountains, but have never seen anything like this country. It is so wild that I cannot find words to describe our situation at times. We had to pass where no human beings should venture . . .' The North-West Territories, or Rupert's Land to the west of Hudson Bay, slowly became settled by an extraordinary hotchpotch of colonists, French-Indian 'half-breed' traders and Indian refugee groups whose options were becoming increasingly limited. The first permanent white colony on the prairies arrived in 1812. The Scottish philanthropist Lord Selkirk, a major shareholder in the Hudson Bay Company, became concerned for the fate of his tenants as the Highlands of Scotland were cleared of crofters. He obtained from the Company a grant of over 100,000 square miles along the Red River, in what is now mainly Manitoba, in order to establish a Scottish settlement there. The siting of this new settlement provoked the most violent hostility from the Company's trade rivals, the North-West Company. Their army of French-Indian traders, the Métis, relied on the Red River area for their supply of pemmican (a mixture of pounded buffalo meat and grease which was the staple diet of both the Indian and fur trader), but this was now to be appropriated by the settlers. In 1816 a group of Métis, trading for the North-West Company, massacred the infant colony, and it was not until the two trading companies were amalgamated in 1821 that the way was reopened for a resettlement programme.

The second wave of crofters settled by the indefatigable Selkirk struggled against the extreme climate, floods and locusts, as well as the hostility of their neighbours. The Métis still resented the settling of land that they were accustomed to hunt and rightly feared the arrival of these industrious Scots as the beginning of the end. Gradually, the settlement grew, and it was soon able to provide the Hudson Bay Company posts with supplies. John McClean, an employee of the Company, described the prairie way of life for the different settlers: 'The half-breeds (Métis) are strongly attached to the roving life of the hunter, the greater part of them depend entirely on the chase for a living, and even the few who attend to farming take a trip to the plains, to feast on buffalo humps and marrow fat. The English half-breeds . . . generally prefer the more certain pursuit of husbandry to the chase and follow close on the heels of the Scotch in the path of industry and moral rectitude.'

This pattern of life was not to last. In 1869 the Hudson Bay Company made arrangements to sell Rupert's Land to the government of the new Canadian Dominion in the east. To the outrage of the Red River settlers, land surveyors flocked to the area from Ontario. The Métis, the Canadian-born English and Scottish communities were drawn together under the leadership of a Métis lawyer, Louis Riel, in a 'Manitoban Government' which demanded the right to self-determination. Riel wrote defiantly in his government's newspaper, the *New Nation*, 'We may be a small community, a half-breed community at that – but we are men, free and spirited men, and we will not allow even the dominion of Canada to trample on our rights. . . .'

A considerable section of Scottish Protestants resisted Riel's leadership and staged an uprising; their leader, Thomas Scott, was captured and executed by Riel. This outrage galvanized opinion in Ontario and Riel's rebellion, which otherwise might well have succeeded, was suppressed by military intervention. Riel fled to the United States and Dominion control over the territory was enforced. Although Manitoba entered the Confederation as an equal partner in 1870, the unsatisfactory outcome for the Métis was to lead to continuing unrest. Riel was eventually captured at another Métis uprising, the North-West Rebellion, and, although strong doubts were cast on his sanity by this time, he was executed in 1875 for Thomas Scott's murder.

British Columbia and the Pacific Coast

It soon became apparent that the Hudson Bay Company's fur-trading interests hamstrung its commitment to settling the region for Britain. In 1849 Vancouver Island reverted to the Crown, although company officials retained effective authority. Next, the discovery of gold along the Fraser River profoundly altered the economy of the region. The hordes of hopeful prospectors who rushed there in 1858 caused the Hudson Bay Company's exclusive trading rights in the region to be revoked; British Columbia became a separate mainland colony. Gold bars on the Fraser were soon played out, but in 1861 and 1862 new strikes were made about 200 miles upriver.

Settling British Columbia and Vancouver Island proved especially difficult. Land access was arduous, expensive and dangerous. There were only two practical routes upcountry, and shipping and merchant companies, touting for custom among the prospectors, made fun of the route their rivals used: 'Take a SPLENDID steamer at New Westminster for Harrison River. Then hire ELEGANT INDIAN CANOES to pole you over the rapids, or walk along the pebble shore. WADE FOUR SLOUGHS and SWIM one small river . . . reach Pemberton; beds 50 cents. Crawlers gratis. (Smallpox blankets carefully washed) . . . swim your horse across (if the ice permits) to Parsonville, then run him up Pavillian Mountain to help circulation.'

American expansionism led Whitehall officials to believe that Britain would eventually lose the area. Subsidized settlement was, therefore, ruled out. One colonial official noted in 1867: 'The fewer Englishmen that are committed to the place, the better it may prove in no distant times.' Nevertheless, settlers arrived from Britain in sufficient numbers to secure sovereignty over the region.

Although many did not make their fortune in the gold fields, the coal seams on Vancouver Island attracted more emigrants from the British Isles, to the extent that the British Navy was relocated to Vancouver Island from Valparaiso in Chile to protect the island's coal resources.

In 1866 the mainland colony was united to Vancouver Island under the name of British Columbia, which was not a cheering prospect for the wealthier mainland community. When the Proclamation of Union was read, the British Columbian newspaper flippantly compared it to a death warrant: 'Not a cheer was given, not a hat was raised; no smile of satisfaction lit up the public countenance, no congratulations offered either to bride or bridegroom as the last words of the Sherrif-parson were heard. . . .'

In 1871 British Columbia exacted the promise of a transcontinental railway as the price for its membership in the Canadian Confederation. In 1865 the Pacific Slope was finally linked by iron by the magnificent engineering feat of the Canadian Pacific Railway to the eastern provinces. The consequences of that enormous railway project would reverberate through every region of Canada in the century to come.

CHAPTER TWELVE

THE END OF THE SLAVE TRADE

The clergymen of Barbados were thunderstruck when the Quaker George Fox posed them a fundamental moral question in 1671: 'Are you not Teachers of Blacks and Tawnies [Indians] as well as of Whites? For is not the Gospel to be preached to all Creatures? and *are they not Men?*' For over a century to come, it was left mainly to the Quaker Society of Friends and to a handful of non-conformists to act as the conscience of the nation. The appalling realities of the slave trade were not generally appreciated in the first half of the eighteenth century. When *Rule Britannia*, written in 1740, declared that 'Britons never shall be slaves', a good many of the Britons applauding the sentiment associated slavery with other nations.

Slavery in England and Empire

Legal precedents, set by the mid-eighteenth century, established that it would be illegal to make an Englishman a slave. The problem was that around fifteen thousand slaves already lived in England, having arrived as part of the households that planters brought back with them from the West Indies. Nabobs who had made their fortunes in India also often brought slaves to England. A fashionable present to a lady in the eighteenth century would be a little black boy, to be petted and idolized. While slavery in England had little in common with being flogged to work in the sugar fields, its mere existence provided the first opportunities to attack the whole system.

In 1772 a test case presented itself. James Somersett was a slave who had been brought to England by his owner and beaten so severely that he was left for dead. He recovered, and was recognized and reclaimed at a chance meeting with his owner, who immediately asserted his right to take the slave back to the West Indies. Lord Chief Justice Mansfield, who was to hear the case, foresaw the uproar that would follow if the law was strictly upheld, and hoped that a compromise might avoid the necessity of setting free all imported slaves in England. When the moment of judgement finally came, however, he was unable to break with legal tradition and declared: 'The state of slavery . . . is so odious that nothing can be sufficient to support it but positive law. Whatever inconvenience may follow, I cannot say that this case is allowed or approved by the law of England and therefore the black must be discharged.'

This decision was a great step forward for the opponents of slavery, but it did not affect the British colonies which already had laws regulating the status of slaves. Although little could be done during the American War of Independence, some of the American colonies saw a contradiction in fighting for freedom whilst maintaining a tradition of slavery. The Quaker state of Pennsylvania and Puritan Massachusetts took the lead in abolishing slavery in 1780, and were joined in this resolution by all of the north-eastern states by the end of the century. The southern colonies depended entirely on slave labour to work the vast plantations and did not follow the north's example. The Mason–Dixon line between Pennsylvania and Maryland divided the two sides, a fracture in the new nation

The Society for the Abolition of the Slave Trade battled for a less barbarous policy towards the rights of primitive peoples.

that would lead to civil war. For runaway slaves who were neither shot nor hunted down by dogs, this line represented the vital frontier in their flight to freedom.

The Emerging Public Voice

While the spirit of Revolution swept through North America during the 1780s, public opinion in Britain was moving from a vague and ill-formed distaste for slavery towards a clearer perception of how this system was at work in the Empire. Slavery had, of course, many supporters, who bluntly upheld the commercial logic of the trade in the face of all other humanitarian arguments.

The fight against slavery was one of the first campaigns undertaken by a pressure group. The tactics were varied and colourful: handbills, pamphlets, poems and cartoons were thrust upon the public in their thousands. A Wedgwood plate was issued, showing a slave in chains surrounded by the slogan 'Am I not a man and a brother?' Two hundred thousand copies were sold. A more practical approach was attempted in 1787 by the founding of the tiny colony of Sierra Leone, backed by private funds. It was intended as a place of refuge for newly-freed slaves and was inspired by what turned out to be the largely mistaken belief that African slaves would wish to return home.

It was clear, however, that the main lever of change would have to come from Parliament, and that this would prove a long haul, since so many vested interests were under threat. The concept of property dominated the slavery debate, as a backbencher argued: 'The property of the West Indies is at stake; and though men be generous with their own property, they should not be so with the property of others.' To object that the black slave was a human being rather than a possession was countered by assertions of his inferiority from both sides. In his treatise, *Of*

National Characters, David Hume mused, 'I am apt to suspect the Negroes to be naturally inferior to the Whites . . . In Jamaica, indeed, they talk of one Negro (Francis Williams) as a man of parts and learning; but it is likely he is admired for slender accomplishments, like a parrot who speaks a few words plainly.' At the same time, the abolitionists were forced to stress the popular image of the simple-minded negro in order to reinforce the moral argument that Christian humanity and protection should be extended for precisely that reason.

The Early Campaigns of William Wilberforce

In 1787 the Society for the Abolition of the Slave Trade was established; its first target was the slave ships. Since ships could be converted to other uses, no one could claim that proprietary rights were being infringed. The fever-ridden West African coast and unhygienic conditions on the slave ships killed off sailors almost as fast as it did the slaves themselves.

The only grim justification for risking these perils was that the ships were considered the 'nursery for British seamen'; indeed, one renowned seaman, Lord Nelson, was among the most vigorous opponents of William Wilberforce, the champion of the abolitionists. Wilberforce was an ideal advocate for his cause. He came from Hull, which had already established itself as an anti-slavery port; he was charming, earnest, passionately eloquent and a close friend of William Pitt (Prime Minister, 1784–1806). He was also a man of impeccable character who could hardly be accused of undermining society with flighty schemes.

The first triumph of Wilberforce's campaign was Dolben's Act, passed in 1788 to regulate the number of slaves a ship could carry. The Act quickly demonstrated how senselessly cruel the treatment of slaves on board had been, since the death rate fell from over ten per cent to three per cent. The anti-slavery campaign was gathering such momentum that in 1790 the House of Commons held hearings into conditions in the slave trade in general. In the following year, Wilberforce moved for total abolition. This was too direct a threat for the planters, however, who raised £10,000 to fight this and any further bills. The opposition of the 'sugar kings' was still so powerful that, despite the support of the Prime Minister and the leader of the

Le baiser de Judas, ou la bonne foi Anglaise.

A French cartoon of 1814 attacks British hypocrisy over slavery, which continued in British colonies long after its official abolition by France.

opposition, Charles James Fox, the motion was defeated. In 1792 and 1793, a 'gradual' Abolition Bill and a bill to stop the trade in slaves to foreign colonies were passed by the House of Commons, but were defeated in the House of Lords.

Revolution in France

Progress would have been swifter had it not been for the perverse effects of the French Revolution. The doctrines of 'Liberty' and 'Equality' were bound to ricochet around the French slave colonies in the West Indies, causing the planters' lobby to associate the cause of the abolitionists with the worst Jacobin excesses. Hoping for slave allies in the Caribbean wars against Britain, the National Assembly freed all slaves in the French Empire in 1794.

When Napoleon continued these colonial wars against Britain, he decided that the idea of liberty had gone far enough. General Leclerc was dispatched with secret orders to return the slaves 'to their original condition, from which it was disastrous to draw them'. Napoleon cut his losses and ceded Jamaica to the

SLAVERY AND THE CHRISTIAN DUTY

Throughout the eighteenth century in the West Indies, there was established opposition to the Christianisation of slaves because, it was uneasily acknowledged, baptism was tantamount to emancipation. It was feared that Christian teaching would breed egalitarian notions among the slaves, making them more difficult to control. The Anglican clergy in Jamaica often tried to ignore the heathens in their midst, with some clergymen even emerging as chief propagandists of the planters. Other Anglican missionaries emphasized biblical references to submission and obedience when preaching to slaves. Nevertheless, the planter assemblies repeatedly tried to restrict or prohibit missionary teachings, which were condemned as 'instruments of Fanatics and Enthusiasts in Great Britain for the purpose of effecting political mischief'.

An eighteenth-century grave of a black slave in a Bristol churchyard.

Their exasperation was directed mainly at the vigorous teaching of Wesleyans, Quakers and the German Moravian Church who condemned slavery as un-Christian, but who were forced to tread a careful line in order to be allowed to remain in the West Indies at all. The black Baptist mission in Jamaica proved too much to tolerate and it was closed in 1807. When emancipation came in 1834, it was to the missions that the slaves flocked for the good news. A Spanish observer described the delight of one missionary as he called out to the slaves: ' "What month of the Year is it? . . . What day of the month is it? . . . What is done today?" – and the children shouted "Negroes all made free!" At this moment several of the little children involuntarily burst out laughing and throwing their bodies about in every attitude of expressive joy.'

A watercolour of William Wilberforce (1759–1833), the father of the parliamentary campaign against slavery.

British. The runaway slaves (known as the maroons) immediately rose in revolt, provoked – it was alleged – by French agents. The British were unable to rout the maroons completely from their forest strongholds high in the mountains of central Jamaica, although rebel leaders were rounded up and sent to the freezing shores of Nova Scotia. Those who survived the first four winters there were finally dispatched to Sierra Leone.

Pitt's acquisitions in the wars against France were regarded by the planters, however, as being of dubious merit. They realized that the revival of the sugar economy on these islands would require a massive and politically suicidal influx of slaves. The anti-slavery feeling was such that George Canning was able to declare solemnly in the House of Commons: 'If there was a question of suddenly cultivating such an island as Trinidad,

we must make up our minds to the destruction of about a million of the human species.'

The New Economics of Abolition

By the early nineteenth century, newly captured sugar markets, especially that of Dutch Guiana which produced thousands of tons of Demerara sugar, were creating a glut which caused prices to slump. The vast sugar plantations in the British West Indies could no longer afford to support the wastefully high turnover of slaves, and the argument that freed slaves lived longer and worked harder was beginning to gain support. What planter resistance remained was divided over the question of the new competing colonies, and was no longer forceful enough to check the progress of the abolition movement. Anti-slavery was now also politically expedient, with even those who had supported slavery now accepting that if British planters were no longer allowed to buy slaves, the whole trade should be abolished in order to put their competitors at an equal disadvantage. Planters in the West Indies were beginning to sell out, and a long-term gloom slowly descended.

In 1806 the slave trade with foreign islands, including those captured in the war, was stopped. In 1807 the entire trade was declared illegal for British merchants: most European states had little vested interest in continuing slavery and had no desire to offend Britain. It was therefore not too difficult for a newly zealous Britain to persuade these states to give up their evil ways. France, too, was now in no position to refuse the humanitarian proposals. Spain and Portugal, however, had been Britain's allies during the last eight years of war. Like Britain they still had slave-based colonial economies. The best compromise that the British government could achieve was to make cash payments in return for undertakings that Spain and Portugal would trade only along selected routes with their own colonies.

In order to police the 1815 settlement with Spain and Portugal, and to make sure that everyone else was toeing the line, the British government created a 'Slave Squadron'. Its purpose was to seize ships with slaves on board, a policy which backfired several times when captains threw their slave cargo overboard on sighting the Squadron. Only after years of diplomacy was it also agreed that ships equipped with the tools of

GOVERNOR EYRE AND THE 1865 REBELLION

Edward John Eyre was appointed Lieutenant-Governor of Jamaica in 1862. In 1865 arguments developed between various factions in the parish of St Thomas-in-the-East over land. George Gordon was a dissenter who held the post of Churchwarden in this Anglican parish and was the leader of one faction. When one of the opposing factions began evicting squatters from the local estates, Gordon took up their cause. Tempers frayed and a group of aggrieved citizens gathered outside the local Court House while it was in session on 7 October 1865; their meeting turned into a riot. Two days later, six policemen were sent to arrest one of the ringleaders, Paul Bogle, and twenty-eight others. They were confronted by an armed mob and had to retreat. On 11 October another mob congregated outside the Court House and this

Sir John Eyre's handling of the 1865 rebellion was attacked in the British illustrated weeklies.

time the local militia were called out. When they fired into the crowd another riot ensued. The Court House was set alight and eighteen of those inside died, including the Vestos, or head of the parish, a friend of Eyre's. The Governor immediately sent in the army. Bogle was hunted down and hanged. Eyre then had Gordon arrested, even though he had been nowhere near the fracas. Gordon was hauled before a court martial, sentenced on what now appears to have been very dubious evidence and hanged. Meanwhile, the army were very active – 354 men were hanged by sentence of court martial, while another 85 were killed on the run. That all those who suffered were black did not escape notice. When the news reached Britain, a storm of protest arose and a Commission of Inquiry was despatched. Eyre was suspended and then dismissed.

slavery – shackles, chains and cramped decks – could be confiscated if they were sailing outside legal routes. Even so, the Squadron had a difficult task. As the slave trade became increasingly illegal, traders were ready to defend themselves by force of arms. The traders resorted to clippers of a lightness and speed that could outsail the Royal Navy frigates. The Slave Squadron never managed to do more than keep the trade within limits and raise the cost of illegal shipment so high that slave-owners, especially in the United States, were driven to running their estates without fresh imports. Putting an end to all slave-trading was not proving the easy victory that the nineteenth-century abolitionists had hoped.

The Emancipation of the Slaves

In 1823 the anti-slavery forces re-organized themselves as the Anti-Slavery Society; they addressed the accusations, which had dogged them a generation earlier, that their demands constituted an attack on property rights. Their first proposal was that the children of slaves should be born free men, leaving owners with plenty of time to adjust to a wage-earning labour force. West Indian legislative assemblies, however, paid little attention to Britain. It was only their dependence on British troops as a defence against continuing slave revolts (Barbados in 1816, Demerara in 1823) that kept them within the imperial fold. Spurred on by the shocked reports of Methodist missionaries in the colonies, the British government pressed new reforms on the hostile planters, such as ending the flogging of women and giving slaves a set day or two off every week to cultivate their own land for food. The Jamaican newspaper *The Courant* fulminated helplessly against such meddling: 'Shooting is . . . too honourable a death for men whose conduct has occasioned so much bloodshed, and the loss of so much property. There are fine hanging woods in St James and Trelawney, and we do sincerely hope that the bodies of all the Methodist preachers who may be convicted of sedition, may diversify the scene.'

The 1832 Reform Bill represented a national desire for radical change after years of largely ineffectual hedging over the slavery issue. It was declared that 'the people must emancipate the slaves, for the government never will', and Jamaican slaves, sensing the mood in Britain and despairing of it ever reaching the colonies, rebelled and were again brutally crushed. The planters and estate owners realized that the moment of emanci-pation was at hand, and their resistance was sullen and resigned.

Dozens of executions followed the revolt, but curiously enough it seemed only to strengthen Parliament's resolve that the system had to end. The reformed House of Commons was no longer prepared to impose taxes to subsidize slavery in the West Indies, and in 1833 an act to abolish slavery was passed. The planters were paid £20 million in compensation – an estimated half of their market value – which was designed as much as anything to enable the planters to pay off their heavy debts and mortgages. Freed slaves were required to work as apprentices for their masters for up to six years, but slavery in countries under direct British rule ended absolutely on 1 August 1834.

About 668,000 slaves were set free in the West Indies, just under half of them in Jamaica. The apprenticeship system, which left ex-slaves in the same position as that of the seventeenth-century indentured labourers, was hopelessly muddled and was soon abandoned as being more trouble than it was worth. All the sugar colonies ended apprenticeship before the dates required by the 1833 Act. Nevertheless, the planters were still left with immense control over their ex-slaves.

Colonial workhouses – every bit as grim as their Dickensian counterparts in England – were left in the hands of the planters, who applied the whip and treadmill to the Negro inmates as freely as they had done on the plantations.

Trade and Empire after Emancipation

Despite a fall in production, the colonies survived well enough throughout the 1830s and 1840s. The strict prohibitions of the Navigation Acts had been replaced by preferential tariffs for Empire products, giving West Indian 'free sugar' enough of a margin over Cuban and Brazilian 'slave sugar' for it to hold its own in the British market, although it could not compete in the re-export trade. By the 1840s an era of free trade had arrived and the preferential tariffs were removed. This really sounded the death knell for the West Indian colonies. Contrary to Adam Smith's arguments that free labour would work better than slave labour, it became obvious that Cuban and Brazilian slave-grown sugar was cheaper. Planters and landowners who remained in the West Indies found themselves clamouring for a worldwide ban on slavery as they had never done before.

Brazil greatly increased her imports of slaves during the 1840s, leading to a horrified outcry in Britain. Palmerston overstepped normal diplomatic bounds by ordering the Slave Squadron to ignore all the rules about territorial waters and to attack slave-traders wherever they were found along the Brazilian coast. Since many Brazilians and slave-owners feared that the massive importation of slaves would upset the social balance, Brazil ended the trade with relief. Cuba, on the other hand, was forced to end slavery only after the American Civil War. The United States committed itself whole-heartedly to cooperating with Britain in the eradication of the Atlantic slave trade. By around 1870 it had finally come to an end.

Emancipation had unforeseen effects throughout the Empire. In India, slavery became legally unenforceable after 1843, which meant that any slave wanting to leave his master and enter the wage-earning economy could do so.

The anti-slavery movement was unable to play an effective role in Africa until the 1860s. A Slave Squadron was established in the Indian Ocean to restrict the Arab importation of slaves from the great East African market of Zanzibar, which was ruled by the Sultan of Muscat and Oman. Again, this proved an expensive process which could do little to eliminate the trade until the interior of Africa had been explored and mapped.

These territories inland were first brought to the attention of the British public by the explorations of Dr David Livingstone. From 1856 to 1873 he lived in East Africa, ostensibly converting the natives, but his heart really seemed to lie in exploring the lands around the great lakes. As this work seemed equally valuable to his superiors, he was allowed free reisn to send back topographical reports, as well as descriptions of the Arab slave trade in which peaceful villagers were kidnapped and marched by force to Zanzibar. Victorian England was outraged and the British government persuaded the Sultan to keep the Zanzibar market a purely domestic affair. Towards the end of the nineteenth century, the struggle against slavery was politically inseparable from the dynamic process of imperial expansion. Inevitably, anti-slavery became a convenient lever with which to push back what were comfortably regarded in the drawing rooms of Britain as the frontiers of darkness. Nevertheless, it is true to say that a deep and sincere public detestation of slavery sustained the drive for emancipation – a policy that was often as difficult and costly for the Empire as it was expedient.

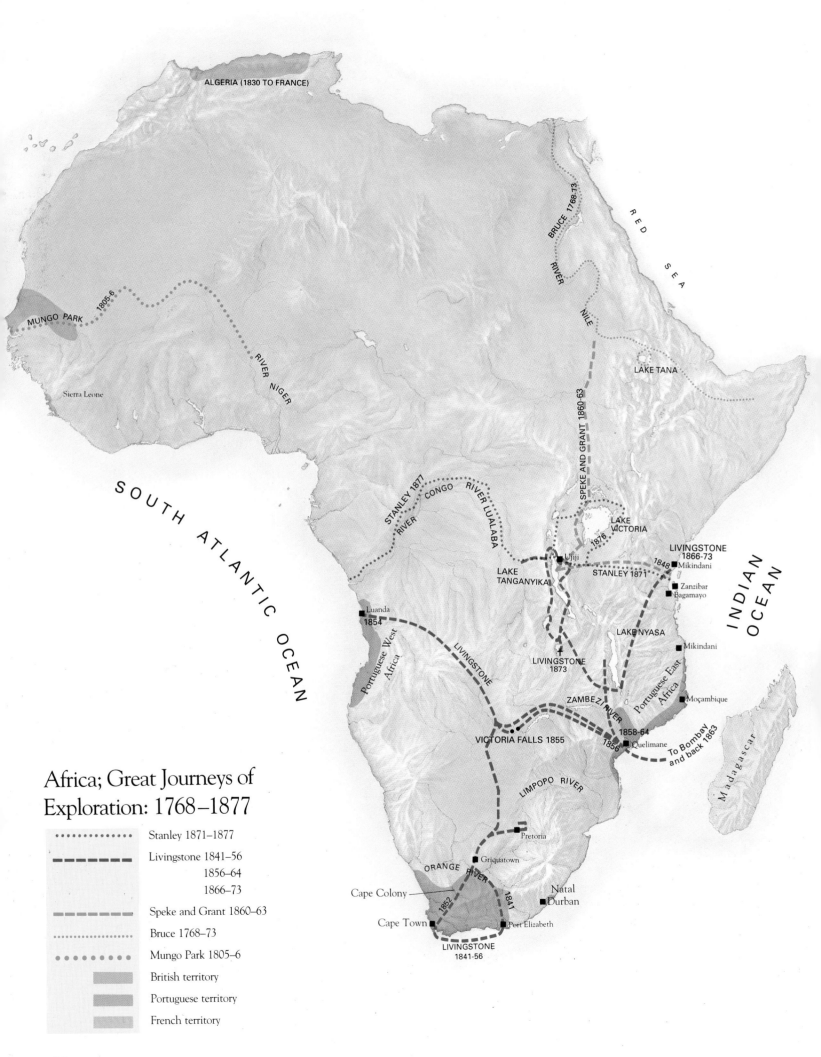

ALGERIA (1830 TO FRANCE)

RED SEA

BRUCE 1768-73

RIVER

NILE

LAKE TANA

1805-6

MUNGO PARK

RIVER NIGER

Sierra Leone

SOUTH ATLANTIC OCEAN

SPEKE AND GRANT 1860-63

STANLEY 1877

CONGO RIVER LUALABA

RIVER

1876

LAKE VICTORIA

Ujiji

LIVINGSTONE 1866-73

Mikindani

STANLEY 1871

LAKE TANGANYIKA

1848

Zanzibar
Bagamayo

INDIAN OCEAN

Luanda
1854

Portuguese West Africa

LIVINGSTONE

LIVINGSTONE 1873

LAKE NYASA

Mikindani

Moçambique

Portuguese East Africa

ZAMBEZI RIVER

VICTORIA FALLS 1855

1858-64

1856

Quelimane

To Bombay and back 1863

Madagascar

LIMPOPO RIVER

Pretoria

Africa; Great Journeys of Exploration: 1768–1877

Griquatown

ORANGE RIVER

Cape Colony

1852

1841

Natal
Durban

Cape Town

Port Elizabeth

LIVINGSTONE 1841-56

∙∙∙∙∙∙∙∙∙∙∙∙∙   Stanley 1871–1877

– – – – – –   Livingstone 1841–56
1856–64
1866–73

– – –   Speke and Grant 1860–63

∙∙∙∙∙∙∙   Bruce 1768–73

●●●●●●   Mungo Park 1805–6

British territory

Portuguese territory

French territory

CHAPTER THIRTEEN

AFRICA: 'THE LAST CONTINENT'

◇

Before the nineteenth century, British interest in Africa had been confined largely to trade. Commerce, however, had been limited to a few coastal areas and had never penetrated far inland. Until Britain abolished the slave trade in 1807, her dealings with Africa were dominated by the appalling traffic in human beings, who were transported in their millions across the Atlantic to supply the West Indian and American plantations. Despite the highly significant role played by the slave trade in the history of Africa and the Americas, neither the Europeans in general nor the British in particular had colonized Africa to lasting effect. The pattern of penetration and settlement that typified European expansion in the west was not evident in Africa until the final decades of the nineteenth century.

The Inhospitable Continent

For centuries, the majority of African states managed to keep the European powers at arm's length, thus controlling the internal trade system themselves. By the seventeenth century, the extensive forest belt of West Africa and the coast were dominated by a number of highly centralized, efficient and militarized states. The largest of these, Asante and Dahomey, controlled millions of people over hundreds of square miles at the height of their power. Their ascendancy was partly due to their ability to pay for firearms out of the proceeds of trade in slaves, gold and dye-woods. The capacity of these formidable states to resist European intervention was greatly reinforced by the disease environment. Ships that visited the Barbary Coast, for example, could lose so many men in a few weeks that they were often burned for lack of a crew. Before medical research caught up with the explorers, malaria and yellow fever killed large numbers of non-immune Europeans.

The handful of British settlements in tropical Africa, like those of other European enterprises in the area, were large trading establishments. The most famous early settlements were those on the James River in the Gambia, in Sierra Leone, at Cape Coast on the Gold Coast and at Accra, which the Royal Africa Company had established in 1676. The profitability and ultimate survival of these settlements depended on the local ruler, who bargained over rent and trading preferences with the white men. But mutual admiration was usually short-lived.

At the same time, the British were also stirring thousands of miles to the south. In the mid-seventeenth century, the Dutch East India Company had established a way-station on the Cape of Good Hope which had grown into a settlement during the eighteenth century. French occupation of Holland in 1795 provided the British with an excuse to invade, and the settlement was finally ceded to the British in 1806. British interest in the Cape was firmly rooted in the needs of her merchant fleet and in the protection of the sea routes to her eastern colonies.

Anti-Slavery and the Early Explorers

By the last quarter of the eighteenth century, the anti-slavery cause was increasingly supported by the public. The abolitionists tried to show, on the one hand, how their policies would not threaten the British economy, but also how 'legitimate' or non-slave commerce in Africa would prove even more lucrative than the slave trade itself. At this stage, the proposition was largely a matter of guess-work and pious optimism. It was an awareness of the depth of national ignorance on the matter that led to the creation of the African Association in 1788. This privately funded club – whose members included bankers and Cabinet ministers, as well as William Wilberforce – existed to promote African exploration. In 1830 the club was renamed and reformed as the Royal Geographical Society.

Some Britons had already explored beyond the African coast, most notably the Scot, James Bruce. He travelled in Ethiopia and, in 1770, declared himself to be the first European to look upon the source of the Blue Nile, although Portuguese explorers had identified the same spot hundreds of years before. Bruce collected fossils and manuscripts during his travels and sketched plants and animals wherever he went. Although he was applauded on his return by the learned academies of Florence and Paris, he was dubbed 'the Abyssinian traveller' by London society. Ridiculed at home, he died irascible, full of grudges and a little deranged.

Twenty-five years later, the African Association funded their most famous explorer, a young Scottish surgeon, named Mungo Park. On an outstandingly successful first trip, Park resolved a question which had been exciting European scientific curiosity for some time, by recording the course of the River Niger in his journal: 'The great object of my mission, the long sought-for majestic Niger, glittering in the morning sun, as broad as the Thames at Westminster, and flowing slowly to the eastward.' Mungo Park died in mysterious circumstances on a subsequent trip to Africa, and it was left to a series of expeditions mounted by Denham, Clapperton and, finally, the Lander brothers to establish that the mighty Niger joined the Atlantic through the intricate delta of the Oil Rivers in what is now modern Nigeria.

Missionary zeal and the gathering momentum of the anti-slavery campaign both drove the British endeavour in Africa forward. Between 1792 and 1813 the Baptist, the London, the

A contemporary engraving from the Illustrated London News *shows the departure of the ex-governor from Freetown, Sierra Leone in 1854.*

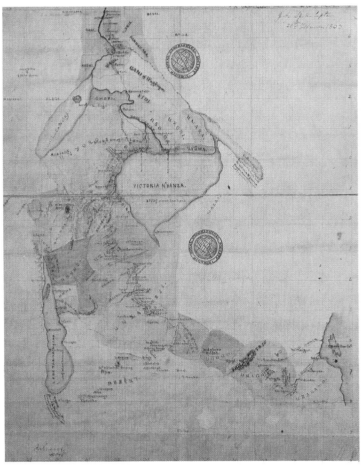

James Grant accompanied Speke in 1860 in his search for the source of the Nile; his 1863 map shows its origin in Lake Victoria.

Scottish, the Church and the Wesleyan Missionary Societies were founded, along with the British and Foreign Bible Society, amid a flurry of fund-raising. These efforts were combined with commercial speculation in a manner that was entirely logical at the time. It was argued that legitimate commerce, if well-rooted in the community, would soon elbow aside the local slave trade. This argument was posed strongly by a society devoted to 'the civilization of Africa', which was founded at Exeter Hall in 1839. Flesh was added to the argument by expeditions up the Niger, which tried to establish trading stations where both the Gospels and cheap, mass-produced Manchester goods could be made available to the Africans of the interior. The various missionary societies financed many expeditions to Africa, of which it would be difficult to say whether missionary zeal or the sheer delight of exploration was the stronger motivating force.

Livingstone in Africa

The London Missionary Society financed the remarkable Dr David Livingstone on a rather loosely defined assignment to, as Livingstone put it, 'go forward to the dark interior'. Livingstone had begun his career in 1841 at the mission station of Robert Moffat, whose daughter he was to marry. Between 1853 and 1856 he undertook a series of impressive expeditions for the Society in which he made an east-west-east crossing of Africa from the middle Zambezi to Luanda on the Atlantic coast and then back to the Indian Ocean coast at Quilimane. In the course of this expedition, he visited, and gave a European name to the magnificent Victoria Falls. He also encountered terrible evidence of the thriving Indian Ocean slave trade. Appalled by the human misery and depopulation, he dedicated himself to the extirpation of the trade. Livingstone embodied the perfect mixture of nineteenth-century British motives in Africa before the age of partition. By 1857, already a considerable celebrity, he told a packed audience in Cambridge: 'I go back to Africa to make an open path for commerce and Christianity.' He was appointed British Consul at Quilimane and, after having resigned from the London Missionary Society, he was granted £5,000 to establish a Universities Mission to Central Africa there. In the following year he led a somewhat disastrous expedition up the Zambezi, using a cumbersome steam-launch which became hopelessly baulked by the numerous falls and rapids on the river. The expedition did manage to move northwards into what is now modern Malawi where Livingstone encountered Lake Nyasa (Malawi) for the first time; when funds ran out in 1863, the expedition returned home.

It was the Royal Geographical Society which next encouraged Livingstone to return to African exploration, not least to resolve a disagreement among explorers as to the head-waters of the Nile. John Speke and Samuel Baker claimed that they had fixed the source to the great Lake Victoria, while their unlikeable but resourceful rival, Sir Richard Burton, maintained that another tributary stream ran beyond Lake Tanganyika further south. The latter argument appealed to Livingstone, although his explorations were later to disprove it. There followed seven years of lonely travel through eastern and central Africa. Livingstone was relatively old by then, his health impaired by illness and his rough life as an explorer. In his travels he found himself alternately protected and blocked by those coastal slave-traders whose activities he had at first deplored. Although Stanley tracked Livingstone down in the celebrated meeting of October 1871, the old explorer had no real wish to return home and continued his journeys in eastern Africa. He died there two years later, apparently at prayer, at the age of sixty.

Livingstone died on the eve of the great European partition of Africa, known today as the 'scramble for Africa'. His life's work had, unconsciously for the most part, contributed to that peculiarly paternal and nationalistic moral environment that fostered the process of colonialism. By 1857 he had become a legend in Britain, enjoying the kind of fame that today is reserved for rock stars or royalty. He regarded his mission as one of bringing light into the darkness. The very phrase, 'the dark continent', redolent as it is of 'un-Christian' ignorance, came to be widely used of Africa by his fellow Victorians. This darkness was perceived melodramatically in the popular imagination. Africa was a largely pagan continent whose major contact with a world religion was with Islam, the faith of the villains of the piece, the coastal slave-traders. Everything non-Christian was misunderstood as cruel and superstitious. There were few doubts that the British brand of Christianity should be diffused to the grateful millions. Nevertheless, Livingstone was not merely a missionary. He was also very much a child of the Industrial Revolution; he was, after all, *Doctor* Livingstone. His missionary training, which had centred on medical studies, gave him an absolute conviction that modern science and medicine should be deployed in exposing Africa both to the Christian God and the second Victorian divinity of scientific reason, and to the material benefits that went with it.

Sierra Leone: A Model Colony?

While Livingstone was exploring the African interior, a most remarkable example of collaborative enterprise was flourishing on the west coast. Sierra Leone had been settled in 1787 by a

David Livingstone (1813–73), reading the Bible. Livingstone was one of the first European missionaries to penetrate the 'dark interior' of Africa. In 1858 he used the paddle-steamer (left) to negotiate the treacherous Zambezi.

group of abolitionists led by the great Thomas Clarkson, who sought to create a free, Christian settlement for the 'black poor' of London and the other port towns of Britain. Some of these people had been loyalist slaves and ex-slaves who had served Britain in her unsuccessful defence of the thirteen American colonies after 1776 and had then added to black communities in Britain which came to be regarded as a 'problem'. Other settlers included some of the fourteen thousand slaves who had been brought to Britain as part of the plantation owners' households. Sierra Leone was intended as a showpiece for the commercial viability of free labour in Africa: 'Civilization, Christianity and the cultivation of the soil', as the sponsors put it. By contrast, it was argued, the evils and unprofitability of slavery would be so apparent that its abolition would follow rapidly. However, the first settlers discovered that Sierra Leone was a precarious refuge rather than a promised land. The financial insecurity of what was initially a private enterprise led to the settlement being taken over by the British Colonial Office in 1808. The population grew rapidly and, by 1864, a Creole from Sierra Leone, Samuel Crowther, had been consecrated as the first bishop of the Niger.

Britain's ban on the slave trade in 1807 had been a unilateral one. Although many policy-makers were driven by idealistic motives, there were commercial reasons for hastening the demise of slavery. So long as other powers were able to import cheap slave labour, the sugar and cotton that their colonies produced would remain highly competitive and would even undercut British prices. Pragmatism and idealism led to the use of about one-sixth of the Royal Navy's high seas fleet as a 'preventive squadron'. This force was designed to intercept suspected slave ships but its powers were limited until all the major countries participating in the trade (except the United States) ceded Rights of Search to the British Navy in the 1830s. The whole anti-slavery enterprise had its own momentum. More and more consuls and political agents became actively involved in the African continent. Their intelligence-gathering revealed not only the local particularities of slave dealing but also much detailed economic information which was used to benefit the growing commercial interest. The presence of the Royal Navy lent a measure of security to these fledgling businesses which were, of course, subject to local laws and customs. As slave trading became systematically outlawed from one African state

BIG GAME HUNTING

In the eighteenth and nineteenth centuries, hunting became increasingly identified as the pastime of Europe's leisured classes. They developed a taste for the large, ferocious quarry to be found and confronted in the wilder parts of the Empire. Africa had already become the scene of the large-scale killing of elephants for their ivory, particularly after fire-arms tilted the balance heavily in favour of the hunters. Further technological developments produced rapid-loading rifles that were effective at very long distances, thereby reducing even further any risk to the hunter. Towards the end of the nineteenth century, the heads of impala and springbok came to hang alongside more

An illustration from Wild Sports of Africa.

traditional trophies in the game rooms of the European rich. Herman Freyburg, recording his elephant-hunting adventures, embodied all

the patronizing swagger of the typical hunter around the turn of the century: 'I speeded up the pace of our march, for the prospect of hunting these monsters fascinated me. Besides, my hunting license would not last for ever . . . I told the bearers how much water they would be permitted to drink daily, for we were obliged to ration our supply – a practice quite unknown to the native and something which is impossible to teach them. The white man has to do the thinking for them . . .'

Butchery abroad disturbed the balance between the animals and the local human population, and pushed many species towards extinction.

after another, Britain set up a series of treaties with European and African rulers.

In the process, the Crown took over a network of small West African trading forts and factories previously run by the Company of Merchants Trading into Africa. The colony of Sierra Leone, which had boasted a Crown-appointed Governor since 1808, now became the base of British control over a scattering of trading stations from the Gambia River to Accra. It was also the headquarters of the Preventive Squadron's West African operations. The Vice-Admiralty Court was set up there in 1819 as an international tribunal, deciding on the fate of intercepted slave ships, their crews and human cargoes.

The colonization of Africa developed an international dimension, as the American Society sent liberated blacks to what is now Liberia and as the French expanded their coastal settlements in Senegal. The Governor of Sierra Leone was forced to define the area of British control in terms of French expansion and, later, in the light of the Monrovia settlement, which was to be recognized as the free Republic of Liberia in 1847. These developments drew the Governor reluctantly into further negotiations with inland African powers. Back in London, the Colonial Office was resolutely opposed to territorial expansion on the grounds of expense and was therefore continually dismayed by the unremitting logic of these expanding political relationships.

The Asante Wars

Many of the European trading settlements had been built on the territories of the Fante kingdoms on the southern Gold Coast, and treaty relationships with these rulers proved particularly problematic. To the north, the interior was dominated by the powerful and extensive Asante empire. The Asante empire was civilized, rich and ruthless and recognized the importance of expanding Atlantic trade. Their incursions prompted the British to counter with the first of several military expeditions in 1824. The British were defeated and the Governor, Sir Charles M'Carthy, killed. When this was followed by a punitive raid in 1826, the Colonial Office decided that enough was enough and resolved to withdraw from the Gold Coast. However, a desperate campaign, mounted by the trading interest together with Britain's local African allies who depended upon the Atlantic trade, persuaded the Colonial Office to resist a full evacuation of the coast.

Much against the wishes of the Colonial Office, the new senior local official, George Maclean, pursued an aggressive policy against the Asante and established a British sphere of influence over much of the coast. In 1850, three years after Maclean's death, the British formalized this control by the purchase of Denmark's last coastal establishment at Christiansborg. Britain's hold on the coast was strengthened in 1872 by a bizarre exchange deal with the Dutch, who ceded their last two coastal enclaves in return for Sumatra. The Asante, however, had enjoyed good trade relations with the Dutch and also claimed the ceded Dutch fort of Elmina for themselves. They raided Elmina and Cape Coast Castle but were repelled by the British. After a solid half-century of caution and opposition to expansion in West Africa, the Colonial Office adopted a strong forward policy. In 1874 a brigade of British infantry under Sir Garnet Wolseley, backed up by a far larger force of African allies and West Indian troops, invaded Asante. One of the invading officers, Hope Grant, expressed the sense of divine mission that still inspired the soldiers of the Queen: 'I cannot help thinking

Sir Garnet Wolseley's (1833–1913) 1874 attack on the Asante, one of the first major British assaults on West Africa.

that it is willed by the all-powerful Ruler above that Africa shall be opened, and that these savage and inhuman tribes be brought to reason, and their horrible iniquities put an end to.'

The defeat of Asante can be seen as the first British move towards partition in tropical Africa. This move into the interior involved the use of physical force which, excepting the French in their bloody conquest of western Sudan, was less frequently deployed in Africa than annexation by treaty diplomacy (which rarely used the big stick it waved). When force was used, as in the 1874 campaign and in the later conquest of northern Nigeria in 1905–6, British troops were in a tiny minority. The use of the armies of local African allies, reinforced by troops recruited in other parts of the Empire, was to be the common pattern in the campaigns that followed.

There were complex reasons for this. Britain's trading interests were slight: by mid-century, annual exports to West Africa were valued at under £500,000. However, the growing industrialization in England and the changing pattern of domestic consumption led to a great demand for vegetable oils (for machine lubricants) and palm oils (for soap). These needs increasingly dictated British policy in Africa. In 1861 Britain acquired Lagos as part of a Foreign Office initiative to harass illegal slave-trading in the area. Although there was strong official opposition to further annexations in the region, it is interesting that palm-oil exports that year topped £1 million. Trade and abolition were, despite the misgivings of the Colonial Office, inseparable.

The Imperial Destiny

By the latter half of the century, the early-nineteenth-century concept of 'mission' had broadened into a wider notion of national destiny – to teach, to preach, to heal and to guide the less fortunate. In 1850 Lord John Russell told the Commons: 'It appears to me that if we give up this high and holy work . . . we have no right to expect a continuance of those blessings, which, by God's favour, we have so long enjoyed.'

The logical conclusion to this thinking was that such intertwined, complex and paternalistic ambitions as the Victorians had for Africa could be achieved only under the umbrella of European political control. The termination of the slave trade, the development of early legitimate trade, the explorers' endeavours and the missionary involvement all served to create spheres of influence in which the British, as well as other governments, became entangled. On the eve of the 'scramble for Africa', a cluster of jealous European 'informal empires' had established themselves in the Dark Continent. The scene was set for the partition of Africa.

CHAPTER FOURTEEN

INDIA: MILITARY CONQUEST
TO MUTINY

◇

By the Treaty of Allahabad in 1765, Bengal was effectively brought under the power of the English East India Company (EIC), which now took all the revenues of India's richest province, paying only a small amount of tribute to the Mughal Emperor in Delhi and a subsistence allowance to the Nawab of Bengal. However, the conquest of Bengal and the subjugation of the rest of the subcontinent in the years that followed was not the result of a consistent drive for power. The anomalous nature of a situation in which a company of merchants was seen to be ruling a vast empire, larger and more populous than the British Isles, was quickly recognized. Hardly had the Company secured this empire than its top officials began to wish it away. Robert James, Secretary of the EIC, told the House of Commons in 1767: 'We don't want conquest and power; it is commercial interest only we look for.' James was not alone in expressing this view. The great Robert Clive, who had done more than most to win Bengal for the East India Company in the 1750s, argued a decade later that expansion was against 'those principles of moderation which are so consistent with the true interest of a trading company'. The problem was that moderation proved hard to define, especially at a time when the political and military balance was so disturbed. Bengal gave the British both a territorial interest and also the means to expand it. Warren Hastings, Governor General of the Company from 1772 to 1785, warned that 'the resources of this country [Bengal] in the hands of a military people . . . are capable of raising them to the dominion of all India.' His words were prophetic.

The Age of the Nabobs

The EIC's takeover bid for Bengal had been prompted by the demands of expanding trade. It succeeded because the Company had a well-trained mercenary army supporting a core of Euroean professional soldiers. Through this army it was able to sell protection to those threatened by the fiscal exactions of the rulers of Bengal, Siraj-ud-Daulah and his successors. Outside Bengal, the Company extended its influence by means of the 'subsidiary alliance' system it had pioneered in Madras. Under this arrangement, Indian rulers were given British military 'protection' in return for payment in cash or land. In practice, the Indian rulers drawn into this system could never raise enough revenue to pay the subsidies. Their courts therefore became a magnet for European adventurers and Company servants with money to lend.

Informal expansion began in the Carnatic. The Nawab of Arcot had been brought under British military protection here in the 1750s, in order to free him from his nominal overlord, the Nizam of Hyderabad. Hyderabad, in turn, continued to labour under the alliance that had been thrust upon it in 1759 to counter French intrigue. In 1765 the Nawab of Awadh (Oudh), whose territories lay along the Ganges plain next to Bengal, accepted garrisons of Company troops in return for an annual tribute. A decade later the Raja of Benares, whose lands bordered the EIC's territory, was allowed to transfer his allegiance from Awadh to the Company on payment of 4.5 million rupees (£450,000) a year.

In 1765 Robert Clive began his second spell as governor of the company and returned to Bengal, the scene of an earlier triumph; in 1757 he had defeated the Nawab of Bengal at the Battle of Plassey.

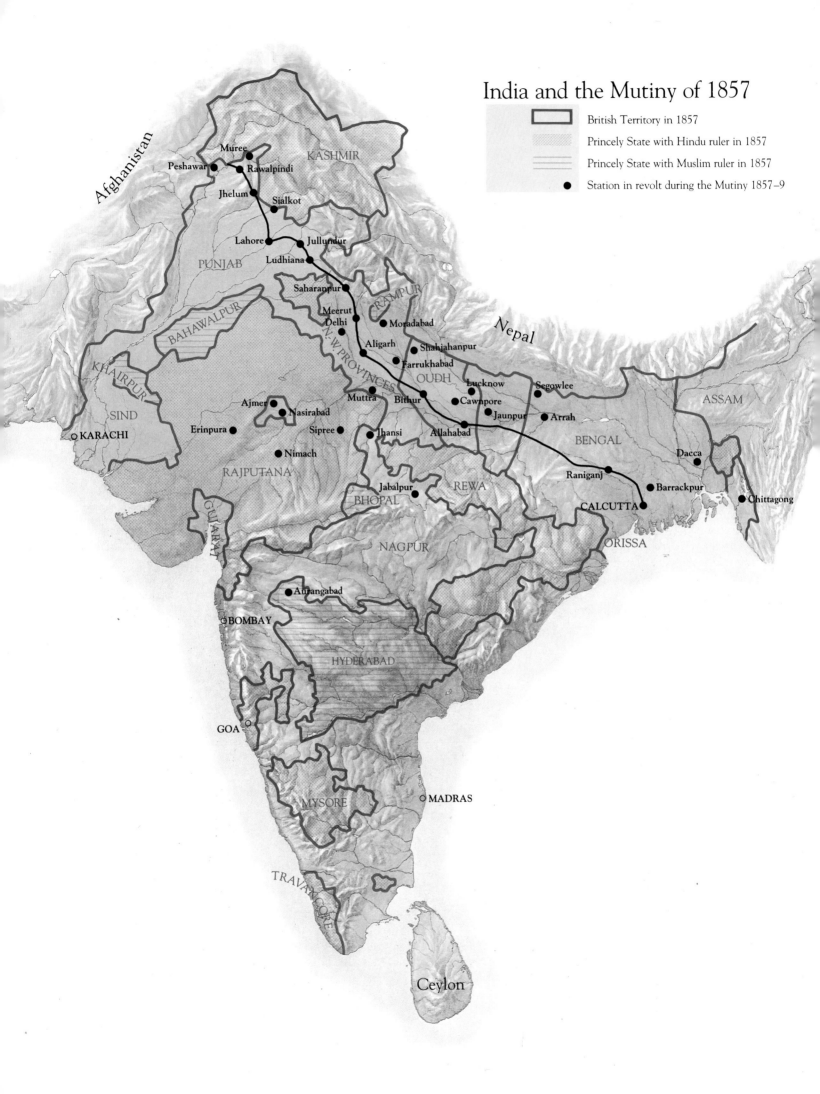

India and the Mutiny of 1857

British Territory in 1857
Princely State with Hindu ruler in 1857
Princely State with Muslim ruler in 1857
● Station in revolt during the Mutiny 1857–9

Afghanistan

Muree
Peshawar ● ● Rawalpindi
Jhelum
Sialkot
KASHMIR

Lahore ● ● Jullundur
Ludhiana
PUNJAB

BAHAWALPUR
Saharanpur

KHAIRPUR
Meerut
Delhi
Moradabad
RAMPUR

SIND
Aligarh
Shahjahanpur
Farrukhabad
N.W PROVINCES
OUDH
Lucknow
Segowlee

Nepal

KARACHI
Ajmer ●
Nasirabad
Muttra
Bithur
Cawnpore
Jaunpur
Arrah
ASSAM

Erinpura ●
Sipree ●
Jhansi
Allahabad
BENGAL

Nimach ●
RAJPUTANA
Dacca

REWA
Raniganj
Barrackpur

GUJARAT
Jabalpur
BHOPAL
CALCUTTA
Chittagong

NAGPUR
ORISSA

Aurangabad ●

BOMBAY

HYDERABAD

GOA

MYSORE
MADRAS

TRAVANCORE

Ceylon

92

A TALE OF TWO CITIES: CALCUTTA AND LUCKNOW

Calcutta was the great city of British India during the first half of the nineteenth century. It was the centre of government, commerce and intellectual life for the subcontinent. Its architecture was self-consciously imperial, especially Government House, commissioned in 1804. The Bengali landowners, merchants and professionals who lived in Calcutta were not always subservient to the Raj, however. In 1826 they petitioned Parliament at the 'political degradation' being inflicted on 'the better classes of the natives of India'.

Lucknow, the capital of Awadh, was also a proudly imperial city, but one more dominated by the Indians themselves. Successive Nawabs, beginning with Asaf-ud-Daulah in the late eighteenth century, set out to combine the best of Western and Eastern architecture in a fantastic *Nawabi* style based on elaborate stucco work and classical decoration. To the British, Lucknow seemed to epitomize the degenerate and sybaritic East, sunk in self-indulgence and torpor; the last King of Awadh, who was deposed for maladministration in 1856, was said to want to become 'the best drum-beater, dancer, and poet of the day'.

In 1857 Lucknow acquired a new significance in British eyes. The long siege of the Residency by rebel sepoys became an important part of the self-image of the Raj. The bullet-marked building was left untouched thereafter, with an inscription bearing the words of Lord Canning: 'There does not stand recorded in the annals of war an achievement more truly heroic than the defence of the Residency of Lucknow'.

These subsidiary alliances corroded the effectiveness and independence of the Indian rulers. They were already weak – hence their need for military protection in the first place – but contact with the Company sapped their strength still further. In Arcot a powerful group of Company servants lent money to the Nawab (raising some of the capital from Indian moneylenders), and reached deep into the economic system of the countryside by financing local magnates and petty chieftains too. In Awadh British officers grabbed trading monopolies and – helped by privileges which included exemption from internal dues – led a commercial penetration into the cloth trade. This diminished the state's revenue and undermined the Nawab's power. In Benares in 1781 the demand for tribute proved too high at a time of warfare and poor harvest; when it was not paid, the Raja was arrested. After a brief revolt, he was deposed in favour of a subservient successor dominated by a British resident.

The word *nabob*, a term used to describe those who returned to Britain having made fortunes in India in the early years of Company rule, became a synonym for conspicuous wealth and dubious morality. Corruption was rife among commercial adventurers, Company servants and military – especially in states such as Arcot and Awadh which were bound up in subsidiary alliances with the Company. According to Warren Hastings, the activities during the 1770s of British soldiers and civilians in Awadh had made its capital, Lucknow, 'the school for rapacity. What will you say of beardless boys rejecting with indignity gratuities of three thousand and five thousand rupees? What will you think of clerks in office clamouring for princi-palities, threatening those who hesitated to gratify their wants with the vengeance of a patronage . . . and what of a city with as many independent and absolute sovereignties as there are Englishmen in it?' The career of Hastings himself – the 'king of the nabobs' – was blighted by similar accusations of corruption when he was impeached before Parliament in 1788.

British outrage at the behaviour of the nabobs reflected, in part, a genuine concern about whether Company rule in Bengal could be controlled from England. Such concern became particularly acute at times when expenditure was high in India, because maladministration and military expansion could eat up all the revenues that Bengal supplied.

When the Company took over the *diwani* of Bengal, it was able to use the tax revenue received to purchase goods for export to England, without needing to export bullion to India. In London it was thought that these revenues were limitless, that they would become, in the words of the Earl of Chatham, 'the *redemption* of a nation . . . a kind of gift from heaven'. Yet it soon became clear that there would be costs to Empire as well. As early as 1772, a financial crisis in India prevented the EIC from paying a dividend, requiring it to ask the Government for assistance. This forced the British Government to face up to the

The bodies of Indian rebels, left unburied by the British, litter the coutyard of Sikandra Bagh in Lucknow.

great riddle of the Raj: whether India was Britain's foremost asset or her foremost liability. The answer seemed to depend on increased supervision from London. This culminated in Pitt's India Act of 1784 which set up a ministerial Board of Control to oversee the Company's administration of its Indian empire.

The First Colonial Civil Service

The first Governor General appointed under this new system was Lord Cornwallis. He came to Bengal in 1786 determined to stabilize the Company's administration. He dismissed corrupt officials, limited private trade and laid the foundations of a system of civil administration (based on the famous 'collectors') that became the backbone of British rule in India for the next century. Indians were now almost completely excluded from administration, as Cornwallis claimed that 'every native of Hindustan, I verily believe, is corrupt.'

It was in land administration that Cornwallis made his most important innovation: the 'Permanent Settlement'. This was intended to solve the problems of agricultural production and of raising land revenues. It gave landlord rights to local magnates (called *zamindars*); fixed a cash revenue for them to pay in perpetuity; and threatened them with forced sale for bankruptcy if they defaulted. In practice, the Permanent Settlement probably increased instability among the Bengal landed society, as many zamindars could not at first work the new system properly. Between 1794 and 1807 the lands on which the government depended for forty-one per cent of its revenue changed hands.

Within twenty years or so, however, a fairly stable landed interest had been established and the 'rule of property' was created in Bengal.

The Rise to Dominion
In the 1780s and early 1790s the Company had fought inconclusive military campaigns against the Marathas and against the newly expansionist state of Mysore in south-western India. In 1795 Richard Wellesley, Lord Mornington, became the new Governor General. Together with his brother Arthur (later Duke of Wellington), he made the Company an aggressive territorial power once more.

Some collision between the major successor states of the old Mughal empire was inevitable. Internal conflicts among the great Maratha chiefs made much of central and western India unstable, while the rapid expansion of Mysore under Haidar Ali and Tipu Sultan threatened the Carnatic, Hyderabad and the spice-producing kingdoms of the Malabar coast. Meanwhile, in Europe, the outbreak of war led to concern about French subversion or invasion. Between 1799 and 1803 Wellesley and the Company armies set out to subdue enemies and friends alike. They were spurred on by the conviction that 'no greater blessing can be conferred on the native inhabitants of India than the extension of the British authority, influence and power.' Among the military successes of these years was the defeat of Tipu Sultan in 1799, and the humiliation of the Maratha chiefs in the Treaty of Bassein in 1802, which brought the Peshwa into an alliance with the Company. During the same period, Hyderabad was reduced to a client state, while the subsidiary states of Tanjore and Arcot were totally absorbed into British India.

These successes were partly due to Arthur Wellesley's military skills: his ability to organize and supply armies, moving rapidly over long distances and equipped with large field guns, brought a new dimension to military strategy. But the Company was also partly responsible for the success because it could concentrate its military resources more easily than its rivals. The size of the army increased by 40,000 between 1789 and 1805, building up its artillery and a strong regular cavalry force in the process and finally swelling to 155,000. The cost of such expansion rose alarmingly: the Company's debt almost doubled in the seven years after 1799. These costs led to Wellesley's downfall, as the Court of Directors in London became increasingly unhappy about a policy that seemed to bring 'little profit except brilliant

gazettes (dispatches)'. War broke out again in 1804; Wellesley's armies suffered defeat at Kotah and Bharatpur; and the British government recalled the Governor General in disgrace the following year.

For the next fifteen years the expansionary dynamic of the EIC spluttered fitfully on, consuming all that it touched. The Company's ability to combine commercial penetration with military dominance proved to be too strong for the native states of central and western India, as it had already proved to be for those of the east and south. The subsidiary alliance system was maintained, in Sir Thomas Munro's words, 'to destroy every government that it seeks to protect; it forced the Marathas into fiscal crises that they could solve only by oppressing their subjects or raiding their neighbours. The aim of Company rule was now to maximize military and fiscal security; it was easy for the Company's headquarters in Calcutta to believe that any substantial Indian autonomy would make this more difficult. The result was that the relationship between the British and the remaining Indian states grew increasingly restless, and this culminated in the Maratha War of 1818 which established British paramountcy over Gujarat, Berar, Maharastra and Rajasthan.

The Decline of the EIC
When the EIC first became a territorial power, it was generally believed that Company profits would increase as the Bengal revenues were reinvested in the purchase of Indian goods for export to London. The reality proved to be rather different, as increased administration costs ate into revenues. In addition, development in the British domestic economy changed fundamentally the economic environment in which the Company operated.

The commercial rationale of the Company had always been the export from India of high-value Indian manufactured goods for sale in Britain and for re-export to Continental Europe. In the 1790s the growth of the British textile industry, and the fragmentation of European trade during the Napoleonic wars, restricted the market for the Company's exports of Indian goods. Raw materials replaced Indian manufactured exports to some extent, but indigo, saltpetre and sugar were not profitable. Even raw cotton could not compete, in the long run, with supplies from the American South.

By the 1800s, the whole pattern of intercontinental trade was changing; industrialization in Britain stimulated bulk shipments

HAILEYBURY AND THE INDIAN CIVIL SERVICE

To improve the administration of the territory under its control, the East India Company established its own training college in 1805. This was moved to Haileybury in 1809. From that time until the 1850s all candidates for the Indian Civil Service had to spend two years there after leaving school, passing examinations in a range of subjects which included Indian classical languages. Most candidates were admitted on the nomination of a member of the Court of Directors. This meant that during its first forty years over a third of the candidates were the sons of men who had served in India. The atmosphere was more evangelical than academic.

The system was changed completely in 1853 with the introduction of competitive entry examinations and the raising of the maximum age for admission to twenty-three so that university graduates could apply. Those admitted were designated as probationers in the Service and their two years' training was a prelude to their departure for India. It was soon realized that graduate entrants could be better trained at their universities and Haileybury was closed in 1858. It was replaced by postgraduate courses in Indian studies at Oxford, Cambridge and London. The historian Thomas Macaulay, who was instrumental in setting up the new system, designed it to present the highest 'intellectual test'. This system remained virtually unchanged until the 1920s.

Until the 1850s the East India College at Haileybury was the forcing ground for young Englishmen serving in India.

An Indian painting of around 1830, showing an Englishman on a tiger hunt.

of raw materials and cheap manufactures at the expense of luxury goods. The EIC, with its high overheads and shipping charges, found it hard to adapt to these changes. Its profits dwindled away and, in 1813, it lost its monopoly of trade between Britain and India. Only the China trade remained a profitable enterprise, and cotton and opium were shipped from India to Canton to trade for tea for the London market. The Company held on to this monopoly until 1833, when it too was abolished.

The Age of Reform

The East India Company had ruled over most of the subcontinent for the last forty years of its existence. During this time, the Indian empire had never seemed entirely secure, external threats prompting conflicts in Burma, Afghanistan and the Punjab in the 1820s, 1830s and 1840s. The Government had also always been short of money: economic development, which might have increased revenue, proved elusive. The Company's officials had thought that peace would bring economic progress of its own accord, but the way in which peace had been achieved had destroyed many internal trade networks.

To overcome these problems, the British submitted India to the best blueprint of civilized society that they possessed: the modernizing ideas of the British Utilitarian philosophers and liberal reformers. Governors General, such as Lord Bentinck (1828–35), aimed to set India on a new path to national greatness. As well as seeking to remove social abuses, such as slavery, female infanticide and widow-burning (*suttee*), the reformers wanted to transfer to a Western-style legal system and to an education system that would promote 'English literature and science'. Military expenditure was to be curbed; and agrarian development was to be encouraged by eliminating 'parasitic' landlords and vesting land-ownership in the hands of the peasants.

Indian society proved largely resistant to Utilitarian social engineering. Many of the detailed plans were based on faulty analysis or skimpy information. Social and intellectual reforms in fact occurred only when the Indians were predisposed to accept them; the largest social movements were religious and owed nothing to British influence. Ironically, British 'reforms' actually helped to create the 'traditional' India of which the reformers had despaired. By classifying and ranking different social groups in legal codes and ethnographic surveys, an official picture of a rigidly hierarchical social order emerged.

The Great Rebellion

The heroic age of Company rule was briefly revived betwen 1848 and 1856 by Governor General Lord Dalhousie. Under his administration, the Punjab and Lower Burma were annexed. Native states within India were challenged too and Jhansi, Satara, Nagpur and Awadh were absorbed, while Berar was transferred from Hyderabad to the Company to repay financial obligations. In addition, Dalhousie stopped the subsidy to Nana Sahib, the adopted son of the last Maratha Peshwa; he refused to accept an heir to the ageing Mughal emperor, Bahadur Shah, unless the imperial title was renounced.

These actions, on top of the political and economic uncertainties of the previous forty years, caused a feeling of unrest to develop nationally, especially among the landed magnates of northern India.

In May 1857 three Indian cavalry regiments mutinied at Meerut, killing not only their British officers but also their families. They then marched to Delhi to 'restore' Bahadur Shah to his former glory. This triggered a succession of military mutinies and civil revolts, leading to a generalized rebellion known as the 'Indian Mutiny'. As far as the army was concerned, the mutiny was inspired by grievances over pay and conditions of service. There was also great resentment at the introduction of new cartridges which were greased with animal fat, and needed to have their ends bitten off before use, thus breaking the dietary taboos of the soldiers.

The British were driven out of Delhi and the Mughal emperor became the titular head of the rebellion, while the deposed Rani of Jhansi and Nana Sahib were among its active leaders. Support came, especially in Awadh, from landlords and magnates who felt that their status and power had been threatened by direct British rule. Many Indians did not revolt, however. The Punjab continued to be loyal; Bengal, Bombay and Madras remained aloof; and there were some magnates in northern India who saw their future as rosier with the new régime rather than with the old. The rebellion never spread very widely; indeed, it failed to establish a secure base for itself, even in the Mughal heartland around Delhi.

Reaction in Britain to the slaughter of officers' wives and children was hysterical, and a ferocious revenge was taken on mutineers and ordinary Indians. General Neill's instructions to his troops during the relief of Cawnpore ran: 'The villages of Mubgoon and neighbourhood to be attacked and destroyed; slaughter all the men; take no prisoners . . .'. Eyewitnesses, following in the wake of Neill's troops, found that 'human beings there were none to be seen, save . . . the occasional taint in the air from suspended bodies upon which the loathsome pig of the country was already feasting . . .'.

Delhi was recaptured in September 1857 after a siege and bitter street fighting. Resistance was strongest in central India, especially in Awadh, where the British troops found themselves fighting village by village against peasant communities who had, in the past, supplied the Company's armies with many of its best soldiers.

The last casualty of the rebellion was the Company itself, accused in London of having fomented a rebellion it could not contain. In November 1858 Parliament passed the Act for the Better Government of India, establishing a Secretary of State for India in London to direct the administration on behalf of the British crown. 'John Company', the embodiment of British power in Asia for the previous 250 years, now gave way to the 'Great White Queen'.

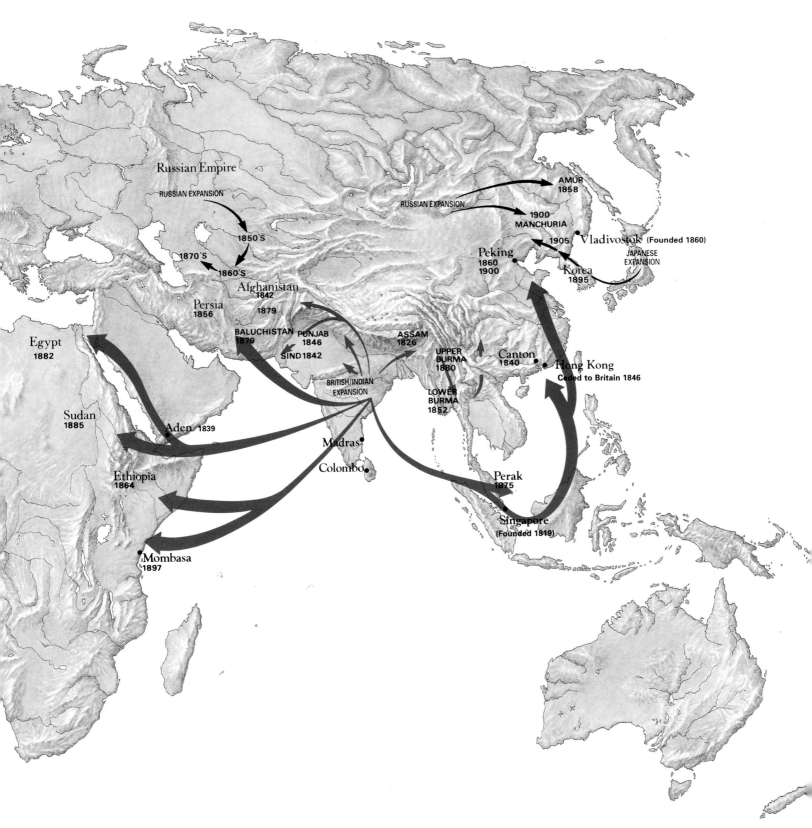

Russian Empire

RUSSIAN EXPANSION

1850'S

1870'S

1860'S

RUSSIAN EXPANSION

AMUR
1858

1900
MANCHURIA

1905

Vladivostok (Founded 1860)

JAPANESE
EXPANSION

Peking
1860
1900

Korea
1895

Afghanistan
1842

1879

Persia
1856

BALUCHISTAN
1870

PUNJAB
1846

SIND 1842

ASSAM
1826

UPPER
BURMA
1880

Canton
1840

Hong Kong
Ceded to Britain 1846

Egypt
1882

BRITISH/INDIAN
EXPANSION

LOWER
BURMA
1852

Sudan
1885

Aden 1839

Madras

Colombo

Perak
1875

Ethiopia
1864

Singapore
(Founded 1819)

Mombasa
1897

The Great Game and the Expansion
of British India: 1800–1900

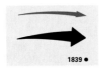

Expansion from British India

Russian and Japanese Expansion

1839 ● Date of Invasion or annexation

96

CHAPTER FIFTEEN

THE ENGLISH BARRACK IN AN ORIENTAL SEA

◇

By 1820 Britain and Russia had become the two formidable powers on the Eurasian land mass. French ambitions had collapsed with the fall of Napoleon, and the Chinese, Ottoman and Persian Empires were failing fast. Other states could not match European firepower or military organization and consequently were of no account. Over the next eighty years the two great powers expanded and consolidated their empires, while diplomats and military planners on each side spent a disproportionate amount of time worrying about the intentions and capabilities of their respective rivals.

'An English Barrack in the Oriental Seas'

India was the key to Britain's imperial position. The maintenance and defence of the Raj was, therefore, the most important single aim of Britain's policy in Asia; given the extent of the subcontinent's contribution to imperial grandeur, that is hardly surprising. In the first place, she represented half the Empire's military might. By 1860 that meant 125,000 Indian and 62,000 British troops and, what is more, local taxes paid for them. Many times during the nineteenth century these troops were used as expeditionary forces to China, Ethiopia, Persia, Malta, Afghanistan, Egypt, the Sudan, and East and Central Africa. As Lord Salisbury pointed out to Parliament in 1867, India was 'an English Barrack in the Oriental seas from which we may draw any number of troops without paying for them'.

Britain's rule in India encouraged further expansion throughout the nineteenth century, and was the base from which her control and influence spread both across the Indian Ocean and China Sea, and deep into inland regions of Central and South-East Asia. Penetration was not only military but also commercial, and Indians played an important role, as soldiers, settlers, labourers, traders and investors. At first sight, this arrangement might sound like a politician's dream come true, but it could turn into a statesman's nightmare. To Lord Salisbury, the 'barrack' was 'bad for England, because it is always bad for us not to have that check upon the temptation to engage in little wars which can only be controlled by the necessity of paying for them'.

Nevertheless, the possession of India – and the availability of the Indian Army – was undoubtedly a stimulus to British expansion in the nineteenth century. It was this temptation that caused the sceptics, such as William Gladstone, to urge caution. But their warnings were usually ignored. Britain, somehow, always needed that little extra piece of territory to secure her Indian base. Much more than regional security was, in fact, at stake. Britain was engaged in a much larger struggle for the mastery of Asia, and the other player in this game was 'the great bear'.

A Nineteenth-Century Cold War

In the mid-1820s experts in London and Calcutta began to worry about the possibility of a Russian invasion of India, prompted by Russia's adventures in the Ottoman Empire and

A contemporary cartoon from Vanity Fair labelled Lord Salisbury, sometime Secretary of State for India, as 'too honest a Tory for his party and his time'.

Persia. This expansionism in Central Asia continued to aggravate Britain's anxieties until the early years of the following century. The result was the 'Great Game' – the Cold War of the nineteenth century – in which the two great powers sought to counter each other's expansion by diplomacy, subversion and whatever informal influence they could muster. Direct hostilities were confined to the Crimean War of the 1850s; the rest of the conflict was indirect and its costs were largely met by third parties. Between 1828 and 1908, Russia and Britain fought, intimidated and sought to control most of the peoples of Central and Western Asia.

Both sides argued that their expansion resulted from problems in the region caused by the turbulent frontiers between states. In the 1820s, Sir John Malcolm, one of India's great soldier–administrators suggested that there was: 'an impelling power within civilization when in contact with barbarism that cannot be resisted'. On the other side, Prince Gorchakov, Russia's Foreign Minister from the 1850s to the 1880s, was a little more practical when he described contact with 'a number of semi-savage tribes, who proved a constant menace to the security and well-being of the empire'. His country had no alternative: the only possible means of maintaining order on the Russian frontier was to bring these tribes into subjection; but as soon as this had been accomplished it was found that the new converts to civilization had in turn become exposed to the attacks of more distant tribes. And so it became necessary to establish fortified posts among the outlying peoples, and by a display of force to bring them into submission.

In reality, the process of expansion was more complex than these explanations suggested. Imperial activity tended to destabilize frontiers, and the men on the spot, often fired by personal ambition, fomented their own convenient crises. Furthermore, distrust between the great powers distorted judgements and encouraged the pre-emptive strike. As Lord Salisbury, when

Secretary of State for India in the 1870s, warned the Viceroy: 'You listen too much to soldiers . . . you should never trust experts: if you believe the doctors, nothing is wholesome: if you believe the theologians, nothing is innocent: if you believe the soldiers, nothing is safe.'

The British Offensive

In the 1820s, Britain's fear of Tsarist expansion dominated her policy towards the buffer states – the Punjab, Sind, Afghanistan and Persia. These states were too weak to withstand an invader themselves and Britain therefore sought to strengthen her position. This meant that Sind was annexed in 1843, the Punjab conquered in 1846–9, and Baluchistan absorbed in the 1870s. By 1887 spheres of influence that were tantamount to an Anglo-Russian partition were carved out in Persia.

There was no great power to rival Britain on the north-eastern frontier, but the expansion of her Indian Empire continued nonetheless. The main threat here came from the Kingdom of Burma which, though no match for Britain, maintained its own aggressive intentions, overrunning, in the years between 1782 and 1819, a number of small states on the Indian border. When informal influence failed to stem Burmese hostility, war replaced diplomacy. In 1826 Britain annexed Assam and other peripheral territories to the north-east of Bengal; in 1852 she took control of Lower Burma; and in 1886 she swallowed the rest of the country.

Afghanistan presented far greater difficulties. The ploy of securing control by imposing a client ruler had twice failed, leading to war in both 1839–42 and 1878–80. In the First Afghan War a large, armed mission was installed to support Calcutta's puppet. In the catastrophic midwinter retreat from Kabul all but one of the 4,500 British and Indian troops lost their lives and a large party of British civilians ended up in Afghan hands. Lady Sale, one of the captives who survived, described the aftermath of the battle: 'The road was covered with awfully mangled bodies . . .. The sight was dreadful; the smell of the blood sickening; and the corpses lay so thick it was impossible to look from them as it required care to guide my horse so as not to tread upon the bodies.'

In 1878 a much smaller party of British officials and soldiers were massacred in a similar way in Kabul, causing the outbreak of the Second Afghan War. A full-scale invasion of the country was launched as a response. By 1880, the Indian Army held Kandahar and Lord Lytton, the Viceroy, had hopes of 'bequeathing to India the supremacy of Central Asia and the revenues of a first-class Power'. But Gladstone's Government in London was less sanguine, arguing that such a 'forward' policy was counter-productive and had already prompted 'the employment of an enormous force and the expenditure of large sums of money [while] all that has yet been accomplished has been the disintegration of the state which it was desired to see strong, friendly and independent'. Rather than proceed, it was decided that Afghanistan should be left as an autonomous buffer state, agreements being reached with Russia and Persia to give her generous borders in the north and west. Finally, in 1893, the negotiation of the Durand Line set a boundary for Indian and Afghan influence over the tribes of the North-West Frontier.

The Russian Advance

Russia had begun to expand into the empty Siberian lands to the east and south of the Urals in the seventeenth century but there were still only one and a half million people there by the beginning of the nineteenth century. Communications with the Pacific coast were maintained by the longest of sea voyages around the Cape of Good Hope. However, by the 1850s interest in the region was growing. Trade had increased, the population had doubled and the anticipated collapse of China suggested new possibilities. In 1854 the Tsar sanctioned the annexation of Amur to curtail the spread of British influence and to prepare the way for further colonization. By 1860, Russia – like the other expansionist powers – had extracted territorial concessions from the Chinese, securing not only access to the Treaty Ports for her

BOX-WALLAHS

By 1900 there was probably more British capital at work in India than in any other part of the Empire. Firms of British expatriate businessmen dominated India's export trade. Most of these firms had their fingers in the domestic pie as well, owning and managing tea plantations, jute mills, coal mines, engineering works and many other sectors of Indian industry.

Many had also cast their nets wider, using the Indian Ocean as their highway between East Africa, South-East Asia and China. In the Indian countryside local sensibilities were cushioned by using Indian businessmen as their agents.

The relationship between expatriate entrepreneurs and the colonial establishment was a complex one. Many colonial administrators affected to despise the box-wallahs and their involvement in trade, just as their contemporary counterparts in Britain might have done. Nevertheless, some successful businessmen acted as advisers to the government, using the contacts they had made

The Lipton tea empire was established in the late nineteenth century by an enterprising Glasgow merchant, Sir Thomas Lipton. He purchased extensive tea, coffee and cocoa plantations in Ceylon in order to supply his shops with cheap products. Portrait of Lord Inchcape (left).

in the process when they wished to lobby on behalf of their own interests. For the energetic, shrewd young man wishing to make his way, India provided a fine opportunity for

advancement, though few were able to travel the distance achieved by Lord Inchcape, who started as a clerk in Scotland and ended his career as the head of an early multinational.

Hobson-Jobson was a glossary of Indian words used colloquially by English speakers, with some suggestions of their derivations and examples of their use. The book was written by Colonel Henry Yule and Arthur Coke Burnell and first published in 1883. The aim of the authors was to trace the way in which such words entered and enriched the English language while frequently acquiring completely new meanings in the process. The book's title is a perfect example of such assimilation. 'Hobson-Jobson' was a term used by the British–Indian Army to describe a religious festival which derived from the cry of *Ya Hasan! Ya Hosian* made by participants. Some words remained close to their original form and purpose. For example: 'bungalow' – a one-storey house with two gable ends built by

A section from the pages of Hobson-Jobson *indicates the origins of the word 'pyjamas'.*

Europeans in Bengal as early as the 1630s; 'loot' – from the Hindi *luut*, first used in English in 1788; and 'dinghy' – first used by the Royal Navy in 1836 but common in travellers' accounts of India in the seventeenth century. Other words became distorted in the transposition: 'juggernaut' was derived from an image of Krishna pulled through the streets of the pilgrimage centre of Puri in the state of Orissa on a gigantic temple cart, under the wheels of which worshippers suffering from painful illnesses frequently cast themselves in a ritual suicide; or 'gymkhana' – a corruption of a Hindi term, *gend-khana*, meaning 'an English racket-court'. To complicate matters further, *Hobson-Jobson* explains such archetypally Indian words as 'caste', 'cobra' and 'curry' which all come from Portuguese.

---

merchants, but also a Pacific port of her own at Vladivostok. In the south, between 1839 and 1864, the Tsar's domain extended slowly over the steppes of Kazakhstan. Forts were built, nomadic tribes subdued and peasant colonists imported to settle the region.

After their defeat in the Crimea in 1856, the Russians began to play the 'Great Game' in earnest. But there were hawks and doves in St Petersburg as well as in London and Calcutta. While Prince Gorchakov, the Foreign Minister, consistently tried to limit the Russian advance, others, such as Prince Baryatinsky, urged a rapid expansion of military control. 'England displays its power with gold,' he argued. 'Russia which is poor in gold has to compete with force of arms.' He concluded that with strategic railways in the Caucasus the Tsar's troops could 'descend like an avalanche on Turkey, Persia and the road to India'.

By the mid-1860s, local commanders had discovered that they could be as aggressive as they liked, provided that they were successful. By the middle of the next decade, the Russians had pacified Turkestan and held most of Central Asia. With the

British annexing Baluchistan in 1876, and the Russians moving on to conquer the Turcomans and to occupy Gok-Tepe in 1881 and Merv in 1884, it seemed that the two empires were set on a collision course. Events were to prove otherwise.

The End of the 'Great Game'
By the mid-1880s the 'Great Game' had effectively been won by the Russians because their influence and control had replaced that of Britain in Central Asia and because they could also overawe the remaining independent states of Turkey, Persia, China and Afghanistan more successfully than their rival. However, St Petersburg's opportunity to exploit this victory was limited and both sides concluded that peaceful co-existence was the way forward. This tacit arrangement resulted in agreements in 1887 on complementary spheres of influence in Persia and on the maintenance of the string of states between them as a buffer zone.

By the beginning of the twentieth century British governments believed themselves to be over-extended and were there-

Afghan forces hide in the Bolan Pass.

The surrender of Dost Mohammad Khan, the Afghan ruler, to Sir William Hay Macnaghten (1793–1841) at the entrance to Kabul. Macnaghten tried unsuccessfully to replace Khan with his pro-British rival, Shuja.

One of the Tibetan wounded, January 1904 (top). To the British, Tibet was a staging post on the trade route to China, but Tibetan resistance in the nineteenth century made the journey a hazardous one. In 1903 a British political mission was dispatched from India in order to overcome Tibet by force, and in the following year a treaty was signed at Lhasa between the two countries. The 13th Dalai Lama (left), one of a line of spiritual and temporal leaders who ruled Tibet, until the Chinese Communists took over in 1959.

fore anxious to play down the possibility of a military threat to India. Thus, when Lord Curzon, Viceroy of India, revived the 'forward' policy by dispatching an armed mission to Tibet in 1904, he was completely disowned by the Government at home. As Lady Curzon pointed out to her husband in a letter, 'the whole Cabinet . . . are frightened to death.' This new policy led both powers towards a broad diplomatic *rapprochement* which resulted in the signing in 1907 of an Anglo-Russian *entente*. Part of the momentum for this new accommodation may well have derived from the disastrous defeat of the Russians by the Japanese in 1905. Now there was a new player on the scene, one that eventually was to prove more than a match for both of the old adversaries. The 'Great Game' was over.

The Indian Diaspora

While India played an important strategic role in the expansion of Britain's Empire, she was also a major centre of economic power. The countries of South Asia had, since medieval times, been part of a regional trade network which stretched from the Persian Gulf to China. However, trade between Europe and Asia was limited until large quantities of silver from the New World became available in the seventeenth and eighteenth centuries. Even though trade with Europe, and especially with Britain, had grown to dominate Indian commercial life by 1800, the old trading relationships still survived and indeed were strengthened by the activities of British imperialism elsewhere.

The most important growth occurred in the trade with China. By 1800 Britain imported large quantities of China tea but lacked any suitable commodity to export in exchange. The production of opium in eastern India made possible a new triangle of trade: tea was exported from China to Britain, cotton goods from Britain to India, and opium from India to China. With encouragement from London, the trade grew rapidly and, by the 1830s, China took more than a third of India's total exports, most of it as opium. The Chinese government tried to

ban the trade but their officials proved too easy to corrupt; the Chinese insisted and the British sent in their gunboats. The trade remained buoyant until the 1860s, when a more conventional demand for Indian cotton and cotton yarn developed.

British businessmen in Liverpool, London, Calcutta and Bombay took the lead in developing India's new regional economic role during the first half of the nineteenth century, but Indian bankers and merchants were not slow to participate. Those in western India were active both in the China trade and in the development of links that extended across the Indian Ocean. Indeed, their success was to cause them problems in South Africa; Gujarati businessmen there were resented and became the focus of racial discrimination. The Chettiar bankers and merchants of South India, however, were the most successful. Concentrating on South-East Asia, they invested heavily in Ceylon, Burma and Malaya, developing new areas of rice production and supplying capital even to European-owned plantations.

The spread of Indian commerce was matched by the emigration of her people in the second half of the nineteenth century. Indian labour was in demand on plantations all over the tropics, especially on sugar plantations in Mauritius, Trinidad, Guiana, Natal and Fiji, on rubber plantations in Malaya and on tea and coffee estates in Ceylon. Much of this labour was supplied through a system of indentures: the workers were contracted for a fixed wage for a fixed period, with the options of a free passage home, permanent settlement or a renewal of the indentures at the end of the contracted period. Migrants also went to Burma, Ceylon and Malaya either as seasonal agricultural workers, or to open up new lands as peasant colonists. By 1911 the *Census of India* estimated that there were roughly two million Indians living abroad, with the largest groups in Burma, Ceylon and Mauritius. This was the foundation of the worldwide diaspora of South Asian peoples, a nexus of culture and language that outlived the empire that officiated at its birth.

CHAPTER SIXTEEN

PRIVATE ENTERPRISE IN THE FAR EAST

◇

After the loss of the North American colonies, British interests appeared to switch to the Orient. Over the next century 'trade not dominion', as Lord Shelburne (Prime Minister 1782–3) said, was to guide the creation of the second British Empire in Asia and Australasia. Although some historians dispute this 'swing to the east', there is no doubt that British activities in the region gathered pace from the late eighteenth century. The main reason for this shift was that Britain's trade with China now appeared to offer massive fortunes.

Merchants in China

In 1784 the Prime Minister William Pitt bailed out the East India Company from its American losses by reducing the duties on China teas. The tea trade generated, in turn, a remunerative commerce in opium which was extracted from the Bengal poppy. Merchants looked for ways around the barriers that had been erected by China against the foreign barbarians. Traders were confined to Canton and, despite occasional efforts to improve relations, they were subjected to what was described as the discrimination and venality of the authorities.

In 1793 Lord Macartney, a former Governor of Fort St George (Madras), went to China on a mission to set up a British embassy there. Macartney and his party were graciously received and sumptuously entertained in Canton; in Peking they skilfully evaded the ritual performance of obeisance (*kow tow*) before the Manchu Emperor. But they returned to England empty-handed. Lord Amherst, subsequently Governor General of India, fared no better in 1816. Regarded as nothing more than a tribute-bearer, he was unceremoniously despatched, without ever being admitted to the Emperor's presence.

South-East Asia: from Way-station to Straits Settlements

The origins of Britain's lucrative empire in South-East Asia were the by-product of a search for bases on the sea route between Bengal and China. The English had been squeezed out of the East Indies by the Dutch in the seventeenth century; they had lost their factory in Bantam (west Java) in 1684 and although Fort Marlborough at Benkulen (south-west Sumatra) was a valuable producer of pepper in the eighteenth century, its use as a centre for regional trade was slight.

In 1786, Captain Francis Light acquired a settlement on the island of Penang for the East India Company. The terms of the deal he struck with the Sultan of Kedah were imprecise but, in the short term, Penang afforded the Company a safe anchorage, supplies of timber and victuals, and the prospect of agricultural development. However, the island lay off the optimum strategic point on the eastern run and barely challenged the Dutch claim to a trade monopoly in the archipelago.

In 1795 however, after French revolutionary forces had occupied the Netherlands, the exiled Dutch Stadhouder (or head of state) issued the 'Kew letters', instructing the Dutch officials in the East Indies to place their territories in British hands for the duration of the hostilities. In this way, Britain gained the Cape, Ceylon and Malacca – none of which, as it turned out, was relinquished after the defeat of France in 1815.

Java, the core of the Dutch seaborne empire, resisted British occupation until Lord Minto, Governor General of India, took it by force in 1811. Minto appointed Stamford Raffles to be its Lieutenant Governor. A man of enormous talent and energy, Raffles recognized the value of South-East Asia and Britain's future in the region. As ruler of Java (1811–16), he devised

In this painting by William Alexander, the Manchu Emperor Chien-Lung receives the British mission led by Lord Macartney in 1793.

101

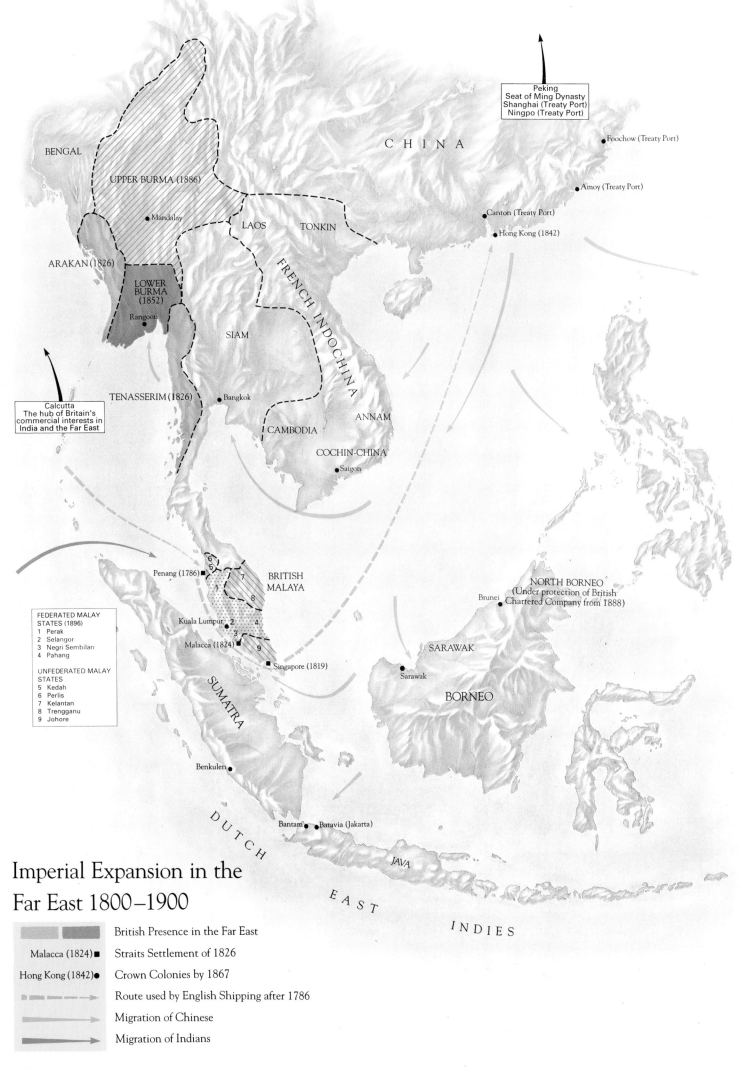

BENGAL

UPPER BURMA (1886)

• Mandalay

ARAKAN (1826)

LOWER
BURMA
(1852)

Rangoon •

TENASSERIM (1826)

Calcutta
The hub of Britain's
commercial interests in
India and the Far East

LAOS

TONKIN

SIAM

Bangkok •

FRENCH INDOCHINA

CAMBODIA

ANNAM

COCHIN-CHINA

Saigon •

C H I N A

Peking
Seat of Ming Dynasty
Shanghai (Treaty Port)
Ningpo (Treaty Port)

• Foochow (Treaty Port)

• Amoy (Treaty Port)

Canton (Treaty Port) •
• Hong Kong (1842)

Penang (1786) ■

6
5

BRITISH
MALAYA

7

1

8

Kuala Lumpur •
2
3   4
Malacca (1824) ■

9

■ Singapore (1819)

FEDERATED MALAY
STATES (1896)
1   Perak
2   Selangor
3   Negri Sembilan
4   Pahang

UNFEDERATED MALAY
STATES
5   Kedah
6   Perlis
7   Kelantan
8   Trengganu
9   Johore

SUMATRA

Benkulen •

NORTH BORNEO
(Under protection of British
Chartered Company from 1888)

Brunei •

SARAWAK

Sarawak •

BORNEO

D
U
T
C
H

Bantam • • Batavia (Jakarta)

JAVA

E
A
S
T

I N D I E S

Imperial Expansion in the
Far East 1800–1900

▭▭	British Presence in the Far East
Malacca (1824) ■	Straits Settlement of 1826
Hong Kong (1842) ●	Crown Colonies by 1867
▸▸▸	Route used by English Shipping after 1786
➤	Migration of Chinese
➤	Migration of Indians

RAFFLES: BOTANIST AND EMPIRE BUILDER

Thomas Stamford Raffles was born at sea in 1781, the son of a sea-captain. He joined the East India Company in London and was transferred to Penang in 1805. By 1811 he was Lieutenant-Governor of Java. Fired by hatred of Dutch methods, a vision of British pre-eminence and an overwhelming curiosity, his administration cost the Company money and antagonized the Dutch. After Java was returned to Holland, he was posted to the backwater of Benkulen in south-west Sumatra in 1818. There he indulged his passion for natural history and built up collections of anthropological, botanical and zoological specimens which brought him fame back in Britain. The climax of his quest came when he discovered the parasite later named after him, *Rafflesia arnoldii*. Its enormous flowers, which can weigh up to 24 pounds, appear for only 5 to 7 days and smell disgusting. In 1819 Raffles visited the island of Singapore where he founded the British colony. Returning in 1822,

Sir Thomas Stamford Raffles (1781–1826) and Rafflesia Arnoldii *(right), the largest known flower.*

he was delighted to discover its economic progress but could not resist interfering with its administration. In 1824 he revisited

Bencoolen before turning for home. Just after he had re-embarked, his ship caught fire and his collection of specimens was totally destroyed.

---

elaborate plans to replace 'barbaric' Dutch practices with British 'civilization'. When Java was restored to the Dutch, Raffles was posted to the backwater of Benkulen. Nevertheless, he won the support of Governor General Hastings (1812–23) to seek another site as a base for the East India Company and, in February 1819, he founded a settlement on the island of Singapore. 'It is all and every thing I could wish,' wrote Raffles, 'and if no untimely fate awaits it, promises to become the emporium and pride of England.' Legally suspect and politically risky, his agreement with certain Malay chiefs was an affront to the Dutch and to those in England who cultivated Dutch support in European affairs. But the trade of the new settlement rapidly outstripped that of Penang. In 1824 the English and the Dutch concluded a treaty, whereby the whole archipelago was partitioned between them: Britain surrendered Benkulen and, in turn, was confirmed in her possession of Malacca and Singapore.

The East India Company made no attempt to occupy its sphere of authority beyond the borders of Penang, Malacca and Singapore. These became the Straits Settlements in 1826, with the capital in Singapore from 1832. Gradually, however, the interests of the government of India and the community of the Straits Settlements diverged. In 1825–6, for example, Henry Burney was sent on a diplomatic mission to Bangkok: Penang merchants and officials hoped that he would succeed in curbing Siam's southerly expansion into the Malayan peninsula; the Government in Calcutta, on the other hand, instructed Burney to win Siam's neutrality at a time when East India Company forces were bogged down in a war against the Burmese.

Policy-makers at the highest level, however, regarded South-East Asia – or Further India as the region was often called – as little more than a nuisance at this time. Burma threatened the security of Bengal while the Indonesian archipelago impeded the flow of trade with China. In order to remove both sets of difficulties, the company acquired some limited territorial responsibilities: in addition to the Straits Settlements, it wrested Arakan and Tenasserim from Burma in the war of 1824–6. It would soon discover, however, that these commitments were neither easily managed nor entirely effective in fulfilling their original objectives. The Treaty of Yandabo in 1826 merely set the scene for further conflict with Burma; the consolidation of

the Straits Settlements in the same year actually stimulated amongst those working there an interest in the region for its own sake rather than a respect for its broader strategic purpose. And the door to the interior of China still remained firmly closed to the Englishmen cooped up in Canton.

The Age of Free Enterprise comes to the Far East

In 1833 the East India Company lost its monopoly of British commerce with China and the era of free trade dawned in the Far East. Larger and larger quantities of Indian opium from Bihar and Bengal were exported to China as private traders flocked into the free market. The Chinese sought with growing desperation to dam the flood, but relations between them and the British government were equally strained.

The crisis came to a head in 1839 when Commissioner Lin Tse-Hsu confiscated and destroyed the stocks of opium. This, he alleged, was causing a drain of bullion from Canton and addiction in southern China. 'Unless this trade is stopped,' he declared, 'before ten years have passed there would not be a man left fit to make a soldier.' His action precipitated the first Anglo-Chinese war which ended in 1842, when the Treaty of Nanking ceded Hong Kong to the British Crown and opened five Treaty Ports (Canton, Amoy, Foochow, Ningpo and Shanghai) to British traders. For all the high hopes placed in the Chinese market by British merchants and manufacturers of textiles, trade was still hamstrung by the obstructiveness of the mandarins, by the vastness of the country and by a sheer indifference to British goods. The *Arrow* incident at Canton, in which the Chinese police arrested the crew of a pirate vessel that was entitled to fly the British flag, precipitated a second bout of Anglo-Chinese fighting in 1856. A joint Anglo-French force seized Canton and, in 1857–8, concluded the Treaties of Tientsin with the Chinese. In 1860 British and French troops occupied Peking, burned the Summer Palace, and extracted yet more concessions before withdrawing. In the following year, the Tsungli Yamen (or foreign office) was created to conduct China's foreign relations on Western terms. This was, at last, an obvious gesture, both politically and culturally, to the 'barbarians' from Europe.

However, there existed a far more dangerous threat to the Manchu dynasty than Western imperialism. This was the cataclysmic upheaval within China, caused by the mid-nineteenth-century rebellions of Muslims, Miao tribesmen, the Nien Fei and the Taiping, in which millions died. Although they were frustrated by the régime, the British – along with the French and the Americans – did not relish the prospect of the collapse of Manchu rule, as this would force foreigners either to flee from the ensuing anarchy or to partition between themselves the expensive burden of governing China. Therefore, from the early 1860s, the British tried to influence rather than oppose Peking. They encouraged the 'self-strengthening' or reform movement; in 1862–3 Major Charles Gordon (later 'of Khartoum') participated in the campaigns of the international 'Ever-Victorious' Army against the Taiping rebels; and, during the next half-century, Robert Hart (formerly of the British consular service but increasingly Sinophile in his sympathies) built up the maritime customs service as the mainstay of government revenue and credit.

Two Asian societies managed to fend off the European empire-builders; one of these was to become the dominant commercial force in Asia. From the middle of the nineteenth century, the more homogeneous and more adaptable society of Japan abandoned a two-century-old isolationism and, in order to keep the West at bay, struck free-trade agreements with Europeans and embarked on the road to modernization.

Siam, in mainland South-East Asia, had a similar history of exclusivism combined, however, with a tendency to bend before the wind. King Mongkut (1851–68), having seen the fate of Burma (which lost a second war with the British in 1852), concluded in 1855 the first of a number of free trade treaties with Western powers. By surrendering border territory to the British and French, by recruiting foreign advisers from a mix of Western nationalities, and by allowing Europeans (especially the British) to dominate the import and export trade, Mongkut and his son, Chulalongkorn (1868–1910), saved the political independence of Siam. As a result Siam (later Thailand) became the only country in South-East Asia to escape Western colonialism.

Empire continued, however, in the Straits. The East India Company's loss of the China trade monopoly in 1833 caused the government in Calcutta to turn its back on the interests of the Straits Settlements at the very time when those settlements, especially Singapore, were benefiting from the general expansion of South-East Asian and Far Eastern trade. The merchant community in the Straits – which consisted of overseas Chinese as well as Europeans – protested at administrative neglect, at inadequate policing of the seas against piracy and at attempts by the government of India to change the currency and raise tariffs. All these threatened the free-trade foundations of their prosperity. Petitions from the Straits community were eventually met in 1867, when the Settlements were transferred to the Colonial Office, and the institutions of Crown Colony rule – notably a representative Legislative Council – were established in the Straits themselves. Nevertheless, to the dismay of local businessmen and, in particular, the Straits Chinese, who were investing in the burgeoning tin-mining industry of the turbulent Malayan frontier, the Colonial Office upheld the old orthodoxy of non-intervention in the Malay states beyond the Settlements.

The Heyday of Empire out East?

From about 1870, Western expansion in South-East Asia and the Far East gathered momentum. The scramble for concessions in China seemed unstoppable, despite attempts at 'modernization'; indeed, the reform movement was baulked by a shortage of capital, and by an ingrained commitment to old ways. The Chinese military was defeated by the French in 1885 and humiliated by the Japanese in 1894–5. The scramble – in which Britain, France, Germany, Japan and Russia all took part – culminated in 1898. It did not ebb in response either to the 'Hundred Days of Reform' (June–September 1898) or to the resistance in 1900 of a secret society called the Boxers to Western religious, cultural and technological influences.

Provincial governors were ordered to execute all foreigners and, in the weeks that followed, more than two hundred foreign missionaries and thirty thousand Chinese Christians were killed.

A colourful example of freelance imperialism during this period was the career of James Brooke, who created his own kingdom from the fief of jungle and mangrove in Sarawak (Borneo) which the Sultan of Brunei had assigned him in 1841, as recompense for help in the suppression of revolt.

COMMISSIONER LIN AND THE OPIUM WARS

On 31 December 1838, after nineteen private audiences with the Emperor, Lin Tse-hsu was appointed High Commissioner at Canton with plenipotentiary powers and the supreme command of Canton's naval forces. Formerly Governor-General of Hupei and Hunan, Lin had earned his reputation as a brilliant administrator and as an intransigent opponent of the importing of opium by the British – a trade that the Emperor had been trying to quash for two decades.

Lin's first move was to confiscate all the opium stored in the Cantonese warehouses by British merchants. Feelings were further

An advertisement for a wax model of Commissioner Lin at Madame Tussaud's.

inflamed when two drunken British sailors killed a Chinese villager. The British refused to hand over the men. Soon the two sides were at war, but the Chinese did not stand much of a chance against even a small British force. The Treaty of Nanking was forced upon them on 29 August 1842. A year later, a supplementary treaty forced them to pay a large indemnity for the war and to open five ports to British trade. It also forbade the Chinese from trying British citizens in their courts.

Lin's reward for following the Emperor's orders faithfully was exile in North-West China until his death in 1850.

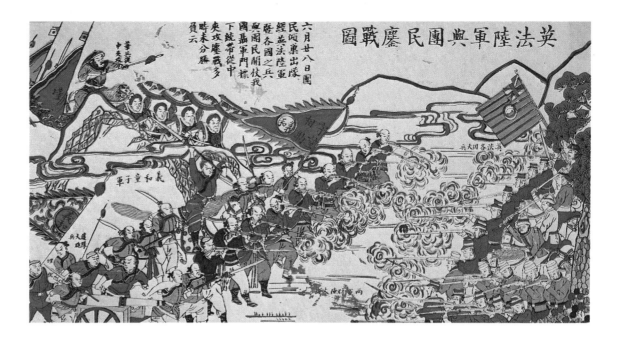

In a contemporary Chinese print, Boxer rebels attack an international force in 1900.

A Western expeditionary force intervened and defeated the Chinese. The Boxer Protocol in September 1900 imposed a ruinous indemnity on the Manchu dynasty, prising it open first to constitutional reformists and then in 1911–12 to republican revolutionaries.

For all its allure and for all the apparent ease with which Western interests were asserted, China never fulfilled the extravagant expectations of some of her European contemporaries. The British pursuit of the 'imperialism of free trade' had encountered major obstacles. Foreign merchants may have been well-established on the coast but they were even less successful in gaining access to the vast interior than the hard-pressed missionaries had been. By the end of the nineteenth century the value of British trade with China was – in relation to Britain's global trade – less than it had been before the Anglo-Chinese war of 1839–42. Because of the intractability of the country and competition from other powers, the British position in China fell far short of what might be termed 'informal empire' – the enjoyment of power in a country without the responsibility of governing its inhabitants.

In South-East Asia during this period, the Dutch asserted an effective presence in the Outer Islands (i.e. those outside Java). The French consolidated their *Union Indochinoise* and the Americans took up the 'white man's burden' when they defeated the Spanish in the Philippines in 1898. The British completed the 'forward movement' in Burma and annexed the former kingdom to India in 1886. In the Malay States considerations of strategy, economics and 'native misrule' induced them to replace the policy of non-intervention with the 'Advisory' or 'Residential' system between 1874 and 1914.

Malaya: a Second Raj in Asia

British control over the Malay States was established by means of a series of treaties and agreements with Sultans and chiefs. Under this system the Malay rulers retained their sovereignty, but were bound to follow the advice of British political officers in all matters except religion and custom. The relationship, which at first resembled British paramountcy in the princely states of India, was ambiguous and immediately ran into trouble when the first Resident in Perak, James Birch, arrogantly made a bid for direct rule. In 1875 Birch was speared to death through the palm-leaf walls of a riverside bathhouse and a nasty little war ensued. Thereafter residents, such as Hugh Low (Resident in Perak), Frank Swettenham (in Selangor and Perak) and Hugh Clifford (in Pahang), handled local rulers more deftly, studiously safeguarding Malay status while building up British power behind

the throne. Administrative convenience soon warranted administrative centralization and, in 1896, four of the Malay States – Perak, Selangor, Negri Sembilan and Pahang – formed the Federated Malay States (FMS). Malay sovereignty was still underwritten in a host of British statements but the fiction wore increasingly thin. Those Malay States which later accepted British protection – Kedah, Perlis, Kelantan and Trengganu, which were acquired from Siam in 1909, and the southern state of Johore, which received a General Adviser in 1914 – sedulously avoided absorption within the FMS. By 1914 British Malaya, an area about the size of England and Wales, consisted of the Crown Colony of the Straits Settlements (Penang, Malacca and Singapore) and nine protected Malay States, of which four made up the FMS with its capital at Kuala Lumpur.

A Mixed Society

In the economically attractive west-coast states, two Malayas had emerged by the eve of the First World War. On the one hand, there was the traditional Malaya of court and *kampong* (village), preserved by British 'protection'; on the other hand, there was the 'modern Malaya' of tin and rubber, railways and roads, banks and agency houses that had been created by British and Chinese capital and by Chinese and Indian labour. The communities of this plural society were not merely differentiated ethnically; they also performed distinct social and economic functions. The British still argued that the immigrant Chinese and Indians, who actually outnumbered the Malays by 1921, were 'birds of passage'. Indeed, apart from the English-speaking Chinese who were well-rooted in the Straits Settlements, it was still true that the overwhelming majority of Chinese and Indian workers had been born outside Malaya and regarded the peninsula as a place of work rather than as a home. Nevertheless, some Malays feared that a fate similar to that of the Maoris, the Australian Aborigines or the North American Indians might befall them.

They were already nervous about their future in a country where political and economic control resided in non-Malay hands; and so they sought to delineate Malay identity by reference to Islam or, alternatively, to the glories of old Malacca. Here lay the cultural origins of Malay nationalism which, in fact, scarcely ruffled the calm of British Malaya before the 1940s. Apart from occasional eruptions of resistance as in Perak in 1875, Pahang in 1891–5, Kelantan in 1915 and Trengganu in the 1920s, the British régime was made stable by abundant revenues and by the collaboration of a still-revered élite of Malay royalty and aristocracy.

Expansion in the Cape and the Great Trek

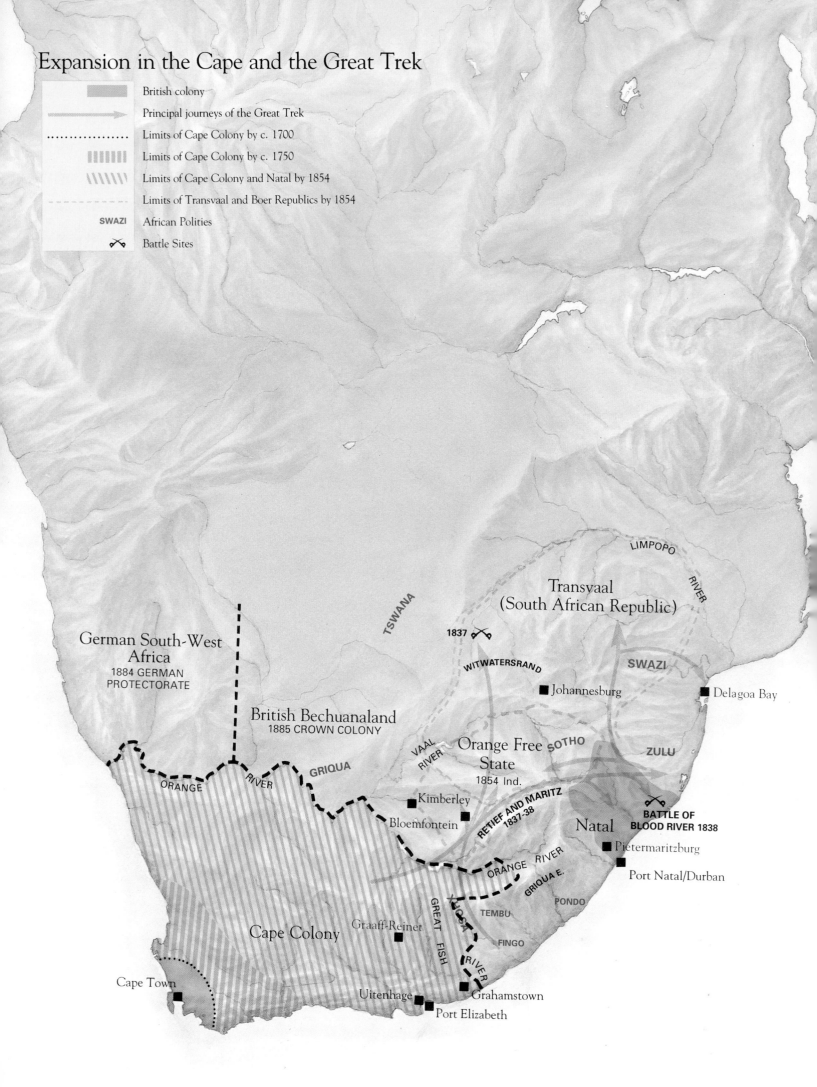

Legend:
- British colony
- Principal journeys of the Great Trek
- Limits of Cape Colony by c. 1700
- Limits of Cape Colony by c. 1750
- Limits of Cape Colony and Natal by 1854
- Limits of Transvaal and Boer Republics by 1854
- **SWAZI** African Polities
- Battle Sites

German South-West Africa
1884 GERMAN PROTECTORATE

British Bechuanaland
1885 CROWN COLONY

TSWANA

LIMPOPO RIVER

Transvaal
(South African Republic)

1837

WITWATERSRAND

SWAZI

■ Johannesburg

■ Delagoa Bay

VAAL RIVER

GRIQUA

ORANGE RIVER

Orange Free State
1854 Ind.

SOTHO

ZULU

■ Kimberley

RETIEF AND MARITZ 1837-38

Bloemfontein

Natal

BATTLE OF BLOOD RIVER 1838

ORANGE RIVER

GRIQUA E.

■ Pietermaritzburg

Port Natal/Durban

PONDO

GREAT FISH RIVER

KOSI

TEMBU

FINGO

Cape Colony

Graaff-Reinet ■

Cape Town ■

Uitenhage ■

Grahamstown ■

Port Elizabeth ■

CHAPTER SEVENTEEN

CONFLICT IN THE CAPE

◇

Before the opening of the Suez Canal in 1869, the southern tip of Africa provided a natural resting point for European merchants *en route* to the East – a fact that proved sad for the historical fate of the indigenous peoples. After the founding of the Dutch East India Company in 1652, the Cape of Good Hope served as a halfway house for Dutch ships sailing to and from the Indies.

The Development of the Cape

By the end of the eighteenth century, the tiny Dutch settlement on the Cape had expanded, comprising more than twenty thousand Europeans and around twenty-five thousand slaves. A small proportion of the population, known as the Khoi, had been persuaded or coerced into providing labour for the port-town and its hinterland. Most of the Europeans were of Dutch extraction, but company policy had encouraged expansion by admitting refugee Protestants from Europe as settlers. Thus, by the nineteenth century, the name 'boer', meaning farmer, was no longer only synonymous with the Dutch, although Dutch was the official language. Some settlers intermarried with the San (known as Hottentots) and Khoi people.

A series of black states had been established throughout southern Africa for centuries before the first Cape settlers arrived. The Xhosa peoples, for example, traded in ivory with passing merchant ships. They were described in 1686 by Simon van der Stel, the Dutch Governor of Cape Town, as 'civil, polite and talkative' and not inclined to 'sell their children as slaves'.

The ability of the Khoi to move from the Cape into the wider interior created a constant labour problem for the small settler population, who had access to an abundance of land but an extremely limited labour pool upon which to draw. Slavery was

seen to be the solution as it had been in the Americas. Slaves were shipped to the Cape from the Dutch East Indies, Madagascar and the eastern African coast; through the movements of these peoples, Islam was introduced to the Cape.

The port-town of Cape Town – forming the core of the settlement – grew rapidly. When the Huguenots were expelled from France, some settled in the Cape and started a wine industry. Immediately to the north and east of the town lay good farming land, where wheat and citrus fruits were grown. The areas closest to the port were the richest; they were the most fertile and could sell their fresh produce without high freight charges. As the population grew, pressure on the most fertile land pushed the Boers further eastwards, where the land was more adapted to stock raising. Here the living was harder.

Days and sometimes weeks of travel separated these scattered populations from the power of the Cape Town Governor, and they created their own local governments which were upheld by the militia, or Kommando, and by the elders of the Dutch Reformed Church. There was almost constant friction between the edges of these settlements and their African neighbours into whose territories they had expanded. Although the settlers tried to dispossess the Africans by force of arms, the Xhosa in particular were a well-organized military force and they firmly blocked Boer expansion in the eighteenth century. After negotiations, a shaky frontier of sorts was fixed at Fish River.

Early British Rule

In 1806 Britain, who regarded the Cape port as a commercial linchpin in her developing Empire, invaded the Cape and paid the Dutch £6 million for legal possession. The conflict with the Boers was about to begin.

The Dutch settlement at the Cape was still very small at the beginning of the eighteenth century. Its primary purpose was to reprovision the ships of the Dutch East India fleet, seen here riding at anchor in Table Bay.

THE MYTHOLOGY OF THE GREAT TREK

The powerful symbolism of the Great Trek was transformed into the cornerstone of Afrikaner mythology in the late nineteenth century. The Battle of Blood River on 16 December 1838, when a small Boer force triumphantly avenged an earlier Zulu massacre, became an anniversary of religious and nationalistic significance. Jan Bantjes recorded the great Vow of the Trekkers: 'We promised in a public prayer, that, should we manage to win the victory, we would build a house to the Lord to be used for worship.' Although the Church that was built ceased to be used for worship in 1861, it was later converted into the

A typical Boer wagon of the early nineteenth century illustrates the privation endured by pioneer families en route to a better life in Natal, the Orange Free State or the Transvaal.

Voortrekker Museum.

The bones of those Boers who had died were collected and buried in a casket in 1895, forming the foundation of what would beome the awe-inspiring Voortrekker Monument. Sir John Robinson, Prime Minister of Natal, described the emotional ceremony: 'In front stood a casket, in which had been deposited all that could be found of the murdered Voortrekkers . . . there were depths of suppressed passion in the extemporized prayers uttered over the crumbling bones, and the written sermon was listened to with profound and unbroken attention.'

Once in control of this valuable way-station, the British could not avoid the issue of slavery. London buzzed with reports of the callous treatment of blacks by their Boer owners. In the opinion of General Dundas, the Boers were 'the strongest compound of cruelty, of treachery and cunning'. Magistrates were enjoined to hear complaints by blacks and were, in turn, accused by resentful Boers of stirring up a black revolt. When a farmer refused to appear before a court to hear a complaint against him, there was a revolt which resulted in the hanging of five Boers at Slagter's Nek in 1815. During the hanging, the rope broke, depositing four of the rebels on the ground. Despite their pleas for mercy, they were picked up and hanged again, and duly became known among the Afrikaners as 'the heroes of Slagter's Nek'.

While some of their Cape subjects railed against the new regulations, Africans along the Cape frontiers regarded themselves as subject to no one but their own political leaders. The British attempted to secure the eastern frontier by building a military fort at Grahamstown in 1812, and then a string of forts along the Fish River. A nearly successful attack on Grahamstown in 1819 led Governor Somerset to expand the frontier eastwards to create a *cordon sanitaire* beyond the Fish valley. Somerset planned to hold this eastern frontier by creating a model farming settlement at Albany which would not have recourse to slavery. The menfolk would, in addition, form a militia to 'police' the eastern frontier. This scheme was initiated in 1819 and the settlers were welcomed by three successive years of crop failures between 1821 and 1823. The experiment was a failure, although those with sufficient capital to withstand the initial reverses successfully introduced the merino sheep into the area and ultimately made considerable fortunes.

Early British rule in the Cape was of the brusque sort expected of an army of occupation. Until 1825 civil rights were virtually non-existent, although trial by jury and some constitutional rights were extended to whites after lobbying from all sides.

The End of Slavery in the Cape

By 1827 English had replaced Dutch as the official language of the colony. British, rather than Dutch, missionaries moved into what promised to be a fertile mission field. They energetically took up the neglected cause of the Africans in order to secure government help and to bring down further condemnation upon the heads of the resolutely Calvinist Boers.

Although no slaves had been imported legally into the Cape after 1803, it was not until 1834 that slavery was finally abolished. By the Proclamation of that year, around forty thousand slaves became indentured 'apprentices' in preparation for their full emancipation. This, however, was no great improvement on their former lot. Compensation was available for slave-owners, but the fine print stipulated that this could be paid only in London: the bulk of slave owners were Boers from the eastern Cape, unwilling or unable to pay agency fees to collect the compensation.

The Great Trek

For one group of Boer farmers – the poorer eastern settlers for the most part – the abolition of slavery was the last straw. A frontier Afrikaner and local commander of the militia, Piet Retief, handed a document to the *Grahamstown Journal* in 1837. It stated, in part: 'We complain of the severe losses which we have been forced to sustain by the emancipation of our slaves . . . We complain of the unjustifiable odium which has been cast on us by interested and dishonest persons, under the cloak of religion, whose testimony is believed in England.'

Retief led three thousand Boers through the Drakensberg Mountains into the green fertile land of Natal, which was beyond the jurisdiction of the Cape Town Governor and British law. The tiny British settlement at Port Natal was overcome and expelled, and the Trekkers set up their Republic of Natalia in its

A Swazi warrior, one of many irregular forces fighting for the British against the Boers in Southern Africa.

In the days when Africa was rich in game, Boer hunters return from the chase, an engraving by Samuel Daniell, 1804.

stead, with Pietermaritzburg as the capital. The British viewed this development with a jaundiced eye and asserted that Cape laws would apply in Natal as well. Most of the Boers loaded their wagons once again and trekked back over the Drakensberg Mountains to the High Veld, where they hoped to be beyond British reach. Somewhat unwillingly, the British annexed what remained of the settlement in Natal in 1843.

The second trek had taken the Boers beyond the curve of the Orange River deep into African territory. Several of the rulers here had treaty relationships with the British. Although the Boer Trekkers were frequently portrayed as romantic, free spirits, they exacted a high cost from the peoples they encountered. 'Orphan' children were appropriated as slaves, cattle were stolen and property confiscated.

The new Governor of the Cape, Sir Harry Smith, sent a force to annex the land between the Orange and Vaal Rivers. This was hardly a solution, however, to the incessant problem of frontier warfare. By 1850 British troops were thoroughly embroiled on their eastern and northern frontiers, mainly intervening between Boer militias and the offended African peoples. Smith was recalled to London under a cloud; nothing annoyed a British government quite so much as costly military campaigns in distant and seemingly unimportant corners of the

Empire. It was suggested in London that some of the costs could be shed by recognizing in part the independence of the Boers. In 1852, at the Sand River Convention, the British disclaimed authority in most areas beyond the Vaal. In doing so, Britain had reneged on some of the treaties of protection she had signed with African allies. By 1860 a number of ramshackle Boer republics had achieved a form of unity and proclaimed themselves the Transvaal Republic and in 1854, by the Bloemfontein Convention, the area between the Rivers Orange and Vaal became the Orange Free State.

Political Divisions in Southern Africa

By 1860 the area which comprises modern South Africa consisted of two British colonies – the Cape and Natal – two Boer Republics and a number of significant and still sturdily independent African states.

White rule in southern Africa consisted at the time of a squabbling sprawl. The Colonial Office in London continued to be hostile towards any sort of costly attempt at 'tidying up', such as the formation of a federation of states. Beyond the frontiers of the two British colonies there was constant tension. The Orange Free State tried gradually to annex the once extensive Sotho kingdom by main force; by 1865 the Sotho king Moeshoeshoe and the Boers were engaged in a full-scale war. LeSotho bordered on Cape Colony as well as the Orange Free State, and so the king's long-stated request for British protection was eventually answered by the new Governor, Sir Philip Wodehouse. The reluctant Colonial Office was persuaded to proclaim what was left of the kingdom – the mountains rather than the fertile plains – a British Protectorate in 1868. Two years later a similar agreement was reached with the Tswana kingdom, to protect it from further Boer encroachment from the Transvaal.

This general lack of resolution on frontier issues appeared to worry few in Whitehall when the victims of this indecision were African. In 1867, however, the discovery of diamonds in the loosely defined territory of Griqualand West on the lower Vaal caused the British to awaken rather suddenly to their responsibilities. The Transvaal, citing the Bloemfontein Convention, claimed the area. The African Griqua, on the other hand, declared that they were entitled to British protection, probably regarding this as the lesser of two evils. An independent arbitrator found in favour of the Griqua and the Transvaal was excluded. By 1871 the British had annexed the area, establish-

THE ZULU WAR MACHINE

The presence of the Zulu in the Natal area can be traced back to the thirteenth century, but their fearsome reputation as warriors was not established until the beginning of the nineteenth century, when competition for land and power intensified. The Zulu kings, Dingiswayo and Shaka, introduced wide military reforms. The *impi ebomvu* (red war or war to the death) replaced ceremonial or haphazard spear-throwing with the use of a short stabbing spear, or *assegai*. The use of this new weapon was enhanced when the old circumcision guilds of young men were transformed into regiments, or *impis*, in which clusters of boys who had been initiated together constituted a military formation. This

developed into a tightly controlled social structure based upon the royal dominion over cattle, the Zulu's wealth, which determined when warriors could assert their independence as married men, with their own herds and home. It became commonplace for warriors to remain unmarried until they had achieved military success or attained royal favour. Such incentives, combined with the use of spies, scouts, decoys and such a strong emphasis on physical fitness that Zulu warriors could run thirty miles without pausing, combined to form a formidable army. When Shaka was told of King George IV, he remarked approvingly: 'Ah! King George's warriors are a fine set of men. In fact, King George and I are brothers;

he has conquered all the whites, and I have subdued all the blacks. But is King George as handsome as I am?'

By 1878 the British had decided that the potential Zulu threat needed to be eliminated. Refusing to accede to Britain's deliberately impossible request that the Zulu army be disbanded, King Cetewayo reluctantly declared war. At Nkambule in March 1879, wave after wave of warriors fell before the firepower of British line regiments: two thousand Zulu died, and only eighteen British. Brushing aside Cetewayo's pleas for peace, Lord Chelmsford overwhelmed the Zulu capital of Ulundi on 4 July, and the Zulu supremacy in Natal was finally broken.

ICONS OF EMPIRE: LADY BUTLER AND THE DEFENCE OF RORKE'S DRIFT

For twelve hours on the 22 January 1879, 84 soldiers of the 2nd Battallion, 24th Regiment held 4,000 Zulus at bay. Eleven Victoria Crosses were later awarded – the highest number ever for a single engagement. As a result, the defence of Rorke's Drift has gone down in history as a symbol for British heroism.

Thanks to the painter Lady Butler, we see the battle now as the Victorian public saw it – in clubs, sitting rooms and schoolboy studies throughout Britain. Lady Butler was the first painter to celebrate the courage and endurance of the ordinary British soldier in a patriotic yet humanitarian way.

The Defence of Rorke's Drift was commissioned by the Queen. Lady Butler's husband, an Anglo-Irish general, disapproved of the conduct of the Zulu War, however, believing that 'five sixths of our African wars have their beginnings in wrongs done in the first instance by white men upon natives'.

'The Defence of Rorke's Drift', 1879, by Elizabeth Butler, who was commissioned by Queen Victoria to portray the gallant defence of this mission station during the Zulu War.

---

ing it as a separate crown colony two years later. The local chief was then prevailed upon to sell his rights and those of his people for an annuity of £1,000 per annum. The leaders of the Boer Republics were understandably incensed by this sleight of hand, arguing that Britain had challenged Boer attempts to annex land while annexing it for themselves.

However, both of the Boer Republics were seriously impoverished – so impoverished, in fact, that the British were able to annex the Transvaal in 1877. The Union flag was hoisted in its capital by the young novelist-to-be, Rider Haggard. The Orange Free State, however, was less open to coercion. Trade had increased as the diamond diggings got under way and many of the diggers repatriated their earnings to the Free State.

The Resistance of the African States

The major impediment to a federation or union in South Africa lay in the various African border states which mounted a series of wars of resistance. The British had fought and lost a long struggle with Sekukuni, as had the Transvaal Republic before. By the mid 1870s, they posed serious problems by challenging land thefts and incursions. Large numbers of British troops became heavily involved along the frontier.

It was the Zulu, however, the strongest military power in the region, who caused the greatest apprehension. In 1872 the Zulu had welcomed a new king, Cetshwayo, a direct descendant of the kingdom's dynamic founder Shaka. Although they had previously enjoyed a fearsome reputation as a military machine, the Zulu people had rarely come into conflict with the British. By the mid 1870s they justly complained of Boer encroachment from the Transvaal. A British boundary commission found in favour of the Zulu, but the High Commissioner, Sir Bartle Frere, decided to use this decision to reduce the Zulu military potential. He declared that the disputed territory would be returned to the Zulu, on condition that Cetshwayo disbanded his huge army, agreed to the presence of a British resident in Zulu territory and promised protection to missionaries in his domain. Cetshwayo simply refused to respond to this provocative ultimatum. In January 1879 the British invaded.

The Zulu Wars

'First comes the trader, then the missionary, then the red soldier,' declared Cetshwayo as he launched himself into the attack. The Zulu forces outwitted and outmarched the main British column, which was attacked and annihilated at Isandhlwana on 22 January. Natal lay open to the Zulu army, which was only checked at Rorke's Drift by a courageous and clever defence of one of the few fords over the swollen Tugela River. The time gained there enabled the British forces to regroup. In June 1879 the Zulu, facing the immensely superior British firepower, were overcome at the Battle of Ulundi. Although the Zulu had been defeated and their territory annexed, the prolonged campaign and the loss of the 24th Regiment at Isandhlwana marked the nadir of British military fortunes.

By the end of 1880, the notion of federation had become more distant than ever before. While British rule had been accepted with resignation in the Transvaal, it had been a deep blow to Boer pride. On assuming control, Frere had promised the Boers eventual self-government. Hopeful Transvaalers had read Gladstone's barnstorming speeches which denounced the evils of Conservative imperialism; but in a politic change of direction, the Grand Old Man declared his opposition to restoring Transvaal's independence in May 1888.

On 16 December 1880 – the anniversary of their victory over the Zulu army at Blood River – the Boers rose in rebellion against the British. Once again, luck deserted the British military. Its sole battalion in the Transvaal was ambushed at Bronkhorst Spruit while marching towards the capital of Pretoria, and 350 soldiers were killed. Sir George Colley, the new High Commissioner, took charge of the situation himself and, with a small force, captured the commanding position of Majuba Hill on the night of 26 February 1881. In the morning, however, this seemingly impregnable position was overrun by a Boer detachment, which killed a further 280 men.

The Secretary of State for the Colonies called for a ceasefire and, in March, a conference was held in Pretoria. The Transvaalers regained their independence, but neither Boer nor Briton was happy with the outcome.

CHAPTER EIGHTEEN

INTO THE OUTBACK

By the beginning of the nineteenth century New South Wales was a well-established colony. It was able to feed itself and its new settlers, as its boundaries were gradually moved farther inland in the search for more productive land. However, the domination of the settlement's commercial life by the officers of the New South Wales Corps, when they were also the only source of physical power, destabilized the organization and running of the colony. They were so powerful, in fact, that on 26 January 1808, the twentieth anniversary of white settlement, they staged a *coup d'état* by rebelling against Governor Bligh, deposing him and running New South Wales as a military junta for two years. For this astonishing mutiny, none of the officers was hanged or even seriously punished. This state of affairs was brought to an end only by the arrival of the new Governor, Lieutenant-Colonel Lachlan Macquarie, on 23 December 1809.

On his arrival, the population barely exceeded ten thousand. He immediately decided that they did not need quite so many drink shops and cut the number from seventy-five to twenty, forcing even these to close during church services as a mark of respect. In addition, the many couples living together without the benefit of religious sanction were encouraged to remedy their omission. On the other hand, Macquarie opened a racecourse less than a year after he arrived. Balls and receptions were also held at the Governor's residence every fortnight; cricket matches were put on the agenda; he built roads, public buildings and hospitals. Yet, in the end, Macquarie was the victim of his own success. While the British were preoccupied with Napoleon,

they could pay little attention to remote colonies. After 1815, however, they were able to criticize at their leisure. Soon, it was felt in London that all these public works had nothing to do with running a penal colony and were a sheer extravagance.

Early Settlers and their Adventures

The truth was that, on the Governor's arrival, convicts comprised only forty-eight per cent of the population although their labour was vital to the colony's success. Before the end of the Napoleonic Wars, very few skilled workmen or ordinary labourers could be induced to emigrate to such a remote spot. The free men included 'emancipists', or freed convicts, and a mixture of retired servicemen, second sons and adventurous gentlemen from Britain who were able to bring with them sufficient capital to buy land and stock and to sustain their workers during the unproductive early days.

Legend has it that the convicts were a mixture of 'murderers and whores'. In fact, the vast majority were petty criminals like fifteen-year-old John Wisehammer, who snatched 'a packet of snuff from an apothecary's counter in Gloucester'. Furthermore, these folk had clearly defined rights while they were serving their sentences; they were even allowed, within limits, to sell their labour on the open market. Once they had served seven years, they became emancipists. Some chose to return to Britain, but others were given land and were even assigned fresh convicts who would in their turn work for them.

As the colony developed and grew, one problem faced by both

CAPTAIN BLIGH'S SECOND MUTINY

Despite the loss of his ship in the notorious mutiny on the *Bounty*, Sir Joseph Banks still held Captain William Bligh in high regard. Thus, when the Governorship of New South Wales fell vacant, Banks recommended his protegé. Bligh got the appointment and arrived in Sydney on 8 August 1806. He had been told to stamp out the illegal trade in rum, which brought him into direct confrontation with the officers of the New South Wales Corps who ran the trade. Captain John Macarthur and Bligh circled one another in an aura of goodwill at first, but they were only manoeuvring for advantage. When Bligh did take action, he was unbending. Macarthur's wife described Bligh as 'violent, rash and tyrannical'. Bligh in turn described Macarthur as 'an arch-fiend, a constant disturber of public society, a venomous serpent to His Majesty's Governors'. Matters came to a head on 26 January 1808. Bligh managed to have Macarthur arrested but he was immediately released by the Commander of the Corps, Major Johnston. A group of drunken soldiers then set off to return

A view of Sydney Cove in 1804 by E. Dayes (left). William Bligh (1754– 1817) (right).

the compliment. Bligh was placed under house arrest, then allowed to embark for England. As soon as he was on board ship, he declared himself Governor again and announced that a state of rebellion was in progress. He sailed to

Hobart to await instructions from London. However, London was more interested in dealing with Napoleon and the situation dragged on for over a year. Bligh was replaced by Colonel Macquarie who restored order.

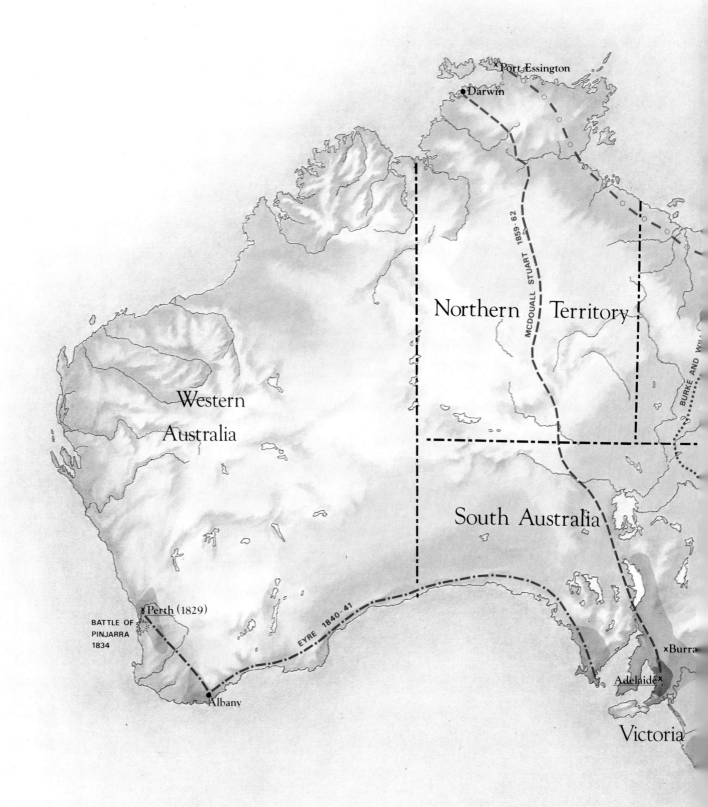

Australia: Settlement and Exploration: 1800–1870

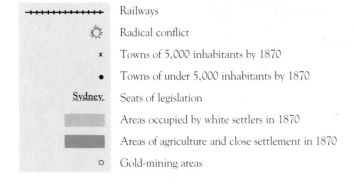

┼┼┼┼┼┼┼	Railways
☀	Radical conflict
×	Towns of 5,000 inhabitants by 1870
●	Towns of under 5,000 inhabitants by 1870
<u>Sydney</u>	Seats of legislation
▮	Areas occupied by white settlers in 1870
▮	Areas of agriculture and close settlement in 1870
○	Gold-mining areas

Townsville

Queensland

LEICHHARDT 1844-45

Rockhampton

Gympie

Brisbane

Hillgrove
MASSACRE OF ABORIGINES
AT MYALL CREEK 1838
Grafton
Armidale

New
South
Wales

OXLEY 1817

Ophir
Maitland
Newcastle
Forbes
Bathurst

Young

Adelong
Sydney and Parramatta

Ovens
MITCHELL 1836
Goulburn
stlemaine
Kiandra
Bendigo
Omeo
rat
Melbourne
Geelong
MASSACRE OF
STOCKMEN AT
BROKEN RIVER
1838

Launceston
Tasmania

ATTEMPT TO ROUND UP
TASMANIAN ABORIGINES 1830
Hobart

Auckland
Thames
WAIKATO
New Plymouth
MAORI
WARS
1860-72
Napier
Nelson
Wellington

Christchurch

Dunstan
New
Zealand
Dunedin

113

emancipists and free immigrants alike was the lack of space. The settlement was hemmed in by the Blue Mountains and, despite the vast area beyond, whose nature the colonists could only guess at, it was pinned to the coast. The first settlers to chaff against these constrictions were George Bass and Matthew Flinders. With the Governor's permission, they made a series of ever more adventurous voyages in small boats before the end of the eighteenth century. In 1798 they discovered that Van Diemen's Land, the future Tasmania, was an island and not joined to the mainland as had been thought hitherto. When this isolated mass was explored further, it was realized that the climate and soil were infinitely richer and more productive than those of the original settlement. The island could also be used as a dumping ground for the most intractable of the convicts. By 1804, the settlements of Hobart, Risdon and Launceston had all been founded. By the time Macquarie arrived, the island possessed about one thousand inhabitants. But that still left the Blue Mountains as an obstacle on the mainland.

Between 1789 and 1804, there were seven attempts to traverse the range. Only in 1813 did three men, together with 'four servants, five dogs and four horses', finally make it across. What they saw on the other side was a revelation: all the grassland that the colony could possibly need for a generation.

In 1797, the first merino sheep had been imported by a group of men which included John Macarthur, one of the most troublesome of the New South Wales Corps. Until the discovery of ample pastureland, the possibilities of sheep breeding were limited. This did not deter Macarthur, however, and he gradually built up his flock. Macarthur was a violently contentious man and a quarrel with his own colonel in September 1801 led to a duel in which the latter was wounded. The Governor was incensed but, being a navy man himself, he foresaw trouble if he tried to hold a court martial of a Corps favourite in the colony. Instead, he sent Macarthur back to Britain for the proceedings. The offender took some wool samples with him. His timing was perfect. The Napoleonic Wars were at their height and the British blockade of Europe in full force. This meant that the British wool industry was starved of the merino wool from Saxony and Spain upon which it depended. Consequently, Macarthur had no trouble in convincing the government of the potential of Antipodean sheep production and was even allowed to buy merinos from a special flock held by the King. On top of that, he inveigled from the government a grant of two thousand acres of the best grazing in New South Wales. In 1805 he returned to the colony, acquitted and in triumph, and set about breeding hybrids by putting his flock to hardier strains.

The Problems of Growth

The breaching of the cordon created by the Blue Mountains in 1813 relieved the pressure of a continually rising population. The numbers of convicts had begun to increase. Between 1787 and 1810, about 9,300 men and 2,500 women had been transported to the Antipodes. Yet, between 1811 and 1820, 15,400 men and 2,000 women made the journey. In the following decade, the traffic grew even heavier – 28,700 men and 4,100 women.

Crime swelled within the chaotic, festering cities of Britain despite the death penalty being enforced for even the most trivial of thefts – its effectiveness as a deterrent was obviously negligible. In 1818, a parliamentary committee recommended that some offences against property be struck from the list of capital crimes: given the totally inadequate prison system (that

Lieutenant-Colonel Lachlan Macquarie (1761–1824), the vigorous Governor of New South Wales.

was to persist for a generation), the only alternative was transportation. Hence the increased volume of convict traffic. At the same time, the social pressure of population growth and economic change was insistent. England and Wales grew from 10.1 million people in 1801 to 18.1 million 40 years later. This growth was at its most rapid in the decade leading up to 1820. Overlaying this pressure was another that arose from changes in industry and agriculture. Factory employment overtook home workshops in some of the country's most basic trades. In the countryside, the steady enclosure of the land drove hundreds of people to the slums and towards the chance of work. Some chose another alternative: emigration.

It was in this context that the voices of post-war criticism over Macquarie's schemes of public works in New South Wales were joined to those doubting the purpose and function of the colony in the Antipodes. Was it a glorified prison or a home for aspiring artisans? In 1819 London appointed a Royal Commissioner, John Bigge, to try to resolve this question.

Bigge spent two years in the colony collecting what he considered to be evidence. This upset Macquarie, who felt the Commissioner's presence to be an implicit criticism of his own conduct. Eventually, he could tolerate the intrusion no longer and tendered his resignation. By the time it was accepted and the former Governor had returned to London, Bigge was in the process of submitting his report, which managed to move in two opposing directions at the same time. The programme of public works, it declared, was utterly unnecessary as 'New South Wales was still a penal colony.' Yet Bigge also favoured free immigration. He recommended that immigrants be awarded land in proportion to their capital. To resolve the tension between the opposing aspects of his conclusions – that New South Wales was both a penal colony and a freewheeling, profitable source of wool – he made the very practical suggestion that the thousands of petty criminals transported each year be trained as shepherds. Thus, in essence, the government's position was confirmed, and no encouragement was given for a radical change of policy. However, the enormous growth in the population wrought its own changes as the settlers spread out to claim more and more land.

The site of Captain James Stirling's bivouac in 1827, fifty miles up the Swan River, near present-day Perth.

The first institutional change to result from this steady enlargement was the separation of Van Diemen's Land from New South Wales. By 1824, the island had developed sufficiently to merit its own administration, particularly as the links to the mainland had to be maintained across eight hundred miles of treacherous waters.

The new Lieutenant-Governor, Colonel George Arthur, made it clear that he intended to initiate a new régime. He was especially tough on the convicts and believed that their work should be 'hard enough to bring home to the miscreants all the abomination of their wrongdoings, while at the same time setting them the example of a righteous master from whom their black hearts might well pick up a sense of goodness'.

The consequences of transportation were also very evident on the mainland in the 1820s: in the words of one French observer, 'The government gangs of convicts . . . marching backwards and from their work in single military file, and the solitary ones straggling here and there, with their white woollen Parramatta frocks and trousers, or gray or yellow jackets with duck overalls . . . all daubed over with broad arrows, P.B.'s, C.B.'s and various numerals in black, white and red; with perhaps the chain gang straggling sulkily by in their jingling leg-chains.'

At the other end of the social scale were the 'Exclusives', the descendants of ex-Corps fathers and free immigrants. These landowners opposed the social advancement of the emancipists at every turn, erecting barriers of snobbery and privilege in a manner that echoed the worst elements of British society a century earlier. Their standards were always gained by reference back to the old country, so that the term 'Australian' was one of abuse well into the 1820s.

New Settlements

In 1827, Captain James Stirling returned from an anti-piracy voyage in the Timor Sea via the western coast of Australia. To his surprise, he came across a navigable river and what appeared to be swathes of fertile land. His report occasioned much enthusiasm, and a private company was formed to settle on what became known as Western Australia. There was no shortage of applicants for the first four hundred places and there were high hopes for the scheme. There was to be no convict labour. But, once the first settlers had arrived in May 1829 and had founded Perth, it quickly became evident that the whole venture was misconceived. Little thought had been given to the layout of the town and few of the settlers were prepared for the hardships of pioneering. In addition, the soil was much less fertile than had first been supposed. After the initial flood of immigrants, the tide slowed to a trickle.

Private initiative was much more successful in founding the colony of Victoria, primarily because the land was much more fertile. This time there was no attempt at a group invasion. First on the scene was the Henty family. Thomas Henty was a successful breeder of sheep and horses in Sussex who, at fifty-three years of age, suddenly decided that he needed new horizons. His family's original destination was Western Australia but a reconnaissance by one of his sons revealed the problems endemic to that settlement. They eventually settled in Portland Bay, virgin territory about 120 miles to the west of the Yarra River where, independently, the two other founders of Victoria staked their claim. John Batman and John Fawker claimed squatters' rights in 1835. The Governor of New South Wales declared this illegal and tried to thwart their plan. But the distances proved too great for the King's representative. By September 1836 he capitulated, recognizing the Port Phillip settlement. A year later he went so far as to pay a gubernatorial visit in which he named the place Melbourne. By 1840 there were 10,000 inhabitants and 800,000 sheep.

South Australia was founded as the realization of the vision of the pamphleteer Edward Wakefield. The colonists hoped to establish 'a paradise of (religious) dissent'. They were entirely misled by the enthusiasm of the explorer Charles Stuart, who had visited the mouth of the Murray River in the late 1820s: although funded through the South Australian Land Company and well publicized, the site chosen was all hills and no pasture. The first settlers arrived in 1838, but it was not until the following decade that their own explorations revealed the existence of fine grazing nearly two hundred miles to the south-east. Only the collapse of the original conception proposed by Wakefield made survival possible.

New Zealand Annexed

Contact between New South Wales and New Zealand was established soon after the arrival of the First Fleet. However, no concentrated effort was made to settle the islands. The ferocity of the Maoris had been noted by Joseph Banks on his trip with Captain Cook and there was no reason to query his judgement.

The first settlers were whalers. They were little threat to the indigenous population because they stuck to the coastline and some of the natives actually became seamen with these deep-sea fleets.

The crop that attracted the traders was the New Zealand flax plant, *Phormium tenax*, the fibres of which the Maori women laboriously wove into cloth. Attempts to mechanize the process failed, however, and the trade diminished in importance in the 1830s. For a decade it was replaced by exports of timber to New South Wales, whose own trees were never so amenable to carpentry as those from the southern temperate forests. The milder climate also allowed the well-organized Maori tribes – working with the missionaries – to develop an export trade in vegetables and cereals. This agricultural potential gradually drew more and more settlers to the area. However, it was the scandal over trade in dried Maori heads that caused the Governor of New South Wales to appoint a British resident in 1833.

At the beginning of the 1830s, between 300 and 330 Europeans lived on the islands; by the 1840s, the number had risen to about 2,000. The settlers sometimes even absorbed native practices. Thus, in 1835, a Maori attack on a British family led to retaliation in the 'battle of the pork' by a British 'tribe' of fifty men led by the Reverend White and Mr Russell, a merchant. Rather than shoot the natives, they 'slaughtered some 150 pigs and burnt the houses of the offending tribe'. The clumsy and amateurish annexation of the islands took place in 1840. The treaty was prepared in both English and Maori, but the texts did not say the same things, particularly regarding some critical areas of sovereignty.

The same Edward Wakefield whose ill-conceived notions had nearly brought the South Australia colony to disaster at the end of the 1830s, was the prime mover behind the New Zealand Company. It used a lottery held in London to involve land speculators in unsurveyed settlements. Indeed, it showed more enthusiasm for absentee investors' cash than for the long-term development of the colony. Yet, this was the organization to which the British Government had ceded the initiative in building up the country. Not surprisingly, given the scale of the mismanagement, agriculture largely stagnated in New Zealand during the early 1840s.

A Social Experiment

Australian economic development experienced a hiccup in the 1840s, but the hiatus was short-lived. Increasingly, the race into the future was fuelled by freely given labour: by 1840 convicts formed only twenty-three per cent of the population of New South Wales, and the proportion was bound to diminish. During the late 1830s, after much prevarication, the House of Commons considered the ending of transportation. Eventually it stopped the traffic to New South Wales although transportation to Tasmania continued until 1853. Western Australia, however, which was having great difficulties in recruiting settlers, began taking convicts in 1849. The practice was finally abandoned only in 1868.

Representation of the people also made significant progress in the original colony. In 1842 the composition of the legislative council was changed: one-third of the council was now appointed by the British Government but the remainder was elected. However, enfranchisement was still only partial as there was a property qualification that excluded most of the population, as it did in Britain. This experiment was such a success that it was extended to Tasmania, Victoria and South Australia in 1850.

The extension of the democratic process to New Zealand was more complex and more complete. As early as 1842, settlers in Wellington held their own elections for a municipal council, but these were disallowed by the Colonial Office. In 1846 the New Zealand Constitution Act was passed in London: this established a substantial local and countrywide democracy. But the Governor suspended it within a year. Then, as in the coming years, the

A cartoon satirizing the British Government's suggestion of 1832 that unmarried women should emigrate to Australia in an attempt to stabilize the colony.

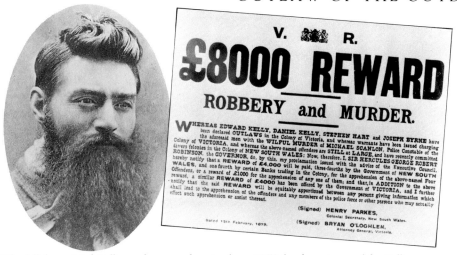

The folk hero, Ned Kelly, and a reward notice from 1879 for the capture of the Kelly gang.

Ned Kelly was born of Irish parents in Beveridge, Victoria in June 1855 and reared to hate the English. He and his brothers grew up in the bush where they were unrestrained by any of the demands of civilization. At the age of fifteen, Ned was arrested for receiving a stolen horse. In April 1878 a constable arrived at the Kelly farm to arrest Dan, Ned's younger brother. The policeman was shot in the wrist. Ned and Dan immediately took to the Warby Ranges.

In October 1878 Ned murdered three policemen. He also began informing all and sundry of his opinions. His enemies, he proclaimed, were the police, the railways, the telegraph wires and the blacks. Since many settlers had similar feelings, Kelly became their spokesman and hero, lauded in song and verse. In December 1878 the gang stole £2,000 from a bank. The following February, Ned and three members of his gang took over the town of Jerilderie. There he dictated a 7,000-word letter to be delivered to people of influence in Melbourne. But, in June 1880, the gang took to drinking and were surrounded. At dawn Ned left the hut encased in his extraordinary suit of home-made armour but was brought down by police fire and arrested. And, despite rumours to the contrary, Kelly went quietly to the scaffold in November 1880.

Maoris were the stumbling block.

Successive British governments took their responsibilities to the Maoris very seriously and were always deeply suspicious of the settlers' intentions – with some justification. Greed and a significant measure of racial contempt underlay the attitudes of many of the Europeans. The natives trusted neither party, an attitude vindicated by later events.

Meanwhile, the Constitution Act of 1853 developed the country's democratic institutions far beyond those of Britain; the franchise was extended to all men over twenty-one years of age who held a minimal amount of property. This measure encompassed both provincial and national assemblies.

The number of settlers in the islands grew substantially as the years passed. In 1851 two-thirds of the population of 26,707 lived on North Island, but the next decade witnessed a shift in the balance as the population of non-native South Island almost quadrupled. This pattern continued throughout the 1860s when the population rose to a quarter of a million, over sixty per cent on South Island.

This expansion intensified the friction with the Maoris, and the pot finally boiled over in 1859. The politically sophisticated tribes had realized that a united front against the 'Pakehas', or white men, whose continual intrusions into their lands were supported by the Crown, might stem the tide. Unfortunately, a trivial mistake over the sale of a property was inflated into a major conflict. The resulting war spluttered for five years on and off until the British had assembled five thousand regular soldiers and could attack in force with the support of artillery. Nevertheless that still did not end the matter. Some Maori tribes were particularly skilled in guerilla warfare and fighting finally ceased only in 1872.

Racial tensions in Australia were, like the Aborigines themselves, less organized. But, with similar expansion into long-held native territory, blood-letting occurred on both sides. Given the size of the country and the dispersal of both populations, however, it was to be expected that such incidents were sporadic.

Gold Rush

The Californian gold rush of 1848 can rightly be described as a fever: it was an Australian prospector who carried this condition back to his homeland. Once men had begun to look, the ore was not difficult to find and, in 1851, the strike was official. In ten years the population of the entire country doubled and, for the first time, significant numbers of non-British immigrants arrived to try their luck. Discoveries were made in both New South Wales and Victoria, and the Governors of both colonies did their best to control the situation. It took only a trivial incident at the end of 1854 to provoke the confrontation of the Eureka Stockade. In essence, the imbroglio was a minor one – a collision between a group of miners and the representatives of authority. But the rhetoric of the moment and of those who used it later as a cypher for a cause inflated its significance.

Much more important than all this, however, were the technological transformations that were recreating Europe and America in the southern hemisphere. It was the advent of these 'prodigious novelties', such as railways and refrigerated ships, that would transform the role of Australia and New Zealand.

The 'Welcome Stranger' Syndicates Mine in Bailieston, 1902.

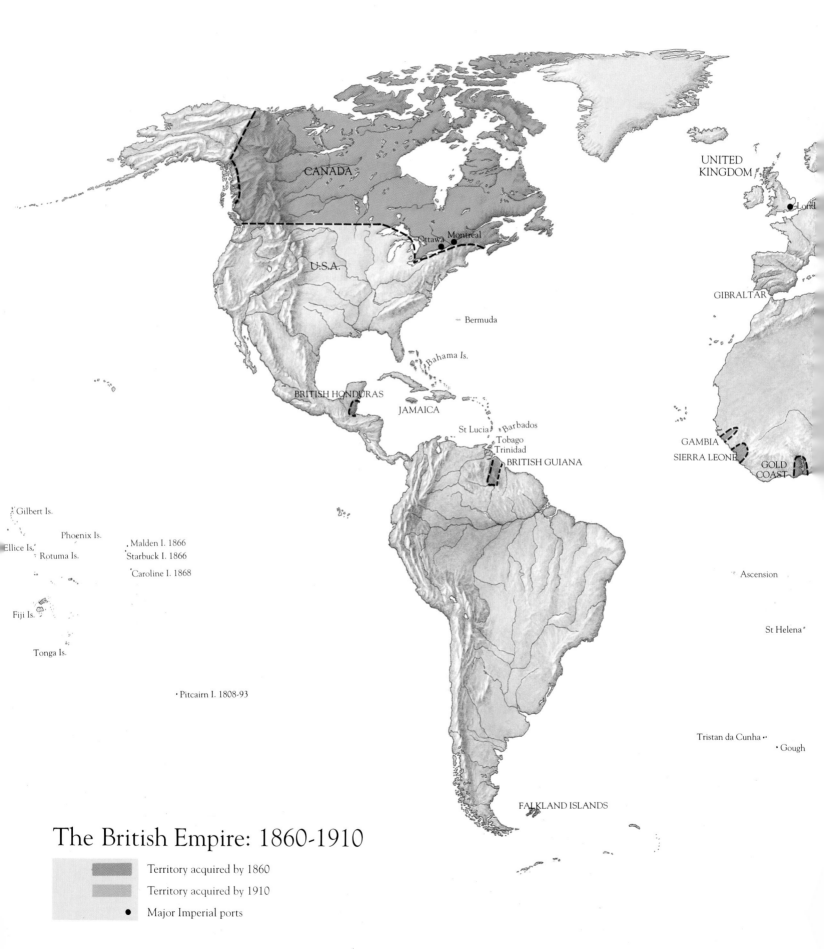

The British Empire: 1860-1910

UNITED
KINGDOM

London

GIBRALTAR

GAMBIA

SIERRA LEONE

GOLD
COAST

Ascension

St Helena

Tristan da Cunha

Gough

CANADA

Ottawa Montreal

U.S.A.

Bermuda

Bahama Is.

BRITISH HONDURAS

JAMAICA

St Lucia Barbados
Tobago
Trinidad

BRITISH GUIANA

Gilbert Is.

Phoenix Is.

Ellice Is. Rotuma Is.

Malden I. 1866

Starbuck I. 1866

Caroline I. 1868

Fiji Is.

Tonga Is.

Pitcairn I. 1808-93

FALKLAND ISLANDS

Territory acquired by 1860

Territory acquired by 1910

● Major Imperial ports

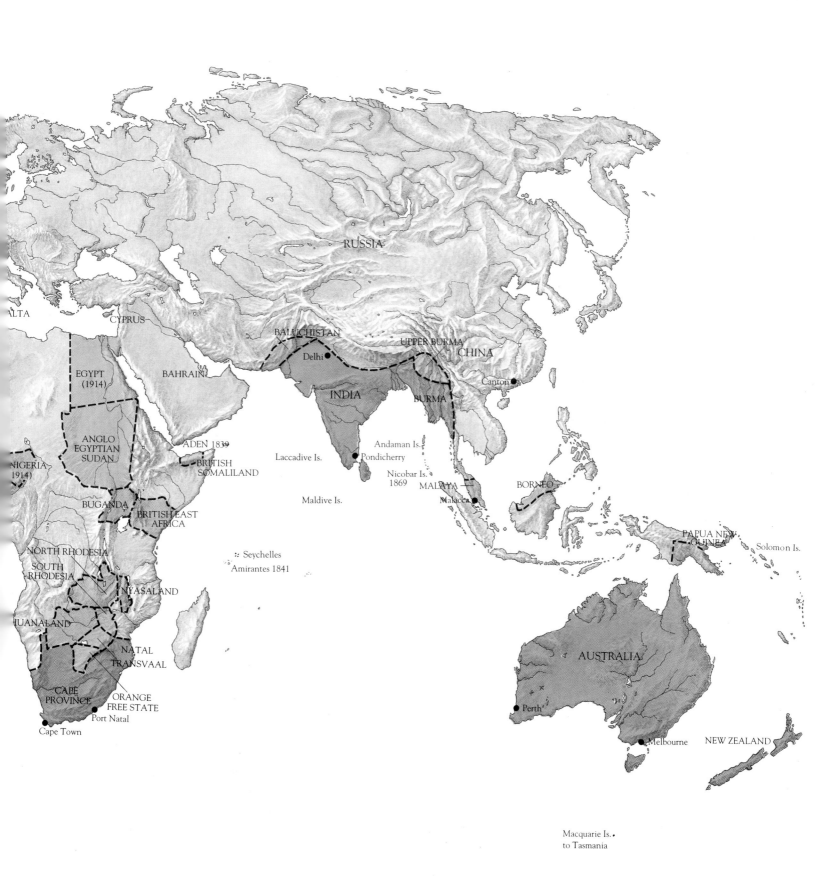

ALTA

CYPRUS

BALUCHISTAN

UPPER BURMA

CHINA

EGYPT
(1914)

BAHRAIN

Delhi

ANGLO
EGYPTIAN
SUDAN

ADEN 1839

INDIA

BURMA

Canton

NIGERIA
1914)

BRITISH
SOMALILAND

Andaman Is.

Laccadive Is.

Pondicherry

BUGANDA

Nicobar Is.
1869

MALAYA

BORNEO

BRITISH EAST
AFRICA

Maldive Is.

Malacca

NORTH RHODESIA

Seychelles
Amirantes 1841

PAPUA NEW
GUINEA

Solomon Is.

SOUTH
RHODESIA

NYASALAND

HUANALAND

NATAL

TRANSVAAL

AUSTRALIA

CAPE
PROVINCE

ORANGE
FREE STATE

Perth

Port Natal

Cape Town

Melbourne

NEW ZEALAND

RUSSIA

Macquarie Is.
to Tasmania

CHAPTER NINETEEN

THE HEYDAY OF EMPIRE

◇

In 1881 John Seeley, Regius Professor of History at Cambridge, delivered a series of lectures entitled *The Expansion of England* in which he argued that 'the diffusion of our race and the expansion of our state' were Britain's greatest achievements during the eighteenth and nineteenth centuries, although this progress, he went on to explain, was almost completely ignored by contemporaries and historians. In a phrase that has since become famous, he suggested: 'We seem to have conquered and peopled half the world in a fit of absence of mind.'

Seeley saw the individual events of the previous two centuries as being of little importance in themselves, except as part of a coherent whole: the development and spread of the English nation. 'The wars with France from Louis XIV to Napoleon fall into an intelligible series. The American Revolution and the conquest of India cease to seem mere digressions and take their proper place in the main line of English history. The growth of wealth, commerce and manufacture, the fall of the old colonial system and the gradual growth of a new one, are all easily included under the same formula.' This vision of Britain however, was not just a theory about the past. It also prepared the citizen 'for what is to come next'.

Seeley's hopes for the future centred on those colonies which he described as having been settled rather than conquered – Canada, New Zealand, Australia, the West Indies and South Africa. Their colonists 'are of our own blood, and are therefore united with us by the strongest tie.' He wished to draw these colonies of settlement into a federal union, which would ensure that 'Greater Britain' remained as strong as those countries which he saw as the great powers of the future: Russia and the United States. If, on the other hand, Britain allowed her colonies to drift into independence, she would be left with moral influence but – being less populous – would be less powerful than either France or Germany. If this were to happen, future historians would look at Britain in the way that Seeley himself was already viewing Holland and Sweden: 'once great, but the conditions of their greatness have passed away.'

Such ideas as Seeley's caught the spirit of the age and were an inspiration. The years from 1870 to 1914 were the heyday of the British Empire, the period during which the British thought of themselves most coherently and consistently as an imperial race. Yet even at the time, Seeley was expressing an extreme view. The solidarity of the Empire existed more in the minds of certain intellectuals than it ever did on the ground. Even when the expansion of England had reached its furthest extent, 'Greater Britain' remained a mirage.

Imperial Consolidation

By 1870 Britain's relations with what Seeley was to call the 'colonies of settlement' had reached a mature stage. The Canadian Confederation had been established in 1867. Her relationship with Britain was based on mutual advantage, as the British Colonial Secretary noted in 1869: 'Canada is part of the British Empire because she desires to be so.' Emotional ties

remained strong, however, in a country that sought to counterbalance such a dominant neighbour as the United States. As late as 1891, Sir John MacDonald won a Canadian general election with the slogan: 'A British subject I was born, a British subject I will die.'

Relations with Australia and New Zealand followed a similar pattern. The institutions of self-government developed without straining the loyalty that the colonies still felt towards Britain. Only South Africa remained a problem for British governments during the last third of the nineteenth century.

The British Debate

Many in Britain were content to see the arms of the Empire proceeding towards self-government, bound only to the mother country by loose ties of mutual trust. In 1871 the Prime Minister, William Gladstone, told the House of Commons that his Liberal Government 'wished to retain the Colonies: but . . . wished to retain them bound to this country by ties of kindred and affection.' On the other hand, a number of outspoken politicians and publicists, such as Seeley and his fellow historian James Froude, were becoming uneasy about this relaxed vision of Empire; they promoted the closer ties of imperial federation as a way of strengthening the Empire. Benjamin Disraeli, the leader of the Conservative opposition in Parliament, seemed to favour such ideas. Made in June 1872, his 'Crystal Palace Speech' called for a 'great policy of Imperial consolidation' to create a 'representative council' in London that would ensure 'constant

'This day is one of the greatest and most glorious days of our lives,' wrote Queen Victoria on the opening of the Great Exhibition of 1851.

Queen Victoria was the first British monarch to take an extensive interest in the colonial territories. She was especially fascinated by India, and the scope for pomp and ceremony that British rule there presented. It was she who, in 1873, proposed that she be given the title of 'Empress of India' (partly to match the status of the Tsar of Russia and the Emperor of Germany). This resulted in the Royal Titles Bill of 1876 that established her as Queen Empress, *Victoria Regina et Imperatix.*

Victoria saw Britain's imperial mission as 'to protect the poor natives and advance civilization'. Her closest emotional identity with the Empire came through her relationship with Abdul Karim, one of two Indian servants whom she employed from 1887 to her death. Karim quickly won her confidence, established himself as her favourite and instructed her in Hindustani. Many at court disapproved of Karim's influence, one Cabinet Minister fearing that he was undermining Victoria's Christian faith.

At the end of her reign, the Queen's interest was caught once more by the very different imperial issue of the war in South Africa, which she saw as provoked by Boer ambitions. In December 1899 she sent every soldier in the field a special Christmas present – a flat box of chocolate bound in a red, white and blue ribbon, with an embossed profile of her head on the lid. This gift from 'the Widow of Windsor', as Kipling imagined her being called by the troops, was perhaps her most explicit act as symbolic head of the Empire.

With Victoria's death in 1901 the style and presentation of the monarchy was fundamentally altered. Shortly after her funeral, Edward VII repatriated his mother's Indian entourage and disposed of other pieces of imperial regalia such as a large hoard of elephant tusks – the annual tribute of many African chiefs. The rectitude and simplicity of the late Victorian monarchy dissolved into Edwardian pomp and high spirits; Kipling's 'Widow of Windsor' was replaced by 'fat Edward – Edward the Caresser' as Henry James called her son.

'The Triumph of the British Empire,' an intricate cameo carved out of a shell by Giovanni Sabbato, who took ten years to complete this masterpiece.

and continuing relations' between Whitehall and colonial opinion. However, during this period as Prime Minister from 1874 to 1880, Disraeli did nothing to implement such a scheme.

During the 1880s and 1890s, awareness of imperial issues increased, but closer formal ties between London and the settler colonies remained a dream. Indeed, colonists in Australia, New Zealand and southern Africa began to take fresh imperial initiatives of their own, expanding into 'empty lands' and asserting their own administrative autonomy.

The Paper Empires of the 1880s

All of the major European nations expanded their empires in the 1880s, most notably in the 'scramble for Africa' in which Britain, France, Germany, Belgium, Spain, Italy and Portugal all acquired new territory. But these European powers sought only what were called 'paper empires' – lines on the map that delineated exclusive spheres of interest which meant little on the ground. For all of them African policy in the 1880s was a means to other ends. Germany's territorial claims, for example, were part of complex schemes of European diplomacy, not just the expression of an overwhelming desire for 'a place in the sun'. Otto von Bismarck, the German Chancellor, sought an understanding with Britain in Europe rather than a rivalry overseas. Thus, in 1890 Germany and Britain exchanged Berlin's control over Zanzibar for London's possession of the Baltic island of Heligoland. To reassure France, Britain signed a convention that ceded control of a vast area of the western Sahara between Algeria, Senegal and Lake Chad. This concession cost London nothing but helped the French to achieve one of their most important objectives. 'We want to get it recognized once and for all,' declared the French Foreign Ministry, 'that no European nation can ever resist our influence in the Sahara and that we shall never be taken in the rear in Algeria.'

Whitehall had two priorities in Africa. The first was in South Africa: here the instability of the Boer republics of the Transvaal and the Orange Free State seemed to create dangers for British settlers in Cape Province and Natal. The annexation of the Transvaal in 1877 was followed by rebellion and defeats for British troops at Bronkhurst Spruit in 1880 and at Majuba Hill in 1881. In consequence, some autonomy was returned to the Boers and, in 1884, the republics were re-established under British protection.

Britain's second priority in Africa concerned Egypt. Here, the classic issues of imperial strategy, financial interests, great power rivalry and local political instability combined to create an intractable problem. Arabi Pasha led a rebellion in 1882 against foreign influence and British troops were sent to occupy Egypt to 'restore order'; in fact this action only exacerbated the problem. Queen Victoria thought that these events provided a heaven-sent opportunity for 'securing to ourselves such a position in Egypt as to secure our Indian Dominions and to maintain our superiority in the East'. The Liberal government, led by Gladstone, hoped instead for a quick withdrawal and drew up a timetable to begin evacuating the troops within a month. The actual evacuation never took place. (An unsympathetic French observer counted sixty-six similar British declarations of intent to withdraw from Egypt in the next forty years.) Egypt remained a British protectorate until 1922.

The High Tide of Imperialism

During the 1870s and 1880s British statesmen had sought to hold the Empire at arm's length, but in the 1890s a strong current of rivalry in Europe combined with political instability in Africa and the Far East to engulf them. There was an intensive scramble for territory which paid greater attention to economic potential than before. In this new rush Britain not only carved out boundaries in Central and West Africa and fresh spheres of influence in China, but also became entangled in a full-scale war in South Africa. Elsewhere, the French completed their territorial expansion in Saharan Africa and South-East Asia; the Russians pushed eastwards into Manchuria; the Japanese annexed Korea and Formosa; the United States took over Hawaii, Guam and the Philippines; and the Germans acquired new territory in South-West and East Africa and in the Pacific. In Morocco, where the interests of France, Spain, Germany and Britain clashed intensely, this rivalry surfaced most bitterly: Europe came close to war during the Agadir crisis of 1911.

This new mood of aggression, which became known as the

'new imperialism', was marked by increased concern in London for the strategic and economic security of Britain and her established imperial possessions. In 1894 Lord Kimberley – the Foreign Secretary in the Liberal administration – identified the maintenance of the Cape Colony as 'perhaps the most vital interest of Great Britain because by the possession of it communication with India was assured'. On the Conservative benches, Lord Salisbury self-righteously emphasized the government's economic motives: 'I think other governments if they seek trade it is in order that they may obtain territory; if the English government seeks for territory, it is in order that it may obtain trade.'

As the century came to an end, Whitehall had to cope with a number of varied threats to the Empire's stability. International rivalry came to be glorified by the fashionable philosophy of 'Social Darwinism', which compared the struggles between nations to those between animal and plant species in nature – the survival of the fittest. Local insurgents still posed a threat to imperial order: the Boxers in China, the Mahdists in the Sudan and the Afrikaners in the Transvaal and the Orange Free State. And the disintegration of weak states could cause as many problems as the aggression of strong ones, as Lord Salisbury pointed out when he talked about China in 1891: 'When a nation dies there is no testamentary distribution of its goods, there is no statute of distribution for what it leaves behind. The disappearance of a nation means a desperate quarrel for what it has possessed'.

By the end of the nineteenth century, Seeley's absent-minded empire-builder had been transformed into a self-conscious imperialist. While many sought to justify this conversion in terms of English virtues, some identified it with English vices instead. The best-known British analyst of imperialism was J.A.

By the mid-nineteenth century British industrial might was supreme: an early photograph shows Brunel's iron ship, the Great Eastern, *under construction at the naval dockyards at Millwall in 1857.*

THE BRITISH IMPERIAL DIET

By the end of the nineteenth century, British consumers enjoyed a wide range of foodstuffs produced in all the regions of the world. The repeal of the Corn Laws in 1846 had established Britain as the leading free-trade economy. In the next fifty years, new technologies and the ever-spreading influence of British capital and enterprise brought new products to these shores. Tea was grown successfully in India from the 1860s, and quickly replaced Chinese tea in the home market. Sir Thomas Lipton even invested directly overseas, buying up tea plantations in Ceylon to ensure his supplies. Tea sweetened with cheap West Indian sugar rapidly became the most popular drink for the poorest classes of British society. In the 1880s refrigerated ships brought meat and dairy produce from Australia and New Zealand; by the 1900s bananas and pineapples were a common sight in the shops. All in all, food for mass consumption made up around a third of Britain's imports during the latter half of the nineteenth century.

Much of the imported food came from the Empire: sago from the Malayan sago-palm and tapioca from the tropical cassava root became the detested staples of nursery diets, while sauces from Indian curry powders usefully flavoured Victorian leftovers. It was a two-way process: British products accompanied the imperial advance into those regions where local food and drink were not trusted, especially in Africa. Camp coffee essence could provide an ingenious touch of home comfort even in the jungle, while whisky was medicinal and safer than local water, if excuses needed to be found.

Religious and philanthropic teetotal campaigns aimed at the British poor had contributed to the success of the Quaker Fry and Cadbury families in manufacturing 'drinking chocolate'. By the early twentieth century the widely available cocoa supplies from West Africa had revolutionized the confectionery industry, creating such a national passion for sweets and chocolate that the British are now said to be among the sweetest-toothed nations in the world.

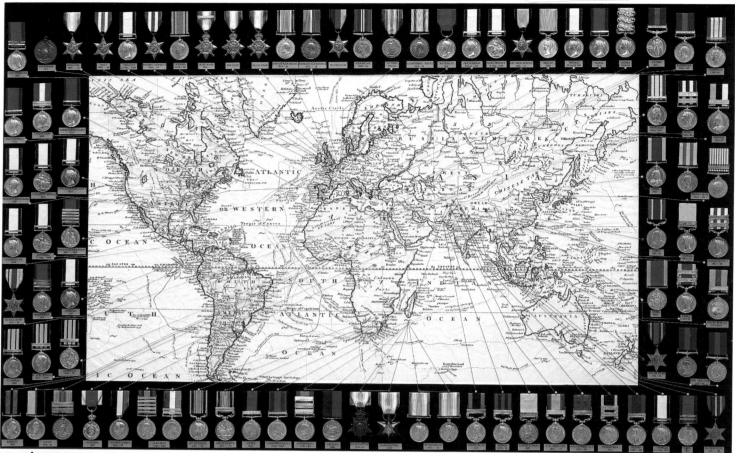

A map of British battles and medals from 1758, prepared by Spink and Son.

Hobson, whose classic account of the economic motivation for imperial expansion, *Imperialism: A Study*, was first published in 1902. Hobson suggested that since the 1870s colonies had been acquired merely to satisfy the greed of capitalists and in fact brought few advantages: 'If, contemplating the enormous expenditure on armaments, the ruinous wars, the diplomatic audacity or knavery by which modern governments seek to extend their territorial powers, we put the plain, practical question, *Cui bono?* The first and most obvious answer is, The Investor'. The interests of such investors, Hobson argued, were at odds with the needs of the country as a whole. Britain did not need her Empire, and the cost of acquiring and maintaining it would impede her progress to true greatness. This viewpoint served as a corrective to the fervour of imperial enthusiasts such as Seeley. Yet the link between imperial expansion and immediate economic advantage was often tenuous, particularly in those parts of Africa acquired since the 1870s. The process and the pay-off were much more complicated than Hobson acknowledged.

The White Man's Burden
Whatever the costs or benefits of acquiring the Empire, maintaining and administering it brought other problems. Britain's colonies in Canada, South Africa and the Antipodes had achieved self-government by the 1870s, but few in London thought that the more recent acquisitions could follow them in this course. The early Victorian notion of assimilation – of a progressive alliance between British 'civilization' and enlightened natives, cemented by free trade, representative institutions and a Utilitarian philosophy – had faded in the light of experience. In India, for example, the Raj had regressed into paternalism, convinced that it alone knew the true wishes of the 'voiceless millions'. Lord Cromer, who served in both India and Egypt argued, 'Free institutions in the full sense of the term must for generations to come be wholly unsuitable'; indeed, he went

on to say, 'It will probably never be possible to make a Western silk purse out of an Eastern sow's ear.'

The colonial territories acquired since 1870 in Africa, Asia and the Pacific were ruled by a new system of 'indirect rule': the traditional authorities retained power – under close supervision from British advisers – avoiding direct bureaucratic administration by expatriates. Under the inspiration of Lord Lugard, this approach was refined during the 1900s in Nigeria and local chiefs were confirmed as 'dependent rulers'. Lugard saw indirect rule as one road to effective political independence. 'Liberty and self-government', he claimed, 'can best be secured to the native population by leaving them free to manage their own affairs through their own rulers'. Such an approach held other advantages for the imperial power, including support from the established power structure in the region, the legitimization of colonial rule, the encouragement of conservative policies and cheap government. The success of the policy in Nigeria caused it to be adapted for use in many other British colonies.

In 1914 the British Empire was larger than ever before. Imperialism had become a global phenomenon that was endorsed by expansionary powers in every continent. The tide of conquest was, however, to recede almost as quickly as it had advanced. In 1898, at the height of the imperial endeavour, Rudyard Kipling composed *The White Man's Burden*, a poem which emphasized that conquest alone cannot capture the minds of subject peoples:

> By all ye cry or whisper
> By all ye leave or do,
> The silent, sullen peoples
> Shall weigh your Gods and you.

Imperialism, as Kipling realized, put the imperialists on trial. The collapse of Britain's Empire in the twentieth century had much to do with the way in which it had been acquired and consolidated in the nineteenth century, especially in the years between 1870 and 1914.

Ireland under the Union

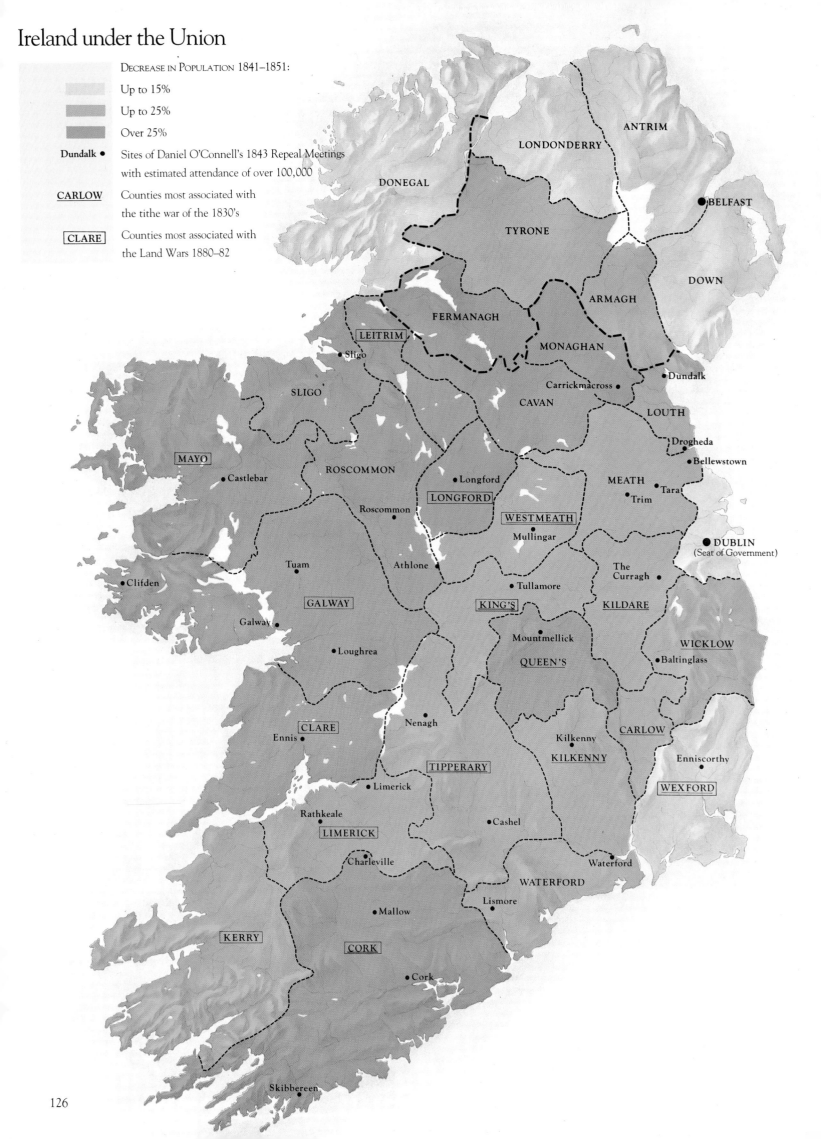

DECREASE IN POPULATION 1841–1851:

Up to 15%

Up to 25%

Over 25%

Dundalk ● Sites of Daniel O'Connell's 1843 Repeal Meetings with estimated attendance of over 100,000

CARLOW Counties most associated with the tithe war of the 1830's

CLARE Counties most associated with the Land Wars 1880–82

ANTRIM

LONDONDERRY

DONEGAL

● BELFAST

TYRONE

DOWN

FERMANAGH

ARMAGH

LEITRIM

MONAGHAN

● Sligo

SLIGO

CAVAN

Carrickmacross ●

● Dundalk

LOUTH

● Drogheda

MAYO

ROSCOMMON

● Longford

● Bellewstown

● Castlebar

LONGFORD

MEATH

● Tara

Roscommon ●

WESTMEATH

● Trim

Tuam ●

Mullingar ●

● DUBLIN
(Seat of Government)

● Clifden

Athlone ●

The Curragh ●

GALWAY

KING'S

KILDARE

● Tullamore

Galway ●

WICKLOW

Mountmellick ●

● Loughrea

QUEEN'S

● Baltinglass

CLARE

Nenagh ●

CARLOW

Ennis ●

Kilkenny ●

TIPPERARY

KILKENNY

Enniscorthy ●

● Limerick

WEXFORD

Rathkeale ●

● Cashel

LIMERICK

● Charleville

● Waterford

KERRY

● Mallow

Lismore ●

WATERFORD

CORK

● Cork

● Skibbereen

CHAPTER TWENTY

THE IRISH QUESTION TO 1914

◇

The success of the French Revolution sent shock waves through the governments of Europe, as they struggled to control popular agitation for reform. Ireland, that thorn in the British crown, was no exception. The United Irishmen clamoured for civil rights to be extended to Catholics, who were still disenfranchised. Wolfe Tone, the great Irish political thinker of the late eighteenth century, wrote of Ireland's political grievances at the time, and appealed for unity against English rule: 'We have no national government. We are ruled by Englishmen, and the servants of Englishmen, whose object is the interest of another country; whose instrument is corruption, and whose strength is the weakness of Ireland.'

Hopes of a secular republic vanished, however, when the 1798 rebellion degenerated into sectarian violence. William Pitt considered an Act of Union between Britain and Ireland as the best way of propping up the threatened Protestant ascendancy while accommodating a degree of civil liberty for the Irish Catholics. This was a new but scarcely radical departure from British policy; it simply demonstrated that Ireland, with its garrison of forty thousand troops, was little more than a subject territory. The problem intensified as Catholics began to demand admission to Parliament and to civil office. Pitt resigned in 1801 because he could not deliver Catholic emancipation, and in 1807 the 'Talents' ministry was ousted for the same reason. The Catholic issue was a deeply unpopular issue with the British public, and the House of Lords, George III and George IV all joined the general opposition to Catholic relief. Indeed, after 1812 the open system of government was operated, whereby ministers were only accepted for office if they agreed to shelve any action on the Catholic issue.

Daniel O'Connell: Champion of the Irish Peasantry

In 1823 Daniel O'Connell started a campaign that was to change all this. He could speak both English and Gaelic, and had attracted attention by defending dispossessed Irish peasants – who could speak only Gaelic – in the English-speaking magistrates' courts. He would munch sandwiches at the back of the

Daniel O'Connell (1775–1847) was elected M.P. for County Clare in 1828 and led the fight for Catholic emancipation.

courtroom and observe loudly 'That's not law!' or 'That's no longer law!' to the astounded judge, who was accustomed to steam-rollering through one conviction after another without being questioned. Declaring that he could drive a coach and horses through any British law, O'Connell soon became idolized as the champion of the Irish peasantry.

He formed the Catholic Association of Ireland in 1823, an organization which proved so popular that it was banned in 1825. The campaign for Catholic emancipation had begun, organized on a parish basis around the priest, with a-penny-a-month subscriptions to promote broad participation. Vast popular rallies were held, known as 'monster meetings' at which prophecies echoing the Gaelic concept of deliverance were declaimed. O'Connell stood in the Clare by-election in 1828, and his victory proved a *fait accompli*. In order to avert civil disorder boiling over in Ireland, the British Government was forced to grant Catholic emancipation in 1829, which allowed all Catholics to vote for the first time.

O'Connell tried to maintain the momentum of success by launching the Repeal Association. The objective was neither social revolution nor a complete break with Britain but 'one king, two legislatures'. Even this, though, was too radical for the British Parliament. But by the time the Repeal Campaign eventually petered out, O'Connell had fathered Irish democracy. The French novelist, Honoré de Balzac, declared that he had 'incarnated a whole nation'. O'Connell had combined the Gaelic cult of the chief with that of the political demagogue, and had associated Catholicism with Irish nationalism in such a way that they would never again be politically disconnected.

British Rule in the Early Nineteenth Century

It has always been necessary to administer Ireland differently from the rest of the United Kingdom: as befitted an internal colony, she retained a separate administration in Dublin Castle, headed by a viceroy. Civil rights were regularly suspended under emergency legislation, such as the 1833 Suppression of Disturbances Act against anti-tithe agitators. The Irish Constabulary was established in 1836 as a paramilitary force; with fourteen hundred barracks throughout the country and around ten thousand men stationed away from their home counties, it was directed by the Inspector General in Dublin.

Ireland was also the first part of the United Kingdom mapped by the Ordnance Survey, a process feared and resented by the Irish peasantry as it enabled landlords to levy new rents on hitherto undefined boundaries. Nevertheless Lord Salisbury declared imperviously: 'The most disagreeable part of the three kingdoms is Ireland, and therefore Ireland has a splendid map.'

The 1830s saw wide-ranging social and economic measures too. State education was instituted to correct Ireland's supposed ignorance and laziness – long before its introduction in England. A Board of Works was set up and a Poor Law enacted. Ireland, like India, became a social laboratory even for those political economists who generally opposed state intervention.

Irish Agriculture before the Famine

Unlike her neighbours, Ireland failed to industrialize. In fact, she had failed the necessary preliminary: the modernization of her agriculture. This was a tragic consequence of the divided society that had been created by English colonization. Protestant landlords with a Catholic tenancy could not modernize their lands (by raising rents and evicting tenants) without risking revenge attacks by the rural peasant secret societies. Instead, revenues were maintained by permitting the subdivision of tenancies. This in turn encouraged an increased reliance on potatoes for subsistence.

Grinding poverty was the norm in the west of Ireland; indeed, the landless classes there were amongst the poorest in Europe. A schoolmaster sent a description of a destitute parish to the Lord Lieutenant: 'Their farms are so small that from four to ten farms can be harrowed in a day with one rake . . . many families cannot afford more than one meal in two days.'

Because of the plantation system in Ulster, however, the common Protestant cultural heritage of landlord and tenant enabled them to enjoy better relations. The land tenure known as 'the Ulster custom' prevented subdivision and resulted in a richer tenantry with greater purchasing power, facilitating in turn a degree of industrialization in the Dungannon–Lisburn–Newry triangle.

The prosperity of County Armagh was visible, it was said, 'even in the countenances of the dogs and cats'. While the industrial wealth of north-east Ulster increased, the rest of the country remained dependent on agriculture. Karl Marx observed in *Das Kapital*: 'Ireland is at present only an agricultural district of England, marked off by a wide channel from the country to which it yields corn, wool, cattle, industrial and military recruits.'

The Irish Famine

In the middle of the eighteenth century Ireland had a population of two and a half million; by the mid-nineteenth century, this figure had risen to nine million, of which three million people existed almost entirely on potatoes and buttermilk. As early as 1805, the travel-writer John Barrow had warned of the disaster inherent in this dependence on the potato crop: 'The great advantage of a potato crop is the certainty of its success. Were a general failure of this root to take place, as sometimes happens to crops of rice, Ireland, in its present state, would experience all the horrors that attend a famine in some provinces of China.'

No one could have foreseen, however, the advance of *Phytophthora infestans*, a blight which turned a luxuriant field of potato plants into rotting slime almost overnight. Between 1845 and 1851 the crop failed year after year. Many simply starved to death but many more died of typhus, relapsing fever, dropsy and cholera – the diseases that prey upon the starving. The poorest regions of the west and south-west were the hardest hit. As Marx observed, 'it killed poor devils only.'

Robert Peel's Conservative Government did recognize the scale of the disaster in its early days, and a relief commission organized food depots. Peel's personal experiences of earlier food shortages in Ireland had affected him deeply: 'Good God, are you to sit in cabinet, and consider and calculate how much diarrhoea, and bloody flux, and dysentery, a people can bear before it becomes necessary for you to provide them with food?'

This, unfortunately, was just what did happen after Peel's Government fell in 1846. The Whig administration in London believed in an adherence to the rights of property and the laws of

Engravings in the Illustrated London News attempted to convey the tragedy of the famine.

SEARCHING FOR POTATOES IN A STUBBLE FIELD.

supply and demand with almost religious conviction. The Whigs were more inclined to put their faith in local responsibility, private charity and free enterprise. Firstly, they adopted a scheme of public works for able-bodied men, which did little to aid the sick and dying; this broke down when local ratepayers refused or were unable to foot the bill any longer. After two years of famine it was decided that outdoor relief would be supplied; by August 1847, three million people were receiving soup-kitchen rations. Although this was the best relief measure, it soon gave way to an amended Poor Law. This included the infamous Gregory Clause which removed any entitlement to relief from those who possessed more than a quarter of an acre of land. Those lucky enough to be admitted to a workhouse faced penal discipline, overcrowding and disease.

By 1849 compassion fatigue was setting in and the Government declared the famine to be officially over, even though it continued unabated into 1850 and 1851. The State had spent £7 million on relief during the famine – a small sum in comparison with the £20 million granted in compensation to the West Indian slave-owners at about the same time. Over one million people had been killed by hunger and disease. Another one and a half million emigrated. The decline of the Irish language was sealed by the death and dispersal of the peasantry. The villagers of Lough Gur remembered: 'Sport and pastimes disappeared. Poetry, music and dancing stopped. They lost and forgot them all and when times improved in other respects, these things never returned as they had been. The famine killed everything.'

The Fenians

The tragedy of the Irish famine focused national feeling. In 1858 the Irish Republican Brotherhood (IRB) was founded – the Fenians. Inspired by a romantic nationalism in naming themselves after the *Fianna*, the warrior band of the legendary hero

Finn Mac Cool, their aim was to rid Ireland of English rule by force. The IRB was organized as a cross between the revolutionary cells of Europe and the oath-bound secret societies of rural Ireland. Most of its members were Catholics from the lower-middle and skilled working classes but the anglophobic emigrant communities in Britain and the United States fostered many more. The American dimension was important because it enabled the Fenians to organize and raise funds in areas outside British control. The IRB also began to penetrate the British Army, swearing in large numbers of troops in Irish regiments, but this conspiracy was discovered and suppressed in 1865. When the rebellion did come in 1867, it proved abortive, with insurgent activity confined largely to parts of Munster. It was outside Ireland that the most dramatic events took place. In North America the Fenians launched three attacks on Canada from the safety of the United States; in Manchester the shooting of a policeman led to the execution (and thereby political martyrdom) of three Fenians. An explosion at Clerkenwell Prison, caused by the Fenians, resulted in a further fifteen deaths. The novelty of these events at that time projected the 'Irish Question' firmly into the minds of the British public.

Gladstone and the Land Wars

The British Prime Minister, William Gladstone, capitalized on this swelling of public opinion and put the Irish Question at the top of his political agenda. He was quite genuinely moved by the plight of a country which had been so mismanaged by Britain over the centuries: 'To this great country the state of Ireland after seven hundred years of our tutelage is, in my opinion as long as it continues, an intolerable disgrace and a danger so absolutely transcending all others that I call it the only real danger of the Noble Empire of the Queen.'

In 1869 Gladstone disestablished the Church of Ireland, thereby taking the fire out of the religious issue. The *Annual Register* called it 'the most remarkable legislative achievement of modern times'. Another long-running grievance was the semi-feudal organization of land in Ireland.

In the late 1860s Gladstone framed the first of a series of Land Bills, whereby the ownership of a great deal of arable and grazing land would eventually be transferred from the landlords to the tenant farmers, who would pay yearly annuities to the government for this purchase. By the time the Bill was enacted in 1870 it had been considerably watered down by Parliament. Nevertheless, Gladstone felt that he was undoing the worst aspects of the English conquest of Ireland by returning the land to the people.

The Land War of 1879–82 brought matters to a head. The spectre of famine hovered over the country once again after three years of poor potato crops. Rent arrears had led to evictions and subsequently to 'agrarian outrages' in retaliation. The peasantry organized themselves into the Land League.

The unrest was exploited by the constitutionalist Charles Stewart Parnell and by two Fenians, Michael Davitt and John Devoy. Parnell was an aristocratic Protestant landlord who detested English rule in Ireland and quickly acquired a position of national leadership. He came to a tacit agreement with the Fenians, who agreed to let him try to achieve the much sought-after radical reforms via a parliamentary route.

Under the presidency of Parnell, the Land League adopted a system of ostracism as its weapon – boycotting, as it came to be called. Captain Boycott, the agent of Lord Erne in County Mayo, was the most famous victim; having evicted families from Lord Erne's lands, he was refused all co-operation from the tenantry. No one would buy from him or sell to him, let alone speak to him, and the harvest was in danger of spoiling because no tenant would touch it. Eventually Ulster loyalists were brought down to Mayo under armed guard to take in the harvest, but the cost was ruinous and Boycott fled the country to England. Other Land League tactics included attacking landlords, their livestock and their agents, and repossessing holdings.

In Parliament, Parnell adopted the constitutional equivalent of the boycott – filibustering. Teams of Irish MPs held forth in debate at interminable length in order to obstruct the passage of unpopular bills. Nevertheless, the Protection of Persons and

THE IRISH DIASPORA

Eight million people left Ireland between 1780 and 1910, forced into exile by land shortage, as well as by the tragedy of the Great Famine. In times of fever and starvation the roads to the ports were thronged with emigrants, lured to the notorious 'coffin ships' by misleading posters which promised an easy passage and a golden land awaiting them. The fare from Belfast to Quebec in 1847 for a couple and four children was £6, a price often paid by landlords either out of philanthropy or in order to clear their lands of tenants. Even though the fare to New York at the time was £21, America was by far the most popular destination. American ships and crews were considered safer and superior to the British 'coffin ships' which were overcrowded, insanitary, and often ignored legal minimum provisions for water and food. Nevertheless, desperation to emigrate was such that thousands risked themselves on any vessel, as Cecil Woodham-Smith commented in *The Great Hunger*: 'There was nothing but joy at their escape from a doomed land.'

Before the transportation of convicts was abolished in 1853, 40,000 Irish prisoners had been sent to the Antipodes. Once they had served their prison terms, the Irish usually adapted well to the new countries where there were at last boundless acres for the taking. Although the Irish sense of identity seems to have been more one of unity against English repression than of any strong sense of nationhood, in the New Worlds they found themselves joined by language, religion and poverty against the hostility of established Anglo-Saxons.

A racist caricature emerged, typified by the words of the distinguished nineteenth-century historian Thomas Carlyle: 'There abides he, in his squalor and unreason, in his falsity and drunken violence, as the readymade nucleus of degradation and disorder.' In America reaction to such prejudice aided the development of what came to be the 'Tammany Hall' Irish political machine which sustained the Democratic Party in the cities.

'The Emigrants' by Erskine Nicol, 1864.

FIGHTING FOR JOHN BULL

Irish soldiers played a vital role in the creation and maintenance of the British Empire. The first half of the nineteenth century, when poverty and population pressure were at their most acute, saw the greatest numbers of Irishmen in uniform. In 1840, for example, the British Army contained 47,394 men from England, 13,388 from Scotland and 39,193 from Ireland, a highly disproportionate contribution. In the private army maintained by the East India Company, the Irish were even more heavily represented, making up half of the European contingent. After the abolition of the Company, six of the nine regiments which assumed the Queen's colours were assigned Irish territorial affiliations.

At the outbreak of the First World War, the Ulster Volunteer Force, a loyalist paramilitary group, offered the services of their best young men to the British Government, hoping thereby to underline their solidarity with Britain. The Government accepted the offer and on this basis formed the 36th Ulster Division. It was exposed to some of the worst fighting and suffered the heaviest casualties of any division in the British Army.

The demand for manpower at the front drove government propaganda to dignify the sacrifice of the nation's youth.

Property Act – which involved 955 internments, the appointment of special resident magistrates and the use of troops – was passed and further exacerbated the situation.

Gladstone followed this act of coercion with a second Land Act, which granted the long-awaited 'three Fs' – free sale, fixity of tenure and fair rents – as well as establishing the Land Commission. This provided no solution, however, to the rent arrears problem which had originally caused the spate of evictions; eventually the Government was forced to pay £800,000 to cover the arrears. Only then did the tenant farmers bring the land agitation to an end.

Parnell and the Liberals

Under the extended British franchise of 1885, the Land League (revived under the new title of the National League) returned eighty-five Home Rule MPs for Ireland. Parnell's highly disciplined party now held the balance of power. Gladstone was anxious to remove the disruptive MPs from the House of Commons. He wanted to devolve powers to Ireland in a way that would still, while being compatible with the security of Britain and her imperial dignity, fall far short of complete independence. His Home Rule Bill proposed an Irish Parliament responsible for Irish domestic affairs but subordinate to Westminster in imperial matters. The conservative Liberals (under the aristocratic Lord Hartington) and the radical Liberals (under Joseph Chamberlain) voted against the Bill. In this way, the 'Irish Question' facilitated a realignment of the right in British politics with Conservatives and Liberal dissidents committed to maintaining the Union. Gladstone had been stopped in his tracks by the 'New Imperialism'. Parnell, maintaining his alliance with the Liberal party, was eventually compromised when the scandal of his relationship with Kitty O'Shea, who was married to one of his party members, reached the divorce courts in 1890. Both Gladstone and the Catholic Church disassociated themselves from the Land League's president and he died in disgrace the following year.

Parnell's achievement had been considerable. He had run the prototype of the modern Irish political party, combining a well-oiled electoral machine with the complete devotion of his followers. The Home Rule crisis had also brought out the intransigence of Ulster Protestants. Both Gladstone and Parnell had overlooked Ulster. One English observer described the Ulster stance: 'Protestant Ulster is incomparably ahead of the rest of Ireland in strength, wealth, prosperity, respect for law and love of personal independence. . . . Rightly or wrongly the northern Protestants believe that to allow Ulster to be taxed and administered by a Dublin Parliament would be to deliver it over to ruin.'

In the summer of 1886 there were three months of sectarian rioting in Belfast, which left 32 dead and 371 injured. At the July general election, the Conservative Lord Randolph Churchill, deciding that 'now is the time to play the Orange card', wooed the Ulster Protestants with the slogan 'Ulster will fight, Ulster will be right.' But any such alliance was conditional, and the Ulster Unionists developed as a distinct group within the Conservative Party.

Heavy Punishments and Light Railways

The Conservatives tried to 'kill Home Rule by kindness'. Arthur Balfour, the energetic Chief Secretary for Ireland, defined Irish nationalism as having been 'born in the peasant's cot, where men forgive if the belly gain'. He backed land purchase schemes which would break up the big estates and turn the peasants into conservative owner-occupiers. Money was poured into backward rural areas, when it could have been more usefully invested elsewhere; in fact, cropspraying and higher farm prices brought more prosperity to the countryside than Balfour's schemes. Strong-arm tactics were employed to enforce the policy: in 1888, for instance, Balfour banned the National League and put twenty-one Parnellite MPs in jail. The national unrest continued: at the turn of the century, more 'agrarian outrages' were committed; more MPs were imprisoned; and Dublin itself became a proclaimed area. The mixture of coercion and reform was widely mocked as 'heavy punishments and light railways'.

The New Nationalism

Catholicism was now more important than ever before as a badge of nationalism. Balfour had not bargained for this 'New Nationalism' which turned to Irish folklore, customs and the Gaelic language to foster the political sense of separatism. At grass-roots level, the Gaelic Athletic Association spread the popularity of 'national' sports and acted as a front for the Fenians. Among the intelligentsia, the Gaelic League promoted the Irish language – a slogan of the period declared that 'a country without a language is a country without soil.'

By the end of the nineteenth century, the Union of Britain and Ireland was a hollow vessel. Victorian Britain could not comprehend the violence of Irish political life. Only Gladstone had been able to make the imaginative leap and recognize Irish nationalism.

CHAPTER TWENTY-ONE

THE BRITISH RAJ:
COLLABORATION AND CONFLICT

◇

By 1860 the façade of British rule in India was securely in place again. The Mutiny had been crushed, and the final abolition of the East India Company meant that British territories in South Asia were now formally governed by the British Crown. The Governor-General Lord Canning, who had weathered the Mutiny with such restraint that army officers had bitterly nicknamed him 'clemency Canning', now became the first Viceroy. The Court of Directors and the Board of Control were replaced by the India Office – a separate department of state headed by the Secretary of State for India, who was a British Cabinet minister responsible to Parliament.

The New Mood

As with many sweeping administrative reorganizations, there was a greater change in the superficial order of precedence than in actual practice. The East India Company had been a commercial fiction long before it was wound up, and many of its employees held the same posts under the Crown as they had under the Company. The Secretary of State was advised on Indian Affairs by the Council of India, a group of 'old India hands' who effectively replaced the East India Company's Court of Directors.

What had changed more profoundly was the mood of the 1860s; the British could never quite relax and trust the Indians in the same way as they had before the Mutiny. Although as Viceroy Lord Canning held the pinnacle of Indian governance, his power was always hedged by London's suspicion and parsimony. His subordinates often hid their entrenched interests behind inertia, poor communications and local politics. As the Queen's representative, the hapless Canning earned the new nickname of 'the Great Ornamental', and his wishes were obstructed at almost every turn. Back in London, Parliament took an occasional interest in Indian affairs and could even be whipped up to near-hysteria on the odd occasion by a whiff of local government corruption or by the threat of invasion. On the whole, however, India never became a real issue in domestic politics to rival the dilemmas of Ireland or Egypt.

The years between the suppression of the Mutiny and the outbreak of the First World War saw the full incorporation of South-East Asia into the British imperial system. It was during this period that India became Britain's 'oriental barrack' and the largest single purchaser of British exports. It was also during this time that India acquired a considerable amount of British investment and played a large part in sustaining London as a currency centre and an earner of invisible income.

In the domestic economy, Indian peasants and British planters grew more cash crops to sell in the international market – cotton in Bombay, jute in Bengal, wheat in the Punjab, tea in Assam, oil-seeds in Madras – while native and expatriate entrepreneurs invested in processing and service industries. Although some of the profits of these enterprises did remain in India, average earnings and standards of living remained low. Prosperity was still largely dependent on a good monsoon, and unfortunately the rains were erratic. Famine and widespread death by starvation were frequent catastrophes.

The late nineteenth century also saw the refinement of the distinctly colonial Anglo-Indian world that we now associate with 'the Raj'. Once the Suez Canal was opened, there were regular P&O steamship sailings to India. A basic understanding of tropical hygiene also began to permeate the family medical encyclopedias, and it became possible at last for a semi-anglicized form of family life to be led. It was a world of clubs and hill stations, and of a Victorian upper-middle-class gentility that had been transposed to the strange beauty and rawness of a country which most would never understand, but which would haunt them all into old age.

An English social structure began to impose itself determinedly on the expatriate community, which had previously integrated itself fairly tolerantly with the local Indians. Kipling described some of the preoccupations of the new arrivals in his short story *Cupid's Arrows*: 'When a man is a Commissioner and a bachelor, and has the right of wearing open-work jam-tart jewels in gold and enamel on his clothes, and of going through a door before everyone except a Member of Council, a Lieutenant-Governor, or a Viceroy, he is worth marrying. At least, that is what ladies say . . .'

Yet commissioners, even marriageable ones, had to have a dominion over which to rule. Nostalgia for the romance of these vanished social complexities should not obscure the fact that India was an occupied territory of the British Empire. The problem that the British faced was how to secure their interests while engineering the co-operation, or at least acquiescence, of the bulk of their subjects.

The most popular solution was to strengthen the paternalistic and bureaucratic elements in the administration. It was an approach that appealed to the conservative-minded – to Tory politicians and ministers in Britain and to old India hands and established bureaucrats in India. Lord Lytton, Viceroy from 1876 to 1880, asserted with impervious confidence: 'We hold India as a conquered country, which must be governed in all essentials by the strong, unchallenged hand of the conquering power.' Men of this school saw themselves as enlightened paternalists, with a duty to 'protect and foster the peoples of India' – the 'voiceless millions' with 'neither education nor civilization', in the words of another Viceroy, Lord Dufferin.

A New Administration

A newly created Indian Civil Service (ICS) was to administer the heavy hand of paternal rule. The ICS was a meritocratic bureaucracy selected by competitive examination, set up in the 1850s as an astringent replacement for the corrupt patronage system of company rule. While the middle ranks were the preserve mainly of able and often intellectually frustrated Indians, the thousand or so top posts were filled by Britons. These men would have spent a year studying for the examinations (which were always held in Britain) and they were required

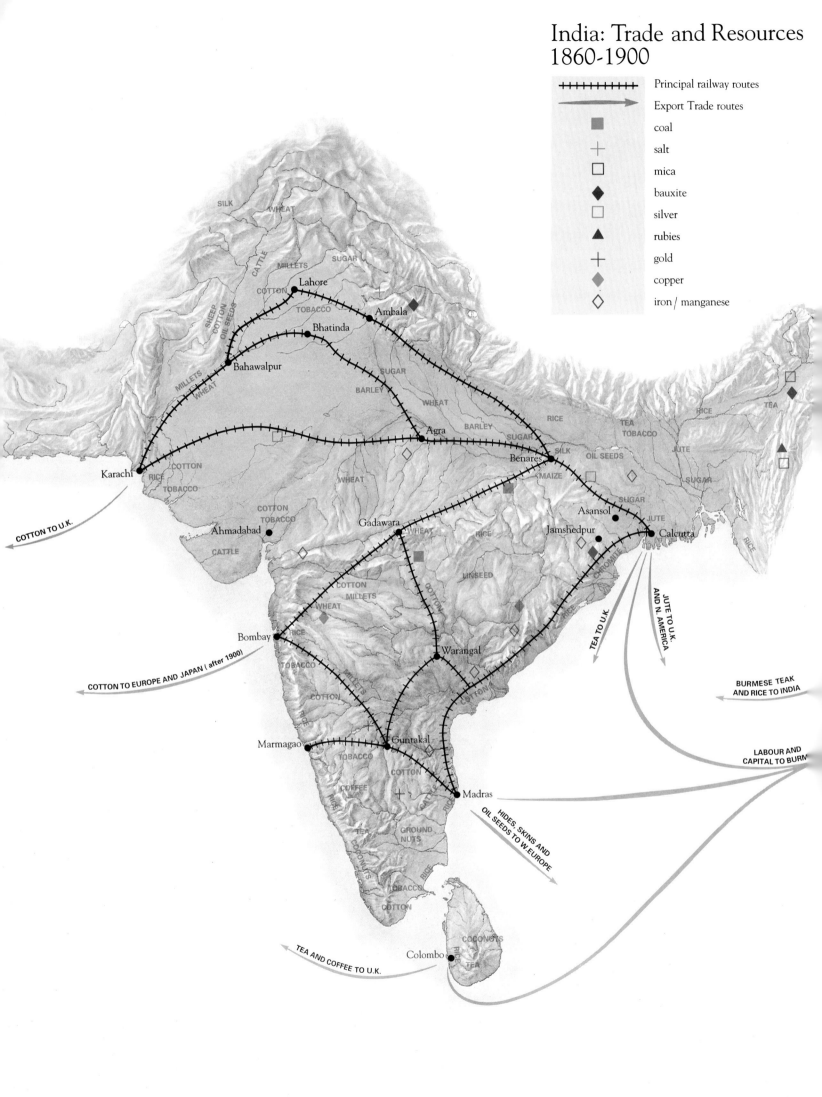

India: Trade and Resources 1860-1900

Legend:
- ┼┼┼┼┼ Principal railway routes
- → Export Trade routes
- ■ coal
- ╋ salt
- □ mica
- ◆ bauxite
- ◻ silver
- ▲ rubies
- ╋ gold
- ◆ copper
- ◇ iron / manganese

SILK
WHEAT
CATTLE
MILLETS
SUGAR
SHEEP
COTTON
OIL SEEDS
COTTON
TOBACCO
Lahore
Ambala
Bhatinda
Bahawalpur
MILLETS
WHEAT
SUGAR
BARLEY
WHEAT
BARLEY
SUGAR
RICE
TEA
TOBACCO
RICE
TEA
Agra
Benares
SILK
OIL SEEDS
JUTE
Karachi
RICE
COTTON
TOBACCO
WHEAT
MAIZE
SUGAR
JUTE
Asansol
SUGAR
COTTON
TOBACCO
Ahmadabad
CATTLE
Gadawara
WHEAT
RICE
Jamshedpur
Calcutta
CHROMITE
RICE
COTTON
MILLETS
WHEAT
LINSEED
COTTON
Bombay
RICE
TOBACCO
COTTON
MILLETS
Warangal
COTTON
TEA TO U.K.
JUTE TO U.K. AND N. AMERICA
BURMESE TEAK AND RICE TO INDIA
Marmagao
TOBACCO
COTTON
Guntakal
COFFEE
RICE
GROUND NUTS
CATTLE
RICE
Madras
LABOUR AND CAPITAL TO BURM
HIDES, SKINS AND OIL SEEDS TO W. EUROPE
TEA
COCONUTS
TOBACCO
COTTON
COCONUTS
RICE
Colombo
TEA
TEA AND COFFEE TO U.K.
COTTON TO U.K.
COTTON TO EUROPE AND JAPAN (after 1900)

Lord Mayo (Viceroy, 1869–1872) and his funeral in Calcutta. Mayo's assassination by a Muslim zealot foreshadowed the new tensions faced by the Queen's Indian Empire.

to show the all-round leadership qualities and 'gifted amateurism' considered to be prerequisites for future rulers of colonial subjects. Such conditions inevitably militated against Indian applicants, only a handful of whom were successful before 1914.

For all its amateur ethos, the ICS was probably the most professional, and certainly the longest-lasting, of all the British colonial bureaucracies. It had a staggering ability to generate facts and figures about the country it ruled. In the 1890s, before Lord Curzon slimmed down the output, over eighteen thousand pages of official statistics were published annually. Despite this documentary tide, not much was ever really accomplished. A detailed knowledge and true understanding of the indigenous population could not be obtained by completing statistical returns and filing memoranda. To some colonial civil servants, such as Sir Walter Lawrence, it seemed that the work demanded almost psychic powers: 'I had the illusion, wherever I was, that I was infallible and invulnerable in my dealings with Indians. How else could I have dealt with angry mobs, with cholera-stricken masses, and with processions of religious fanatics? It was not conceit, Heaven knows: it was . . . the illusion which is the very air of India. They expressed something of the idea when they called us the 'Heaven-born' . . . They, the millions, made

us believe we had a divine mission. We made them believe they were right.'

In reality, the 'Heaven-born' did not always live up to their name, and by the end of the century the appeal of the ICS as a career had become distinctly limited, with India seen as getting only the 'leavings' of the Home Civil Service. Official concern about the poor calibre of the new British recruits, their 'lack of manners, decline in social status, and want of consideration for Indians' was now so marked that the Royal Commission on the Public Services in India made ponderous note of the frequency of the complaints.

The Rise of Indian Nationalism

Once the Mutiny had been crushed, subsequent armed insurrections were almost entirely local, apart from one rebellion in 1872 led by so-called Wahhabi Muslim reformers in which the Viceroy, Lord Mayo, was assassinated. These were rebellions inspired by small extremist groups and were not seen as indicative of any general social unrest. Yet, by the time Queen Victoria was declared Empress of India in 1876, her Indian subjects had adopted a new and more subtle form of disloyalty. The validity of British rule and colonial policy began to be

THE INDIAN RAILWAYS

The Indian railway system is often seen as one of the greatest achievements of Victorian India. The first line, which ran for twenty miles from Bombay to Thana, was opened in 1853; by 1906, when all the main trunk routes in use today had been built, there were almost thirty thousand miles of track.

Railways had a considerable impact on the Indian economy and on internal migration and social mobility. They aided famine relief, linked large parts of the interior country to the ports, and facilitated the movement of goods for domestic and foreign trade. But there were disadvantages as well. Many of the lines were built for strategic, rather than economic reasons, and tended to stimulate the import–export trade rather than the internal economy.

The organization of the railway system brought problems of its own. Most of the track was built by an alliance of state and private capital, but under a number of different

arrangements. The first lines were of 'broad gauge' (66 in); later, metre-gauge track was laid for branch and feeder lines, and for some main lines as well. By the 1900s there were as

many as ninety-six different lines open to traffic, managed under one of ten different systems, and supervised by thirty-three separate railway administrations.

The Burma Railway extension: by 1890 the railway network extended over the entire subcontinent.

questioned in a disconcertingly similar way to the liberal nationalism that was sweeping through the *anciens régimes* of eastern and southern Europe.

British rule had offered the Indians limited scope to use the power of the Raj for their own ends. The British had brought European-style administration, law-courts, newspapers, businesses and public utilities to India, and employment in the lower levels at least was open to Indians. Education in English was the key to these opportunities and university graduates were at the forefront of the Indian invasion of government service and law. These men demanded more than mere employment. During the 1870s criticism of colonial policies intensified, especially of those policies thought to limit Indian aspirations in government. The educated élites of the major colonial cities claimed to speak for an Indian nation that had discovered itself through the same action of British rule that was now holding it in check. A newspaper editorial of the mid-1880s bemoaned the 'denationalization of the Indian people': 'With the loss of our country we have lost our national religion, our national science and philosophy, and our national traditions. It is not surprising that under such circumstances, the growth and progress of the Indian people as a nation should be in abeyance . . . in our present denationalized condition, we are neither fish nor flesh, neither Indian nor British.'

Nationalist sentiment was expressed in the founding of a number of political associations. Out of this activity emerged the Indian National Congress (INC), which met for the first time in Bombay in 1885. The INC was to become the vehicle for the mass nationalism that accompanied India's achievement of independence from Britain in 1947. At first, however, it was little more than a forum for annual debates, most active in the early days at its London branch, which lobbied Parliament. There was then a touching spirit of trust in the British sense of 'fair play', as one delegate argued at the inaugural meeting: 'All of us have the utmost faith and confidence in the justice and fairness of the English people and we have only to solicit an enquiry into the facts, being content to leave the issue in the hands of their great political leaders. . . .'

The most difficult task that faced the first leaders of the Congress was how to unite the geographically distinct regional élites that formed its basic support. Educated Indians in Bengal, Bombay, Madras and elsewhere had some concerns in common, but were also involved with local issues that had little universal appeal. This threatened the unity of the Congress. The British found it easy to ridicule the early nationalist leaders, caricaturing them as *Babus* (clerks) and dismissing them as self-serving representatives of narrow, sectional interests.

It was true that early active support for the INC stemmed from a limited base, but there was a genuine idealism for social reform and economic progress which would improve the lot of all Indians.

Leading figures began to emerge from the ranks of the INC: men such as Dadabhai Naoroji (who became the first black MP at Westminster in 1892), R.C. Dutt and M.G. Ranade. They devised a searching socio-economic critique of the material and spiritual poverty in India, demonstrating that colonialism could never solve the problems of growth and development that it had helped to create. They argued that British rule led to a 'drain of wealth' from India, which made the cost of the imperial connection too high to bear.

RITUALS OF EMPIRE

Durbars were traditional court rituals of Mughal India, which the British revived in order to express dominance over their colonial subjects. In 1876, 1903 and 1911 durbars were held to mark the accession of Victoria, Edward VII and George V to the imperial title. The ceremonies were designed to gratify Victorian notions of Gothic chivalry and to bind the colonial aristocracy to its monarch. All three imperial durbars took place on a specially selected site north of Delhi, the old Mughal capital. Victoria and Edward did not attend in person, but the main feature of the 1911 durbar was the ceremony in which George V crowned himself Emperor of India.

The 1903 durbar symbolized Edwardian ideas about India, and, in particular, about Lord Curzon's proconsular style. Curzon personally spent six months organizing the programme down to the last detail. The key to the event was the participation of the Indian princes who, for the first time, offered direct acts of homage to their new Emperor. The emotional high point was the assembly of Mutiny veterans of all races, who marched around the parade ground to the strains of 'See the Conquering Hero' and 'Auld Lang Syne'. As Curzon recorded, it was a spectacle that 'brought tears to the eyes of strong men and a choking in every throat'.

The Imperial Durbar of 1903, held in honour of Edward VII.

This clerihew, written at Oxford, dogged Curzon all his life:
'My name is George Nathaniel Curzon
I am a most superior person
My cheeks are pink, my hair is sleek
I dine at Blenheim once a week.'

The Lieutenant General of the Punjab in the splendid company of his tea-time guests: five maharajas, two rajas and one nawab.

Officers of the 93rd Highlanders posing with their Indian game trophies in the 1860s.

Political Developments within India

The intellectual vitality and moral fervour of the INC leaders were not enough to win them political success. Their message embraced the subcontinent, but their audience remained small. An additional problem was that the process of securing reforms tended to be divisive; when reforms actually came, they were often designed to diffuse protest and to draw new splinter groups into politics, thereby nullifying the influence of the established nationalists. These self-defined interest groups, bound together by caste status, language, religion or regional identity, all pressed their claims for special treatment. The leaders of such movements used cultural symbols to foster emotional solidarity and political awareness that often identified Indian enemies as well as British ones. This type of sectarian and socially regressive politics caused terrorist movements to develop in Bengal and inspired violent mass campaigns in defence of Hindu symbols and customs in western and northern India. Those who felt threatened mobilized in turn and some, especially the Muslims, appealed to the British for help. The founding of the All-India Muslim League in 1906 to press Muslim claims upon the government was the culmination of a long campaign to counter the threat of social and political change.

It was for these reasons that the Congress leaders who aimed for a nationwide appeal always found that action was much more difficult than words. There was some truth in the jibe that, by the 1900s, the INC was little more than a trades union for the educated élite. There was widespread dissatisfaction with the established leadership, and nationalist leaders with greater charisma in Maharastra and Bengal agitated for radical changes in tactics and programme. In 1907 the Congress split into mutually hostile 'moderate' and 'extremist' wings after an acrimonious meeting at Surat. As a consequence, the organization was gravely weakened.

Action, not Words

The political problems of the Raj were not just those of intellectual debate with liberal nationalists. British rule in India depended on raising large amounts of revenue. For various reasons – including currency depreciation, new administrative standards and external expansion – the cost of administering India was rising rapidly. In order to extend taxation, it was necessary to increase local representation, which meant that Indians had to be allowed into government. This was not seen as a threat to British control. Evelyn Baring, Finance Minister of the Government of India, declared his reasons for supporting the Government of India Resolution on Local Self-Government in

1882: 'We shall not subvert the British Empire by allowing the Bengali Baboo to discuss his own schools and drains. Rather shall we afford him a safety valve if we can turn his attention to such innocent subjects.'

But progress was slow. By the 1880s Indian representatives had been admitted to a modicum of power on municipal councils and, in 1909, elected Indians made up a majority in the provincial legislatures, although there was no executive power attached to these positions. These reforms were aimed at a much broader spectrum of opinion than that represented by the INC.

Divide and Rule

At Queen Victoria's death in 1901, the foundations of British rule seemed as firm as when the Queen had been declared Empress of India a quarter of a century before. The Viceroy during this period, Lord Curzon, carried on the paternalist tradition; he believed it the duty of the Raj to protect the 'voiceless millions' whose life was one of 'mute penury and toil'. Yet, over the previous twenty-five years, the means to this paternalistic end had changed. It was now necessary to buttress the traditional bureaucratic administration and scrupulous racial fairness by active alliances with Indian supporters. Curzon and his successor, Lord Minto, saw the Indian princes, the rural propertied classes and the Muslims as British rule's natural allies against Hindu militants and liberal intellectuals.

By the first decade of the twentieth century, the driving force of Indian political activity seemed increasingly sectarian. The British, who had always denied the existence of an Indian nation, now set out to fulfil their own prophecies. Innumerable local particularisms were stressed and potentially loyal minorities (or majorities) were fostered in the name of impartiality. In 1905 the most nationalistic of the Indian provinces, Bengal, was partitioned into two lesser provinces, one mainly Muslim and the other mainly Hindu. In the Provincial Legislative Councils set up by the Morley–Minto reforms of 1909, reserved seats and special constituencies were created for Muslims, landlords and other interest groups. Minto was deaf both to Indian protest and unease in Westminster, writing staunchly back to London: 'If we are weak enough to yield to their clamour now, we shall not be able to dismember or reduce Bengal again, and you will be cementing a force already formidable and certain to be of increasing trouble.'

It was the classic imperialist tactic of 'divide and rule' in action, and the temptation to adopt it must have been overwhelming. To the Edwardian rulers of India, however, it seemed that it was the ruled who were clamouring for division.

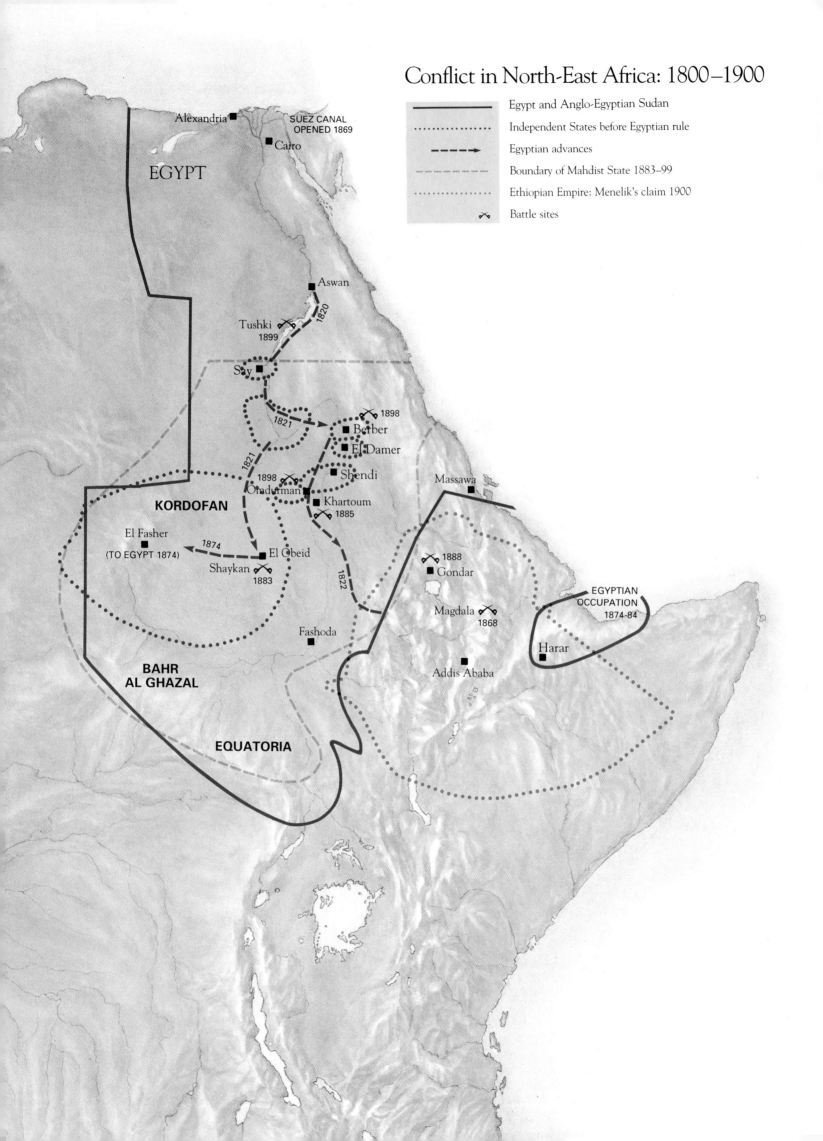

Conflict in North-East Africa: 1800–1900

Egypt and Anglo-Egyptian Sudan
Independent States before Egyptian rule
Egyptian advances
Boundary of Mahdist State 1883–99
Ethiopian Empire: Menelik's claim 1900
Battle sites

Alexandria
SUEZ CANAL
OPENED 1869
Cairo

EGYPT

Aswan
Tushki
1899
1820

Say

1821
Berber
1898
El Damer
1821
Shendi
1898
1821
Omdurman
Khartoum
1885
Massawa

KORDOFAN

El Fasher
(TO EGYPT 1874)
1874
El Obeid
Shaykan
1883
1822

1888
Gondar

EGYPTIAN
OCCUPATION
1874–84

Magdala
1868

Fashoda

Harar

BAHR
AL GHAZAL

Addis Ababa

EQUATORIA

CHAPTER TWENTY-TWO

THE EMPIRE ON THE NILE

◇

The countries of the eastern Mediterranean were the centre of much political intrigue during the nineteenth century. France and Britain competed on the south-eastern shore to secure command of the short route to the East, which ran overland from Alexandria to Suez. Russia pressed for easier access to the Mediterranean from the north, claiming rights of passage to the world's oceans while intensifying British anxieties that St Petersburg was, in reality, more interested in threatening India.

The eastern Mediterranean had been dominated by the Ottoman Turks since the sixteenth century and, in 1800, their empire stretched from Belgrade to Baghdad and from Algiers to Armenia. The Sultan's North African provinces guarded a trade network that brought slaves from south of the Sahara, coffee from the Yemen and Ethiopia, and grain and textiles from Egypt. However, by the eighteenth century, Ottoman rule had long been shaky and the Sultan's provinces had become a 'confederation of anarchies'. The competing powers now had to decide on how to resolve the confusion. Britain hoped that Ottoman rule could be revived, whereas France wanted the dissolution of the empire so that the independent countries could be brought under western sway.

The French made the first move in 1798 when they sought to defend their Revolution by invading Egypt and threatening the British route to India. Napoleon's expedition was a military disaster. His fate taught Europe two lessons: that Egypt's occupiers must expect resistance and that nothing could be achieved without the Sultan's sanction, for it was an Anglo-Turkish force that evicted the French in 1801. Lessons were also learned by the Muslims, who realized that they needed to adopt the western style in military and political matters to remain free from direct European control. Muhammad Ali, 'founder of modern Egypt' and the governor of the province from 1805 to 1848, tried to apply this lesson. The problems that he and his successors encountered in modernizing their country were complicated to an almost insoluble degree by the interference and mutual jealousies of the great powers.

An Attempt at Modernization

Muhammad Ali came to Egypt from Albania as an officer in the Turkish army of reoccupation; he then fought his rivals to gain the governorship and set about founding an independent kingdom. Quashing all intermediary levels of power between village and state, he abolished tax-farming, forced peasants to sell him cotton for a pittance and replaced craft guilds with state factories. He used the revenue derived from this coercion to support a huge, conscripted army. To further the national cause, the country's French-trained officer corps, still largely of Turkish origin, began to promote the sons of Egyptian landowners. With these changes, Muhammad Ali transformed Egypt, as Josiah Condor pointed out in his travelogue on the Near East published in 1827: 'During the sixteen years of his energetic administration, a mutinous soldiery has been transformed into a regular army; the revenue has been prodigiously increased; new articles

The Mamelukes' submission to Napoleon following his invasion of 1798 signalled Egypt's incorporation into the western sphere of influence.

of produce have been raised; trade has been carried on to an extent previously unknown; several important public works have been undertaken and executed, and the whole country from Alexandria to Syene has been rendered perfectly safe for the European traveller.'

Once the country was in good order, Egypt took the offensive. Crushing rebellions in some of the other Ottoman provinces while undermining the Sultan's control of others, Ali pressed for Egyptian independence. Whitehall, however, did not consider such a change in the status quo to be in Britain's interest. Egypt's secession might bring about the final collapse of the Ottoman Empire, removing a very useful buffer between the British and the Russians. Egyptian independence also seemed likely to reinstate Muhammad Ali's friends, the French, in power in Cairo.

Under the banner of free trade, which Britain was able to impose on the Sultan as the price of continued friendship, the commercial penetration of Egypt by Europeans subverted Muhammad Ali's modernization drive. Thus, by the 1860s the pernicious private interests that Ali had sought to remove from the economy had become re-established. Protected by consular courts, Europeans controlled much of Egypt's trade. European bankers lent the capital which the state could no longer raise in taxes, since the land had reverted to politically privileged owners – a fifth of Egypt's cultivated area being in the royal domain.

On the other hand, cotton exports had quadrupled in price and doubled in quantity in the early 1860s as a consequence of the disruption of the trade caused by the American Civil War. France had managed to retain a toehold in the country, despite Anglo-Turkish opposition, by excavating the Suez Canal, which opened in 1869. By the early 1870s, Egypt had a railway and telegraph network built to European standards, and an embryo parliament in the unrepresentative and entirely consultative council of notables. Modernization seemed well under way and independence in sight. Yet by the end of 1882, in an extraordinary turnabout, Egypt was under British occupation.

The Egyptian Collapse

The growing enfeeblement of the Ottomans forced Britain to concede that, by the late 1870s, maintaining a dominant influence in Istanbul no longer guaranteed the exclusion of European rivals from the Near East. Each province would have to be dealt with on a case-by-case basis. In 1878 Britain took Cyprus and let the French know that, if they wished, they could have Tunis – an option that was exercised in 1881. Thus, the Anglo-French balance in the region was maintained. Egypt, however, was a more complicated question. As the former Foreign Secretary, Lord Salisbury, ponted out in 1881, Britain had three alternatives. She might, in his words, 'renounce – or monopolize – or share. Renouncing would have been to place the French across our road to India. Monopolizing would have been very near the risk of war. So we resolved to share.' But sharing required a watchful eye now that the pretence of Ottoman suzerainty had worn so thin; Egypt had to be watched in Cairo, not from Istanbul.

Egypt in the meantime had gone bankrupt. The causes were clear and not untypical of several nineteenth-century economies. Autocratic governments which pursued modernization frequently outdistanced their ability to tax agrarian economies which lay under powerful private ownership. This is exactly what Stephen Cave, a junior member of Disraeli's Government, reported in 1875 after a fact-finding mission: 'The Khedive has evidently attempted to carry out with a limited revenue in the course of a few years works which ought to spread over a far longer period and which would tax the resources of much richer exchequers.' Moreover, while a country's production was expanding fast it was particularly vulnerable to external trade fluctuation. When the bottom fell out of the cotton market as the South resumed exporting after the end of the American Civil War, Egypt lost out. The greed of Egypt's 'friends' did not help either. The French off-loaded most of the costs of constructing the Suez Canal on to the Khedive, Ali's grandson Ismail, who ruled the country. To meet that debt, he had to sell his 44 per cent of the company's shares to the British. Bankers of all nations extorted high commissions. Thus, out of her £100 million foreign debt in 1875, Egypt had only seen £68 million, although she was charged interest on the full amount. Even nature conspired against the country, as an unusually low Nile in 1877 left the harvest shrivelled and tax revenues in a similar state.

The Khedive, who was obliged to agree to any conditions which would preserve his credit-worthiness, had to call in the receivers. An internationally recognized debt commission, with representatives from all creditor states, was assigned the revenues from a number of specified taxes. The British and the French

THE POLITICS OF SUEZ

While all mid-nineteenth-century British governments knew that India was the chief external source of Britain's prosperity, they resisted schemes to make passage easier along the short route between them. Britain had controlled the Cape route around Africa since 1806; it was long but it was secure. The Mediterranean alternative was considerably less appealing. To the north, the Mesopotamian route promised plain sailing at either end, from London to the Levant and from Basra to Bombay, but in the middle it involved a hair-raising ride overland through decaying Ottoman provinces and insurgent Arab chiefdoms. To the south, via Suez, the overland politics remained easy so long as Egypt was dependent on Turkey or at least not in thrall to France, but there was treacherous sailing down the Red Sea. Steam rewrote the laws of navigation. But it was not until the 1840s that iron hulls, screw propellers and high-pressure engines were combined to make steamships competitive with sail, and then only with a state subsidy for the carriage of mails. The Suez route, with a string of camels to tie the shipping lines together, could now cut the return-journey time between London and India from two years, subject to the monsoon, to three months, dictated by a timetable. The commercial arguments for a

canal became irresistible. The political nightmares remained: a canal would seal Egypt's independence; the Ottomans would collapse; the Russians would steam freely through the Bosphorus; and the French would have their thumb on Britain's new Indian windpipe. French engineers and diplomats had been busy in the half-century since Napoleon had had the route surveyed. When the freelance de Lesseps won a 99-year canal concession in 1854, which granted his company the land along its banks and around three-quarters of the total profits on 56 per cent of the share ownership, while the Egyptian government was saddled with 44 per cent of the investment in return for only about a quarter of the profit, he had two generations of French influence behind him. Construction started in 1859. It took ten years, using enormous numbers of forced peasant labourers until Anglo-Turkish protests on ostensibly humanitarian grounds obliged the company to invest in steam-powered excavators. Britain and Turkey came round to accept the canal only as it was completed. It was too late for the British royal family to be represented at the extravagant opening ceremonies, which turned into a French festival. The British press expressed a sense of humiliation: 'The Queen of England has opened the Holborn Viaduct,

The Khedive Ismail (viceroy 1863–79), who was bankrupted by the building of the Canal.

and the Empress of France is going to open the Suez Canal.' But political reverse was soon converted into commercial triumph; by 1880, three quarters of the canal's traffic was British-owned. Two years later the strategic logic of Empire put a largely French waterway into effectively British hands.

Port Said in the late nineteenth century, when it was the world's largest coal bunkering station.

assumed administrative control of the Egyptian treasury, a most unusual invasion of sovereignty. Banks were normally expected to make private arrangements for debt conversion with their foreign defaulters, with no more state support than a ministerial word in an ambassador's ear. However, unlike the nations of Latin America, Egypt had no protective Monroe doctrine to keep other powers at bay. Ironically, as their country was being auctioned off, the anger of the Egyptians at last gave them common cause.

Benjamin Disraeli (1804–81), purchased Suez Canal shares for Britain.

Egypt Finds its Voice

The foreigners did not interfere in finance alone. Two years after the country had been declared bankrupt, Ismail was forced to accept ministerial government. However, this was not the kind of representative régime which might have made heavy taxation easier for the people to stomach. The Prime Minister was a Christian Armenian, Nubar Pasha; the finance minister was English; and a Frenchman was in charge of public works. The Khedive had lost the autocratic powers of patronage but had gained no constitutional authority in return.

Local leaders took great offense at this intrusion. Landowners who were fearful of higher taxes, officials who were angered by the influx of expatriate advisors, Egyptian colonels who resented the retention of Turkish generals, and religious leaders were all drawn together in opposition. A few liberal intellectuals and a critical section of the press gave a nationalist voice to the traditional grumbles of displaced officials and disappointed favourites of the Khedive. However, when Ismail tried to assume the Egyptian mantle in 1879 by putting himself at the head of this opposition, the Anglo-French controllers wrapped themselves in the faded remnant of Ottoman suzerainty and persuaded the Sultan to depose the Khedive in favour of his son Taufiq.

The Europeans determined to exploit their initiative and, in return for some concessions on the country's debt, demanded more cuts in public spending. In response, Egyptian resistance boiled over and the régime was unable to enforce the economies that were demanded of it. Mutinous regiments took to the streets, led by Colonel 'Urabi, an Egyptian of rich peasant origin. His actions brought him great popular acclaim and on 3 October 1881 he harangued a huge crowd: 'The Khedive has called an Assembly based on the old ordinances of Ismail who, as you know, treated the Assembly like a pack of slaves. . . . henceforth the Parliament, made up of our own flesh and blood, will stand between us and Tyranny. Justice and the People will provide its strength.' But the politicians could only fight among themselves. Factions split between Turks and locals, the propertied and the salaried. Peasant unrest and Islamic fundamentalism caused further divisions. Some were frightened by popular enthusiasm while others grew bolder. Rather than become involved, France and Britain sat on their hands and waited. Neither wanted to imperil the balance of power between them.

The Intervention

Eventually, Britain and France had to act. To preserve the status quo, the French government under Gambetta persuaded the British to sign a joint note, which was delivered to the Egyptians in January 1882, threatening to intervene on behalf of the embattled Taufiq. Far from being intimidated, the Egyptian opposition under 'Urabi intensified its demands for a repatriation of financial control under more responsible government – without repudiating the debt. By this time, the Gambetta ministry had been replaced by more cautious politicians who were quite happy to stand by and let Britain take the strain. The British 'men on the spot' now made sure that Gladstone's government would have to act; the consul-general in Cairo insisted that xenophobia, not nationalism, was taking to the streets and threatening European lives and property. Thus, when an Anglo-French fleet appeared off Alexandria, the mob played right into his hands when they massacred 50 Europeans. Admiral Seymour ignored his instructions to dismantle the harbour denfences and bombarded them instead on 11 July, killing 1,000 Egyptians. The security of the Canal was now at risk from an incensed Egypt, which might well have turned to France in its hour of need. A force of more than 30,000 embarked from Britain in sixty steamers. They were joined by another 7,000 from India. After a thirty-five minute dawn attack on 'Urabi's main fortress at Tel-el-Kebir, they marched into Cairo in September 1882, intent on restoring the Khedive and external financial control.

The British Burden

Gladstone's critics called it a bondholder's war but such political sloganizing ignored the actual sequence of events. The cries of bondholders did not prompt the invasion. Nor was nationalist resistance sufficient to call down imperial repression; indeed, Anglo-French policy sometimes looked to constitutional reform to unite Egyptians and Europeans in an enlightened self-interest. Concern for the Canal was raised less for itself than to strengthen the hand of British officials who, after four years of agitation, wanted to conduct affairs in a more orderly manner. Their professional impatience was aligned to an unchallengeable confidence in the British way, the obverse of which was a disdain for people who were different; educated orientals, after all, preferred to speak French. Trade may have fuelled Her Majesty's ship of empire, but gentlemen were on the bridge.

Britain claimed immediately that her supervision of Egypt was a temporary affair and repeated the assertion at frequent intervals. The intention was to create an orderly, constitutional form of government that was friendly to Europe yet resilient enough to withstand foreign manipulation. For some years the hope was doubtless sincere, but the more the British tried to withdraw, the more firmly they became stuck in the Egyptian sand. As Sir Evelyn Baring, the consul-general known to his staff as 'over-Baring', commented in a confidential report to the Foreign Office in October 1883: 'I do not see why the policy of withdrawal should not be carried out but it can only be carried out with safety if, on the first symptoms of disturbance, the Khedive and his government act with vigour and put it down with a strong hand.' In the same memorandum, however, Baring had to admit that the actions of the British were only weakening the position of the Khedive further. Moreover, it was difficult to get any leaders of substance to cooperate – still more to get them to reform an agrarian tax and tenure system which served them so well but the public revenues so badly. With the passage of time, Egypt became a habit, as engineering the Nile or irrigating cotton became as fascinating as trying to organize the natives. It was fun to be Pharaoh. But, even if they could have resisted the pleasures of colonial administration, the British found themselves trapped by the legacy of Muhammad Ali.

The Sudanese Quicksands

Muhammad Ali had invaded the Sudan in 1820 to snuff out the last remnants of the old Mamluk military rulers of Egypt, to capture slaves for his army and to find gold. These were all cogent reasons for conquest. His successor Ismail was more interested in European recognition and, to that end, compromised his rule in the Sudan. He affronted the trading communities of the upper Nile by ostentatiously employing European officials to end the slave trade. And he wasted his

---

'OVER-BARING'

Sir Evelyn Baring, Resident British Minister in Egypt.

Evelyn Baring was born into the famous banking family in 1841 but trained for service in the military. As he matured, he came to dislike his life as a soldier and when his cousin, Lord Northbrook, was appointed Viceroy of India in 1872, Baring became his private secretary. He soon proved to be a fine administrator, but treated his subordinates in such a patronizing way that he was nicknamed 'Over-Baring'.

He first visited Egypt in 1877 as the British Representative on the Debt Commission. He returned again in 1879 and then in 1883, when he was appointed British Agent and Consul General. For the next 20 years he was the effective ruler of Egypt. His control of the public purse, when combined with his encouragement of irrigation works and other agricultural projects, returned Egypt to financial solvency by 1887. As he got older he became more and more distant in his manner, losing touch with events. He certainly found it impossible to control the capers of General Gordon who, he concluded helplessly, was 'half cracked'. Baring underestimated the significance of the rising star of Egyptian nationalism, but nevertheless his service was recognized in 1892 when he was made Lord Cromer.

Throughout his life Baring was a hard worker, starting at sunrise and continuing until two hours after sunset, with a two-hour break in the afternoon for exercise. A good linguist, his opinions were much respected at the Foreign Office, where his judgements on Egyptian affairs were the last word. He retired in 1907 and divided the last ten years of his life between writing and the House of Lords.

General Horatio Herbert Kitchener (1850–1916) as Sirdar of the Egyptian army.

Looting after the Battle of Omdurman, 1898.

army in disastrous campaigns against Ethiopia. As a result, the Arab peoples of the Sudan rose against their Turco-Egyptian rulers in 1881. Their lightning rod was Muhammad Ahmad, an ascetic holy man who proclaimed himself the Mahdi – as many Muslim rebels had before – chosen by God to scourge oppression with justice at the end of time. His armies made short work of the Egyptian garrisons.

Back in Cairo the new Khedive, Taufiq, was keen to prove his independence of the British. So he sent an expeditionary force under General Hicks, to ensure that the Sudanese toed the line. In late 1883 the force was annihilated. Gladstone decided that Egypt had no option but to evacuate the Sudan. To conduct the retreat he despatched a former governor-general of the Sudan, Charles 'Chinese' Gordon – a disastrous choice. Gordon reached Khartoum and dug in rather than evacuated, determined to resist the Mahdi's siege. The British public immediately proclaimed Gordon a hero and the Conservative opposition in Parliament tabled a Censure Motion, 'That this House regrets that the course pursued by Her Majesty's Government has not tended to promote the success of General Gordon's mission, and that even such steps as are necessary to promote his personal safety are still delayed.' Gladstone was forced to send a relief column. It arrived two days after Gordon had been killed and beheaded. Imperial disaster was added to Egyptian deadlock. Meanwhile, the Egyptian puppet ministry in Cairo had resigned rather than accede to the withdrawal from the Sudan. The only chief minister that Baring could find was Nubar the Armenian. Attempts to square British aims with Egyptian consent had to be postponed.

Whitehall was in no hurry to reconquer the Sudan in Egypt's name. The Muslim state was well able to resist other potential colonists of the region. Even when Lord Salisbury's Government accepted Britain's permanent commitment to Egypt in 1889, it contented itself with diplomatic trading and peripheral defences. German ambitions in East Africa were traded for sovereignty over the Baltic island of Heligoland. Italy was encouraged to confine herself to Ethiopia; and a British protectorate was proclaimed over Uganda. Only the French represented a threat to the 1,000 miles of the Nile still in independent African hands.

The impatience of Parisian governments with the British dominance of Egypt increased every year. If France could control the upper Nile, it could dictate terms to Cairo and hence London. At last, in 1896, they had their chance. The Italians were routed at the battle of Adowa by Menelek of Ethiopia, who encouraged the French to think of him as their ally. With Menelek's support in the east, the French could march on the Nile from the west. It was time for the British to make their move. General Kitchener marched a largely Egyptian army on Khartoum and routed the Sudanese at Omdurman in September 1898. In the words of Colonel Smith-Dorrien, who commanded the Eleventh Sudanese in the battle: 'It was a sight never to be forgotten. The endless columns of warriors, led by mounted Emirs, moving steadily on, the morning sun flashing on their white garments and long spears, with countless banners fluttering in the light breeze; but it was also a pitiable sight to see the awful effect of our fire all along the line: they were simply mown down at long ranges and in very few parts of the line did they approach nearer than 600 yards, although in one or two instances a few men got very much closer before they were killed.' Eleven thousand followers of the long-dead Mahdi were slaughtered in one day. Continuing on his way with five gunboats, Kitchener confronted an army of seven Frenchmen and one hundred Africans who were already encamped on the Nile at Fashoda. The French concluded that discretion was the better part of valour and the Sudan was once more Egyptian – but also British. Kitchener celebrated his victory by digging up the Mahdi's bones and throwing them in the Nile. Meanwhile, downstream in Egypt, cotton yields per acre were declining while the population was growing. The savagery of conquest was less complicated than the problems of administration.

Congo Free State
(Belgian Congo)

Uganda

British East Africa

☼ BUNYORO
REBELLION 1894-7

**KIKUYU
EMBU**

BUNYORO ■ **NANDI**

BUGANDA Entebbe

OGADEN

GUSII

German East Africa

GIRIAMA

☼ MAZRUI
REBELLION
1895-6

NYAMWEZI

☼ ARAB RESISTANCE
(FOLLOWERS OF TIPPU TIB)
1891-4

HEHE

☼ ARAB-SWAHILI
REBELLION
1888-9

Karonga ■

Angola

*British
Central* ☼ Africa

☼ ARABS OF KARONGA
RESIST, 1887-95

CEWA

Mozambique ■

R h o d e s i a

NYANJA

☼ CHILEMBWE
RISING 1915

Wankie ■

Mozambique

South West Africa

**WANKIE
MINERS' STRIKE
1912**

☼

Madagascar

MOZAMBIQUE CHANNEL

SHONA–NDEBELE
REBELLIONS 1893-7

Bechuanaland

Pretoria ■

Johannesburg ■

Swaziland

**SOUTH AFRICAN NATIONAL
CONGRESS FOUNDED 1912**

Bloemfontein ■ Basutoland

☼

**ZULU REBELLIONS
(BAMBATHA) 1888, 1906**

☼ Durban ■

**'GUN WAR'
1880-1
(BASOTHO v. CAPE)**

South Africa

SOUTH ATLANTIC OCEAN

INDIAN OCEAN

Anti-Colonial Rebellions in Southern
and Central Africa: 1880–1914

☼   Areas of rebellion or sustained resistance

      Areas of Arab resistance

HEHE   Native Polities

– – –   Political boundaries by 1914

CHAPTER TWENTY-THREE

THE SCRAMBLE FOR AFRICA

◇

The British Empire in Africa was founded on a paradox. Never had such large areas of the map been coloured red so rapidly, nor with so little apparent effort. But never were the British forced to move so hurriedly to cover up their weaknesses. Throughout the nineteenth century, the continent of Africa had been regarded by Britain as its own reserve, protected, if largely unexploited. In the last two decades of the century, however, Africa was broken into by a number of European powers, principally France and Germany, and also King Leopold (acting in a private capacity rather than as monarch of Belgium). The last great spectacle of British imperial expansion, which so excited the Victorians, was in reality a grim rearguard action by a country whose statesmen half knew that it was already past the peak of its power. Emerging European rivals found British pretensions to be not only increasingly irksome but also, when tested, encouragingly empty. While other nations scrambled for a share in Africa, Britain had to scramble to remain there.

In 1860 Britain produced half of the world's iron and coal, bought nearly half of its raw cotton, and owned one third of all merchant shipping and probably still more of all foreign investment. The country was at the height of its power. Thereafter, economic growth continued more slowly; countries which had started to industrialize later now began to grow much faster, notably the United States and Germany. By the 1870s Britain's continuing global dominance no longer seemed secure, whether on the world stage, or, on a smaller scale, on a number of African coasts and rivers.

The Defence of the Empire

Britain was over-extended strategically. As a liberal state, hostile to government expenditure, she was unable to translate industrial wealth into equivalent military power. The Crimean War had shown up the slothful inefficiency of the British army; a decade later, the wars of German unification demonstrated frightening energy in the army of a new rival. The confident assumption of the Royal Navy's ascendancy was similarly shattered in successive naval scares in the 1870s and 1880s, as the industrial powers stepped up their rate of naval building. These newcomers found it easier than did Nelson's heirs to innovate in gunnery. Outside Europe, with so much territory to defend, Britain found herself embarrassingly prone to frontier disasters, defeated by those whom she had dismissed as savage tribes. In 1879 the Zulus, armed with spears, wiped out a British regiment at Isandhlwana, the Afghans another one at Kabul. Two years later the despised Boers destroyed a British force on the seemingly unassailable Majuba Hill. The Cape High Commissioner, Lord Milner, wrote gloomily of 'an avalanche of military incompetence over good lives . . . thrown away by idiotic leadership. . . . What between the stupidity of our generals and the frivollings of fashionable females I often feel desperately ashamed of our country'.

Worse still, there were signs that the very design and purpose of the Empire, far from being an unwavering source of strength

to Britain, might be deeply flawed. In the 1850s the Indian Mutiny had suggested, shockingly, that British rule was by no means gratefully received by the unenlightened. In the following decade, recently liberated slaves rioted in the West Indies, while white settler colonies in South Africa and the Antipodes were continuously troublesome, despite their potential value as fields of investment and trade or as nurseries of loyal manpower and white leadership. They were constantly in conflict with their non-white neighbours, which brought Britain fresh military expense and extensions of responsibility she could well do without. Even on England's doorstep, the Irish Home Rule debate about self-government for a subject people was an unwelcome issue that would not go away. By the 1870s the nerves of Empire were getting frayed.

British Trade in Africa

Britain had long been established on important stretches of African coastline: in West Africa, where the slave trade had given way to a growing trade in vegetable oils and timber; on the east coast, mainly around the Arab island of Zanzibar which was the main port in the region and a centre of investment for Bombay traders; and in the south, where the strategic naval ports of Simons Town and Durban depended for their security on hinterlands settled by whites who had proved themselves at least as dangerous as the blacks. All three areas caused Britain anxiety in the 1870s. There was no single reason for this, but all commercial relations with Africa were shaken by the downturn in the trade of primary commodities. As tropical export prices fell in a European market place thronged with ever more producers, so African growers, chiefs and traders – black and white – squabbled over their dwindling profit margins.

On the west coast, with the Navy's anti-slavery squadron ready to hand, the British consuls responded to their traders' demands for punitive action against grasping 'middleman chiefs'. In the east, the British had to compensate their ally, the Sultan of Zanzibar, for the banning of his slave exports by providing training for his army; this expertise, of course, gave him a firmer hold over the eastern ports. At the southern end of the continent, Britain took advantage of the discovery of diamonds at Kimberley to extend its Cape Colony at Boer expense, and then forced the Colony to assume the financial duties of responsible government in 1872.

Something more was afoot, however, than reflex British responses to isolated clashes with existing trading partners or to opportunities for putting local allies into stronger positions. Rather, these were the surface eddies of a deeper current. Industrialization forced European states to try to control their sources of raw materials (such as cotton), their sources of food for their growing populations, and the markets which would keep them in employment. Such control could not always be secured by diplomatic treaty or by peaceful investment. It was for this reason that economic competition remained armed, an affair of state.

The First Scramble

It could be said that the first scramble for Africa started with a parliamentary vote in Paris for French-built railways to cross the Sahara to the western Sudan. These were the first railways planned for tropical Africa, and were obvious portents of conquests to come. The first scramble ended less than six years later around a conference table in Berlin, possibly because other interests had stepped into the African arena, unnerving both the French and the British. The first intruder was Leopold, King of Belgium. Since 1876 he had sponsored a number of activities in the Congo, the failure of which pointed to the need for closer European control. When, in 1882, Leopold tried to put his International Association on a firmer footing with African treaties and European negotiations, the French feared that if his enterprise collapsed, the Congo would be opened up to the British. The French consequently insured themselves by ratifying a treaty with Chief Makoko to the north of the River Congo. The British, for their part, had the same fears about the French and virtuously sponsored the claims of their Portuguese allies to the south, who had been there for nearly three centuries. With his eye on the forthcoming German elections, Bismarck led the opposition to this new British attempt to keep Africa to herself. Competing consuls scuttled around the western and central African coasts with treaty forms for African chiefs to sign. Then, anxious that national rivalries might become more heated than the African prize was worth, the European powers decided at Berlin to calm each other down.

This was achieved by reaching an agreement on three main issues. The swathe across the middle of Africa that had not yet been staked out by any European state would be a free trade zone – this included Leopold's Congo and the area eastwards to the Indian Ocean. Next, the Niger would be open to free navigation under the guarantee of France and Britain. Finally, no power could lay claim to African soil without establishing 'effective occupation' and some degree of administration. The first measure made future colonization less attractive, since conquest would not result in a protected market. The second took some of the heat out of the developing Anglo-French competition for the Niger, and the third was designed to put up the costs of annexation. The Berlin Act was a package deal of disincentives. And it worked. What followed has been called a 'loaded pause'. Emil Banning, one of the principal collaborators with Leopold in the establishment of the Belgian Congo, congratulated the Conference members on their tidy work: 'These regulations, inspired by the most liberal ideas and discarding all whims of selfish exploration, will protect both the natives and the Europeans . . . the partition of Africa on both sides of the Equator . . . was achieved peacefully, without any of the onerous and bloody conflicts which accompanied and notably impeded the colonisation of the two Americas.'

The Background to the Second Scramble

In the late 1880s, Europe was in the trough of a widespread depression. Trade with tropical Africa, which had never been very significant, slumped. There was little to be gained by forcefully opening up new African markets. Formal annexation would not only put up the costs for traders, but would also force Europeans to confront the problem of slavery. The abolition of slavery, it was believed, would destroy the basis of African social order and economic production; on the other hand, to tolerate what the reforming rhetoric of the century had denounced in other corners of the Empire would be difficult and embarrassing. The answer seemed to lie either in establishing 'paper protectorates' or in allowing mining and trading interests to provide what active government was required, rather than in setting up expensive administrative structures. The panic of the first scramble for Africa was over, and the other tempting investment fields of eastern Europe, the Ottoman Empire, Russia, China and the Pacific began to suggest themselves. The opinion of the British Vice-Consul in the Niger delta in 1886 was widely shared: 'So long as we keep other European nations out, we need not be in a hurry to go in.'

By 1890 a second, quite different scramble was underway and it was marked by another conference, this time at Brussels. The topics of discussion – the trades in liquor, arms and slaves – would have been inconceivable five years earlier. In the first scramble for control of African coasts and customs duties, few armies had been employed or African lives lost. The second scramble was to control the Africans and, more especially, their labour. This time Africans were to die in ever growing numbers, from disease and starvation as well as through combat.

The French Empire in Africa

Three white imperial spheres of interest, all on the periphery of tropical Africa, were to dominate the fortunes of the continent into the next century. Each had turbulent frontiers of insecurity and competition which drew them, and their rivalries, forward into the tropics. The first was the professional, almost private, imperialism of the French marines who had appropriated for themselves the task of subduing the warrior Muslim empires of the western Sudan. Scarcely a dry season had passed in the last twenty years without a French expedition setting off on another

THE PEASANT SCRAMBLE FOR AFRICA

The early colonial states were not well equipped to support the new capitalist farming systems introduced by the second Scramble for Africa. The slender public goods they supplied, such as railways and peace, liberated small men from the protection of big; and the public burdens, such as tax and coercion, which might have driven men into employment were not effective so long as households retained cheap access to land. South Africa was the most aggressive colonial régime in this respect, under pressure from white farmers and mine-owners to produce black labour. But even here the strength of black resistance and the weakness of white farming left Africans with enough land to be able to choose whether or not to become wage-workers. No other British colonial government was as ruthless. In West Africa, the Muslim chiefs of the savanna were content that many of their former slaves stayed on as tributary peasants, while the lords of the coastal forests made windfall profits by selling land to timber companies or peasant corporations. In the east, the chiefs of Buganda turned down the chance of becoming big commercial farmers, choosing to retain tributary rights over peasants; the white settlers of Kenya too, with more land than capital, lived off the rent and traded the produce of their African tenants rather than employing them as farm labour. The real producers in every case were peasant households, controlling their own labour and much of its product. They often worked corporately, buying virgin forest to plant cocoa in coastal West Africa, or pioneering agricultural settlements on the former pastures of Kenya's 'white' highlands. What had happened was a peasant scramble to colonize.

The imperial powers sort out their African differences at the first Berlin Congress in 1878.

campaign against the Muslim rulers, who presented Africa's most visible military challenge. It took the French almost ten years, from 1883 to 1892, to subdue the Tukulor empire of the upper Niger; and fifteen years of intermittent struggle, between 1883 and 1898, to destroy the armed mercantilism of Samori Toure in the western Guinea highlands. As the French fought eastwards into the interior so, during the 1890s, the British had to move in westwards from their coastal bridgeheads in Sierra Leone, on the Gold Coast and in what became Nigeria, lest their productive hinterlands should become French. In the last few years of the century, the British in Northern Nigeria were fighting campaigns of an intensity not witnessed in their sphere of influence in Africa since the Asante wars of 1874, before the first scramble began.

The New Economics of Southern Africa

Diamonds were discovered in southern Africa in 1869, and in 1885 the discovery of gold at the Witwatersrand in Johannesburg, which lay in what was unequivocally Afrikaner territory in the Transvaal Republic, lent a new urgency to the long struggle between Boer and Briton over the control of lands and the labour of the Bantu. The repercussions were to spill over into tropical Africa as well. The British government was happy to back the ambitions of the English-speaking Cape Colony when the diamond millionaire Cecil Rhodes bought a monopoly control of Kimberley in 1888. In 1890, combining patriotism with profit, Rhodes sent a volunteer pioneer force (composed largely of well-bred young Englishmen) north across the Limpopo. They settled in a land to be named Rhodesia, after their patron. Apart from hoping they would find gold, Rhodes intended that the Afrikaners should be encircled by the British. This would draw a firmer line between the Afrikaners and their German allies in South West Africa, and knock a geographical wedge between the Portuguese colonies of Angola and Mozambique. In this way, local imperialisms inevitably involved larger ones. Whereas, in the first scramble, Africa comprised a series of adjacent coasts, in the second it was woven together into one continent.

The British in Egypt

The third white sphere of interest in Africa was that of the British in Egypt. Their presence at the crossroads of the Middle East had been an irritant to European relations in Africa since their invasion in 1882. Nevertheless, this had little actual effect on the competition for tropical Africa until 1888, when Lord Salisbury had to acknowledge that he could not extricate himself from Egypt on terms that would satisfy both national and international interests, despite persistent claims from Britain that she wished to do so. It was then that Salisbury was prepared to move forward into East Africa, something which he had previously resisted. If this meant offending the Germans, or buying them off elsewhere (as in a treaty of 1890 whereby the North Sea island of Heligoland was traded for a free hand in Uganda), almost any price was considered worth paying for a British presence to safeguard the head-waters of the Nile.

Queen Victoria regarded herself as the mother of her peoples, and in Africa she seemed to be genuinely beloved. The King of Basutoland in a famous declaration said he preferred to be 'a flea in the Queen's blanket'(i.e. under Crown protection) than annexed to the Boer republics.

This African carving portrayed Queen Victoria's physical attractiveness by giving her neck a most desirable three rolls of fat: symbols of wealth and protection against famine.

THE CIVILIZING MISSION

Africa's conquerors were mostly recruited from Europe's new middle classes, schooled in self-mastery, disciplined by an ethic of official duty, spurred by the ambitions of bureaucratic control, fired by belief in racial destiny and driven, some of them, by an evangelical sense that they must save others from sin. They were as appalled by African governments as they would have been by their own of a century earlier. Returning from the west coast kingdom of Dahomey in 1864, Richard Burton observed that 'A Dahoman visiting England but a few years ago would have witnessed customs almost quite as curious as those which raise our bile now.' African rule was personal rule and its rewards, therefore, were bureaucratic vices, ostentation, arbitrary judgement, cruel punishment, personal favours, and private retinues of clients and servants, some of them sexual. Part of its offence lay in the very temptations it offered to white 'men on the spot', personal rulers themselves in their own petty tropical fiefdoms and far from professional restraints upon personal licence. It was only when the British faced the problem of ruling

Drawing by Joseph Dupuis, whose book Journal of a Residence in Ashantee *of 1824, describes the early forays of British traders into Asanteland.*

Africa themselves that they accorded to chiefs and their rituals a moral authority which was questioned more often by Africans than by Empire officials. After such civilizing efforts it was ironic how the British came to mistrust the new African élite they had created: the literate Christians who had freed themselves from tribal customs.

Arms, Slaves and Liquor

In the 1890s trade terms began to revive for primary producers. Africa's growing import capacity was able to finance the buying of arms. The main African arms importers were those along the most threatened European frontiers: the Muslim empires of the western Sudan and the Swahili-Arab slavers of eastern Africa. This influx of weapons helped to break up the old African political systems. Power fragmented and warfare escalated, its captives swelling the horrific internal slave trade which was now more zealously publicized than ever before by European missionaries and traders. European liquor importers also benefited from the African free-for-all, although they were strenuously opposed by missionaries and by employers who claimed that their labour supply was 'demoralized' by the spirituous inducements offered by less scrupulous competitors.

Although no European power was anxious to lead a crusade against slaving, arms or liquor, disorder and commodity prices escalated to such an extent in the mid-1890s that the new British Colonial Secretary, Joseph Chamberlain, began to see a need for the scientific development of Europe's tropical estates.

This concept drew the British into the mêlée as self-interested policemen. In eastern Africa, they were forced to support missionaries and planters against Arab slavers in Nyasaland. They also intervened in civil war in Buganda in order to gain a foothold on the upper Nile, and were drawn in further as Buganda's allies against neighbouring Bunyoro. Through the Yoruba wars and internal Asante conflicts, Britain advanced her influence in the west and along the Gold Coast. In East Africa, the German and British governments supplanted the paper administrations of company rule; the Royal Niger Company was also bought out. Only two areas of chartered company activity survived into the next century: Leopold's concessionary hell of enforced rubber collection in the Belgian Congo, where conditions at least as bad as slavery prevailed; and Rhodes's British

South Africa Company, with its unique asset of a South African mineral foundation. Even Rhodes, however, was lucky to fend off an imperial takeover in the mid-1890s when the gold discoveries did not materialize and the company had to rely for its returns on settler farming. This provoked such risings among the local population that they were beyond the company's control and imperial troops had to be called in. By the time Britain had to decide whether to bail out bankrupt capitalists or to leave Africa altogether in the mid-1890s, the economic climate had changed once more. There was a world boom in commodities and also a resource scare, with the United States increasingly buying up products such as cotton and coffee, which it had previously exported or re-exported to Europe.

The Effects of European Domination

The politics of conquest gave way at the turn of the century to the politics of administrative control and economic exploitation of the scarce labour supply. Slavery had been common because free labour was so expensive; in the wake of white conquests, the labour supply became even tighter, through private employers and through an insatiable demand for labour on public works. Now that slaves had fled home in droves as the authority of their African masters collapsed in military defeat, the problem arose of how best to harness the production potential of ex-slaves, most of whom were now labouring peasants.

Former African friends and foes alike had to be made to pay tax, and to work in ways which would profit traders, employers and the new colonial states. As Africans tried to reconstruct their lives after fleeing from slavery or the tax collector, they imposed their most effective constraints on their conquerors. They had to be allowed a large self-interest in the expansion of the colonial economies and they chose to pursue their interest as peasants and migrant workers rather than as proletarians. The second scramble, like the first, was largely incomplete.

CHAPTER TWENTY-FOUR

THE STRUGGLE FOR SOUTH AFRICA

◇

Before the end of the nineteenth century, the area that is now the Republic of South Africa consisted of two Boer republics, two British colonies and a number of independent African kingdoms: a fragmentation common in other regions of Africa at the time when the Europeans began to impose their rule in the 1870s. The similarity was reinforced by the nature of South Africa's economic life. The governments of both the British and the Boer-dominated states were limited by the small revenue they could draw upon. The vast majority of their subjects were poor farmers whose capacity to pay tax was severely limited. Customs revenue was also small, depending as it did on the volume of import and export activity. Few citizens could afford highly priced imports, while most farmers were too under-capitalized to gear their production towards specialist exporting. Black or white, most inhabitants were poor, illiterate and provincial in contemporary European terms. Had it not been for the economic and political changes that were looming, the region could easily have developed into a typical European settler colony like Kenya, supported by a small agricultural export economy.

The Discovery of Gold and the Growth of the Transvaal

In 1884 it was confirmed that one of the bleakest areas of the Transvaal was in fact a significant goldfield. The field was sited on the Witwatersrand, a dry, thinly vegetated highland to the south of the Transvaal. This unpromising area turned out to be an enormous find; the field was around 170 miles long and 100 miles wide and appeared to contain a seemingly inexhaustible supply of gold. But no goldfield is quite like another, and the Witwatersrand ore formed a low percentage of the rock in which it was embedded. Then, as today, its extraction demanded a very high level of initial investment and the most modern and expensive techniques. The seams ran deep into the earth's crust, and mining costs, which included draining and ventilating the mines and raising the ore to the surface for local rail transport, were enormous.

It was impossible, however, to raise the capital required locally. The Boer farmers were simply 'transplanted' peasants and their ramshackle republic was unlikely to provide the outlay required. The investors, therefore, were mainly German and British speculators. Similarly, the skills necessary for developing the area were not to be found locally. The mining houses employed technologists from other gold-mining areas such as California and Australia, and from the tin- and coal-mining regions of Britain. Only the manual labour was recruited from the indigenous populations. Many Africans travelled far to the 'Rand' (as the region became known), for a wage which helped them to entrench their independence through the buying of weapons, farm animals and machinery. As the tent-city of Johannesburg, in the middle of the goldfield, grew into an industrial city, many of its inhabitants were non-Boer outsiders – or *uitlanders*, as they were called in Afrikaans.

In 1884 the Transvaal was virtually bankrupt; only five years

President Paul Kruger (1825 – 1904) photographed in Pretoria.

later, its gold resources gave it a revenue of £1.5 million and, by 1896, gold accounted for 97 per cent of the Transvaal's export revenue. An intriguing problem began to develop, however. The Transvaal was a landholders' republic, its citizens poor farmers imbued with a fundamentalist Calvinism. Their lives were intimately bound to the soil they tilled, which fostered a strong conservatism that regarded change as the work of the devil. They were not about to vote large sums of money to foster the comfort of cities which many viewed as sinks of iniquity.

The Transvaal farmers were insistent on their rights. They were also, being Dutch-speaking, developing a strong sense of independence, which had sprung initially from the original trek into the African interior. This sense of racial independence embraced a hatred of the British newcomers, who had denied them the elemental freedoms they demanded, and a dislike of the indigenous tribes who resisted their expansion. Now that this great underground treasure chest had been discovered, there was at last an opportunity to stand up to the British on the basis

The Kimberley Open Gold Mine, photographed before its closure in 1915.

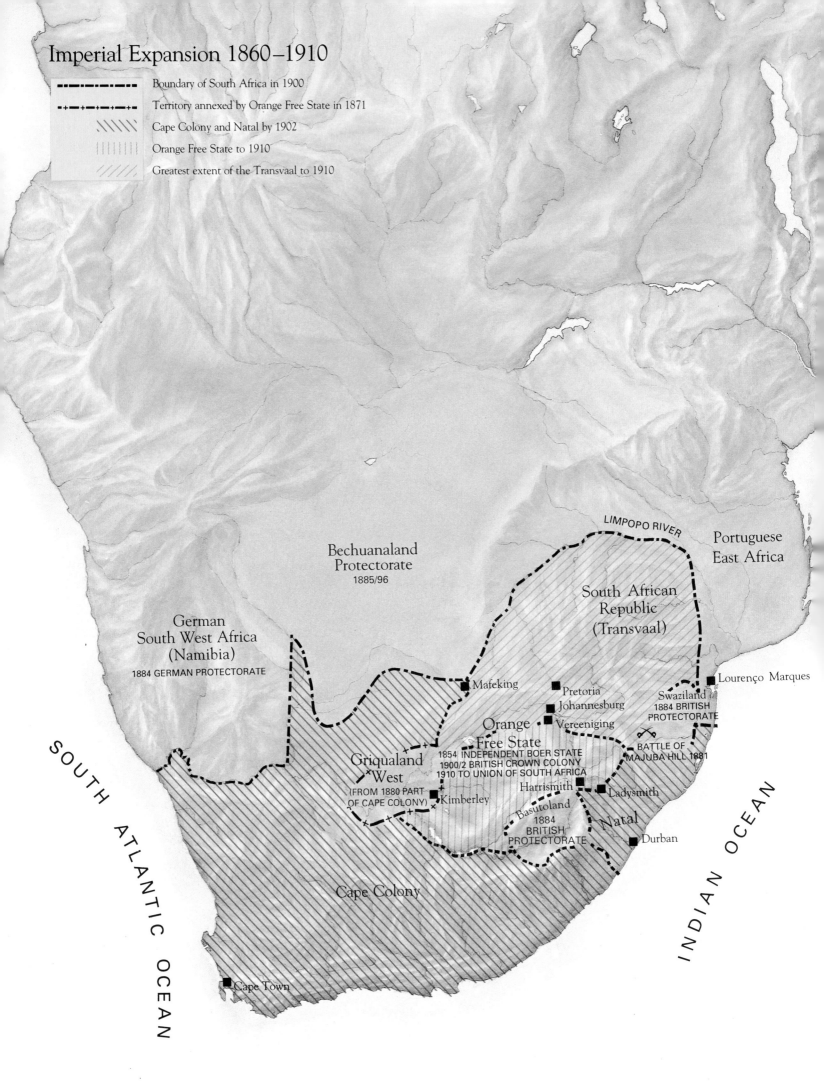

Imperial Expansion 1860–1910

—··—··—··—	Boundary of South Africa in 1900
—+—+—+—+—	Territory annexed by Orange Free State in 1871
▨	Cape Colony and Natal by 1902
▥	Orange Free State to 1910
▧	Greatest extent of the Transvaal to 1910

SOUTH ATLANTIC OCEAN

INDIAN OCEAN

German
South West Africa
(Namibia)
1884 GERMAN PROTECTORATE

Bechuanaland
Protectorate
1885/96

LIMPOPO RIVER

Portuguese
East Africa

South African
Republic
(Transvaal)

■ Mafeking

■ Pretoria
■ Johannesburg
■ Vereeniging

Orange
Free State
1854 INDEPENDENT BOER STATE
1900/2 BRITISH CROWN COLONY
1910 TO UNION OF SOUTH AFRICA

Swaziland
1884 BRITISH
PROTECTORATE

■ Lourenço Marques

Griqualand
West
(FROM 1880 PART
OF CAPE COLONY)

BATTLE OF
MAJUBA HILL 1881

■ Kimberley

Harrismith ■

Basutoland
1884
BRITISH
PROTECTORATE

■ Ladysmith

Natal

■ Durban

Cape Colony

■ Cape Town

THE IMPERIAL VISION OF CECIL RHODES

By the age of thirty, Cecil Rhodes was among the richest men in the world and had become one of the most influential figures in the history of Africa. Born in 1853, the son of an East Anglian clergyman, Rhodes was packed off to South Africa because he suffered from a 'weak chest'. At first he grew cotton in Natal, but failed. Then, in 1871, he set out for the Kimberley diamond fields and found an enormous fortune. Determined to overcome his feeble education, he enrolled as a student at Oriel College, Oxford. After his graduation, he expressed his gratitude through enormous bequests which still sustain the university. In 1880 he founded the De Beers company and in 1887 he diversified into gold, founding Consolidated Goldfields.

Cecil Rhodes (1853–1902), by Sir Luke Fildes.

Meanwhile, his eye had turned to politics. He dreamed of a pink strip on the map stretching all the way from Cape Town to Cairo. Such ambitions intimidated the Colonial Office, however. Undaunted, Rhodes had the muscle to achieve his ends without them. By 1888 his negotiators had induced the king of the Matabele to cede all his mineral rights and in 1889 the British South Africa Company achieved its royal charter. Rhodes' incursions northwards brought him into disrepute as he attempted to bully his way to his goal. Nevertheless, although Rhodes was under fifty when he died, such a canny observer as Mark Twain still had to admit that 'When Rhodes stood upon the Cape Peninsula his shadow fell upon the Zambezi.'

---

of economic equality. But the Transvaal needed external investment, and Britain had considerable international clout. The British also controlled the coasts of southern Africa. Imports and exports to and from the land-locked Transvaal had to pass through Cape Colony or Natal on the way to the coast.

The Transvaal was frustrated by this dependency but it was equally keen to profit by it. Tax after tariff were slapped on goods that moved in and out of the Rand; part of the resulting profits built a railway line, completed in 1889, which ran outside British territory to Delagoa Bay in the north. A tariff war between the British colonies and the Boer republics soon followed. The battle for railway routes continued too, spreading to the Cape and Natal. The result was a proliferation of competitive routes, each serving local interests.

Cecil Rhodes and the British South Africa Company

In the Cape, politicians continued to work towards a mutually beneficial customs union. The premier, the diamond millionaire Cecil Rhodes, and his Dutch-speaking ally, Jan Hofmeyer, initially sought closer cooperation within the area. Rhodes was an imperial dreamer, and those dreams were involved with the development of the railways. His ultimate goal was to drive the Cape railway system northwards through the Transvaal, to the land between the Limpopo and Zambezi rivers where, it was speculated, there might be as much gold as there was to the south. The Orange Free State and the Transvaal, however, were not keen on the idea of a customs union. In 1889, they signed a defensive alliance. The Parliament of the Transvaal, the *Volksraad*, remained deaf to all entreaty and cajolery. They had no faith in the British, and the British, in turn, dismissed them as 'inflated toads, incapable of any united action'.

Rhodes decided eventually to lock horns with the Transvaal and to prevent its northward expansion by privately annexing lands to the north. In 1889 he won a Royal Charter for his British South Africa Company and, the following year, a heavily armed BSAC 'pioneer column' stormed into MaShona and Ndebele country. The Colonial Office in London was still extremely uneasy about expansion and unnerved at the possible expense of war with an enraged Transvaal. It offered the republic the prospect of building a railway line through Swaziland to Kosi Bay on the condition that it entered into a customs union. The Transvaal President, Paul Kruger, turned the offer down and demanded unhindered control of the Swazi coast. In so doing, he appeared to invite German support for the republic. German military officers were soon seen in Pretoria, and a small German fleet was moored in Delagoa Bay.

The Build-up to War

The British, who had been unwilling imperialists up to this point, pre-emptively warned off both Germany and the Transvaal by insisting in 1893 that the *whole* of South Africa was a British sphere of influence. The declaration solved nothing and the tensions continued until the dramatic change of mood brought about by Joseph Chamberlain, who became British Secretary of State for the Colonies in 1895. Unlike his predecessors, Chamberlain was a 'forward imperialist', an enthusiast for extending the Empire and for colonial domination. By 1895 the absolute value of the Rand had become clearer. Available technology had caught up with the demands of the gold-mining industry, and nothing but the obduracy of the Transvaal stood in the way of long-term profits. Men like Chamberlain and Rhodes were frustrated by their inability to exercise leverage, let alone political control, over the gold-mines.

The mine sites were like states within a state. Although 70 per cent of the white population were *uitlanders*, they were denied the franchise and were treated with a mixture of envy and contempt. Under Rhodes, the British and the opponents of the Transvaal republic in the Cape seized on the denial of civil rights to the *uitlanders* as a pretext for denigrating and harassing the Transvaal government.

On New Year's Day 1896, Cecil Rhodes's agent, Dr Jameson, led five hundred horsemen from Bechuanaland into the Transvaal in an attempt to provoke the *uitlanders* into revolt. The raiders were rapidly arrested by Boers – who had intercepted their telegraph messages – and were tried in the Transvaal. A subsequent commission of enquiry ruined Rhodes's political career, but Chamberlain, who was undoubtedly complicit in the raid, was left with his reputation intact. The Transvaal emerged as the victim of big-power bullying and Kruger turned once again to Britain's many rivals for support. He signed treaties with both Germany and France, who distrusted Britain after the Fashoda incident. British warships were despatched to South Africa.

Milner's War

In April 1897, Chamberlain sent Sir Alfred Milner to the Transvaal as High Commissioner. Although he sought a settlement short of war, both he and Chamberlain seemed convinced that the British mining interest was suffering as a result of Kruger's continued intransigence. There was a stronger reason, however, for Chamberlain's irritation. In the final decade of the nineteenth century, the British South Africa Company had expanded British suzerainty: in 1893 the Ndebele had been defeated, and Ndebele and MaShona risings had been put down in 1896. By 1897 the Cape railway reached Bulawayo in modern Zimbabwe. From the Zambezi southwards, the independence of African states had been destroyed and British rule installed in its place. The British now had political control over a huge potential pool of cheap labour which could be persuaded to serve the industrial revolution initiated by the gold fields. A large central and southern African empire was virtually complete, but the British still lacked the freehold to the region's most significant economic asset. The Transvaal stood in their way.

With the assent of the home government, Milner sought every excuse to snipe at Kruger. In October 1899, after months of mounting provocation, Kruger sent an ultimatum to Queen Victoria, insisting that no further British troops be sent to South Africa. The British Prime Minister, Lord Salisbury, rejected the ultimatum, thereby signalling the outbreak of the Boer War.

The Anglo-Boer War

In October 1899 there were twenty-two thousand British regular soldiers in South Africa, the bulk of them in Natal. It was a war which they confidently expected to be over by Christmas, but this confidence was soon drained. The Boer militias or *kommandoes* began the campaign with a series of lightning victories. In the east, their forces besieged the British position at Ladysmith, where the young correspondent of the *Morning Post*, Winston Churchill, was captured. In the west, the Boers invaded and annexed British Bechuanaland, dominating in the process the vital railway link that ran north to Mafeking and south to Kimberley. During the first months of the war, disaster followed upon disaster for the British. Attempting to raise the siege at Kimberley, they suffered massive losses at the hands of General Piet Cronje's forces. Between 9 and 15 December 1899, which became known as 'the Black Week', the British lost or surrendered thousands of troops at Magersfontein, Stormberg, Ladysmith and Colenso. It became clear that the Boers were no ragged army of farmers and that the British troops, heavier in numbers but slower in speed and strategy, were no match for the Boers' horsemanship and knowledge of the terrain. 'We must face the facts', wrote Churchill, 'that the individual Boer, mounted in suitable country, is worth from three to five regular soldiers.' The Boers were driven by a fight for freedom, and young boys in their early teens swelled their ranks.

Lord Roberts, with Lord Kitchener as his deputy, was ordered to South Africa to rescue the situation. In January 1900,

Sir Redvers Buller lost vast numbers of troops at Spion Kop and Vaalkranz, whilst maintaining pressure on Ladysmith. By February, however, Roberts was advancing across the Orange River. The Free State troops withdrew from Ladysmith to defend their homeland, permitting Buller to take Ladysmith at last.

Cronje's Surrender

Roberts brought three divisions together to assault the Free State. On his flanks, General French relieved the siege of Kimberley. The Boer commander Cronje, en route for the defence of Bloemfontein, evaded the British until trapped on the wrong side of the Modder River by thirty thousand British troops. Kitchener ordered an attack but was repulsed with losses of over a thousand men at Paardberg. Cronje and the main Boer army, together with women, children, wagons and animals, were besieged in a river ravine with no hope of relief. They fought back in despair, growing weaker daily, until Cronje was forced to surrender on 27 February 1900. Roberts entered Bloemfontein on 13 March, which was a mixed blessing for the British, who endured a terrible typhoid epidemic there. Nevertheless, the Free State was annexed in May 1900, while Colonel Robert Baden-Powell's legendary defence of Mafeking was ended by relief on 17 May. The following month Johannesburg and Pretoria were captured, and the two Boer republics finally fell into British hands.

Although their governments had fled, three guerilla armies of Boers stayed in the field. Their campaigning under Botha, De la Rey and De Wet became the stuff of heroic legend. Lightly armed and battle-hardened, they kept a diminished British force pinned down by lightning raids. It was a classic guerilla struggle and one which brought out the worst in Kitchener's strategy. Frustrated by the guerillas' success and their support from civilians, he initiated the infamous 'scorched earth' campaign. Boer farmsteads were razed, their property stolen. Their wives, children and African servants were herded together in institutions known for the first time as 'concentration camps'. In March 1902 the Boer commanders knew that they were finished and in May 1902 a peace was negotiated at Vereeninging.

It had been a bloody, dreadful war. More than twenty-two thousand British troops had died, more than half from disease and infected wounds. More than a hundred thousand had been hospitalized. The Boers had lost around five thousand troops and a further thirty thousand were prisoners of war. Many of their

THE FIRST CONCENTRATION CAMPS

The concentration camp – an idea that had been used by the Spanish in nineteenth-century Cuba – was developed when the British isolated the Boers from the settler communities that sustained them. The civilians from scattered farmsteads across the battle zone were invited to congregate in a series of ill-planned camps in which they were promised food and shelter. However, the British had no idea how to cope with the camps once they had been established. Their population swelled rapidly in one year from 50,000 in 1900 to over 150,000 the following October. Nearly a third of the interned were Africans whose stock and crops had been confiscated by both sides. Food soon ran short,

During the Boer War, over 40 concentration camps were set up by the British, mainly for women and children from Boer farms. Official records admit that as many as 26,000 died, of whom 20,000 were under the age of 16.

and sanitation in the overcrowded camps was often non-existent, with disastrous consequences. Far more than either Boer bullets or shrapnel, a sequence of diseases had killed or hospitalized many British soldiers. This made them unwitting carriers of disease amongst a largely rural population highly prone to contagion. General Kitchener attempted to lay the blame on the 'unhygienic' Boer women: 'The inmates are far better looked after in every way than they are in their own homes,' he said; 'the doctors' reports of the dirt and filth in which the Boer ladies from the wilds revel are very unpleasant reading, and I am considering whether some of the worst cases should not be tried for manslaughter . . .'

The Boer 'kommandoes' drew desperately on all resources to combat the British troops. Fourteen-year-old boys fought, and were killed, alongside their fathers and grandfathers (left and below).

Dead British soldiers in the first trench at Spion Kop.

wives and children had died in the camps. Their farms and countryside had been ravaged. Ramsay Macdonald, the future Labour Prime Minister of Britain, visited the burnt-out site of the village of Lindley in 1902 and wrote: 'Every house, without a single exception, was burnt ... Grass grew upon broken hearthstones and lizards crawled upon deserted doorsteps. The whole journey was through a land of sorrow and destruction, of mourning and hate.' The British Treasury did its own calculations and estimated that the war had cost around £200 million, an astronomical sum.

The Fate of the Africans

Africans have figured little in this account since the war has generally been seen as one between whites. Africans fought and died on both sides, however; most black South Africans had supported Britain in the hope that the British Cape Colony franchise would be extended northwards. Their sufferings were compounded in the aftermath of war by Milner's many-faceted policy of 'reconstruction'. This was a partly successful attempt to repair the physical damage done to communications, industry and the agricultural sector, aided by large grants from Britain. Reconstruction also meant reconciliation between Boer and Briton, an altogether more difficult task, for which a terrible price would have to be paid.

The citizens of the republics found themselves at a disadvantage after the war: they spoke the wrong language, they had no assets, and many had lost access to the land. Few had suitable skills to cater for the huge economic changes taking place. Had they not attempted to create a position of relative privilege for themselves by statutory racial discrimination, poor Afrikaans-speaking whites would have been forced to compete in a labour market with the far more numerous Africans.

Most employers, who were English-speaking, found this demand for statutory discrimination irksome – not out of any liberal sentiment but because they thought that racial privilege would push wages up. An unsegregated pool of unskilled labour, on the other hand, allowed low wage levels across the board. Unskilled wages fell as skilled wages rose and many Africans,

who still had access to agricultural land, refused to work for such meagre returns. Big employers demanded increasing coercion from the state to force Africans to work for low wages, but the Liberal Government in Westminster proved a serious impediment to such a development at this stage.

The Act of Union in May 1910 brought together all the disparate parts of South Africa as a self-governing dominion, with the exceptions of the British protectorates of Basutoland (Lesotho), Bechuanaland (Botswana) and Swaziland. All the delegates to the Convention, which thrashed out the agreement, were white; Africans were not consulted on the eventual shape of their motherland. Their rights to vote, to own land, and even their freedom to work were no longer open to question or defence in the British Parliament, but were subjected to the local political process, which effectively denied them a voice.

The Native Land Act of 1913 denied Africans the right to own land on 87 per cent of the Union's land area. The 13 per cent reserved for Africans contained marginal scrub and, of course, no town, no port of significance nor any industrial area. A black South African, Sol Plaatje, wrote: 'Awakening on Friday morning, June 20th, 1913, the South African Native found himself, not actually a slave, but a pariah in the land of his birth.' The Africans outnumbered whites by at least four to one, but the vestiges of their independence were destroyed. The reserves could not support their numbers and Africans were increasingly forced onto the labour market. In time, successive Pass Laws and stern employment regulations forced unskilled wages down, while white workers were automatically defined as skilled. Substantially unchanged, this thirteen per cent of African land now constitutes the black 'homelands' designated by the South African regime today. The animosity between Boer and Briton was solved by crushing the rights of the majority African population; the Liberal Government, in its anxiety to make amends for Britain's brutal part in the war and, more importantly, to secure dependable Afrikaner allegiance, had abandoned all principles of liberalism. Britain's Anglo-Boer War had been a disaster and, in sowing the seeds of apartheid, her peace was more disastrous still.

Alaska (USA)

YUKON RIVER

●Dawson

Yukon
Territory
(1898)

Chilkat Pass

GOLD (1898)

District of
Mackenzie
(1895)

British Columbia
(1871)

Alberta
(1905)

BLACKFOOT

Edmonton

PLAINS-CREE

Saskatchewan
(1905)

Vancouver
Victoria

OKANAGAN VALLEY

KOOTENAYS

Calgary

Saskatoon

CROWS NEST
PASS

ASSINIBOINE

Regina

The Development of Canada: 1870–1914

··················	International boundaries
– – – – – – –	Provincial borders
+++++++++++	Canadian–Pacific Railway (completed 1885)
BLACKFOOT	Indian Nations
●	Provincial capitals
•	Towns

Greenland
(Denmark)

INUIT

INUIT

District of
Franklin
(1895)

th West Territories

District of
Keewatin

District of
Ungava
(1895)
1912 to Quebec

British
Colony of
Newfoundland

Quebec
(1867)

PRINCE EDWARD
ISLAND (1873)

Sydney

INTERCOLONIAL
RAILWAY (1876)

Charlottetown

oba

1898 Boundary

Ontario
(1867)

NEW
BRUNSWICK
(1867)

Fort William

Quebec
City

Fredericton

NOVA SCOTIA (1867)

Port Arthur

Halifax

Saint
John

North Bay

Montreal

Ottawa

CPR 'SHORT LINE' (1890)

Hamilton Toronto

London

Windsor

153

CHAPTER TWENTY FIVE

CANADA: FROM COAST TO COAST

———————————————— ◇ ————————————————

In the two generations preceding the First World War, Canada discarded her status as a collection of rural colonies and emerged as a wealthy Western power. At the heart of this rapid transformation lay the development of the railroad. By extending the trade and industry of the St Lawrence valley westwards over the prairies, the Canadian Pacific Railway enmeshed the young country in a web of commerce. The railways encouraged immigration and industrial growth. However, in the face of undefended boundaries with America, the railways became something more than engines of economic change. They became a clear assertion of political sovereignty, integrating the remotest prairie township with the hub of government in Ontario.

Building a Nation

The speed at which the railways covered the face of Canada was remarkable. In 1867 there were only about 2,200 miles of track in the whole of British North America. From then until 1914, this doubled almost every decade. In itself, the growth of the railways was not a sign of economic viability. If considerations of profit and loss alone had determined the fate of the Canadian Pacific Railway, it would hardly have crept farther west than Lake Huron. However, one of the conditions that British Columbia had attached to joining the Confederation in 1871 had been that the railway should reach her within ten years. The expensive burden of building this railway was to be handed down from government to government.

Some politicians, however, succumbed almost too much to its spell. The railroad was a central plank in Prime Minister Sir John Macdonald's programme. But finding financial backers for the project was not easy. These had to be wooed with cash subsidies and land grants along the line's right of way. In 1872 the Montreal-based railway promoters, afraid of losing these generous incentives, subscribed more than $350,000 to the election fund of Macdonald's Conservative Party – money which was earmarked for electoral bribery. The disclosure of this back-room conspiracy – known as the 'Pacific Scandal' – forced the immediate collapse of the Macdonald Government.

The Liberal administration of Prime Minister Alexander Mackenzie, which followed, embarked upon a more cautious plan of building connecting railway links between navigable rivers and lakes. This was mocked by the Conservatives as the 'amphibious route'. In any case, Macdonald was back in office by 1878, the Canadian Pacific Railway was reorganized and its progress to the Pacific resumed. In November 1886 the first Canadian Pacific Railway engine steamed into Vancouver.

Taking a railway line north of the Great Lakes incurred huge transport and labour costs. During the long winters, the railway labourers had to dig themselves in and out of camp sites in freezing conditions, as they migrated with the progress of the tracks. They formed motley communities of itinerant labourers, cooks, foremen and engineers, many miles from the nearest settlement or any form of law enforcement. In order to protect the line from sabotage or from attack by marauding Fenians from America, the eastern arm of the railway between Montreal and Nova Scotia followed an all-Canadian route which greatly added to its length and expense. The western arm to British Columbia was equally problematical since its route was determined partly by strategic considerations. Because it was to serve as a reinforcement of the 49th Parallel – the unmarked and undefended boundary with America – it was obliged to follow another sparsely populated route. As it crossed the Rockies in British Columbia, it demanded hair-raising feats of engineering. But its success was vital, both politically and symbolically, to a country of such disparate immigrants as Canada.

Peopling a Nation

Immigration was officially encouraged. Pamphlets were distributed in Britain by agents of the Canadian Pacific Railway, offering free or subsidized rail travel to the provinces, and advising: 'PERSONS WHO SHOULD EMIGRATE . . . Persons with capital, either in large or small amounts, seeking investment . . . Tenant farmers with limited capital . . . Agricultural labourers, skilled and unskilled . . . Mechanics of various descriptions . . .'

However hopeful of attracting wealthy immigrants the Canadian government may have been, it was predominantly the poor who flooded into Canada, attracted by cheap land. The isolation of tiny settlements accessible only by sleighs in winter was a crushing and unexpected difficulty, however. 'I would suggest long and earnest hesitation before they decide on fixing themselves here as agriculturalists,' wrote a young immigrant to his 'bachelor friends' back in Ireland, 'and I would more strongly advise them to marry before they come out, if they can meet with cheerful, accommodating, and economizing lasses with a little of the NEEDFUL, indeed, whether possessing this last qualification or not, such girls would be in themselves a TREASURE here . . .'

Immigrants poured into Canada from all corners of Britain and Europe. At the time of Confederation, there were perhaps three million Canadians, all but a fraction of whom could be found in Ontario and Quebec; in British Columbia, for example, the native peoples still outnumbered the whites by three to one. By 1911 Canada's population had doubled and both the source of its immigrants and their distribution had shifted. At the turn of the century, arrivals from Scandinavia and central Europe overtook in numbers the traditional immigrants from the British Isles; their houses and steepled churches became a new characteristic of the Canadian prairie horizon. The Pacific coast of British Columbia attracted many Chinese and Japanese immigrants who laboured under terrible conditions in the Canadian Pacific Railway construction camps and in the Vancouver Island coal mines.

In 1871 only 18 per cent of Canadians lived in urban areas; by 1911 that figure was nearly 42 per cent. The older towns, sited along harbours, rivers or lakes, expanded with the flow of

VIEW OF GANADA SOUTHERN TRAIN PASSING NIAGARA FALLS.

A Canadian railway construction gang in 1911, west of Missanabee (left).

immigrants and the development of industrialization and agricultural mechanization. But there were new cities too, such as Vancouver, Regina and Winnipeg, which had grown up around the rail junctions, swelling with each trainload of immigrants. The railway tracks and yards carved these towns into two distinct districts – rich and poor – which intensified class and racial tension. Anti-Asian sentiment became an ugly feature of British Columbia and there were riots in 1908.

The Boom Years

As the land and its inhabitants became more settled, new industries developed, including pulp and paper manufacture. Coal mining expanded into northern Ontario, southern Alberta and the Crowsnest Pass in the Rockies. From about 1900 steel production increased dramatically, mostly around Hamilton, Ontario. Tinned salmon and prefabricated housing materials were traded eastwards from the Pacific coast to ease the lot of the prairie settlers.

Although the prairies were very fertile, the extremes of climate required that new and hardy strains of wheat be developed which would ripen before the autumn frosts. Red Fife wheat was widely grown for this reason, until the Dominion Experimental Farms developed the Marquis seed in 1910. Rising grain prices throughout the 1890s, the rapid population growth in the western grain belt and the use of this hardier wheat had a cumulative effect; an effect which can be seen in the figures of wheat output, which leapt from 2 million tonnes in 1904 to 7.7 million tonnes in western Canada in 1913.

The great success of the wheat economy in the west allowed the farmers of valuable agricultural land in Quebec, Ontario and the Maritime regions to turn to dairy and cattle farming and to fruit. As Canadian agriculture became more specialized by region, cattle ranching in the dusty Okanagan valley of British Columbia was replaced by fruit farming. None of this regional specialization – across a continent some 4,000 miles wide – would have been possible, however, without a transcontinental railway and a veritable fleet of paddlewheel steamers.

Meanwhile, however, the Maritimes were in decline. Of all the provinces, these were the staunchest bastions of loyalists, proud of their origins as political refugees from the American War of Independence. Many still lived in the crumbling splendour of their old colonial mansions. But they were too far from the centres of commerce in New York, Toronto and Montreal, and the young of each generation were drawn away from Prince Edward Island, New Brunswick and Nova Scotia to the prairies or far away to the goldfields of the west.

THE ROYAL CANADIAN MOUNTED POLICE

The scarlet tunics of the Mounties have been one of Canada's most enduring symbols. Formed in 1873 as the North-West Mounted Police, the force was modelled on the British constabulary in Ireland and India – hence the red uniforms and distinctive hats. However, unlike colonial law-enforcers elsewhere, the Mounties quickly endeared themselves to the young nation by their impeccably upright yet manly image, fostered by a vigorous selection process. The purpose of the Mounties was to extend the arm of Ottawan law into Canada's far west; in 1874 they marched to the Alberta badlands to staunch the illegal whisky trade conducted by a group of American interlopers based at Fort Whoop-Up. On the way they established a series of posts from which they were able to patrol the area by means of regular circuits or 'beats' covering thousands of miles. In the 1880s they became the focus of a political controversy but they were already too well-established to be disbanded. The prefix 'Royal' was added to their name in 1904 after members of the force had distinguished themselves in the Boer War. In 1919 they were merged with the Dominion Police and renamed the Royal Canadian Mounted Police. Yet, despite these changes in their function, the Mounties will always be associated with interminable treks across the frozen prairies in pursuit of disreputable fur trappers and whisky salesmen: the men who always got their man.

'The Mountie gives his man one more chance' by Frederic Remington.

The North-West Rebellion

The Maritimers were not the only victims of the westward shift in population and economic activity. Canada was, even in the late nineteenth century, a frontier land. On these frontiers, the mining and lumber camps were extremely isolated and native groups were still in a position to protest against the Europeanization of the territories claimed by Britain. By 1885 trouble was brewing on the prairies. After the uprising of 1869–70 the Métis had moved from Red River to the vast area between the north and south branches of the Saskatchewan River. Here they had hoped to re-establish their way of life, which depended on hunting and subsistence farming. However, the westward migration of the Euro-Canadians and the threat posed by surveyors measuring up their land soon caught up with them again. Both the Plains Indians and Northern Cree Indians had also been reduced to desperate straits by the near-extinction of the buffalo, and by the land treaties in which the Dominion Government had parcelled up most of their traditional hunting grounds in sale lots. These Indians joined the Métis in general protest, and Louis Riel returned from exile in the USA to lead the uprising. The Métis confronted the North-West Mounted Police at Duck Lake; troops were swiftly sent out along the completed sections of the Canadian Pacific Railway: after a short campaign, the rebellion crumbled at the Battle of Batoche. Riel himself was not allowed to escape a second time and was hanged in the winter of 1885 for his execution of Thomas Scott, during the Red River uprising, fifteen years before. The ringleaders, Chiefs Poundmaker and Big Bear, were imprisoned and the Métis were eliminated as an obstacle to prairie settlement.

Political Developments

The transportation of troops to the scene of the rebellion was evidence of the extent to which the western prairies had been absorbed into Canada by the railways; and the way in which the uprising was crushed proved that Ottawa could now police even its farthest settlements efficiently. It also revived the old animosity in the east between the English and French, the Protestants and Catholics. Quebec demanded that, as a Catholic and a French Canadian, Riel should be spared; Ontario, on the other hand, insisted that he should die. This issue divided opinion in central Canada and undermined the Conservative Alliance: under the leadership of the French-Canadian Laurier, Quebec became a Liberal stronghold.

Louis Riel, leader of the Métis rebels in Western Canada, who was eventually hanged for treason.

After the death of Macdonald in 1891, the traditional two-party political system weakened. In 1905 two new provinces, Saskatchewan and Alberta, were created from the grain-rich prairies. Farmers in these provinces were suspicious that the old Liberal and Conservative parties were controlled by eastern business interests, and bitterly resented Ottawa's ownership and control of prairie resources. Their agitation for equal benefits coincided with demands made by disaffected farmers in Ontario. The coalition of interests resulted in the new Progressive Party which called for 'political purity', low tariffs and an end to monopolies.

Another dimension was added to the political scene by the growth of working-class organizations that were a consequence of Canada's industrialization. British immigrants to Canada brought with them the traditions of friendly societies, labour protest and unionization. Another influence was the experience of the great American industrial cities across the border. The Canadian Trades and Labour Congress was founded in Toronto in 1883, with the support of the Knights of Labor Assemblies, which had spread north from the United States. The Western Federation of Miners also crossed the frontier, giving rise in the early twentieth century to the Industrial Workers of the World Organization. In the 1890s and 1900s socialist MPs

SPORT IN THE DOMINIONS

As the distinct cultural traditions of the Canadian immigrants began to merge towards the end of the nineteenth century, Canadian sport began to blossom. In 1874 McGill University took on Harvard at rugby, using the freely adapted rules that were then current in Montreal. From this match onward, the game took off on the American side of the border and became 'American football'. In 1876 lacrosse was introduced into Britain, having been adapted by the Canadians from a game played by the Algonkin Indians. Around the turn of the century, popular British sports such as cricket and riding began to decline and a more egalitarian sporting culture developed in their stead. The nationwide popularity of ice hockey

was established by the time that the Stanley Cup was introduced in 1893 as its premier trophy. By 1920 the game had become an Olympic sport.

After World War II, some provinces established training programmes and sent field workers to far-flung communities to promote the concept of sport and recreation. A certain amount of obstruction was sometimes encountered, such as came from one genuinely puzzled mine manager: 'Hell, man, we don't need any more recreation, we've got fourteen prostitutes and seven bootleggers now. We don't really need you fellows.'

By the 1960s sport in Canada formed part of a well-developed national policy.

The Victoria Ice Rink 'the largest and best in the world', opened in Montreal in 1862.

were elected to provincial assemblies and to the Dominion House of Commons, watching with interest the New Unionism and the growth of Lib-Lab politics in Britain.

Lucky Strike

No chapter on Canada's history would be complete without a description of the gold rush. In the second half of the nineteenth century, there had been several gold strikes along the Fraser River in British Columbia, each of which had started a stampede of hopeful prospectors. A young Englishman, Robert Byron Johnson, had described the gold fever in the town of Victoria and the profiteering of local hotel proprietors, who 'reckoned that any man that 'ud raise a growl on such an occashin was darned small pertaters; I might spread out on the side-walk, or turn in with an Injin, if I was a mind to, but his charge to a white man for nightly accommodashin was fifty cents, and niggers rigidly *excluded* . . . the whole place was utterly wild . . . emigrants thronged the streets, buying broken-down mules and Indian ponies, and loading them with provisions and mining implements, packed in so ill a manner that one could well imagine how little skin would remain on the backs of the wretched quadrupeds once the journey was completed . . .'

The Klondike gold rush of 1896 was the largest yet, attracting not only Canadians but also many Americans, who arrived on rusty steamers from San Francisco in such numbers that Canadian sovereignty in the Yukon region was threatened. The journey to Klondike, 300 miles from the Arctic Circle, was a difficult one. Those who could afford the fare arrived on the dozens of steamboats plying the Yukon river; others struggled over the daunting Chilkat Pass on foot, pared of all but their most essential tools and belongings which they carried on their backs. The city of Dawson was the epicentre of the gold rush, and became notorious for the scandalous types it attracted. By 1900 there were 30,000 inhabitants: saloon girls and cardsharks preying on the miners, Asians and Indians, and preachers vainly attempting to stem the tide of iniquity around them. There was

also at least one poet in Dawson, Robert W. Service, whose sagas of the north – *The Cremation of Sam McGee* and *The Shooting of Dan McGrew* – found a readership throughout the Empire:

> There are strange things done in the midnight sun
> By the men who moil for gold;
> The Arctic trails have their secret tales
> That would make your blood run cold;
> The Northern Lights have seen queer sights,
> But the queerest they ever did see
> Was the night on the marge of Lake Lebarge
> I cremated Sam McGee.

When gold was discovered farther north in Alaska in 1899, much of Dawson's motley population moved away. However, by this stage, Canadian claims to the Yukon territory had been confirmed, both by the strength of settlement there and by the presence of the North-West Mounted Police.

Foreign Affairs

The relative autonomy allowed by Canada's constitution, except in the field of foreign affairs, enabled the colony to develop quite freely. Between 1870 and 1914, Canada's role within the British Empire matured to a new independence. Canadian soldiers participated in the Boer War, which broke out in 1899, and were acknowledged to have been some of the finest colonial soldiers there. The country became increasingly confident and trade with Britain declined.

As Britain concentrated her imperial efforts in Asia and Africa, it was up to the sparsely populated colossus to deal directly with its wealthy and ambitious southern neighbour. By the 1890s Canada had become increasingly locked into trade and finance from America, a dependency that would become almost a stranglehold in the twentieth century. Even in this Indian summer of Empire, Canada was moving with increasing speed from being part of an integrated global system towards playing a junior role in a continental partnership.

The main street of Dawson City, July 1899, thronged with wealthy miners who came to spend their newly-found wealth in the gaming houses

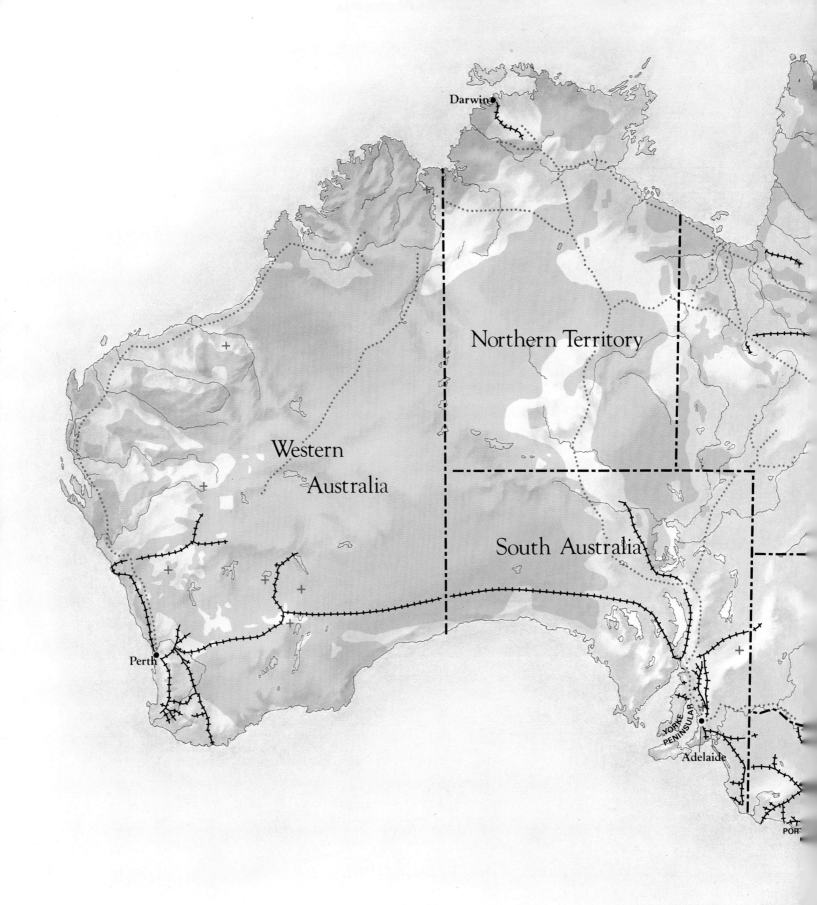

The Development of Australia: 1850–1914

Darwin

Northern Territory

Western Australia

South Australia

Perth

YORKE PENINSULA

Adelaide

POR

	Areas of Aboriginal occupation
┼┼┼┼┼┼┼	Railways
··········	Stock routes
─·─·─·─	State border
┼	Goldfields

Queensland

Brisbane

ew

uth

ales

Sydney

Wagga Wagga

Canberra

Albury

Victoria

Heidelberg

Melbourne

Tasmania

Hobart

Auckland

Rotorua

AUCKLAND

Tarawera

Taupo

New Plymouth

Te Whaiti

TARANAKI

Nelson

HAWKES BAY

WELLINGTON

Napier

NELSON

Wellington

Hokitika

Blenheim

MARLBOROUGH

WESTLAND

CANTERBURY

Christchurch

OTAGO

SOUTHLAND

Invercargill

Dunedin

159

CHAPTER TWENTY-SIX

AUSTRALIA COMES OF AGE

◇

In the last decades of the nineteenth century, Australia enjoyed considerable prosperity. Before 1890, national wealth was increasing at rates comparable to those current in the United States, and twice those of Britain. The population was growing at an annual rate of around 3 per cent, while the imbalance in the numbers of men and women had begun to even out.

Never was it so true that 'Australia rode the sheep's back'. The flocks penetrated farther and farther inland, while investment in buildings, fences, transport and water-storage increased the land's capacity. Much of this capital derived from profits, but an increasing share came from loans raised in Britain. Whereas total British investment during the 1860s amounted to £23.4 million, in the 1880s it had reached £175 million. Since Britain imported much of Australia's agricultural output, anything that affected Britain was bound to have serious consequences down under. Thus, the worldwide drop in agricultural prices that began in the 1870s had a knock-on effect in the Antipodes and profits diminished after 1875.

The situation of the small farmers was a very vulnerable one. While certain areas, such as the Yorke Peninsula in South Australia, remained prosperous, there was continual failure in other areas and many abandoned their farms in despair.

The goldfields discovered in the middle of the century never quite lived up to expectations but the workings in Victoria remained productive throughout the 1870s. More varied mineral deposits were discovered as the century progressed, the most spectacular among them being Broken Hill, which was a mound of pure silver, lead and zinc. Copper was found at Mount Lyell, and more gold at Charters Towers and Mount Morgan.

Australian enthusiasm for imperial adventures against their neighbours is captured by a contemporary print of Queenslanders raising the Union Jack over eastern New Guinea in 1883.

The flood of money from London fuelled not only genuine investment but also a rash of land speculation in the cities, particularly Melbourne; as a result, the period became known as the era of the 'land-boomers'. Urban building became a significant part of economic activity in the Australian colonies. Factories for processing food and for making clothing, metal goods and the like appeared. Housing spread out, creating sprawling suburbs of detached cottages of which 50 per cent were owner-occupied by 1911. Back in Britain at that time, the comparable figure was 10 per cent. These suburbs became an important element in the development of Australian society.

Politics of the Late Nineteenth Century

By the second half of the nineteenth century, all of the Australian colonies, except Tasmania, had roughly similar political systems. Each possessed two parliamentary houses: the Legislative Assembly, the lower house, elected by manhood suffrage, and the Legislative Council, the upper house, whose members were either appointed by the governor or elected by a constituency of the rich and landed gentry. At first, however, there were no political parties on the Westminster model and ad hoc alliances would form and dissolve with great rapidity. This meant that the governments themselves rose and fell with similar speed: in forty years, South Australia had 41 governments, New South Wales 29 and Victoria 28.

The Rise of Australian Nationalism

Although many Australians were quick to articulate their country's interests, they strove to protect them by emphasizing their Britishness rather than rejecting it. For example, rather than develop their own national sport, the Australians took up the mother country's game of cricket with fervour.

One 'national' cause that united most politicians throughout the colonies was the issue of the Pacific Islands. The proximity of

Collins Street, a remnant of Melbourne's heyday.

German and French interests provoked sustained campaigns against what was seen as the complacency of the Colonial Office. Only after one of these campaigns in 1884 did Britain assume control of Papua New Guinea. At the imperial conference three years later, Australian politicians angered their hosts by their insistence on further annexation.

This stance led, quite naturally, to the support of British imperialism in other areas of interest. Thus, in 1885, one of the people most active in support of Britain's adventure in the Sudan was James Service of Victoria, a politician who had vehemently attacked Britain over her inactivity in New Guinea.

Anniversaries became effusive occasions and Queen Victoria's Golden Jubilee tapped floods of exuberance among the populace. As the *Sydney Bulletin* complained, the centennial celebrations in 1888 often applauded the imperial tie as much as they did the Australian achievements. For many of the descendants of British immigrants, however, those two notions were indissolubly linked.

Racism underlay many nationalist impulses. The *Sydney Bulletin*, for example, proclaimed 'Australia for the white man'. The desire to annex the Pacific Islands had been underpinned by racial contempt. It helped to foster enmity towards minorities such as the Chinese and the Melanesians who, since the 1860s, had been recruited to work on the sugar plantations in Queensland. As one journalist observed, 'As to the virtues of the Chinese as citizens: who has seen them? Wherever the Mongol settles, be he rich or poor, his neighbourhood reeks of physical and moral pestilence. His house is rarely washed out; the windows are never open, and the blinds are eternally down – that is to say, unless he has a fresh white paramour, who has not become accustomed to breathe an atmosphere charged beyond Caucasian endurance with human exhalations and opium fumes.' Racism also sustained the contempt with which the native Aboriginals were treated. The colonial parliaments showed less concern than Westminster had done in the past. Massive expropriation continued on the distant frontiers.

The victims did not just acquiesce, however. Some showed great resilience in combating the contempt with which they had to contend. Many Chinese insulated themselves from the hostility by maintaining much of their traditional culture. The Melanesians proved less malleable than their employers had hoped and wrung concessions from their would-be exploiters. The Aboriginals even found places in the colonial order, if only as policemen, stockmen or as workers in the northern fisheries. Still this did not induce them to integrate further into the white man's world. The extent of their suffering is revealed in a petition presented in 1881: 'all the land within our tribal boundaries has been taken possession of by the Government and white settlers; our hunting grounds are used for sheep pasturage and the game reduced and in many places exterminated, rendering our means of subsistence extremely precarious, and often reducing us and our wives and children to begging.'

The Slump of 1890

Australia's economic bubble burst in the 1890s. The growth rate had been declining in the 1880s and, as we have seen, its dependence on both the British financial markets and on patterns of consumption in the United Kingdom made it very vulnerable to any disturbance on the other side of the world. Already, during the 1880s, Australian businessmen had attempted to shore up their flagging economic performance with more borrowing. Thus, when one of Britain's great merchant banks, Baring Brothers, crashed in 1890, an enormous shudder rippled through the Australian economy. Victoria was most seriously affected by the slump, Western Australia least.

With the onset of the Depression came the sharpening of class tensions. Skilled labour had been at a premium ever since the landing in Botany Bay, which meant that wage rates had always been high and that the working men's organizations had considerable leverage. Even before the difficulties of the 1890s, Australia had possessed a tradition of very active trade unionism. Thus, when employers responded to the economic downturn with their traditional remedy of a cut in wages, strikes were inevitable. In the docks the situation grew so inflammatory – literally – that cargoes of wool were set ablaze. In their turn, the employers and the various colonial governments resisted bitterly and so the battle lines were drawn.

In response, radicalism and mainstream working-class movements toughened their stance. Trade unions sponsored their own 'labour party' parliamentary candidates and had a number of notable successes, first in Queensland and then in New South Wales. For a few heady days in December 1899, Andrew Dawson headed a labour ministry in Queensland, probably the world's first. The growth of these groups representing the interests of labour began to polarize Australian politics.

The Triumph of Federation

One cause endorsed by many middle-class politicians at the time was the federation of the Australian colonies, an idea that went back a number of years. A rudimentary 'federal council of

ALFRED DEAKIN AND THE FORTUNES OF FEDERATION

Alfred Deakin was Australia's first important politician. He was born in Melbourne on 3 August 1856 and rose to prominence in the Victoria legislature. However, his real claim to fame lay in his domination of Australia's transition to Federation. Throughout the 1890s, he promoted the national cause with missionary zeal, ignoring the vagaries of the moment and the tactics of other politicians. As he wrote in his history, *The Federal Story*, 'The fortunes of Federalism have visibly trembled in the balance twenty times during the past ten years . . . Again and again it was made the sport of Ministries and Parliaments

Alfred Deakin (1856–1919), the apostle of federation.

and local agitations and just as often, indeed at every step, it benefited by their necessities and purely selfish actions. . . . The enthusiasm for union without which the merely selfish energy

would have died down . . . was the dominating factor among the young, the imaginative, and those whose patriotism was Australian or Imperial. This feeling of loyalty was the mainspring of the whole movement and its constant motive power.' Despite the many hurdles, and the need to hold two referenda in order to ensure that a clear majority in all the participating colonies wanted to come together, the goal was achieved on 1 January 1901 with the swearing in of the Governor-General in Centennial Park, Sydney. Alfred Deakin soon became the Australian Prime Minister.

Australia', with the brief participation of Fiji, had begun meeting in 1885, culminating with a major conference on the topic in 1890. The idea then went out of fashion and it was only in the middle of the 1890s that it resumed its place on the agenda. Among those bodies reviving it was the Australian Natives Association. Political leaders, such as Alfred Deakin in Victoria and Edmund Barton in New South Wales (both of whom would later head national ministries), saw it as a movement of nationalist idealism. Some conservatives saw federation as helping to develop an efficient capitalist unit in a worldwide, British-orientated, economic system. Many ordinary people supported the movement because they hoped that it would benefit their particular region.

Between 1897 and 1898, a conference of state representatives and other interested parties sat to draw up a constitution. Their deliberations were put to the test in a referendum the following June but the endorsement by the New South Wales electorate was not quite large enough for the measure to be passed. A year later, the matter was referred to the voters for a second time after a vigorous campaign and on this occasion was passed with a resounding majority. The politicians then had to travel to London to get imperial approval and, in September 1900, the act which brought the Commonwealth of Australia into being received the royal assent.

The Politics of the Early Commonwealth

The governments of the early Commonwealth pursued policies that both embodied Australian 'national' values and reflected the progressive liberalism then prevalent in Britain and the United States. Racism walked hand in hand with tariff protection. The exclusion of Asian immigrants, justified as 'the White Australia policy', became tighter. The recruitment of Melanesian labour was ended and many of the people previously induced to emigrate were repatriated, frequently against their will. In 1905, the Commonwealth assumed responsibility for Papua New Guinea. In 1911–13 the Commonwealth even backed an expedition to the Antarctic.

Federation also meant internal free trade. The former colonies were now called states and they wished to capitalize on all commercial opportunities. The complement of uninterrupted inter-state trade was a substantial tariff wall erected against the rest of the world.

The first Prime Minister was Edmund Barton, but the dominant personality during the early years of the Commonwealth of

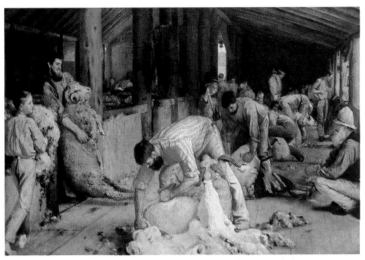

The busiest time in the sheep station's year was the annual shearing, captured here by Tom Roberts in 1890.

Australia was his successor, Alfred Deakin, who became part of the polarization process and, from 1910, led a loose association of middle-class elements against Labour. As he wryly pointed out at the time, 'It cannot be pretended that upon either side of the House we have reached a fusion of parties. We have reached a confusion, but not a fusion.'

Notwithstanding its trade union base, Labour affirmed its allegiance to the national interest. This alienated some radicals but, in April 1910, it permitted the electoral endorsement of their policies. The new Prime Minister, Andrew Fisher, maintained the opposition's policies, merely placing a stronger accent on health and welfare, land taxation and state involvement in banking. Fisher lost office in 1913 but regained it at the outbreak of the First World War.

All federal governments had to consider military and strategic issues. In 1908, while Deakin was Prime Minister, the Royal Australian Navy was established. As one of his fellow politicians warned, 'For a maritime state unfurnished with a navy the sea, so far from being a safe frontier is rather a highway for her enemies; but, with a navy, it surpasses all other frontiers in strength.' In addition, the United States' Navy was invited to visit Australian ports during its Pacific-wide voyages that same year. These moves reflected the anxiety caused by Japan's triumph over Russia in 1905. Deakin's Government also asked Lord Kitchener's advice regarding the defence of the Commonwealth. The Labour

NEW ZEALAND NOVELIST

Katharine Mansfield was born in Wellington, New Zealand, on 14 October 1888. In 1908 she came to London, publishing her first collection of short stories, *In a German Pension*, in 1911. When her brother died in the First World War she was shocked into nostalgia and began to write the stories for which she is still famous today – lyrical evocations of family life in New Zealand. In 1918, after divorcing George Bowden, she married the critic and essayist Middleton Murray. This brought her into contact with D.H. Lawrence, but the friendship was a stormy one, with the character of 'Gudrun' in *Women in Love* allegedly based on Katharine.

Her best collections of stories were published during this period, including *Bliss* in 1921 and *The Garden Party* in 1922. The last five years of her life were overshadowed by tuberculosis. She died in France on 9 January 1923. Several of her works were published posthumously by Middleton Murray, including her journal in which as a nineteen-year-old she had recorded her intense delight in the New Zealand countryside: 'Start very early. Titiokura – the rough roads and glorious mountains and bush. The top of Turangakumu. Next day, walking and bush, clematis and orchids. At last come to the Waipunga Falls, the fierce wind, the flax. . . .'

A family snap of Katharine Mansfield with her nephew in 1907.

Maori culture was still thriving in 1857, when these drawings of their elaborate food storage bins on stilts were made.

opposition endorsed these actions and upheld them when they came to power.

The umbilical cord between Australia and Britain was still strong. Already, the colonial governments had sent troops to the Boer War. Thus, when war broke out in 1914, there was no hesitation. Prime Minister Fisher proclaimed, 'Australians will stand behind our own to help and defend her to our last man and our last shilling.'

New Zealand Starts to Grow

New Zealand, too, entered a fresh phase of its development around 1870. While exports of wool remained strong, other areas of the economy flagged. The most vigorous response to this stagnation came from Julius Vogel, a British immigrant who had stopped off in Victoria on the way. Vogel was first elected to parliament in 1863 but within six years had become Colonial Treasurer. On his initiative, the central government borrowed money, mostly from London, in order to develop the islands' infrastructure.

The scale of this investment in relation to the size of the country's economy meant that most people were affected by the consequent prosperity. When Vogel sought to rid himself of the frustrations and obstructions put in his way by the provincial councils, especially in North Island, he easily succeeded in so doing. In 1875 he went to London to represent the colony in loan negotiations and his place was taken by H.A. Atkinson, who lacked his predecessor's bold approach. The reduction in government spending that followed might have appeared prudent to the conservatives but it certainly contributed to the hard times experienced by the islands in the 1880s.

Stagnation in the price of wool had its effect as well. Many settlers suffered distress, some suffered disaster. Yet, in the decades to come, technological changes would transform New Zealand's position. By 1890–91, meat, chilled and transported to Europe in refrigerated ships, had assumed a place second only to wool in the list of the colony's exports.

During the 1870s and 1880s, the politics of New Zealand were remarkably similar to those of Australia. Factions ebbed and flowed around particular personalities and few people seem to have stayed in parliament for any length of time. In 1890, labour discontent spread across the Tasman Sea. The success of its political wing was virtually instantaneous and five labour candidates were elected. Furthermore, the liberal factions which came to power in the same elections, under the leadership of John Ballance, were very radical in their policies. Under him and his successor, R.J. Seddon, legislation was passed which established government support for small farmholders, women's suffrage, industrial arbitration and old age pensions.

Accompanying this radical turn of events was a prosperity that set New Zealand apart from Australia and was to sustain it until the 1920s. Wool prices gradually rose, but it was the burgeoning dairy and frozen meat businesses that made the greatest difference to the economy. The farmers were now no longer dependent on just one product.

Conflict and Culture

After their defeat at the hands of the British army, the Maori suffered a sharp decline in morale. Their sense of identity seemed to disintegrate. Furthermore, as Pakeha (European) agriculture expanded, the Maori tribes were forced farther and farther back into less fertile land until they became almost a peripheral irrelevance in a land that, within living memory, they had dominated. Assimilation became the canon of the Young Maori Party, many of whose affiliates were young professionals who had already crossed the divide. Nevertheless, Maori culture was not so easily discounted. In the two censuses conducted around the turn of the century, most of the 4,000 inter-racial couples counted were living in Maori communities.

The problem for the Pakeha in dealing with the Maori was largely one of imagination, or lack of it. Many took pride in asserting the superiority of their indigenous compatriots when compared with the Aboriginals or the South African Bushmen. Yet even a well-meaning clergyman could describe that superiority only in terms that measured the Maori's ability to absorb the alien culture: 'On the West Coast of this island, the natives have made splendid progress. They have abandoned the whares [Maori huts], and are living in cottages which would compare well with those in the cities. They have a water supply laid on, and their slaughter-house is an up-to-date building which would be an object lesson to many European communities, the abbatoir being floored with concrete.'

The new century saw a gradual erosion of the value of real wages. And in 1901 the New Zealand Socialist Party was formed. In the coalfields, the combination of these two developments encouraged a militant attitude. Drawing on ideas formulated in the United States and Australia, the militants were strong enough by 1908 to win a strike in defiance of the arbitration court. The following year, the more widespread but still militant Federation of Labour was formed. As in Australia, this movement polarized the political forum and an equally militant conservative opposition, the Reform Party, rose to power, under W.G. Massey. Even the war failed to heal the rift and, in the decades to come, politics in New Zealand were as divisive as those in Australia. The awarding of dominion status in 1907 almost seemed an irrelevance.

While the political battle lines were being drawn, a first generation of Pakeha artists, writers and thinkers was starting to emerge. Yet the islands were still a provincial society and it is very noticeable that the short story writer, Katherine Mansfield, and the physicist, Ernest Rutherford, had both left their homeland before they produced their greatest work.

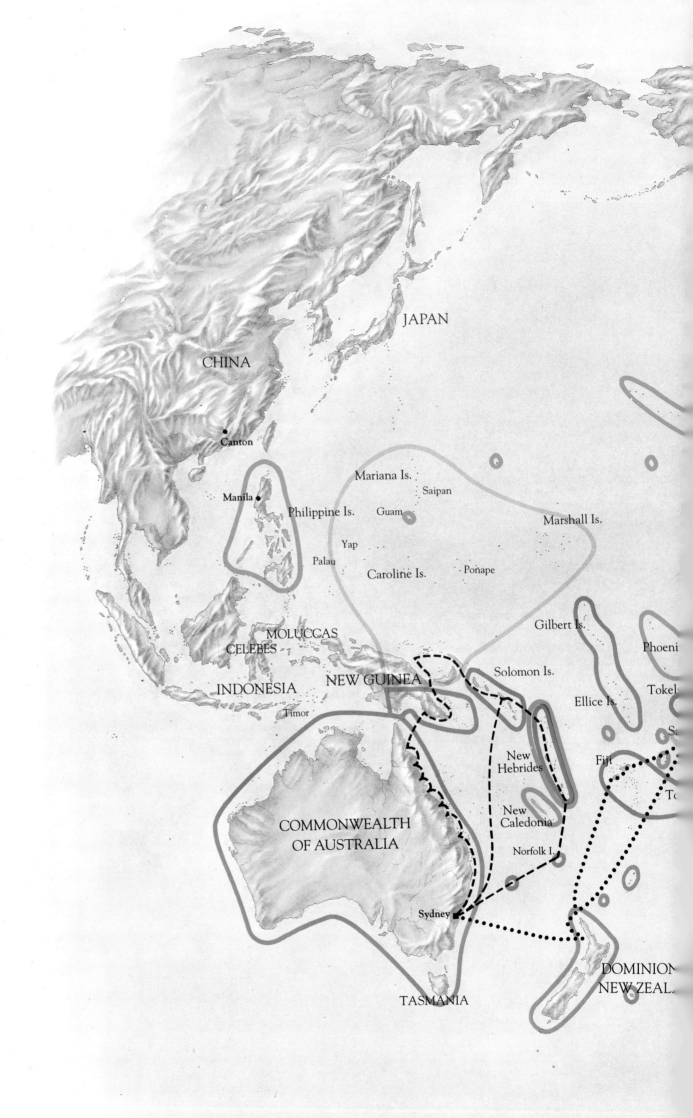

CHINA

JAPAN

Canton

Manila

Philippine Is.

Mariana Is.

Saipan

Guam

Marshall Is.

Yap

Palau

Caroline Is.

Ponape

MOLUCCAS

CELEBES

Gilbert Is.

Phoeni

INDONESIA

NEW GUINEA

Solomon Is.

Tokel

Timor

Ellice Is.

Sa

New
Hebrides

Fiji

COMMONWEALTH
OF AUSTRALIA

New
Caledonia

To

Norfolk I.

Sydney

DOMINION
NEW ZEAL

TASMANIA

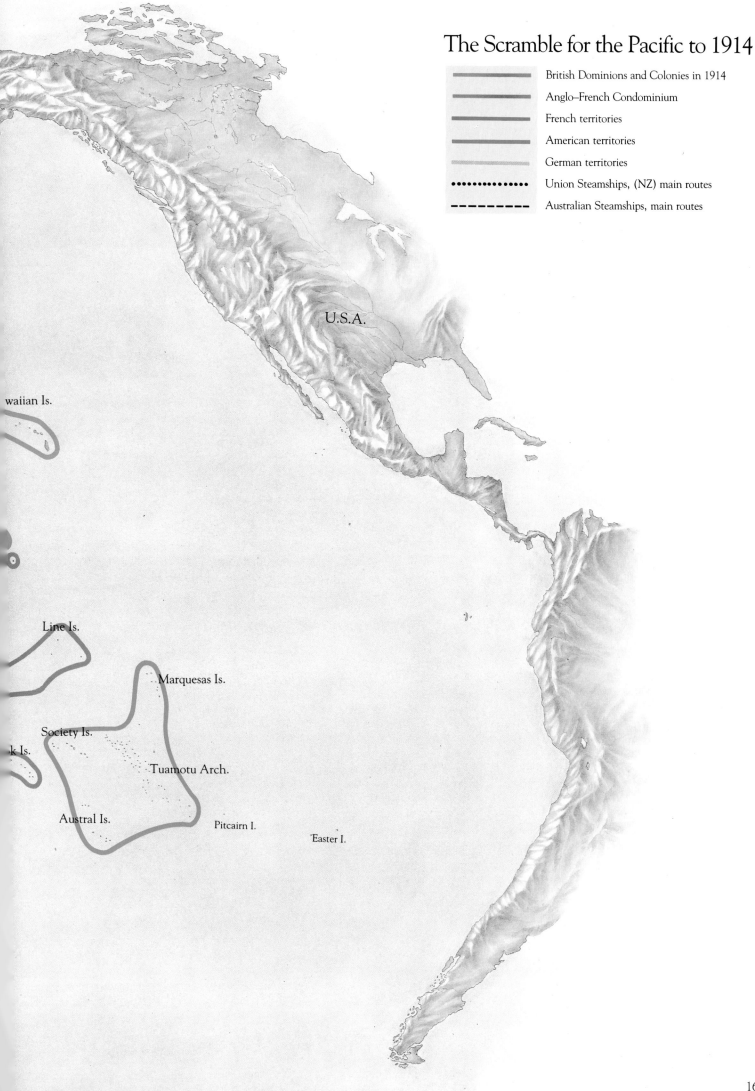

The Scramble for the Pacific to 1914

British Dominions and Colonies in 1914
Anglo–French Condominium
French territories
American territories
German territories
Union Steamships, (NZ) main routes
Australian Steamships, main routes

waiian Is.

Line Is.

Marquesas Is.

Society Is.

k Is.

Tuamotu Arch.

Austral Is.

Pitcairn I.

Easter I.

U.S.A.

CHAPTER TWENTY-SEVEN

A PATTERN OF ISLANDS: DIVIDING THE PACIFIC

◇

It was not a matter of chance that the islands of the Pacific Ocean were among the last places on earth to be touched by British imperialism. The vast ocean wastes, dotted with islands, many of them tiny and with negligible populations, offered little to tempt empire-builders. Not surprisingly, European contact after Captain Cook's death in 1779 was only intermittent for nearly half a century. A prolonged period of informal penetration followed and it was only in the 1880s and 1890s that this remote sector of the globe was finally partitioned between the European powers. Even then, it was largely carried out as a measure of political housekeeping and was performed with little enthusiasm.

Whalers, Traders, Missionaries and Beachcombers

Waves of settlement and influence have swept across the Pacific for millennia. As the nineteenth century progressed, European traders, missionaries and planters joined this ancient succession, but their intrusion was accompanied by the new values and pressures which would eventually bring annexation.

After New South Wales was settled in 1788, the colonists began looking to their Pacific frontier for trade and supplies. Soon their vessels were busily engaged in procuring pork from Tahiti for their own market, and in collecting sandalwood and culinary delicacies (*bêche-de-mer*) for the Chinese. The local chiefs and their people absorbed this change in their way of life fairly easily. Hundreds of Fijians, for example, were mobilized to cut sandalwood or to build curing-houses. But they returned to their former occupations when the supply of wood was exhausted, the lagoons fished out and the traders had moved on to other islands. Similarly, in the seal and whaling trades, there was no competition for land or resources, and the islanders could easily accommodate new demands.

On rare occasions, however, these contacts degenerated into bloody violence. There was the notorious *Boyd* massacre in 1809 in the Bay of Islands, New Zealand, when the crew of a whaling vessel were slaughtered and eaten. In 1829 the *Sophie* was forced to abandon 113 Tongan sandalwood labourers on a hostile New Hebridean beach. In 1842 Andrew Cheyne's sandalwood ship, with its crew of fifteen, ran into trouble at Lifu in the Loyalty Islands: 'At 3 p.m. on the 30th a large war canoe came alongside from the other side of the bay, carrying 50 men, they brought a little Sandal Wood but did not seem anxious to sell it, having come apparently for the purpose of taking the schooner. They came like wild Bulls, and boarded the vessel in spite of us – we drew our men up across the quarter deck two deep while we were buying their wood, and after allowing them to remain on board nearly two hours, we were at last obliged to charge them with our bayonets and drive them overboard. They fought hard for some time but were at last obliged to give way.' However, of the many thousands of trading transactions that took place during these years, the forty or so violent incidents recorded were very much the exception to the rule. As one trader said, 'You cannot trade with these people and fight them too.'

Gradually, small communities of Europeans grew up around the islands to help service the passing trade. Camping initially on the sand, they became known as beachcombers. By the 1850s there were about two thousand, of whom a quarter were escaped convicts from Australia. They were completely outnumbered by and almost totally reliant upon the islanders, who numbered over four million. Muskets soon became the key trading item and those chiefs who obtained them had their power greatly enhanced as a result. In Tahiti, Pomare I had a missionary draft a letter to Governor King of New South Wales to accompany a pork shipment dispatched in 1801: 'May it please your excellency, Your letter and present I kindly accept. I love King George and his subjects, and will, while I live, be a protector to those who put themselves under my care; but I must tell your excellency, I at this time stand in fear of the commonality, many of them being disaffected towards me, and their disaffection, I

Whalers off the coast of North Island, New Zealand, in 1838.

Historians and commentators have described the European penetration of the Pacific as a disaster, or what the writer Alan Moorhead described as a 'fatal impact'. Entire populations were slaughtered by European diseases, such as smallpox and measles. The use of firearms against traditional weapons increased the carnage, undermining traditional authority and the will to survive. 'Blackbirders' kidnapped tens of thousands of islanders against their will, to work as virtual slaves on colonial plantations. The Pacific paradise was irreversibly corrupted by the worst evils of Western civilization.

During the 1970s and 1980s, this cheerless picture has been compared with surviving information about pre-colonial times. The results have been remarkable. Life expectancy was about 40 years before the Europeans

The cry of the blackbird helped Jamaican slave-owners to locate runaway 'blackbirds' – a perjorative term which later spread to the Pacific.

arrived; degenerative diseases and periodic starvation were common. Violence was institutionalized and life was cheap. Although European diseases were new, the islands had been ravaged by epidemics before. Indeed, the Pacific population was not decimated. It actually increased in many areas after the arrival of the Europeans. New technologies, such as firearms, were soon incorporated into existing social traditions. The Pacific had been a great trading community for centuries and the idea of paid work was understood. By the 1890s half of the Solomon Islanders working in Queensland were labourers who had returned for a second or third contract.

---

fear, is encouraged by some seamen who are in the island; and therefore I wish your excellency to present me with a few fire-arms, whereby my authority may be maintained and the peace of my kingdom preserved.'

King immediately dispatched the muskets and Pomare put them to use with considerable effect. However, such weapons did not, as is often thought, cause great loss of life or disruption amongst the island societies. Rather, they became a critical asset in customary internecine warfare; it was the island factions, not the white interlopers, who used the guns to maintain and extend their domination.

The Conversions Begin

Missionaries arrived on the islands at the same time as the whalers and the traders, fired with enthusiasm by the Evangelical revival then current in Britain. The nonconformist London Missionary Society established a toehold on Tahiti in 1797. The Church Missionary Society (the Anglicans) began their work in New Zealand in 1814. By the 1820s most Tahitians were nominally Christians. French Catholics arrived in the south-west Pacific in the late 1830s and, during the following two decades, large numbers of Maoris, Tongans, Fijians and Samoans declared their allegiance to one denomination or another.

Polynesia, with its stratified societies and healthy climate, proved a fruitful field of operation for the missionaries, who quickly became intermediaries between chiefs and traders. In Tahiti, for example, the missionaries' support for Pomare II, and the guns they brought with them – not to mention the fifty-tonne, missionary-built vessel he was given – ultimately helped him to conquer the whole island. The missionaries then assumed a role as both spiritual and temporal advisers to the new 'state'. Thus, it would seem that the chiefs used the missionaries as much as the missionaries used the chiefs: in the beginning, conversions were rather more politically, than spiritually inspired.

Those islands of the western Pacific known as Melanesia (situated immediately to the north-east of Australia and inhabited by Oceanic negroid peoples) were far less fertile recruiting grounds; they were rife with malaria, social authority was much more diffused and the locals more warlike. John Williams, the doyen of the Polynesian L.M.S. missionaries, was killed in 1839 during the Mission's first attempt to land in the New Hebrides. Although he was quickly succeeded by others – most notably the Presbyterians – the conversion rates were very much lower and the area proved relatively unattractive for Europeans throughout the nineteenth century.

The Maoris fiercely opposed foreign interlopers and massacred the entire crew of the Boyd in 1809.

Planters and Blackbirders

Increased European penetration of the islands in the second half of the nineteenth century was largely the result of a growing demand for tropical products in the European economy. Vegetable oil, derived from copra, became an increasingly marketable commodity in Europe from the 1850s, and the German firm, Godeffroy and Sons, started the first Pacific copra plantation on Samoa in 1857. Sugar cane, cocoa and cotton plantations followed in the 1860s; the growing of cotton increased rapidly when the blockade of the South during the American Civil War interrupted supplies from the world's primary source. European planters moved into North Queensland, Samoa, Fiji, Tonga, New Caledonia and even the New Hebrides to grow these crops.

Indentured labourers were recruited to work these new plantations, and while there were only 2,760 Europeans in Fiji in 1871, 22,000 workers had flooded in from Melanesia by the turn of the century, with a further 60,000 Indians arriving between 1879 and 1920. Missionaries stigmatized recruiters in the islands as 'blackbirders', claiming that many of the labourers were kidnapped or taken against their will, although this was rarely the case after the initial contact period.

The plantations – with their European owners and managers, and thousands of immigrant workers – placed an unprecedented strain on the indigenous governments. Native kingdoms, even with the aid of guns and missionary advisers, could not cope, or so it was thought. Cakobau, a Fijian chief legendary in the 1840s for his barbarity, was tied in knots by litigation initiated by the planters when he became a constitutional monarch in the 1860s. Planters refused to pay local taxes, or to abide by the decisions of the local land courts and they formed private armies. Island chiefs and law-abiding planters alike appealed to the European authorities in the hope that annexation would stem such anarchy. As a result, and with considerable reluctance on the part of those powers, the serious partition of the Pacific began.

Dividing the Cake

New South Wales had demanded that Britain should annex various islands on regular occasions from the 1820s onwards, but this had generally fallen on deaf ears. In London, such acquisitions were seen as mere drains on the exchequer. The first change of heart came in 1840 with New Zealand. At the Colonial Office, a very reluctant James Stephen agreed that the only way to curb the speculative exploitation of the New Zealand Company, and to protect the Maoris in land deals, was for Britain to take over the administration of the territory. The failure of the local missionaries and traders to keep a civilized peace had forced the British government's hand.

That there was no concerted imperial plan in the Pacific is evident from British acquiescence in the French annexation of Tahiti and in America's takeover of Hawaii during the 1840s, despite Britain's prior claim to both groups of islands. Nor were the French out to amass large territorial gains. Once they had established a base in Tahiti, they remained content until 1853 when, again without protest from the other powers, they annexed New Caledonia for use as a penal colony, just as Britain had taken Botany Bay sixty-five years earlier.

However, the arrival of trade and the Bible did not necessarily mean that the flag would follow. Occasional visits by the French and British navies kept the peace in the other islands. On some, such as the New Hebrides and Samoa, British Protestant missionaries and French Catholic priests, and the traders and planters from many countries all worked cheek by jowl, supporting competing chiefs, generally upsetting each other's plans and perennially calling on their respective metropolitan forces to step in and assert their authority – something the home governments were loath to do.

Investment in large-scale plantations and the recruiting drives of the 1860s caused greater disruption than before. From Fiji especially, where most of the planters were Australian, there were insistent calls for British annexation. In 1858, even Cakobau joined the chorus, hoping that his debt to the United States of $45,000 for razing the American consulate to the ground (among other minor peccadillos) would be seen as a fair exchange for sovereignty over his kingdom. In the face of this pressure, the Colonial Office wriggled for as long as it could, appointing consuls and advisers and even suggesting, without success, that New South Wales should take over Fiji. Finally, in 1874, when the humanitarian lobby added its weight to the cause by pressing hard for controls on labour recruitment, the Crown acquiesced. Similar calls for the annexation of the New Hebrides, Samoa and New Guinea were unsuccessful, however. Instead, the Governor of Fiji was made a high commissioner of the western Pacific, to enable him to police British subjects throughout the islands.

That, of course, failed to silence the Antipodean imperialists, but the British were adamant. In Lord Salisbury's estimate, the

FIJI'S INDIANS

In May 1987 Fiji hit the world's headlines when Colonel Rabuka led the Fijian army in the overthrow of the country's elected government and then four months later, in a second coup, took Fiji out of the Commonwealth. The roots of this action stretch back over a hundred years into the imperial past. In 1879, five years after Fiji's annexation, the governor allowed the importation of indentured Indian labourers in order to protect the native Fijians from capitalist exploitation.

These *Girmitiyas*, as they called themselves, worked on the sugar plantations but were forbidden to own land, a restriction of their freedom that still applies.

Today the Indian community produces 90 per cent of the country's sugar crop, Fiji's main export, but the native Fijians own 80 per cent of the land. The Indian population has multiplied faster than the ethnic Fijians and by the 1980s it outnumbered them. The Indians have been dominant in the labour movement, urban commerce and in public service, contrasting with the more conservative Fijians who have worked their land, followed their traditional chiefs and made up virtually all of the armed forces.

With Rabuka's coup, an imperial ghost from the nineteenth century had claimed a twentieth-century victim.

Old Girmitiya songs lamented the luring away of Indians by the Fijian recruiters:

Indians working on a Fijian sugar plantation.

Oh, recruiter, your heart is deceitful
Your speech is full of lies! . . .
I hoe all day and cannot sleep at night
Today my whole body aches
Damnation to you, recruiters!

Wellington Harbour, New Zealand, one of the world's finest natural harbours, depicted in 1840 by an unknown artist. Wellington was named in 1840 in recognition of the help given to the New Zealand Company by the first Duke of Wellington.

Australian colonists of the New Hebrides were 'the most unreasonable people I have ever heard of. . . . They want us to incur all the bloodshed, and the danger, and the stupendous cost of a war with France . . . for a group of islands which to us are as valueless as the South Pole?' Not surprisingly, the colonial governments took a different view.

To the Australians the islands were strategic outposts. The fear of potentially hostile European powers establishing themselves close by was a very real one. French planters were already challenging the British in the New Hebrides, and the Presbyterian missions there had great support from the colony of Victoria, which did not want to see them ousted by French Papists. Furthermore, France seemed ready to send more convicts to the area – a sensitive issue in New South Wales where there were complaints of escaped French convicts landing and plying their former trade.

A keen sense of unease was also aroused in Samoa and the other islands by the German presence. Matters came to a head in 1883 when, to pre-empt a German occupation, the Queensland government declared that New Guinea was part of Australia, only for the move to be declared illegal by the Colonial Office. Seizing their chance, the Germans moved in. This provoked such an outcry in both Australia and New Zealand that the British were forced to alter their long-established policy, and to accede to colonial pressure. An editorial comment in a contemporary newspaper reveals, however, a less than edifying motive behind the action: 'Queensland is bound to look for cheap labour for . . . semi-tropical agriculture, and New Guinea is one of our probable fields for seeking that. Once in the hands of the Germans that would be cut off.' Consequently, after some negotiation, New Guinea was partitioned; the Germans took the north and the British the south. The Dutch were already in control of the west of the island. Eventually, pressure in other places had some effects. France and Britain established joint dominion over the New Hebrides. Then in 1888, much to New Zealand's relief, the Cook Islands were annexed.

The fact that at home the cause of imperialism was waxing may have had its effect in the corridors of power. The scramble for African domains was approaching its conclusion; the Pacific remained as one of the last areas with lines as yet undrawn. Britain annexed the Gilbert and Ellice Islands in 1892 and the Solomon Islands in the following year (both of these groups were British missionary and trading areas). In 1899, Germany and the United States partitioned Samoa, while the Americans alone annexed Hawaii. Tonga became a British protectorate in 1900. The final move came in the following year when Ocean Island – a particularly large pile of guano – was added to the imperial crown.

The Australians were proud of the part they played in the process; as one newspaper rather dramatically put it, they had prevented 'jewel after jewel' being 'torn from the diadem'. More than the British, they had something to protect. By the 1880s, the Fijian sugar industry was dominated by one Australian company, Colonial Sugar Refineries, while the shipping to all the islands was increasingly under the control of the Sydney firm, Burns Philp, which had nine steamers and forty-one smaller sailing-traders in service by 1900. Although this made little difference to the economies of either Britain or Australia, it was of importance to the companies and cities involved. In addition, the possession of strategic outposts helped the colonists' sense of security. Thus, the persistence of Australia and New Zealand had finally paid off.

Their role was made even more explicit in the early years of the new century when New Zealand took control of the administration of the Cook Islands, and Australia ran New Guinea. At the outbreak of war in 1914, the two Antipodean colonies took the process one stage further when the Germans were expelled from New Guinea and Samoa. The Japanese in their turn claimed the Marshalls and Carolines. All were retained at the end of the war under mandates from the League of Nations. The scramble for possessions was over – at least for a generation.

LUMBER
WHEAT

22
CANADA 8

139
USA 20

U.S.A

LUMBER
WHEAT
NICKEL

Halifax

Bermuda

2 4
WEST INDIES
SUGAR

Kingston

PANAMA CANAL
(UNDER CONSTRUCTION)

BEEF

28 24
SOUTH AMERICA

221 118
EUROPE

United Kingdom
MACHINERY
COAL
STEEL
COTTON
GOODS

27 21
MEDITERRANEAN
REGION

Gibraltar

Malta

PALM OIL

Simonstown

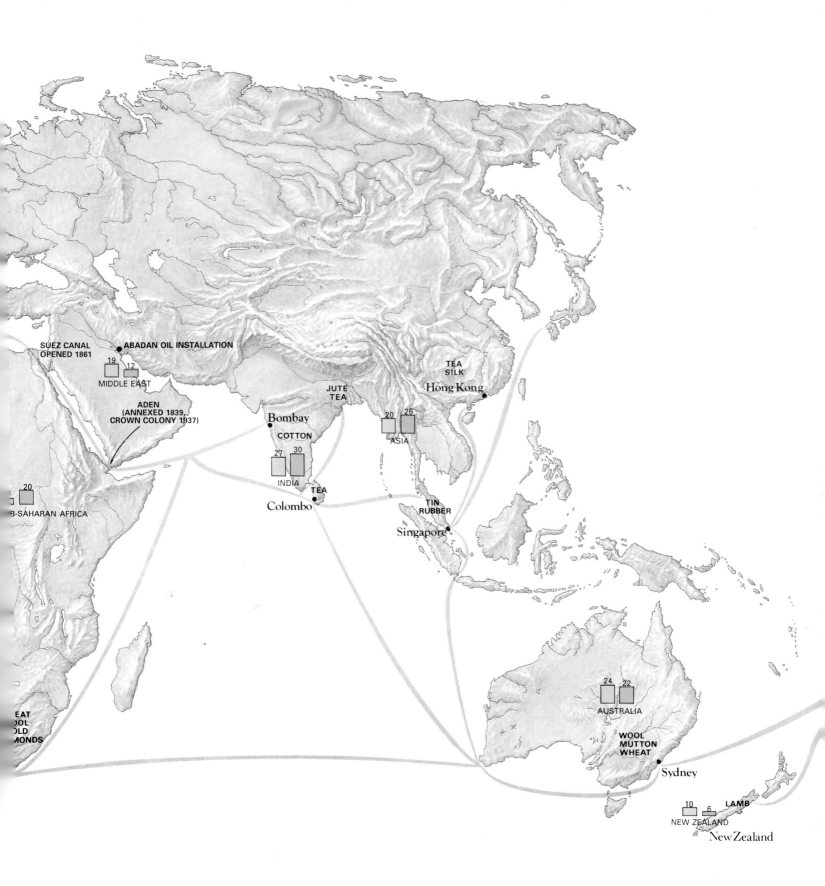

SUEZ CANAL
OPENED 1861

● ABADAN OIL INSTALLATION

19 12
MIDDLE EAST

ADEN
(ANNEXED 1839,
CROWN COLONY 1937)

TEA
SILK

JUTE
TEA

Hong Kong

20 26
ASIA

Bombay

COTTON

27 30
INDIA

TEA

Colombo

TIN
RUBBER

Singapore

20
B-SAHARAN AFRICA

EAT
OOL
OLD
MONDS

24 22
AUSTRALIA

WOOL
MUTTON
WHEAT

Sydney

10 6
LAMB
NEW ZEALAND

New Zealand

Britain's Balance of Trade with the Empire in 1900

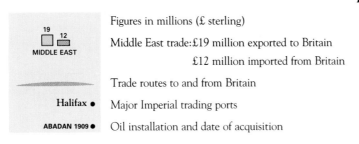

19 12
MIDDLE EAST

Figures in millions (£ sterling)

Middle East trade: £19 million exported to Britain
£12 million imported from Britain

Trade routes to and from Britain

Halifax ● Major Imperial trading ports

ABADAN 1909 ● Oil installation and date of acquisition

CHAPTER TWENTY-EIGHT

THE WEARY TITAN

◇

The years between the end of the nineteenth century and the outbreak of the First World War appear, in retrospect, as a golden age of prosperity, stability and international dominance for Britain.

The spread of Britain's dominion was a dazzling concept in itself. Queen Victoria's Diamond Jubilee in 1897 was marked by a London parade attended by soldiers from all corners of the Empire. The Duke of Argyll informed Victoria: 'Although your Majesty's Home Troops were far the finest, we were much interested in the Colonials. Their uniform is dun-coloured. But we could not help remembering that no sovereign state since the fall of Rome could muster subjects from such distant lands.'

Comparisons with imperial Rome were popular; imperial heroes in fact and fiction moulded middle-class opinion and enriched the popular culture of the day. Such images were not always comforting, since even Rome had fallen to the barbarians in the end, and to the policy-makers of Edwardian Britain new dangers seemed to threaten at every turn. Joseph Chamberlain predicted gloomily to the Colonial Conference of 1902 that Britain was a 'Weary Titan that staggers under the too vast orb of his own fate'. The problems were threefold: economic, strategic and social. Each one called official policies into question and seemed to require major new political initiatives.

Economic Decline

Although Britain was still playing a large part in the international economy around the turn of the century, her industries no longer dominated the world as they had done fifty years before. In 1870 British factories had produced thirty-two per cent of the total world output of manufactured goods; by 1900 the percentage had fallen to less than half of this. The United States took over Britain's position as the world's largest single manufacturing economy in the early 1880s, and by 1900 Germany had moved into second place. America's rate of manufacturing growth was more than twice that of Britain.

The rapid spread of industrialization abroad was bound to affect British exporters hoping vainly to remain 'the workshop of the world'. By 1890 the industrial countries of Europe and North America had pushed British exports out of their home markets, and were challenging them elsewhere. Britain could obtain only partial relief from this pressure by retreating into the Empire although, by the turn of the century, this was absorbing a third of British exports. In 1913 India was Britain's best market and Canada her fourth best, but Germany stood second, Belgium and Holland third, France fifth and the USA sixth.

This problem was to become an economic feature of the twentieth century, but it was not until the 1920s that major disruptions to the balance of payments became evident and that the role of sterling as the linchpin of the international monetary system became threatened. Nevertheless, the decline of British manufacturing was already plain to see. It was a damaging trend and was aggravated by increasing imports of manufactured goods, which rose to become a quarter of all British imports by 1900, compared to only five per cent forty years previously.

The alleged 'failure' of the late Victorian economy was attributed at the time to now-familiar whipping boys: low capital investment, a reluctance on the part of manufacturers to adopt new production techniques and high wages. But there were other, more complex factors at work. The rate of market growth was very slow, and Britain was no longer at the forefront of

Eighty-nine regiments, from the Canada Field Artillery to the Sierra Leone Frontier Force, represented the romance of an Empire which was celebrated by the poet-laureate Tennyson: 'One with Britain, heart and soul, one life, one flag, one throne!'

'Iron and Coal' by William Bell Scott, depicting the dignity of honest toil against the industrial background of the River Tyne.

innovation and technical change; America and Germany had again taken the lead in developing the new manufacturing economies of electrical goods, chemicals and metal processing. It has recently been calculated that between 1873 and 1913 there was no real growth in productivity at all.

Other observers blamed the retardation on the flow of capital out of the country. Already in 1899, the *Contemporary Review* warned: 'The gain which the moneyed class draw from their investments abroad cannot possibly last for ever, and cannot compensate us for the misfortune which will overtake us if we allow our great national industries to be sacrificed.'

The industry which seemed most likely to be sacrificed in this way was the strategically vital one of iron and steel. While Britain had once produced almost half of the world's output of pig iron and a third of finished steel, by 1913 a third of Britain's iron ore had to be imported. British firms were slow to adopt the new capital-intensive processes that were enabling the Americans and Germans to make high-quality steel from cheap raw materials. Home producers, in their turn, argued vehemently that much of the competition was 'unfair trade' – the result of excess steel being deliberately dumped at low prices by continental manufacturers. Whatever the underlying reason, this decline was threatening the armament development of the army and navy which, in the face of an aggressive German military build-up, was very disturbing indeed.

These concerns were more publicly voiced in the years before the First World War. They seemed well-founded: in 1914 it was discovered that Germany had produced all the magnetos used in British engines and all the khaki dye for military uniforms.

Problems of Defence

The sheer size of the British Empire during the last quarter of the nineteenth century exacerbated defence problems. Britain's per capita defence costs were much higher than those of any other country in the world, even in the early twentieth century, and accounted for over a third of total government expenditure.

With the exception of India, it was hard to wring direct contributions for imperial defence from the colonies themselves. It was argued that any contribution would defend Britain's interests and not their own, and the self-governing colonies of Canada and Australasia would not consider contributions unless they had a controlling right as well (although they did send volunteer troops to fight for the Queen in South Africa). The British argued rather compellingly that the Empire needed a supremely powerful navy to defend it, and that this was possible only by maintaining a single, unified command.

The Boer War of 1899–1902 was a shock to British army morale. The fighting lasted two and a half years, instead of being a three-month skirmish as had been jauntily predicted in *Punch*. When the war finally ended, the government formed the Committee of Imperial Defence to reform tactics and strategy, to assess possible threats and to draw up future defence priorities. Invasion scares and xenophobia fuelled a national paranoia about foreign designs on British territory. Sir Thomas Sanderson of the Foreign Office commented wryly: 'It has sometimes seemed to me that to a foreigner reading our press the British Empire must appear in the light of some huge giant sprawling over the globe, with gouty fingers and toes stretching in every direction, which cannot be approached without eliciting a scream.'

During its first five years, the Committee of Imperial Defence was concerned with countering a major threat to the Empire: the invasion of India by Russia. The completion of the Russian rail link to Tashkent meant that a potential invasion force of hundreds of thousands of troops could be sent south into India across the Oxus river. To repulse them, it was calculated, the British must take up defensive positions in Afghanistan. To achieve this, the Indian army needed to be reinforced by between one hundred and fifty thousand and five hundred thousand British troops (far more than the peacetime strength of

WITH THE FLAG TO PRETORIA

The inglorious conduct of the Boer War from 1899–1902 jolted the British government out of its late-Victorian complacency. The warfare of the Boer farmers in South Africa was a disturbing phenomenon. They were superb horsemen with an expert knowledge of the veld, able to vanish into the hills as quickly as they had appeared. Despite the blusterings of generals such as Kitchener, who expected the tiny Boer army to stand ground and be mown down honourably 'like the Sudanese, who stood up to a fair fight', the new guerilla tactics were extraordinarily effective. For the first time the British army had to develop counter-insurgency techniques. These included pacification measures, such as the infamous

A wry look at the new fashion for on-the-spot reporting, with Kipling at the typewriter.

concentration camp system, in which twenty thousand died of hunger and disease.

It took more than two years for a British force to defeat the Boers. As well as causing a massive crisis of confidence at home, it was the first time a war had been reported regularly in the press. One correspondent was the young Winston Churchill of the *Morning Post*. The Harmsworth Brothers produced illustrated accounts and explicit criticism of the conduct of the war in their paper, *With the Flag to Pretoria*. These photographs and sketches helped to provoke an unprecedented wave of anti-war agitation: 'The mistakes of generals in the field kill hundreds, the ignorance of ministers in the Cabinet slays thousands.'

FEAR GOD AND DREAD NOUGHT

Lord Fisher of Kilverstone, Admiral of the Fleet, was one of the most influential figures in British defence policy-making in the years before the First World War. His succession of reforms of the Royal Navy amounted to a revolution at the Admiralty. In particular, he was responsible for scrapping large numbers of obsolete ships (he described the Naval Reserve as 'a miser's hoard of useless junk'), and replacing them with new vessels that combined speed with fire power. The most famous of the ships his vision inspired was the *Dreadnought*, a big-gun battleship with strength, speed and fire power that made all other battleships obsolete. When 'Jacky' Fisher was made a peer in 1909, he took as the motto for his coat of arms the phrase 'Fear God and Dread Nought'.

The completion of the *Dreadnought* in 1906, coupled with the Tangier crisis of 1905, began an arms race between Britain and Germany for command of the seas. The new battleships made all current naval designs outmoded and negated the large advantage in numbers of existing ships that the British possessed. By the

Norman Wilkinson's vision of 'The Royal Navy', painted in 1907, made the Dreadnought a symbol of British sea-power.

autumn of 1914 Britain had built thirty-one modern capital ships but the cost of naval construction had risen alarmingly. In the 'dreadnought crisis' of 1909, the building programme could be sustained only by contributions from Australia, the Malay States and New Zealand. A dreadnought cost about £2 million: the Old Age Pension Scheme set out in the Budget of 1908 cost about £8 million. By 1914 HM Government was spending £12.5 million on pensions and £51.5 million on the Royal Navy.

---

the entire British army) and more than three million camels.

The costs of defending the army were spiralling ever upwards. Lord Selborne observed that it was 'a terrific task to remain the greatest naval power when naval powers are year by year increasing in numbers and in strength, and at the same time be a military power strong enough to meet the greatest military power in Asia'. Lord Esher, the leading Edwardian defence expert, could see that the bonds of imperial solidarity were wearing terribly thin. In 1905 he prophesied that one major military reverse, such as that which Russia had just suffered in her war with Japan, would destroy the Empire: 'We should inevitably have an overwhelming party in favour of reducing the sacrifice in blood and money on the altar of imperial rule.' It would, he continued, be a case of 'India is not worth a shilling on the Income Tax, or the lives of fifty thousand street-bred people.'

'A Bread-and-Butter Question'
The economic depression of the 1890s fuelled humanitarian campaigns to improve the lot of the poor in the industrial cities of Britain. Researches, such as those of Rowntree in York and Booth in London, suggested that there was a large underclass of the semi-employed, living a life of near-destitution and unable to exist without charity. Recruitment for the Boer War revealed that the strength of the nation in arms was much diminished: many of those enlisting had existed almost entirely on a diet of bread, tea and margarine, and were severely undernourished. Violent swings in the trade cycle subjected workers in the vulnerable manufacturing industries to erratic employment. It was feared that this could lead to social unrest and political extremism, especially now that the franchise was percolating down the social hierarchy. It was a slow process, however; by 1913, forty per cent of men and all women were still denied the vote.

It was claimed that the failing British economy could not feed, defend or employ the growing population without new overseas resources. Cecil Rhodes, for example, saw the Empire as too

important an asset not to be exploited to the full: 'In order to save the forty million inhabitants of the United Kingdom from a bloody civil war, we colonial statesmen must acquire new lands to settle the surplus population, to provide new markets for the goods produced by them in the factories and mines. The Empire, I have always said, is a bread-and-butter question. If you want to avoid civil war you must become imperialists.'

To Lenin, such an analysis suggested that Britain had become 'the rentier state . . . the state of parasitic, declining capitalism'. Some Edwardian socialists saw the problems as soluble only if firm and drastic action were taken. Beatrice Webb and the Fabians thought the Empire could supply resources, such as cheap food, which would improve the lot of the working class. Die-hard imperialists such as Lord Milner and Lord Curzon, on the other hand, supported domestic social reform as a means of providing stronger soldiers to defend the Empire. The national crisis expressed itself, therefore, not only in declining industrial competitiveness and military over-commitment, but also in the sense that it seemed to be corroding the very core of British manhood, as Lord Curzon remarked in 1910: 'We can hardly take up our morning paper without reading of the physical decline of the race . . . beaten in cricket, then in polo!'

1906: Watershed of Empire?
Imperial propagandists of the left and right were mostly on the political fringes in the 1890s and 1900s, while successive governments adopted much more cautious approaches. The Unionist government (as the Conservatives were known in this period) was under increasing pressure to find and spend more money on social reform at home, if only to meet the needs of a generation of newly enfranchised voters. Joseph Chamberlain, Colonial Secretary until 1902, tried to face these problems squarely; he proposed protection for ailing British industry, discouraged capital exports, set up a modest social welfare programme and proposed a tariff on food imports. The prospect of this last policy was so unpopular, conjuring as it did the

spectre of a 'dear loaf', that in 1906 the Liberals won a landslide victory.

The policies of the Liberal government between 1906 and 1911 are often seen as representing a 'watershed' in the history of Britain's relations with her overseas colonies, marking a decisive stage in the transition between Empire and Commonwealth. The growing tensions in Europe prompted Britain to try to put her colonial house in order as far as possible, setting relations with Canada, South Africa, Australia and New Zealand on a new and more equal footing. In 1907 the defeated Boers in the Transvaal and the Orange River Colony were given new constitutions, allowing local leaders to control internal affairs once more. In the same year, the Imperial Conference in London decided on a new term – 'dominions' – to describe the self-governing colonies and to emphasize their status as nations approaching full independence.

During the early years of this administration, a fortuitous boom in world trade moderated the problems of excessive overseas commitments and inadequate resources to meet them. Social unrest receded, in turn, and social reform became more affordable. The Liberal government was influenced by humanitarian concerns and socialist ideas which argued the moral case for a welfare state. Social expenditure became the most important priority. As industry revived, the issue of raising extra revenue through tariffs became less relevant. Indirect taxes, such as a corn duty, were considered to be regressive, taking too high a percentage of income from the poor. In his famous Budget of 1909, the Chancellor of the Exchequer, Lloyd George, set out instead to 'soak the rich' by increasing direct taxation on property and income in order to fund his pensions and National Insurance schemes.

The Liberals dealt with the strategic crisis that had gripped the Empire by turning to diplomacy. An Anglo-Japanese Alliance of 1902 had already shored up Britain's position in the Far East, and an entente with France in 1904 soothed the inflamed rivalries in tropical Africa. Finally, Britain reached a détente with Russia in 1907 – much to the surprise and dismay of India

Conservative opinion in Britain equated any loosening of the imperial bonds with complete disintegration.

– which left her free to concentrate on European politics. An effective treaty with France and Russia could be achieved only if Britain promised to send her troops to their aid if Germany declared war. Plans were drawn up for what was to become a British Expeditionary Force, and Britain's continental commitment was revived for the first time since the days of Wellington. In this way, the foundations for British involvement in the First World War were created out of the impossible cost of defending India from the Russians.

The Army was committed to Europe and the burden of imperial defence fell on the Navy once again, expected as it was to command the Mediterranean as well as the Channel, the Atlantic and the North Sea. The Navy's resources were not infinite, however. As a result, the Chiefs of Staff admitted the necessity of allowing the Dominions some control over the small squadrons left in their waters.

A New Hercules?

As the Edwardian Age drew to a close, the looming crisis of Empire seemed to have been averted. In reality, it had only been pushed into the shadows. By 1910 the old problems were reasserting themselves, as money for new ships and for the rearmament programme was desperately needed. Domestic industry, especially steel, was becoming hard-pressed again. Worst of all was the threat to the social programme inside and outside Parliament. The Liberals lost much ground in the 1910 general election and only held power in a coalition with the Irish MPs, who demanded Home Rule in return for their support. The Labour Party, the Unionists and the House of Lords all opposed the Liberal programme on National Insurance, education, housing, unemployment and the Poor Law.

The only man who seemed to have any clear idea of a way out of the impasse in 1910 was Lloyd George. He proposed that the Unionists and Liberals join forces to push legislation through Parliament, thereby forestalling the threat of 'national impoverishment' brought about by foreign competitors. In order to accommodate the Irish Nationalist MPs in his coalition, Lloyd George hoped that a reorganization of the Empire into a Federation of Britain and the Dominions would reconcile Ulster to some form of Home Rule.

These plans came to nothing, although they formed the basis for the wartime coalition government in 1916. They were also straws in the wind, indicating the British political state of flux. The difficulties facing Britain at the end of that great age of economic expansion and empire-building seemed immense. Even the diplomacy that had been used to shore up Britain's position in Asia began to come unstuck between 1908 and 1914. The Anglo-Russian détente was soon strained by the revival of traditional rivalries in Persia, where the Russians made moves to occupy Azerbaijan. In the Middle East, Britain became increasingly sensitive to German activities in the Ottoman Empire, which were focused around railway building; it was thought that these activities would alter the strategic balance in the area and threaten Britain's position in the Persian Gulf, where oil had recently been discovered. In 1911 the Russians and Germans met, to consider extending the German-controlled Baghdad Railway through Persia – an initiative that forced Britain to open self-protective negotiations with both nations about spheres of influence in the region. As the world slid into war, fresh crises were brewing at home and abroad. By August 1914, the rulers of the greatest imperial power since the fall of Rome were aware of their weakness as they had never been before.

Canada

United Kingdom

Jutla

WESTERN FRO
1914-1918

Gibra

Bermuda

Bahamas

British
Honduras   Jamaica

St Lucia   Barbados
Trinidad & Tobago

Gambia

Sierra Leone

Gold Coast

British Guiana

Gilbert Is.

Washington I.
· Fanning I.

Ocean I.

Phoenix Is.
· Jarvis I.
Malden I.

Ellice Is.

Rotuma

Manihiki   · Caroline I.

Samoa

Starbuck I.

Ascension Is.

Fiji Is.

Tonga Is.   · Cook Is.

St Heler

· Pitcairn I.

CORONEL
1. Nov 1914

FALKLAND IS.
8. Dec 1914

South Georgia

South Orkney Is.   South Sandwich Group

South Shetland Is.

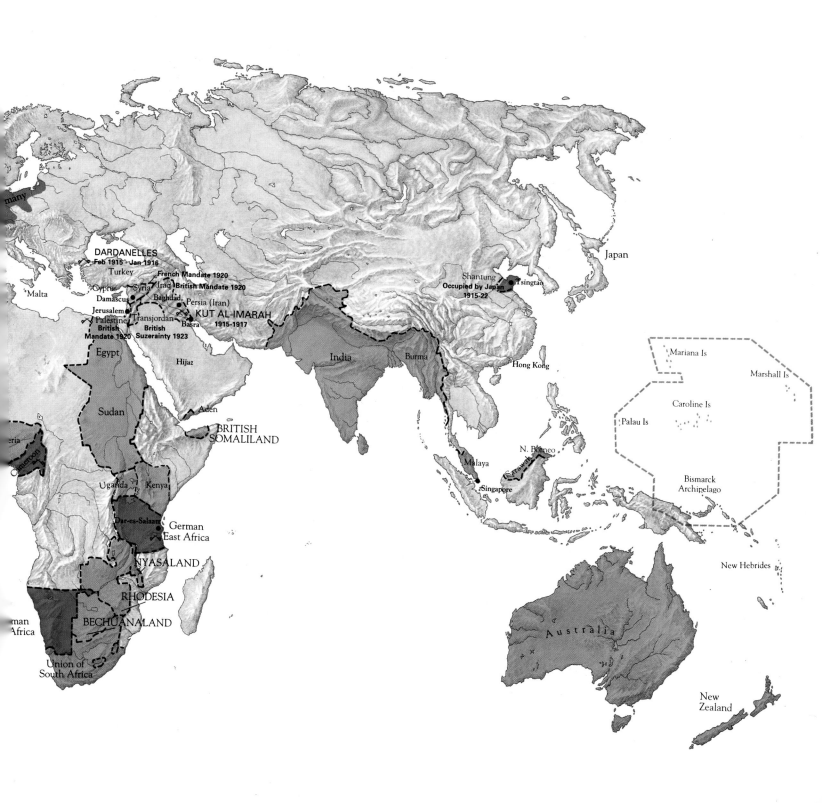

Germany

DARDANELLES
Feb 1915 – Jan 1916
Turkey

Malta

Cyprus

Syria   French Mandate 1920
Damascus   Iraq   British Mandate 1920
Baghdad

Jerusalem   Persia (Iran)

Palestine   Transjordan   Basra   KUT AL-IMARAH
British   British   1915-1917
Mandate 1920   Suzerainty 1923

Egypt   Hijaz

Sudan   Aden

BRITISH
SOMALILAND

Cameroon

ria

Uganda   Kenya

Dar-es-Salaam   German
East Africa

NYASALAND

RHODESIA

BECHUANALAND

man
Africa

Union of
South Africa

India   Burma

Shantung
Occupied by Japan   Tsingtao
1915-22

Japan

Hong Kong

N. Borneo

Malaya   Sarawak

Singapore

Mariana Is

Marshall Is

Caroline Is

Palau Is

Bismarck
Archipelago

New Hebrides

Australia

New
Zealand

The Empire and the First World War

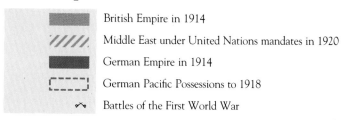

British Empire in 1914

Middle East under United Nations mandates in 1920

German Empire in 1914

German Pacific Possessions to 1918

Battles of the First World War

CHAPTER TWENTY-NINE

DILEMMAS OF EMPIRE: THE WORLD BETWEEN THE WARS

◇

On 3 August 1914 King George V declared war on behalf of the whole Empire, and pledges of allegiance and aid poured in from all quarters. In November of that year Lord Kitchener wrote: 'I have no complaint whatsoever to make about the response to my appeals for men. But I shall want more men, and still more, until the enemy is crushed.' By the end of the war, in November 1918, a total of 5,704,416 men (around 22 per cent of the entire male population of the United Kingdom) had served in the British army. They were joined by two and a half million men from the Empire beyond the British Isles. The largest contribution was made by India: some one and a half million volunteers joined up, 62,000 of whom died in battle. Imperial troops were backed up by thousands of non-combatants, including 82,000 Egyptians and 92,000 Chinese serving in labour units in November 1918. Imperial financial contributions were similarly significant: Canada, Australia and New Zealand bore the cost of their forces; South Africa paid for the South-West Africa campaign and much of the maintenance of its troops in the East Africa theatre. India's military expenditure rose from £20 million in 1913–14 to £140 million in 1918–19, and in 1916 she also took over £100 million of the British government's war loan. In addition, unprecedentedly large demands were made of imperial producers of food and other commodities vital for the war effort.

A propaganda poster published by the Parliamentary Recruiting Committee encourages the women of Britain to back the war effort. It was not uncommon, during the First World War, for women to accuse men in civilian clothes of cowardice by handing them a white feather.

The Navy in Wartime

Britain's world power in peacetime and her survival during war depended on the security of the sea lanes. In August 1914 the Royal Navy was superior to the German fleet – twenty-four dreadnoughts to Germany's fifteen – and had more in the process of construction than Germany. A British squadron under Admiral Sturdee destroyed four German ships off the Falkland Islands on 8 December 1914, enabling the safe transport of troops from Australia and New Zealand. Britain's very survival depended upon the regular supply of food and materials from overseas, particularly after Germany had mounted a submarine blockade of the island in February 1915. It was in this context that the fortress colonies of Malta and Gibraltar, the scattered coaling ports like Aden or the Falkland Islands, and the communications points such as the cable stations of St Helena and Ascension came into their own.

The Campaigns in Africa and the Far East

The very first engagement of the war was the small but successful raid upon the German cable station at Lome (Togoland); Britain and France then partitioned the country uneasily between them. The campaign in the Cameroons was more prolonged: a force from Nigeria took Duala in September 1914 and the French invaded from the south and east, but the Germans were not driven out into Spanish territory until February 1916. Despite some initial resistance from Afrikaner nationalists, the Union of South Africa followed Britain into the war in German South-West Africa, where 3,500 German and colonial troops

capitulated to General Botha at Otawi in 1915. Although a British landing force of Indian troops was defeated by General von Lettow-Vorbeck at the battle of Tanga in November 1914, the British finally won naval control of Lake Tanganyika in 1915. The following year Tanga was taken by General Smuts; Dar-es-Salaam, too, fell in September. However, Lettow-Vorbeck took the war into Portuguese East Africa in October 1917 and, at the time of the Armistice in November 1918, he was mounting an invasion of Rhodesia.

German colonies in the Pacific and Far East were targets of the Allies as well, with New Zealand occupying Samoa and the Australians forcing a German surrender in New Guinea. Meanwhile, Japan, which had been Britain's ally since 1902, declared war on Germany. In violation of China's neutrality, the Japanese occupied the Shantung peninsula, where the German fortress of Tsingtao capitulated on 7 November 1914. Two months later, Japan issued the Twenty-One Demands by which she laid claim to much of the peninsula. The Japanese navy also occupied German islands in the Pacific, including the Marshall Islands, the Mariana Islands, the Palau Islands and the Caroline Islands.

The Middle East

In November 1914, the Allies of Russia, Britain and France declared war on Turkey, thereby spreading the war to the Near and Middle East. Britain swiftly reinforced the position she had previously assumed within the Ottoman Empire, annexing Cyprus (occupied since 1878) and proclaiming a protectorate over Egypt (occupied since 1882). The Khedive Abbas Hilmi was summarily deposed and his uncle installed in December

1914 as a Sultan independent of the Turkish Caliph in Constantinople. By now, however, a stalemate on the Western Front prompted Winston Churchill and other ministers to evolve an 'Eastern strategy', hinged on Egypt, with the aim of piercing the 'soft underbelly' of the Central Powers. The strategy was at first a disaster, as Britain and France launched a huge naval assault on the heavily fortified Dardanelles, hoping to blast their way through to Constantinople. Turkish guns, embedded on either side of the narrow strait, crippled the fleet in a single day. A second attempt to take the strait by landing half a million imperial troops (including over thirty thousand Anzacs) on the Gallipoli peninsula dragged on for eight months of slaughter and defeat. General Townshend's attempt to sweep the 6th (Poona) Division through Mesopotamia towards Baghdad also ended dismally in April 1916 after four months of besiegement at Kut-el-Mara.

Meanwhile, German and British troops had dug themselves into nightmarish trench warfare in the fields of Flanders, fighting for a few yards of territorial mud at a time. As one soldier wrote in a letter home, 'I shall never look on warfare either as fine or sporting again. It reduces men to shivering beasts: there isn't a man who can stand shell-fire of the modern kind. The Anzacs are fine fellows, but they say Gallipoli was a garden party compared to this show'.

The Fall of the Ottoman Empire

By March 1917, however, the general tide of the war had turned. The British had occupied Baghdad and, in December, General Allenby went into Jerusalem. The Ottoman Empire began to crumble and the British entered into a number of embarrassingly contradictory agreements, by which their Arab Hashemite allies understood that they should rule over Syria,

Transjordan, Palestine, northern Iraq and most of the Arabian peninsula. At the same time, by the 1916 Sykes-Picot agreement, the British and French had divided Syria, Lebanon, Transjordan and Iraq between them, with the ports of Haifa and Acre going to Britain. A third contradictory initiative was the fateful Balfour Declaration of 1917 by which support was promised for 'the establishment in Palestine of a national home for Jewish people' (Palestine's population at the time was 93 per cent Arab).

Empire Unrest

War had stretched the resources of the Empire to the limit, making colonial regimes even more susceptible to internal threats. Indian troops mutinied at Singapore in 1915 and, in the same year, the Sheikh of Senussi (in the Western Desert) launched a holy war (*jihad*). There was a rising at Darfur in the Sudan in 1916 and riots at Bongo on the Gold Coast. Britain's campaigns against the Turkish Caliph angered the Muslims of British India, and British reverses in the Dardanelles encouraged Tilak of the Indian National Congress in his agitation for home rule, and drove Congress and the All-India Muslim League into each other's arms (the Lucknow Pact, 1916). There was such concern about Indian instability that on 20 August 1917 the British committed themselves to eventual 'responsible government' in India. This Delphic pronouncement was interpreted differently by British conservatives, who were unable to entertain the thought of Indian self-rule, and by nationalists, who were excited by the prospect. Meanwhile, at Easter in 1916, Ireland erupted into rebellion. The Irish Republican Brotherhood, led by Patrick Pearse, took over the Dublin Post Office. Although the insurrection was suppressed, nationalism gathered momentum until Independence was declared in 1922.

A platoon of soldiers wait crouching in a trench in Flanders, preparing to go 'over the top'.

The Impact of the War on the Empire

Nationalist struggles within the Empire were obscured by the bombast of victory in 1918. A month after the November Armistice, the Commander-in-Chief in India wrote: 'Now that it is all over and the Empire stands on a pinnacle built by her tenacity and courage – never did our reputation stand as high.' Britain considered her imperial record to have been vindicated and Germany, by implication, was deemed unfit for colonial responsibilities. This was a view which coloured contemporary propaganda and hung over the peace conference at Versailles.

The Empire, at least, had not fragmented under external attacks or from rebellions from within. With their imperial reputations enhanced, the Allies re-partitioned the world. It was agreed that Germany's former colonies and the non-Turkish possessions of the Ottoman Sultan should be ceded to the newly established League of Nations, and then administered as mandates by France, Britain, the Dominions and Japan. Britain acquired responsibility for Palestine and Transjordan, Iraq and Tanganyika (formerly German East Africa), and shared the Cameroons and Togoland with France. Japan was confirmed in the occupation of those Pacific islands she had wrested from Germany, and her troops remained on the Shantung peninsula until it was restored to China in 1922.

The Dominions, too, were determined to share in the spoils. Australia gained German possessions in the Pacific south of the Equator; the mandate of German Samoa went to New Zealand; and South Africa took over German South-West Africa. A new national pride grew out of the exploits of war, with Canada remembering the heroism of Vimy Ridge while the sacrifices at Gallipoli were to be annually commemorated on 25 April as Anzac Day in Australia and New Zealand. The South African and Canadian Premiers, Smuts and Borden, declared that they looked forward to an autonomous and equal status within the Empire and to being jointly responsible for imperial foreign policy. Outside the Empire, however, the fallibility of the European systems which had resulted in the carnage of Flanders unleashed a wave of anti-imperialism in America and Russia.

Post-War Imperial Crises

The imperial problems during the years from 1918 to 1922 sprang from the yawning rift between British commitments and British capacity. The war had killed one million men, wounded two million more and had resulted in an expenditure for Britain of over £8 billion. Despite the euphoria of victory, an unprecedented wave of anti-war bitterness swept the country. As one veteran of the Somme recalled, 'When the war ended, I was elated, naturally. But I felt sad for my friends who had been killed. I still do. There was no point in the war at all – it was all totally futile.'

After the huge majority of the 'Khaki election' in December 1918, Lloyd George's Coalition Government tried to grapple with the conflicting demands of policing world peace and creating a British society 'fit for heroes'. The electorate had trebled through the Representation of the People's Act, and the burden of debt had increased to ten times its 1914 level. The conscript army was demobilized without delay and channelled into the factories, so that by 1919 the army had shrunk from five million to one million men. Financial constraints, as much as anti-war feeling, encouraged international agreements on disarmament. Yet, with Lloyd George, Milner, Balfour, Curzon and Churchill in power and with the world in uproar from Archangel to Afghanistan and from the Liffey to the Yangtze, it was inconceivable that the British government would either stand idle or withdraw the legions to Little England.

Ireland was the major imperial trouble spot, followed by India, Egypt and Mesopotamia. Widespread unrest followed a Government of Ireland Act, which provided separate parliaments for Northern and Southern Ireland. The Act was accepted by the North but rejected by the South, where Sinn Fein refused to participate. Lloyd George was forced to seek a settlement with the Republicans, and a treaty establishing dominion status for the Irish Free State in the South was accepted by the Dáil (the Irish Parliament) in January 1922. De Valera, later President of the Republic, denounced the treaty, however, and the new state was plunged into a civil war.

GEORGE V'S BROADCASTS TO THE EMPIRE

The King first broadcast to the nation on April 23 1924 when he opened the British Empire Exhibition. Although the service was limited, his estimated audience numbered ten million. Even the press, who were very suspicious of radio, responded enthusiastically. The inauguration of an overseas service by the BBC was held back until 19 December 1932 by technical and financial constraints. A few days later, the King's Christmas message was transmitted. George V was 'very pleased and much moved' by the response and these broadcasts at Christmas became an institution, opening up the monarchy and aiding the development of the BBC's Empire network. Although the Indians complained that the messages were too short, the Canadians that they were too late and the Australians that reception was too weak, technological developments at least made them more accessible. When Edward VIII went on the air to make his abdication speech in December

King George V (1865–1936) addresses the nation over the radio in his Christmas Day broadcast of 1934.

1936, bar room receipts in New York diminished significantly because everyone was at home listening. By 1939 the BBC had acquired an international reputation for reliability and impartiality in its reporting which would serve Britain and the Empire well in the contest with Dr Goebbels' propaganda machine.

British Prime Minister, David Lloyd George (1863–1945) (right), and General Joffre (1852–1931)

Field Marshal Douglas Haig (1861–1928) (left)

The British approach to India was a similar blend of coercion and conciliation. The Rowlatt Acts, which allowed internment without trial and trials without juries, were passed in March 1919. The following month General Dyer ordered his troops to open fire on a crowd of unarmed demonstrators in Amritsar, killing 379 and wounding 1,200. Although the Government of India Act in 1919 provided an elected majority on the Indian legislative assembly and a measure of responsible government, in the provinces, Gandhi, who had previously supported the imperial war effort, began his India-wide boycott of the new councils. In alliance with the Muslims, he transformed the Indian National Congress into a mass movement striving towards self-rule (*swaraj*) by peaceful means.

Although they were suppressed, revolts in Egypt by the nationalistic Wafd party, resulted in Lord Milner's recommendation for a conditional independence hedged about by many safeguards of Britain's interests. The British protectorate in Egypt ended nominally in 1922, and the Wafd won a landslide victory in the 1923 elections, under a constitution promising universal suffrage and ministerial responsibility. However, there was a frustrating stalemate over certain 'reserved questions', including defence, the security of communications, and the future of the Sudan.

In Iraq, the Arabs rose in revolt against the British mandate. The way out of the problem lay in transforming the mandate into a client-state. Emir Faisal, the former ruler of Syria, was proclaimed King of Iraq and, by 1930, a series of agreements had converted the mandate into an independent Iraq in return for military concessions to Britain. In Persia (Iran) Reza Khan resisted British ascendancy and seized power in 1921. In 1925 he was proclaimed the new Shah.

In 1921 there were Arab riots against the immigration of Jews into the British mandate of Palestine. In Turkey, too, the peace settlement provided fresh grounds for conflict. Under Mustapha

Kemal, a renewed nationalism threatened the Straits and the Allied base at Chanak. Lloyd George appealed to the Dominions for help, but apart from New Zealand and New-foundland, they were unwilling to be drawn into what was seen as Britain's squabble. Although the crisis passed peacefully, they took no part in the redrawing of Turkey's boundaries at the 1923 Treaty of Lausanne.

Inter-War Naval Policy

One of the terms of the peace treaty was the internment of the German fleet (which was later scuttled) at Scapa Flow, a move accepted by Germany, as a contemporary observer, Jacques Bainville, wrote, 'only with a knife at their throats'. Between 1914 and 1918 the Royal Navy had failed to win a decisive victory, despite British supremacy in the naval rivalry with Germany during the build-up to war. It was obvious that Britannia no longer ruled the waves. The naval armaments treaty at the 1921–2 Washington Conference established a ten-year break from any naval construction. Future construction of capital ships was to be fixed at a ratio of five British to five United States to three Japanese ships. Britain's position in the Far East and the Pacific was further weakened in 1921 when the government decided not to renew the Japanese alliance which had been in effect since 1902. Building work on a new naval base at Singapore, which would help Britain defend the region, began in 1924 but delays meant that the base was not opened until 1938. Defence chiefs were not blind to the risks they were running. They knew full well that the strategy of sending the main fleet to Singapore at a time of Far Eastern crisis would fail if Britain was simultaneously engaged on another front. When war did hit South-East Asia in 1941, the Royal Navy was fully occupied in the Mediterranean and Atlantic.

Imperial Regeneration between the Wars

As the post-war boom was succeeded by depression, politicians of the left and right turned to the Empire for an economic solution. During the 1930s, there was marked expansion of British trade with the Empire and Commonwealth: imperial imports rose to over thirty-seven per cent in 1937, while the Empire's share of British exports increased to almost forty per cent. Shortages of manpower and money forced Britain to lean heavily on the Dominions for support. In return for this support, Britain was prepared to trade constitutional concessions. The 1935 Government of India Act granted responsible government to the provinces. This was hardly a magnanimous concession since it was designed to reinforce British control over central government by deflecting Indian nationalist energies into struggles over provincial spoils. Likewise, the granting of internal self-government in Egypt, the construction of client states in the Middle East and the practice of Lord Lugard's principles of indirect rule in Africa were all devices by which Britain relieved herself of direct administration and yet retained overall power.

However, India took advantage of her constitutional position by vetoing the deployment of Indian troops outside India. Similarly, in Egypt the Wafd became more openly defiant of British officials in the Sudan, while Britain's conflicting commitments to the Jews and Arabs of Palestine turned the region into a liability from which she was eventually forced to withdraw. Nevertheless, the Government did not accept that the war had set the Empire into irreversible decline. Rather, it acknowledged the need to adjust the way it continued to pursue the pre-war objective of global authority.

Ireland: Crisis and Partition

Membership of Sinn Fein, 1919

up to 200 per 10,000

up to 400 per 10,000

up to 600 per 10,000

Ulster Districts where over 50% of population are Protestant

British Military Areas

◁ ◁ ◁ ◁ ◁ ◁ Martial Law Area, maximum extent Jan. 1921

▶ ▶ ▶ ▶ ▶ ▶ Dublin District, maximum extent June 1921

□ Brigade H.Q.

◪ Divisional H.Q.

LONDONDERRY

◪ Londonderry

ANTRIM

DONEGAL

Belfast ◪ ■

TYRONE

DOWN

FERMANAGH

ARMAGH

MONAGHAN

SLIGO

◪ Dundalk

LEITRIM

CAVAN

LOUTH

MAYO

ROSCOMMON

MEATH

LONGFORD

WESTMEATH

□ Dublin

Athlone ◪

The
Curragh

△ DUBLIN

GALWAY

KING'S
OFFALY

KILDARE

◪ Galway

WICKLOW

QUEEN'S
LAOIS

CLARE

CARLOW

TIPPERARY

KILKENNY

◪ Limerick

WEXFORD

LIMERICK

WATERFORD

◪ Buttevant

KERRY

◪ Fermoy

CORK

Cork
◪ □

184

CHAPTER THIRTY

THE DECOLONIZATION
OF IRELAND

◇

Ireland can be regarded as a microcosm of many of the fundamental colonial issues that faced Britain in the twentieth century. Here was an ancient people struggling with the constitutional, economic and cultural problems of building a new state after centuries of colonization. Here, also, was an entrenched group of settlers who were well aware both of their position as a minority within the island and of their ambiguous relationship with the mother country. Finally, there was Britain herself, an imperialist power partly responsible, partly negligent and mostly perplexed about developments in her oldest and nearest colony.

The Ulster Question

Since 1870 Irish nationalists had been demanding a measure of self-government known as Home Rule. Their opportunity came in 1910 when the election results revealed that the Liberal Party had lost their overall majority. The Irish Parliamentary Party – led by John Redmond – was then able to drive a hard bargain for Home Rule as the price for allying itself with the minority Liberal government. Victory was almost complete when the powers of the House of Lords, which had vetoed the second Home Rule Bill in 1893 and had more recently blocked Liberal social reforms, were curtailed by an Act of Parliament in 1911.

At the same time, there was a growing threat of rebellion by the Protestants of Ulster. Descended from seventeenth-century colonists, these Protestants were well organized at grass-roots level by the Orange Order and were represented by the Ulster Unionist Council. They distrusted the Ulster Catholics who were regarded not just as economic competitors but as followers of the Anti-Christ as well; Home Rule was therefore denounced by the Ulster Protestants as Rome Rule and as inimical to civil and religious liberties. The Protestant opposition was led by Edward Carson but the organizing genius was James Craig. On 28 September 1912 a pledge – Ulster's Solemn League and Covenant – to refuse to recognize a Home Rule Parliament in Ireland was signed by 250,000 men. A 100,000-strong Ulster Volunteer Force was established.

The nationalists were soon drilling a private army of their own – the Irish Volunteers – while the Socialists acquired the smaller Irish Citizens Army. It seemed that the British were losing their grip, especially after the 'Curragh Incident' in which fifty-seven army officers refused to obey orders in a pre-emptive move against the Ulster Volunteers. The outbreak of the Great War in 1914 came as something of a godsend for the authorities; Home Rule, with the prospect of special treatment for the Ulster Unionists, was shelved for the duration.

The Easter Rising

Both Carson and Redmond committed volunteer forces to the British effort. This commitment split the Irish Volunteers, many of whose members belonged to the secret Irish Republican Brotherhood, a self-proclaimed revolutionary vanguard which maintained that 'England's difficulty is Ireland's opportunity'.

On Easter Monday 1916 a force of Irish Volunteers, organized by Sean MacDermott and assisted by the Irish Citizens Army, took over the main public buildings in Dublin. An Irish Republic was proclaimed on the steps of the General Post Office. The city was taken completely by surprise, but the British forces rallied and there followed five days of fighting. Three thousand

THE EASTER RISING

The tricolour of the Irish State flies today over the high, classical portico of the General Post Office in Dublin. Inside there is a vast bronze statue of the legendary Cuchulain, a Celtic warrior who bound himself to a shattered pillar so that he might die facing his enemies upright.

It was here, on Easter Sunday 1916, that a handful of men, women and boys erected barricades, sandbagged windows and pinned up a scrap of paper declaring an independent Irish Republic. Other strategic sites throughout the city, including Bolands Mill, Trinity College and Liberty Hall, had been similarly seized and fortified in the peaceful early hours of the morning. There were never more than 15,000 rebels, and only half of them were armed. The British Army was taken completely by surprise: the General was on holiday in England, and the majority of his officers and men were attending the Bank Holiday races. Hastily gathering what resources there were, the Army laid siege to the centre of the city and the

A British officer and two privates stand guard over Dublin buildings devastated in the Easter Rising of 1916.

gunboat *Helga* lobbed shells at the rebel-held buildings.

In five days it was over, with the leaders executed at Kilmainham gaol. A previously unsympathetic nation was roused to outrage, and the popular mythology of nationalism soon began to date the disintegration of British rule in Ireland from the uprising of 1916.

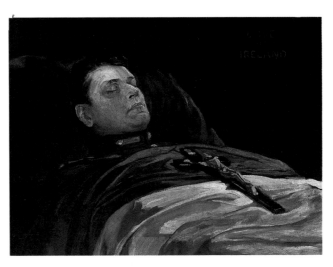

Michael Collins (1890–1922)
on his deathbed, by
the Irish painter,
Sir John Lavery.

were killed and the centre of Dublin was left a burnt-out shell. The British, in their turn, regarded the rising as a stab in the back, and so did many Irish citizens whose sons and husbands were fighting on the Western Front. Nevertheless, public disgust transformed suddenly into anti-British hostility when Dublin Castle overreacted, executing fifteen of the rebel leaders and interning thousands more. The rising of 1916 had triumphed in failure.

Sinn Fein: We Ourselves

This polarization was inevitable. Redmond lost leverage when the Liberals joined the Conservatives in a wartime coalition. The growing threat of conscription after the German spring offensive in 1918 eroded the credibility of the Irish Parliamentary Party. It was replaced as the rallying voice of nationalist Ireland by *Sinn Fein* (meaning 'we ourselves') at the general election after the Armistice. *Sinn Fein* was founded in 1905 by Arthur Griffith, and had been infiltrated by the Irish Republican Brotherhood during the war. Its uncompromising policy was to abstain from British institutions and to repudiate British authority. In January 1919 it established its own parliament: *Dail Eireann*. At the same time a guerilla war began in which the Irish Volunteers quickly transformed themselves into the Irish Republican Army (IRA). There were small-scale operations throughout 1919, followed by a sustained IRA attack on the Royal Irish Constabulary barracks – and on the British legal system – throughout most of 1920. Late that year Britain launched a counter-offensive; because of her reluctance to call the disturbances a war, however, the main burden fell on the Royal Irish Constabulary, assisted by ex-army recruits known as 'the Black and Tans' (from their motley uniforms). On 'Bloody Sunday', the commander of the IRA, Michael Collins, ordered the assassination of fourteen British agents. The Black and Tans retaliated by shooting twelve spectators at a Gaelic football match in Croke Park.

In 1921 Britain, faced concurrently with revolts in the Middle East and India, moved towards a settlement. In June a Home Rule parliament was established in Belfast. The state of Northern Ireland was born amidst a storm of violence which continued for two years, and which left 428 killed and 1,766 wounded. It encompassed Down, Antrim, Tyrone, Armagh, Fermanagh and Derry. The British forces were gaining the upper hand over the IRA in the south, but public opinion at home was weary of war. A truce was agreed in July with the very men who had earlier been denounced as thugs and gunmen. In December a Sinn Fein delegation – led by Griffith and Collins – signed a treaty which failed to secure an outright republic; instead, the Irish Free State was established with dominion status, like

Canada. An oath of allegiance to the British Crown was still required and Britain, mindful of her strategic interests, retained port facilities at Berehaven, Queenstown and Lough Swilly. Michael Collins felt that in signing this treaty, he had signed his own death warrant.

From Dominion to Republic

Although the treaty was accepted by a majority in the Dail and by most of the electorate, it caused an irrevocable split between pragmatists and purists in Sinn Fein and the IRA. The sticking point was not the partition of Ireland but the oath of allegiance. Collins was killed in the ensuing civil war. The Free State Government stamped out 'the irregulars' – as they called the Republicans – in a military campaign more systematic and ruthless than any waged by the British.

The successes of the pragmatists paved the way for the triumph of the purists. In 1932 Eamon de Valera came to power. His policy was clear from the outset: 'Let us remove these forms one by one, so that this state we control may become a republic in fact, without the consent of the parliament of Northern Ireland.'

Fifty years later Canada and Australia are only now stepping onto the road so deftly trodden by De Valera in the 1930s. It is ironic to think that this man be hailed as one of the great statemen of the British Commonwealth, someone who in 1933 abolished the much-hated oath of allegiance and began the steady down-grading of the office of Governor General.

The way was now clear for the new constitution, which was approved by referendum in 1937; this declared Ireland a sovereign state with a president as titular head of state. It also recognized Irish – a language struggling against extinction – as the national language, and afforded Roman Catholicism a special status as the religion of the vast majority. Significantly, Article 2 of the constitution pronounced the *whole* island as the national territory. When, in 1938, the mood of appeasement in Britain gave De Valera an opportunity to secure the treaty ports, he declared that his agreement with Chamberlain 'recognizes and finally establishes Irish sovereignty over the twenty-six counties and the territorial seas.' Ireland remained neutral during the coming Second World War – much to the chagrin of the Allied Powers. In 1949 Ireland became a republic and left the Commonwealth.

A Protestant Government for a Protestant People

Meanwhile, the Second World War had reinforced Northern Ireland's position within the United Kingdom. Its languishing economy was boosted by the production of food and war materials; she was also well-placed strategically both to help win the Battle of the Atlantic and to act as an assembly point for American troops before the D-Day landings. The people suffered with the rest of the United Kingdom, most notably in the German air-raid on Belfast which killed 745 people. Churchill expressed in a wartime speech what he hoped would prove to be a new unity: 'The bonds of affection between Britain and the people of Northern Ireland have been tempered by fire and are now, I firmly believe, unbreakable.'

This new mood of unity was underlined by the constitutional guarantee made by the British Government in the 1949 Ireland Act, which was passed in response to the establishment of the Irish Republic: 'In no event will Northern Ireland or any part thereof cease to be part of His Majesty's dominions.'

Unfortunately, Northern Ireland was not a homogeneous political unit. The Catholics, who made up a third of its population, were considered disloyal by the dominant Unionist party, who consistently discriminated against them. Even if Unionist leaders realized that this was not justifiable, they were unable to change course for fear of the influential Orange Order ousting them from power. In 1923 local-government electoral boundaries were redrawn so that Newry Urban District was the only important council that remained in nationalist hands. This feat of gerrymandering was accomplished 'to give effect to the views of Unionist rank and file.'

The Orange Order unofficially monitored recruitment and promotion in the Northern Ireland Civil Service. The most blatant discrimination in jobs and in the allocation of public housing was practised by the councils in border areas. The security forces were largely Protestant too. The B-specials, a part-time paramilitary force, was especially feared. The Special Powers Act, a draconian piece of emergency legislation, was regularly invoked to suspend civil rights. The net result was that Northern Ireland became effectively a one-party state, in which the 1931 Wild Birds Act was the only legislation ever sponsored by a non-Unionist MP.

The British Government was partly to blame; eager to wash its hands of Ireland, it had set up a devolved government in Belfast which the Ulster Protestants had not requested. It had then failed to supervize the actions of a parliament which was forbidden to pass laws aimed at religious discrimination.

The manoeuvre by which Lloyd George divided Ireland provoked cynical humour.

Eamon de Valera's career followed the classic twentieth-century pattern for the nationalist – from prison to the presidency.

The Troubles

The 1950s and 1960s were relatively prosperous times for the province. But it was also during this period that the Ulster Volunteer Force (UVF) came into prominence – partly as a reaction to the IRA campaigns of the '50s and partly as an attempt to control increasing Catholic objections to discrimination.

In the late 1960s, Northern Ireland collapsed into chaos. Terence O'Neill, the aristocratic Unionist Prime Minister, had embarked on a tentative reform programme, only to be hounded by the Reverend Ian Paisley, an extreme Protestant and political agitator. Catholic students and activists, committed to non-violent protest, formed the Northern Ireland Civil Rights Association. They demanded reforms aimed at equality of opportunity within the northern state. Nevertheless, the Civil Rights movement was dismissed by Unionists as a front for IRA objectives.

Impatience grew at the painful pace of reforms and Derry, where Unionist gerrymandering was most blatant, was the main flash point. In 1969 a bombing campaign by Protestant extremists, disguised as the work of the IRA, 'quite literally blew me (O'Neill) out of office.' After a three-day riot in August 1969, known as 'the Battle of the Bogside', British troops arrived, to be welcomed initially by the Catholic minority as protectors from the Protestant mob and the local security forces.

Jack Lynch, the Irish Prime Minister, called for a UN Peace-keeping force in the belief that British troops were unlikely 'to restore peaceful conditions in the long term.' The presence of British troops and the re-arming of a section of the IRA, the

HEROES FROM A DIVIDED COUNTRY

A massive statue of Edward Carson stands outside the parliament buildings in Belfast. It is ironic that his monument should guard the institution whose creation he had steadfastly sought to obstruct.

Born in Dublin in 1854, Carson combined a lucrative career at the bar with politics. This led to his appointment as Solicitor-General for Ireland in 1892, followed eight years later by his promotion to the same position in England. Carson was an implacable opponent of Home Rule, believing that the consequences would be disastrous for all of Ireland. But the only serious opposition to the proposal centred on Ulster. This led to an alliance between Carson and the Ulster Unionists. Carson proved a brilliant orator at the large set-piece rallies held in the years that led up to 1914. However, this only forced the nationalists further down the separatist road. When the British government gave the six northern counties their own parliament, Carson was appalled.

One of the early heroes of the nationalist cause was Patrick Pearse who, for five days in April 1916, was President of the Provisional Government of Ireland and commander-in-chief of the republican forces. These were improbable roles for someone who had made his reputation as a poet, playwright and educationalist. But Pearse was inspired both by intense nationalism and by religious devotion. Late in 1913 he joined the Irish Volunteers and the Irish Republican Brotherhood. Soon he was the mouthpiece of the nationalist movement, giving a celebrated oration at the funeral of O'Donovan Rossa in August 1915. Although he had no military experience, he was chosen to lead the rising of Easter 1916 because he was a member of both the Supreme Council of the IRB and its Military Council, as well as Director of Organization of the Volunteers. On 24 April 1916 Pearse read out the Proclamation of the Irish Republic. By 3 May he was dead, executed by a firing squad.

Provisionals, stimulated the nationalist aspirations of the Catholic community, which intensified the violence between the IRA and the British Army. Internment without trial was introduced; this exacerbated the situation still further, until in March 1972 the British Government abolished the Home Rule Parliament at Stormont and imposed direct rule. Since then, successive British governments have been unable to solve the Northern Ireland problem, although Conservative attempts have been more constructive than those of Labour.

In 1973 the Conservative government carefully constructed a power-sharing administration as a result of the Sunningdale Agreement. However, in the following year, the minority Labour government (represented in Northern Ireland by Merlyn Rees) allowed this remarkable initiative to collapse in the face of intimidation by the Ulster Workers' Strike. Subsequently, internment without trial was phased out but the 'special category' status for political prisoners was also halted, an action which eventually caused the IRA hunger strikes of 1982. IRA violence against the security forces, outlawed Protestant paramilitary groups and even civilians has continued.

The most recent initiative has been the 1985 Anglo-Irish Agreement. Both countries, however, have different objectives: the United Kingdom wants better security cooperation on the border, while the Irish Republic wants reform within Northern Ireland. The only real value of this agreement is the crisis-management exercised by a joint secretariat of civil servants.

Poorest of the Rich

Since the Republic was established, Dublin governments have paid lip-service to the ideal of Irish unity. Most citizens of the Republic have been more interested in bread-and-butter issues – especially since economic growth has been so difficult to foster in post-colonial Ireland.

At the time of independence, the farming and export sectors were dominant politically and economically; the small population could not generate the internal demand needed for industrial take-off. The political division between those who supported and those who opposed the treaty has been reflected in a similar divide in economic thinking: *Fine Geal* (Tribe of the Irish) tended towards fiscal control and free trade, while *Fianna Fail* (Soldiers of Destiny) advocated budgetary expansion and internal development.

In the 1920s the government kept taxes low and maintained free trade in the interests of the farmers, while a decade later De Valera and Fianna Fail put tariffs on imports and attempted to foster self-sufficiency and native industry. De Valera's Ireland, with its stress on 'frugal comfort', was more spiritual than materialist. The Irish, however, voted increasingly with their feet: in the 1950s 400,000 people emigrated and the population dropped to 2.8 million, 5 per cent below the level at independence. A new approach came from T.K. Whitaker, the top official at the Department of Finance: beginning in 1958, there was a five-year and then a seven-year plan. Foreign investment was encouraged by tax-breaks for companies; and the state sector expanded. Free trade was resumed first by establishing the Anglo-Irish Free Trade Area and then by joining the European Economic Community.

There was a boom period during the early and middle 1970s, especially for the big farmers who milked the EEC subsidies. This was too much of a good thing for the Irish political system, however. In order to maintain the boom and to stay in power, politicians resorted increasingly to extravagant public expenditure, bigger loans and higher taxes. After the recession, which hit the country in the early 1980s, unemployment increased to twenty per cent. Emigration began again, but this time the best-educated rather than the least-skilled left the country. The national debt doubled in four years to stand at IR£25 billion by the autumn of 1986.

In March 1987 Charles Haughey became Prime Minister for the second time and began a programme of drastic retrenchment. The economy improved in 1988, but only due to a dramatic improvement in the British market, which sucked in imports. A large part of Ireland's exports are now industrial goods, but their production is largely an assembly job for foreign firms based in Ireland, who repatriate their profits and do not reinvest locally. Employment in native manufacturing declined by forty-nine per cent between 1951 and 1984, and Irish capitalists find it more profitable to expand abroad than at home.

The major structural problems of the Republic's economy remain unaddressed. The IRA pursues its objective of bombing the six northern counties into an all-Ireland republic. The Ulster Protestants, increasingly beleaguered in their own laager, want to remain British subjects but have less and less in common with the rest of the United Kingdom. Meanwhile, the British state shoulders what obstinately remains their 'white man's burden', in keeping planter and Gael from each other's throats.

CHAPTER THIRTY-ONE

THE MEDITERRANEAN AND THE MIDDLE EAST: 1914–47

◇

It is easy to overlook the scale and importance of Britain's former interests in the Mediterranean and the Middle East, extending as they did from Gibraltar to the frontiers of the Indian Empire. It may seem incongruous that Britain should have had colonies in Mediterranean Europe: indeed, on one occasion, Cypriot leaders angrily rejected the constitution that London offered them as 'something for Zulus'. By 1914, however, Britain had been a Mediterranean power for over two hundred years. Since the end of the eighteenth century she had also been deeply interested in the Middle East. Paradoxically, during the final fifty years of Britain's reign as a world power, her involvement in this huge region expanded enormously, and expensively.

Before the First World War

Even before 1800, Britain's presence in the Mediterranean had been greatly extended. Several factors drew Britain deeper and deeper into Middle Eastern politics: the expansion of her rule in India; fear of French, Russian and, later, German penetration into the crumbling Ottoman and Persian Empires; and the constant threat of a hostile partitioning of the Middle East. For much of the nineteenth century, Britain's policy was to champion the Ottomans as the policemen of the Persian Gulf and as the main rivals to Russian influence in Teheran. When the Suez Canal was opened in 1869, dramatically shortening the sea route to India, Egypt was elevated to become the centrepiece of British Middle Eastern strategy. In 1882, the so-called 'temporary occupation' was imposed, and the country became a *de facto* British protectorate, garrisoned and guarded by British troops.

After 1900, the exploitation of oil which began in southwest Iran gradually transformed the economic prospects of the countries of the Persian Gulf. In British eyes, however, the strategic and political character of the region was more important than the economic. By the eve of the First World War, the British had developed an elaborate defensive system to uphold their interests in the strategic corridor running from the Strait of Gibraltar to the mouth of the Red Sea. They held two great naval fortresses at Gibraltar and Malta, as well as Cyprus (which had been taken from the Ottomans in 1878 as a potential strongpoint in the eastern Mediterranean) and garrisons in Egypt and Aden. This spinal cord of bases required a diplomatic defence in depth, and British diplomacy, therefore, remained committed to preserving the Ottoman Empire as a buffer state against Russia. Skilful and ruthless as it was, this pragmatic amalgam of diplomacy and force was swept aside in the maelstrom of 1914. The partition of the Middle East, so long deferred, now seemed imminent.

The War Years

When war broke out in Europe in August 1914, there was good reason to believe that the Ottoman Empire might remain neutral and that the Middle East would be affected only indirectly. It was a vain hope. The Ottomans entered the war at the end of October 1914. There were divisions among the leadership of the nationalist Young Turks who ruled the Empire; and a sense of self-protection which may also have prompted the country to join the Central Powers rather than the Allies (Britain, France and Russia). The long-standing Anglo-Ottoman friendship was shattered. Instead, the British had immediately to provide for the defence of the Suez Canal and Egypt (now formally a British protectorate) against Ottoman armies advancing from Palestine. To forestall the Ottoman threat to the Persian Gulf, where Britain possessed a small oil installation at Abadan, a contingent of imperial troops was dispatched from India to Basra, at the head of the Gulf. Most dramatically of all, the British now had to plan how the Dardanelles from the Mediterranean to the Black Sea could be forced open in order to allow Russia to trade freely and obtain vital war materials. This operation, if successful, was expected to result in the capture of Constantinople and the Ottomans' capitulation. The future of the Ottoman Empire had become an urgent question.

British thinking was cautious at first. Any wholesale dismemberment of the Ottoman Empire was likely to bring Russia's imperial frontiers closer to the Mediterranean, the Suez Canal and the Persian Gulf. Britain's first choice was, therefore, to keep the Ottoman Empire going, but to emasculate it by some form of decentralization. It soon became clear that such a policy would be poorly received in St Petersburg. Russia had already successfully demanded that Constantinople should be a war gain for Russia. As the abandonment of the ill-fated Gallipoli expedition drew closer, the British, French and Russians negotiated a tripartite agreement on the partition of the Ottoman Empire, the terms of which clearly reflected Britain's nervousness about Russian expansionism. Under the Sykes-Picot plan of 1916, Russia was to acquire much of what is now eastern Turkey; France would receive modern Lebanon, Syria and the northern third of modern Iraq. The British, modestly, were to take the rest of Iraq, overlooking the Persian Gulf. Palestine was to be internationalized. This scheme not only exploited France's hunger for some tangible recognition in the Middle East; it also avoided the dangers of a common frontier between Britain and Russia, whose glacier-like irresistibility was part of the mythology of British foreign policy. With the buffer of a French-ruled Syria, the inconvenience of the Ottoman Empire's liquidation would be reduced to a minimum.

Of course this was only one – and not even the most notorious – of the pacts into which the British entered as the war in the Middle East demanded more and more of her resources. The Ottomans had no intention of giving up without a fight. Widely despised as the 'sick man of Europe', the country inflicted a series of humiliating defeats on British and Indian armies. Ottoman guns blasted the British fleet as it defended the straits to Constantinople. The British admiral resigned in disgust. 'Damn the Dardanelles!', he exclaimed 'They will be our grave!' On the peninsula of Gallipoli, 250,000 British and Anzac (Australian and New Zealand) troops were mown down

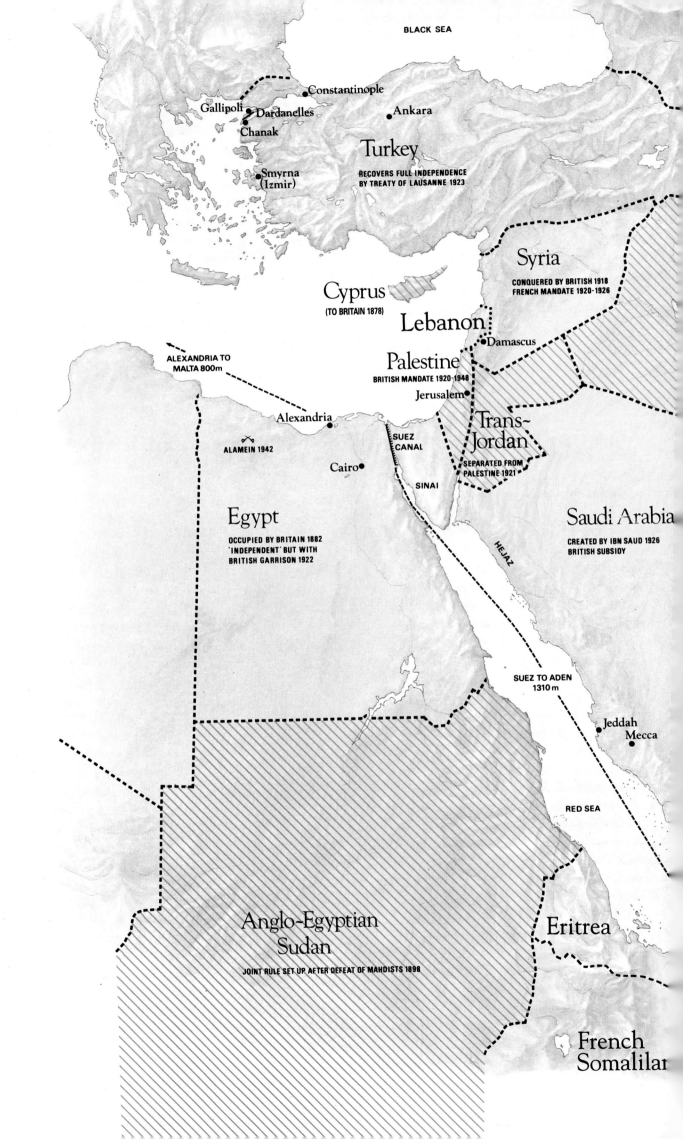

BLACK SEA

Gallipoli
Dardanelles
Chanak
Constantinople
Ankara

Smyrna
(Izmir)

Turkey
RECOVERS FULL INDEPENDENCE
BY TREATY OF LAUSANNE 1923

Cyprus
(TO BRITAIN 1878)

Syria
CONQUERED BY BRITISH 1918
FRENCH MANDATE 1920-1926

Lebanon

Damascus

ALEXANDRIA TO
MALTA 800m

Palestine
BRITISH MANDATE 1920-1948

Jerusalem

Alexandria

ALAMEIN 1942

SUEZ
CANAL

Cairo

SINAI

**Trans-
Jordan**
SEPARATED FROM
PALESTINE 1921

Egypt
OCCUPIED BY BRITAIN 1882
'INDEPENDENT' BUT WITH
BRITISH GARRISON 1922

Saudi Arabia
CREATED BY IBN SAUD 1926
BRITISH SUBSIDY

HEJAZ

SUEZ TO ADEN
1310 m

Jeddah
Mecca

RED SEA

**Anglo-Egyptian
Sudan**
JOINT RULE SET UP AFTER DEFEAT OF MAHDISTS 1898

Eritrea

**French
Somalilar**

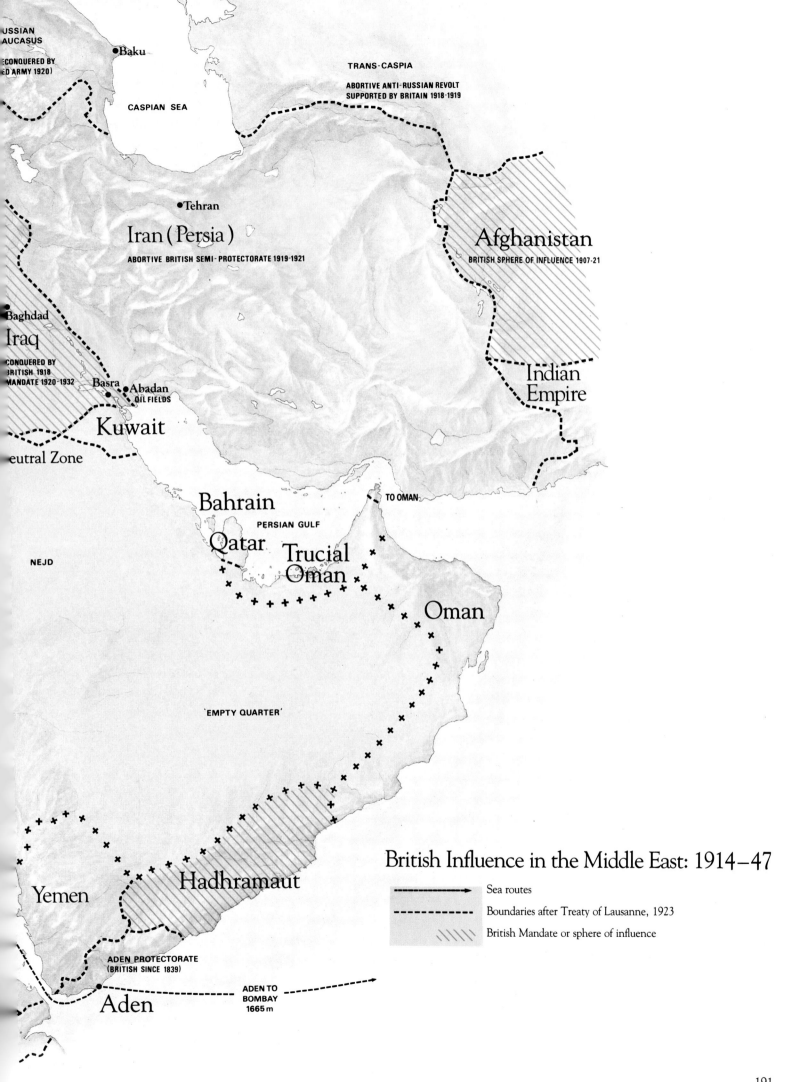

RUSSIAN
CAUCASUS
(RECONQUERED BY
RED ARMY 1920)

●Baku

CASPIAN SEA

TRANS-CASPIA

ABORTIVE ANTI-RUSSIAN REVOLT
SUPPORTED BY BRITAIN 1918-1919

●Tehran

Iran (Persia)

ABORTIVE BRITISH SEMI-PROTECTORATE 1919-1921

Afghanistan

BRITISH SPHERE OF INFLUENCE 1907-21

●Baghdad

Iraq

CONQUERED BY
BRITISH 1918
MANDATE 1920-1932

Indian
Empire

Basra ● ●Abadan
OIL FIELDS

Kuwait

Neutral Zone

TO OMAN

Bahrain

PERSIAN GULF

Qatar

NEJD

Trucial
Oman

Oman

'EMPTY QUARTER'

Yemen

Hadhramaut

British Influence in the Middle East: 1914–47

- - - - ▶ Sea routes

- - - - - - Boundaries after Treaty of Lausanne, 1923

////// British Mandate or sphere of influence

ADEN PROTECTORATE
(BRITISH SINCE 1839)

Aden

ADEN TO
BOMBAY
1665 m

The day of the Gallipoli landing, 25 April, became a day of national remembrance in Australia.

by machine-gun fire in a campaign that lasted more than eight months.

In 1915, as part of their effort to stir up resistance to the Turks among the Arab peoples of the Ottoman Empire, the British formulated the Hussein-McMahon agreement with the Sharif of Mecca (the Ottoman-appointed Arab Governor of the Holy Places). To this day bitter controversy surrounds the terms of this agreement, by which the Sharif's support for the Arab rising (made famous by the legendary participation of T.E. Lawrence) was secured. What is clear, however, is that the terms were carelessly drafted and misleadingly translated. Sir Henry McMahon, the British High Commissioner in Egypt, did not think it in Britain's interests to define these terms too closely: 'What we have to arrive at now is to tempt the Arab people into the right path, detach them from the enemy, and bring them on to our side. This, on our part, is at present largely a matter of words, and to succeed we must use persuasive terms and abstain from haggling over conditions.'

The Sharif and his son, Faisal, claimed that the treaty promised a great self-governing Arab state under their dynasty. This promise was plainly in conflict not only with the Anglo-French partition plan made a few months earlier, but with any project for the creation of a Jewish homeland in Palestine, 'greatly confusing the issue of principles', as Churchill observed. For their part, the British denied that they had intended the creation of an Arab state under the Sharif's Hashemite dynasty, or that Arab independence had been conceived in such sweeping terms. Nor did they willingly concede that it conflicted with Balfour's declaration of 1917 to create a Jewish homeland in Palestine.

Until the Ottomans were defeated, of course, such promises and pacts were mere scraps of paper. As the war entered its final year, British hopes of victory appeared more elusive than ever. The collapse of Russia opened up the Ukraine, Georgia and the Caucasus to the great German advance of 1918 and raised the nightmarish prospect that Iran, hitherto docile under a joint Anglo-Russian occupation, would become the client of Germany and the Ottomans, providing a channel for attacks on British armies in Iraq and even in India. Although the war ended before these worst fears were realized, small British contingents had established themselves in northern Iran and Russian Central Asia.

The Peace Settlement

When the Ottomans shared defeat with Germany and Austria-Hungary, their fate at the hands of the victor powers was at first uncertain. Britain had borne by far the largest share of the Middle East war after the collapse of Russia and was determined that her views should prevail when the Peace Conference turned its attention from Europe to the East. From a British point of view, the war had totally transformed the old strategic issues of the Mediterranean and the Middle East. The Ottoman Empire had been blown apart; there seemed little point in trying to put it together again. Moreover, the Ottoman leaders had been revealed as treacherous xenophobes, ready to exploit Europe's diplomatic rivalries against Britain's regional interests. The British felt that they could afford to indulge their resentment. The prime value of the Ottoman Empire had once been that of excluding Russian power and influence. But Russian imperialism had collapsed like a house of cards in 1918 as Armenian, Georgian and Turkoman nationalism asserted itself in former Tsarist provinces.

THE LEGEND OF T.E. LAWRENCE

The writer Robert Graves, who knew Lawrence well, wrote this description of him in 1927: 'He is short (five feet five and a half inches), with his body long in proportion to his legs. He has a big head . . . his hair is fair (not blond) and rather fine. The upper part of his face is kindly, almost maternal; the lower part is severe, almost cruel. His eyes are blue grey and constantly in motion . . . He is, or was, of great physical strength.' In retrospect Lawrence appears a hero, anguished by self-doubt and confusion, the object first of adulation and then of savage debunking.

Before 1914 Lawrence had acquired a knowledge of Arabic and the Arab Middle-East while working as an archaeologist at Carchemish, and had served on a semi-official survey party in the Sinai desert. When the war came, Lawrence found his way back to Egypt

T.E. Lawrence (1888–1935), the romantically renowned 'Lawrence of Arabia'.

and into the Arab Bureau which oversaw British contacts with the Arab peoples of the Ottoman Empire with which Britain was now at war. When the Arabs under the Sherif of Mecca rebelled against the Turks, Lawrence joined Faisal, the Sherif's son as his military adviser, revealing a remarkable talent for desert warfare and relations with the Arab tribes. After the war, Lawrence made himself a spokesman for the nationalist aspirations of Faisal and his followers. His charismatic personality attracted many admirers, including Churchill. But Lawrence had little influence on the post-war settlement in the Middle East, which he regarded as Britain's betrayal of former allies. His quest for personal obscurity ended with death in a road accident in 1935, but not before his *Seven Pillars of Wisdom* had created a literary memorial.

CHURCHILL AT CAIRO

Winston Churchill (1874–1965), Gertrude Bell (1868–1926) and T.E. Lawrence in front of the Sphinx near Cairo.

By the end of 1920 the British had become thoroughly disillusioned with their wartime conquests in the Middle East. Their relations with the Arab peoples of the former Ottoman Empire had deteriorated sharply, as the prospect of a 'national home' for Jews in Palestine, the handover of Syria to French rule and the imposition of direct Indian-style rule in Iraq all served to inflame Arab hostility. To make matters worse, in 1920 there was a major Arab revolt in Iraq against the British – partly inspired by the supporters of Faisal, the most influential member of the Hashemite family which ruled in Mecca and aspired to rule over much of the Arab Middle East. This was the situation Churchill inherited when he became Colonial Secretary with responsibility for the Middle East in 1921. Churchill assembled a conference of British officials at Cairo, including Gertrude Bell and T.E. Lawrence, both of them admirers of Faisal. A series of sweeping decisions emerged. Palestine was divided into an all-Arab Jordan and Palestine proper where the Jews could settle (Churchill was a keen Zionist), while Iraq was to be placed under Faisal as king, and direct British rule given up. In this way, much of the modern pattern of the Arab Middle-East was laid down. Even so, difficult negotiations lay ahead before Faisal was persuaded to agree to the treaty terms the British required. 'Has he not got some wives to keep him quiet?', grumbled Churchill at one point. What Churchill could not have foreseen was how the Second World War would destroy any slender hopes for a reconciliation of Arab and Jewish interests in Palestine.

The main embarrassment of 1919 was the French expectation that the Sykes-Picot bargain of 1916 would be fulfilled. The British, however, could no longer see why a French presence in the Arab Middle East should be necessary, and craftily invoked American sympathy for Arab self-determination as a means of establishing a loose British protectorate over the Arab lands. At the same time, while reluctantly abandoning Lord Curzon's wilder projects for British protectorates in the Caucasus and Central Asia, Britain contented herself with imposing a virtual protectorate on Iran. Turkish rule was to be expelled from Constantinople and the Straits. In the Mediterranean and the Middle East, at least, there was to be no doubt as to who had won the war.

This was an astounding, almost visionary, transformation of the cautious and limited strategy pursued by the British before 1914. The Foreign Secretary and former Viceroy of India, Lord Curzon, provided the real reasons for this change of attitude: 'You ask, why should England do this? Why should Great Britain push herself out in these directions? Of course the answer is obvious – India.' For Curzon, and for others in the British government, the outcome of the war had provided an historic opportunity to dig deeper and better defences around India and its communications with Britain. The Anglo-Indian strategic system was at the heart of British world power. Never again should it be threatened, as it had been by Ottoman perfidy during the war.

However, this grandiose vision of a new British imperium in the Middle East did not survive beyond 1920. At home, the demand to end conscription was soon reinforced by pressure for financial economies. Garrisons in the Middle East proved an easy target. To make matters worse, the British found themselves assailed in the hour of their triumph by nationalist revolts against their rule in Ireland, Egypt and India. Although these revolts and chafings against the Empire seemed containable for the moment, there was also industrial unrest at home. Expansion no longer looked so easy. Without much cash or coercion at his disposal, Curzon was forced to abandon the informal protectorate over Iran. The French refused to give way gracefully over Syria and the Lebanon, and eventually gained most of what they had been promised in 1916. In Iraq, there was a costly and embarrassing revolt against British rule. As a final blow, the Greek army, which had been expected to keep the Turks away from the Dardanelles and to guarantee Turkish subservience, was defeated by the extraordinary rise of Turkish nationalism under Kemal Ataturk.

Once the dust had settled, it was clear that the prospects for British influence in the post-war Mediterranean and Middle East were less discouraging. The British had been forced to abandon the most far-reaching of their acquisitions. Although Iran and Turkey had recovered their independence and were now ruled by determined, modernizing dictators – Reza Shah and Kemal Ataturk – there was little to fear from them. In fact, the success of these rulers in welding together cohesive states made them much more effective barriers against any revival of Russian ambitions than they had ever been before 1914. In the Arab Middle East, Winston Churchill, as Colonial Secretary, devised an imaginative solution for modifying Britain's top-heavy presence in Iraq. He selected Faisal, the disappointed beneficiary of the defunct Hussein-McMahon agreement, to govern the disparate parts of Iraq, thereby appeasing local feeling and preventing any return of Turkish power. Since Iraq was technically a mandate of the League of Nations, a referendum was considered necessary to show that Faisal was the choice of the people. A referendum was duly stage-managed with this result. Faisal set up an Arab government and struck a bargain with the British. He bound himself to accept British advice in foreign affairs and defence, in return for which the British would provide him with the means to coerce his often recalcitrant subjects. At the first sign of tribal rebellion, the RAF would drop a timely and explosive indication of governmental displeasure.

Until the late 1930s, these arrangements seemed sufficient to uphold Britain's strategic interests in the Gulf. But in Egypt and Palestine, the defence of imperial interests was a more complex matter. In Egypt a powerful nationalist movement had grown up, and in 1919 the British had faced a major revolt. Despite arduous negotiation, no agreement had been possible with the nationalist leaders. In frustration, Britain made a unilateral declaration in 1922 which stated that Egypt was 'independent' and that Britain would not interfere in Egyptian internal affairs. Foreign policy, however, would be directed from London. A British garrison remained, and the divisions in Egyptian politics, especially between the King and the Wafd – a nationalist party dominated by landowners and professional people – ensured that no united patriotic front threatened the British with expulsion. It was not until 1936 that Britain was able to regularize her position in Egypt by a treaty. This recognized British strategic rights in the Canal Zone, that base area which had been so vital to Britain's worldwide system of imperial defence during the First World War and which was to be so again as the skies darkened after 1935.

JEWISH TERRORISM

There were two main Jewish terrorist organizations in Palestine during the period of the British mandate over the territory: the Stern Gang and the Irgun. Both emerged in the 1930s as hostilities intensified between the Arabs and the growing Jewish settlements. Arab fears of eventual Jewish domination increasingly found expression in acts of violence which the official leaders of the Jewish community were unwilling to reciprocate. The terrorist organizations grew up in opposition to this 'moderate' attitude. The Stern Gang was, however, always as much anti-British as anti-

Part of a poster seeking details of the Stern Gang.

Arab and carried out attacks on British officials and police with more and more daring after the outbreak of war in 1939. The Stern Gang's main success was in murdering a British minister, Lord Moyne, in Cairo. After 1945 the Irgun was much the more important of the two organizations, carrying out a large number of bomb attacks and assassinations, including the attack on the King David's Hotel when dozens of Arabs and Jews as well as British were killed. A number of the leading politicians of recent times in Israel were prominent in the terrorist organizations.

Kemal Ataturk (1881–1938), founder and first President of the Republic of Turkey.

Egypt and the Palestinian Imbroglio

Palestine had become a mire of difficulties for Britain. The mandate in Palestine had been casually assumed, mainly to protect the northern approaches to the Suez Canal. Britain was also pledged to promote a Jewish homeland. The eminent Zionist Chaim Weizmann envisaged a Palestine 'as Jewish as England is English'. Even before 1930 there had been signs of serious communal conflict between Jewish settlers and the Arabs who were resentful that they, unlike the Iraqis, had been denied self-rule. But it was the rise of Hitler and the subsequent surge of Jewish refugees from Europe that transformed Palestine into a battleground. Between 1936 and 1939 the British faced an Arab revolt. To appease them, Britain eventually agreed to admit no more than 75,000 Jews without Arab agreement. In the meantime, a campaign of Jewish terrorism had begun with the formation of the Irgun and Stern Gang.

Before 1939, however, the British were reasonably confident that the dominance they had achieved in 1918 could be preserved indefinitely, provided that they ran their Middle East client states on a loose rein and provided that no hostile Great Power entered the region. It was believed that tactful diplomacy would defuse Arab nationalism and that the Arabs would always be divided. Nevertheless, even before the outbreak of war, the situation was far from secure. Germany and Italy besieged British influence in the Middle East, and Iran, Iraq and Palestine all hoped that the demolition of British power would give them the chance of independence that they had been waiting for. The final erosion of British primacy in the region had begun.

The Middle-Eastern Citadel

On the face of it, as in the First World War, the British won a decisive military victory. However, for much of the war, the Mediterranean was far too unsafe to play its old role as a corridor to Britain's Asian possessions. (Britain's principal naval base at Malta lay under siege from 1940 to 1942.) Moreover, not even victory enabled Britain to re-establish her dominance in the Middle East.

The reluctant cooperation of the Arab states had been obtained only at great cost. Threatened by what they saw as the 'disloyalty' of the Egyptian government and the open sympathy of Iraq for Germany, the British threw aside their inter-war policy of tactfully concealing their influence and openly deployed military power to enforce their political ends. Indeed, from an Arab point of view, the result of the war was a great enlargement of overt British domination – an obvious target for Arab nationalism once the war was over.

Political resentment was powerfully reinforced by economic grievances. The peoples of the Middle East suffered all the inconveniences of a complex system of economic regulations imposed on the region by the Anglo-Americans. The popular appeal of nationalism was broadened and deepened by drastic price inflation and the invasion of economic and social life by foreign agencies.

There were other factors which aggravated these local grievances until they became an unmanageable problem for the British in the post-war years. The war signalled an end to Russian dormancy in the Middle East.

Indeed, even before the war had ended, Britain had become fearful of Russia's designs on Turkey, Iran and the region in general. Similarly, American influence was growing rapidly, both as a reflection of the role played by the United States in the Mediterranean war against Italy and Germany and because American oil interests were determined to break the old British monopoly in the Arab states.

These emerging interests were to show their strength when the British were forced to confront the greatest Middle Eastern problem of all: the emergence of Palestine as an *international* problem beyond Britain's sole jurisdiction. Try as they might, the British could not prevent the destruction of their influence among the Arab states after 1945 and ultimately of their whole pre-war primacy in the region.

In many ways, the years between 1914 and 1945 had marked the apogee of British power throughout the whole Mediterranean and Middle Eastern region. The fall, after 1945, was to be both sensational and rapid.

CHAPTER THIRTY-TWO

DIVIDING THE SPOILS: INDIA PARTITIONED

The figure of Mohandas Karamchand Gandhi – universally known as the Mahatma or 'great soul' – dominates the history of Indian nationalism from 1915, when he returned to India from South Africa, until his assassination in 1948, six months after India and Pakistan had achieved independence from Britain. For much of this time, Gandhi was the prominent personality of the Indian National Congress, devising and instigating new methods of civil disobedience that would disrupt British rule. In the last decade of his life, he became the key negotiator; the British, the Muslims and all other political groups had to deal with him.

However, the history of the Indian freedom movement, and of the forces that led to the independence and partition of the Indian Empire in 1947, is too complex to be explained by the ideas and activities of a single leader. Even between 1915 and 1922, when Gandhi stamped his brand of leadership indelibly on the Indian political scene, he was but part of a process that was stimulated by forces beyond his control. The outbreak of war in 1914, along with the reactions to it in both India and Britain, had created a set of circumstances that allowed the new techniques and goals of Gandhi's nationalism to spread rapidly.

The War and its Aftermath

In August 1914, when India entered the First World War as a loyal member of the imperial family, the foundations of British power in India seemed solid enough. Substantial sacrifices in men and money followed, however, as Indian troops fought on the Western Front, in the Middle East and even conducted their own campaign against the Turks in Mesopoamia (Iraq). As a result, opinion in the subcontinent demanded political concessions as the price for continued support.

The British responded in August 1917, when the Secretary of State, Edwin Montagu, announced that the goal of British rule was to be 'the gradual development of self-governing institutions, with a view to the progressive realisation of responsible government in India as an integral part of the British Empire'. In 1919 the passage of the Government of India Act gave substance to this declaration, as elected Indians were allowed some power to determine policy – even if only on non-contentious issues and at nothing more than provincial level.

The 1919 Act failed to meet the aspirations of the embryonic nation, however. The Indian National Congress had returned to the centre of the political stage in 1916 by reuniting its 'moderate' and 'extremist' wings, as well as by concluding an alliance with the Muslim League. Congress leaders had also organized 'Home Rule Leagues' in Bombay and Madras during the war years, while Muslim activists in north India had started the *Khilafat* campaign, in protest at Britain's proposal to break up the Ottoman Empire at the end of the war.

Confronted by these challenges, the Government of India decided to retain its special wartime powers of press censorship and internment without trial, encapsulating them in the Rowlatt Act of 1919. The resulting protests in the Punjab led not only to the imposition of martial law in Amritsar but also to

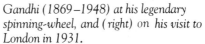
Gandhi (1869–1948) at his legendary spinning-wheel, and (right) on his visit to London in 1931.

the infamous massacre in the Jallianwallah Bagh Gardens on 13 April 1920. Here, according to the official account, 379 Indians were killed and almost 1,000 wounded. Brigadier-General Dyer, the local commander, took 50 troops to disperse an illegal demonstration. 'I realized that my force was small and to hesitate might induce attack. I immediately opened fire and dispersed the mob . . . .. My party fired 1,650 rounds.' The men fired into the unarmed crowd for 10 minutes; there had been no warning given. The dead, who included women, were left in the afternoon sun for the dogs to pick over.

Gandhi's defence of the rights of Indians in South Africa, and his career after returning to the subcontinent in 1915, ensured that he was well-qualified to coordinate the new political movements. In 1917 and 1918 he had launched limited campaigns of passive resistance over local issues in Bihar and Gujarat, using the technique of civil disobedience – imbued with the philosophy of *satyagraha* ('soul force') – that he had devised in South Africa. In 1919 he led the protest against the Rowlatt Act, organizing a *hartal* (a traditional expression of moral outrage involving a work stoppage). He used the same tactic to draw attention to the *Khilafat* campaign of the Muslims. Finally, in 1920, he organized a campaign of total non-cooperation with the Raj. It began in the autumn, and he promised self-rule within a year.

Gandhi planned that through this campaign the educated Indians would be given the opportunity to withdraw from British-run schools and colleges, the law courts, legislatures and official posts, showing their alienation from colonial life. This would be supplemented by ritualized law-breaking, a boycott of foreign cloth and alcohol, and the formation of organizations to coordinate non-violent protests on approved local issues. However, Gandhi's greatest strength was his appeal to the masses, and the campaign spread the influence of the Congress throughout the subcontinent. As a British official commented early in 1921: 'The currency which Mr Gandhi's name has acquired in even the remotest villages is astonishing. No one

THE GREAT CALCUTTA KILLING

Savage communal riots, with Hindus and Sikhs on one side and Muslims on the other, disfigured the last two years of the British Raj. Communal violence was nothing new in the India of the 1940s, but the scale was unprecedented, especially in rural areas. Whether the outbreaks were spontaneous or the result of incitement by political agitators remains a bitterly argued question. What is certain, however, is that the level of violence in 1946–47 took all the leading politicians by surprise, and made it harder for them to avoid full-scale partition with massive transfers of population.

The spiral of communal hatred and mistrust was provoked by events in Calcutta during a day of direct action called by the Muslim League on 16 August 1946. At least 4,000 people were murdered during the following three days, while 10,000 were injured in barbaric attacks that left buildings gutted and

Vultures pick at the remains of those massacred in Calcutta in 1946 in this photograph by Margaret Bourke-White.

the streets littered with dead bodies. Attacks on Hindu landlords and traders at Noakhall in eastern Bengal, and a mass upsurge of Hindu

peasants against Muslims in Bihar followed. Further riots and killings in the Punjab lasted until six months after Partition.

---

seems to know quite who or what he is, but it is an accepted fact that what he says is so, and what he orders must be done.'

Gandhi's great achievement was to devise a set of widely understood symbols that drew on Indian tradition. By creating a new political language for nationalism he involved the mass of the people in politics for the first time. However, even a leader with Gandhi's command could not control the responses induced by the campaign. Threats to his leadership were posed by sporadic violence and by the growth of peasant movements demanding action against landlords and moneylenders, at a time of price inflation and social insecurity. He consequently delayed his call for the non-payment of land revenue. When twenty-two policemen were slaughtered in a village in north India, Gandhi abruptly halted the entire campaign. Non-cooperation was formally suspended on 11 February 1922. In March the Government plucked up the courage to arrest him and, without its focal point, the movement collapsed.

Dominion Status

By the end of 1922 the moment had passed. Gandhi remained in prison until 1924; he then withdrew from public life and organized the All-India Spinners' Association, whose purpose was to promote *khadi* – hand-woven cloth made from hand-spun yarn. Not only would such manufactures strengthen traditional Indian village life, they would also undermine the economic imperialism of the Lancashire cotton industry.

For five years the fortunes of Congress languished. In 1927, however, the Simon Commission was established by the British government to review the working of the 1919 Act and to propose further reform. Because the Commission was a parliamentary body, no Indians could participate. This provoked howls of protest on the subcontinent.

To counter this, in 1929 the Viceroy, Lord Irwin, and Ramsay MacDonald's Labour Government took a new initiative in constitutional reform. In October Irwin issued his famous statement: 'It is implicit in the declaration of 1917 that the natural issue of India's constitutional progress . . . is the attainment of Dominion Status.' Quite what that meant was never defined precisely. The Viceroy proposed that the recommendations of the Simon Commission be supplemented by a full-scale constitutional conference (the Round Table Conference) in London, to which all interested parties could contribute.

These proposals did not satisfy the nationalists. Gandhi had returned to the centre of the political stage in 1928 when Vallabhbhai Patel, one of his closest followers, launched a classic *satyagraha* against the land tax increases in Bardoli in Gujarat. In December 1929 the British offer of constitutional discussions was decisively rejected by the Congress, while Gandhi started a nationwide campaign of civil disobedience.

Mass Law Breaking

The second great Gandhian mass movement began in March 1930. It began with a 240-mile 'salt march' from Gandhi's headquarters at the Sabarmati *ashram* (religious retreat) in Ahmedabad to the sea at Dandi where salt was made, illegally, on the shore. The subsequent campaign of civil disobedience ran, with interruptions, until 1933. For the first year it was a well-disciplined undertaking based on symbolic acts of mass law-breaking that challenged the legitimacy of British rule and exposed its repressive nature. However, a halt was called in March 1931 so that the Mahatma could attend the Round Table Conference in London. The broken momentum was never regained, particularly after the nationalists had returned from Britain empty-handed.

In January 1932, when Congress tried to restart the campaign, circumstances had changed. The worldwide slump in agricultural prices that had occurred during the previous twelve months had created a dramatic effect on the Indian peasantry. The peasants were now more concerned with protesting about land revenue, rents and interest rates – matters with which Congress was not yet equipped to cope.

Gandhi was demoralized. Encouraged by their opponents' disarray, the Viceroy and his administration moved on to the offensive: they suspended a wide range of civil liberties and refused to return the assets of those whose land had been confiscated as a result of no-revenue campaigns. Within a year, the agitation was at an end and most of the prominent Congress leaders were in jail. Just as he had done in 1924, Gandhi backed away from politics and switched his attention to a social issue: in May 1933 it was the discrimination practised against the untouchables, the bottom rung of Indian society. 'Have we not practised Dyerism . . . on our own kith and kin?' he wrote. Shortly afterwards he implored all members of Congress to abandon politics and to work for social uplift instead.

The 1935 Government of India Act

The long and complex process initiated by Lord Irwin in 1929 resulted, eventually, in a new constitution. The 1935 Government of India Act gave significant powers to Indian politicians by establishing fully autonomous provincial governments – elected by a much wider franchise than before – in which ministers responsible to the legislature controlled all aspects of the administration.

In making these arrangements, the British were anxious to reward those who had rejected the calls for mass action, in particular the Muslims. They were also keen to represent minorities and they introduced a system of reserved seats to ensure that this happened. Muslims were given a statutory majority of seats in the Sind, the Punjab and Bengal, with a significant minority stake in the United Provinces and Assam.

The Act envisaged that power would eventually be transferred to Indian ministries at national level, but only in a new federal structure that would incorporate the Indian States as well as the territory controlled directly by the British. It was calculated that if representatives from the Princely States were brought into the national legislature, they would blunt the thrust of the nationalist challenge. However, even under this scheme, defence policy, currency and exchange policy, debt servicing, and external and ecclesiastical affairs were still to remain in the hands of the British.

Congress Takes Control

The new system of central government described in the 1935 Act was never implemented because the Princes never agreed terms on which to join the Federation. The new provincial governments did go ahead, however, with the first elections being held in 1936; the administrations assumed responsibility in most provinces the following year. Congress swept to power in Madras, Bombay, Central Provinces, United Provinces, Orissa and Bihar, where they ruled until they resigned on the outbreak of war in 1939. This political dominance was achieved because Congress was the best organized party in India and the only one with a truly national basis. However, their apparent cooperation had a sting in the tail. As Nehru, the President of the Congress party, said in 1937, 'We are not going to be partners and co-operators in the imperial firm . . . We go to the assemblies or accept office . . . to try to prevent the federation from materializing, to stultify the constitution and prepare the ground

for the constituent assembly and independence.'

The scale of the Congress victory in the 1936 elections served to warn other politicians that they would need special protection to survive. This lesson was particularly well learned by the Muslim League, under Mohammed Ali Jinnah, which had also tried to campaign on a nationwide basis. In the event, the League won less than a quarter of the Muslim seats in the elections and was excluded from power everywhere. In the important Muslim majority provinces of Bengal and the Punjab, governments were formed by independent parties with the support of Hindu voters. The League could redress its rejection by the electorate only by appealing to the British. It did so by claiming that Congress was practising religious discrimination. Jinnah was both shrewd and determined, and the campaign culminated in the adoption by the League of a plan for a separate Muslim state of Pakistan. A resolution was passed asserting that the areas in which the Muslims were in a majority, as in the north-western and eastern zones of India, should be grouped to constitute 'independent States', in which the constituent units should be autonomous and sovereign.

The Triumph of the League

During the Second World War India was a major asset to the Allied cause. Her troops saw action in North Africa, the Middle East and Burma, while the country itself functioned as an important supply base and staging post. Not surprisingly, the war critically affected the country's future.

In the early stage, while the conflict was centred on Europe and the Mediterranean, India's administration seemed to be in control. The Muslim League dominated Muslim political activity in the north, while continuing to build up support in the Punjab and Bengal; Congress was very tentative in exploiting the situation. Matters changed completely when Japan and the United States entered the war.

The Japanese invaded South-East Asia but America was reluctant to fight for British imperialism; the Raj was made to look anachronistic. The Labour members of the War Cabinet, led by Clement Attlee, pressed for a new initiative that would win nationalist support for the war effort. The Cripps Mission of 1942 offered full independence after the war in return for political support during the hostilities. Congress declined to offer its support, however, without immediate concessions. Shortly afterwards, its last great mass campaign was launched –

INDIAN NATIONALISM AT WAR

Subhas Chandra Bose, known to his followers as 'Netaji', meaning 'beloved leader', was one of the most charismatic of Indian nationalists. He rose to prominence in 1920 during the non-cooperation campaign in Calcutta and became the spokesman of Bengali urban radicals. In 1924 the British interned him on suspicion of involvement with terrorism; but on his release he was elected Mayor of Calcutta. During the late 1920s he combined with Nehru to try and push Congress towards more militant action. Ten years later Bose failed in a bid to challenge Gandhi's dominance of the nationalist cause.

The Second World War changed Bose's life. In January 1941 he escaped from house arrest and made his way to Berlin where he tried to

Subhas Chandra Bose (1897–1945).

organize an Indian Legion to liberate his country. But he reached an impasse with Hitler, who wanted to use the force on the Russian front. In July 1943 the Japanese summoned him to Singapore to collaborate with them in creating the *Azad Hind* (Free India) Government, with himself as Head of State. He formed the Indian National Army with 20,000 Indian prisoners of war, released for the purpose from Japanese POW camps, and with 40,000 Indian volunteers from Singapore and other places in South-East Asia. I.N.A. soldiers saw action alongside Japanese troops in Burma in 1944 but they were badly supplied and made little impact on the campaign.

A GREAT IMPERIAL CAPITAL

At the Coronation Durbar of 1911, George V announced that the imperial capital was to be moved from Calcutta to a new site in Delhi. Although Delhi was a traditional centre of Mughal power, the new city was to be designed as an explicit symbol of British strength. Herbert Baker, who planned the city and designed most of its principal buildings in conjunction with Sir Edwin Lutyens, encapsulated their approach to the style to be employed: 'First and foremost it is the spirit of British sovereignty which must be imprisoned in its stone and bronze . . . to realise this ideal the architecture of the Roman Empire . . . should be used as the basis of the style, while Eastern "features" must be woven into the

The Legislative Assembly, home of India's Parliament in New Delhi.

fabric as a concession to Indian sentiment.' To the architectural critic Robert Byron, New Delhi was to be the 'Rome of Hindustan'.

However, the Viceroy's House took so long to construct that it did not come into use until

the late 1920s, and was still not completely finished by the time of Independence in 1947. In fact, New Delhi became a monument to the decline of the Raj, as it descended from the glory of 1911 to the chaos of the last days.

---

the 'Quit India' movement. This was designed to make India ungovernable, forcing both an end to the war and the ejection of the imperialists. In August and September 1942 strikes, demonstrations and *hartals* paralysed the cities, while mass action in the countryside disrupted communications and threatened the war effort. The campaign was the most powerful direct threat to British rule to have been encountered since 1857, but

A cartoon by David Low of 1945, entitled 'Unrest in India', depicts the artist himself, Pethick-Lawrence, the Secretary of State for India, and Attlee, carrying banners, while Jinnah and Gandhi look on.

Jawaharlal Nehru (1889–1964), the first Prime Minister of independent India.

it was effectively neutralized within seven weeks. All known Congress leaders were in jail by the end of the first week while troops were used to restore order. By the end of 1943 more than ninety thousand arrests had been made and one thousand people were dead. On at least five occasions, aircraft were used to machine-gun crowds indiscriminately. Congress and the Raj were at an impasse. The way was open for a third force.

Jinnah took full advantage of the situation. The Muslim League managed to form provincial governments in four areas not dominated by Congress – Sind, Bengal, Assam and the North-West Frontier province. Only the independent Muslim politicians of the Punjab still held out. Here, the League used the Pakistan issue to undermine its rivals. In the provincial elections of 1946 the League won eighty-eight per cent of the Muslim seats. Now there was a third force with which to contend in the constitutional discussions.

The Great Divide

The existence of three conflicting desires became apparent during the final set of negotiations. Congress, led by Jawaharlal Nehru, wanted a strong central government; the Muslim League wanted more power for the provinces; the last Viceroy, Lord Mountbatten, wanted a stable state with which Britain could maintain close ties. In the end, none of these aims could be realized, and each party had to settle for second best. Congress had to accept partition; the League got a 'moth-eaten Pakistan'; and the British were landed with two mutually antagonistic states, close cooperation on defence with either, therefore, being made impossible.

But the highest price was paid by the people, a million dead in communal rioting and almost seven million refugees migrating across the new borders. In the words of the *Hindustan Times*: 'By dividing the Army, the police and the Civil Service on communal lines, they let loose a Frankenstein.' In human terms, this was the Empire's greatest defeat.

On 15 August 1947 India and Pakistan rose from the blood and suffering of the old British Indian Empire. The separate sovereignty of the Indian Princes was abolished and other minorities, such as the Sikhs, were ignored. Whereas the rule of the League in Pakistan was never secure, Congress has dominated independent India ever since.

The outstanding achievement of Gandhian nationalism was not just in winning freedom, but in creating a political organization strong enough to withstand the traumas of nation-building as well. Few other colonial nationalist movements have been able to match such a feat.

CHAPTER THIRTY-THREE

THE TROPICAL COLONIES: 1914–47

◇

As the costs of imperial rule became more pressing from the end of the nineteenth century, British ministers, colonial governments and entrepreneurs began to consider the need for economic development. Progress was painfully slow, but in under-developed tropical colonies such as Africa and Malaya, or in the over-exploited areas, such as the Caribbean, the effort quickened in the twentieth century.

Africa: the Instabilities of Growth

As the slave trade was brought to an end, a less barbaric trade between Europe and Africa arose in its place. In 1848, a British official on the Gambia reported that 'the Sera-Wollies and Telli-Bundas frequently come from distances of not less than five or six hundred miles in the interior, and on paying a small custom [a tax] to the chief of the country in which they settle, are permitted to cultivate the ground under his protection for one or more years . . . and to sell the produce to the European merchant. The greater proportion of the ground nuts exported is raised in this manner.'

Colonization presented the Europeans with the opportunity to control both the African producers and the economies of the countries in which they lived. By levying taxes, for example, Britain could try to force the indigenous population to grow the cash crops, such as cocoa or sisal, which alone yielded the monetary income necessary to pay the tax, and to buy the consumer goods, produced by Europe, such as cotton fabrics. As Cecil Rhodes put it, rural producers might be removed from what he saw as their life of sloth and idleness, and made to give some return 'for our wise and good government'. A Gold Coast newspaper viewed it slightly differently: 'The old slavery is dead, but a more subtle slavery may take its place.' Extending the network of paid officials, both European and African, to impose and collect taxation meant, however, that money had to be spent on salaries and facilities. Similarly, creating the physical infrastructure of roads and railways linking areas of production and local markets with ports, entailed capital expenditure. The funding of such projects depended upon success in securing low-interest, long-term loans and upon the generation of revenue to pay for incidental costs. Securing such monies was a difficult task.

Britain's initial solution had been to sanction chartered companies, such as the Royal Niger Company or the Imperial British East African Company, which would administer the territories and extract whatever profits they could – privatization in effect. But these organizations failed completely in their commercial objectives and, by 1924, the Colonial Office had assumed responsibility for all the areas of tropical Africa under their control.

It was a classic chicken-and-egg situation. Development depended on investment and revenue, but investment could only be attracted by evidence of development. The problem was that putting money into tropical Africa was something of an unknown quantity for prospective shareholders, who were

King Ja-Ja of the Opopo in discussion with the British Consul. The King had become such a successful exporter of palm-oil from West Africa that the British deposed him in 1887 and took over his trade for themselves.

intimidated by the high risks and uncertain rewards. Far better rates of return were obtainable from European or from North or even South American stock. Private finance, therefore, was always slight. Public funding, on the other hand, was limited by the restraint shown by the Treasury and by the constantly inadequate revenues generated by taxing low-income countries. Not surprisingly, the economic value of tropical Africa to Britain before the First World War was marginal.

Boom and Slump 1914–45

The wartime demand for raw materials and the ability of colonial administrations to increase production by various means

A poster illustrates the 49 countries of Britain's colonial Empire standing solidly with Britain in the war against oppression.

– including the recourse to forced labour and compulsory cultivation – had created, by 1917, an illusory impression of economic success. The combination of war-induced demand and wholesale destruction on the battlefield boosted the prices for most African-produced commodities. This boom was short-lived, however, and the prices had begun to drift down again by the end of 1922.

Matters were further complicated during the inter-war years by Britain's shifting economic position. British goods found it harder to compete with more efficient producers in world markets as newer industrial powers, such as Japan and America, were able to undercut British prices. Imperial markets, on the other hand, provided a degree of protection. Similarly, these same markets enabled Britain to buy raw materials, such as tin and copper, without having to cope with fierce competition from the rising industrial nations. By 1938 both imports and exports from the Empire had doubled – as a proportion of total trade – when compared to figures for 1913.

The problems arising from inadequate investment in the tropical colonies were merely intensified after 1929 with the Great Depression. In an attempt merely to maintain income levels, the producers were induced to adopt a variety of measures, including the cultivation of more land and diversification. Many Africans exercised these options with remarkable vigour. Yet despite the farmers' increased productivity, the drop in world commodity prices was so great that the monetary value of colonial exports and their income decreased. Thus, Tanganyika's exports of sisal increased by 4,000 tons between 1929 and 1930. Yet the larger quantity sold for £300,000 or 35 per cent less.

As their revenue from indirect taxation diminished, the colonial administrations retreated. Measures such as the Colonial Development and Welfare Act of 1929 failed to attack the roots of the problem because, ultimately, in the words of the act, it was more concerned with 'promoting commerce with or industry in the United Kingdom' than with directing investment to the colonies. Whitehall's lack of interest can be gauged by the sum spent during the 1930s on all the African colonies: £4.2 million. However, that was not the whole story.

The European Settlers

European settlement in East and Central Africa was encouraged during the 1920s – according to a Cabinet minute – as a way of 'relieving abnormal unemployment', although the largely unspoken but absurd belief that the local population was congenitally idle also made its contribution. It did not seem to occur to those in power in London that the Africans did not have the same objectives as themselves. European farmers, it was believed in Whitehall, would modernize local agricultural practices, creating massive export surpluses. These would yield revenue which the colonial administration could then re-invest to enhance development further. Sir Philip Mitchell, the Governor of Kenya, put it most clearly in a memorandum to the Colonial Office: 'It is of the greatest importance . . . for the future wellbeing and prosperity of the native people that there should be a vigorous and well established British settlement . . . for without it there is no hope of successfully overcoming the immense problems which confront us . . .. The British people in East Africa are the key-stone of the arch.'

Unfortunately the Europeans proved less productive than the supposedly feckless natives. The overheads of the immigrants were greater and their often extravagant lifestyles seriously eroded the proportion of their incomes that could be ploughed back into the soil. Furthermore, many Europeans were inexperienced and undercapitalized. Where they settled in any numbers, as they did in East Africa, they spent considerable amounts of time and energy manipulating the political process to their own advantage, while taxes raised from African producers were redirected to cushion white settlers.

By the late 1930s, Whitehall had become disillusioned with the Europeans. Their political domination and poor economic performance in the colonies of East Africa was contrasted

ENGLISH PLANTERS IN MALAYA

Malayan society before independence in 1957 was stratified along racial lines. On the estates this meant that the Europeans were employed as managers or their assistants. Beneath them, a small number of Eurasians or Indians worked in the office or supervised the workers. At the bottom was the large Tamil work force. Even those Europeans who disregarded differences of origin found that economic circumstances reinforced the segregation between the races.

This segregation was not practised in sexual matters and, before 1920, many English planters had a Malay mistress. However, improvements in their financial circumstances changed the options open to the planters and, between 1911 and 1931, the number of married men rose from 33 to 53 per cent of the total male population of Europeans over twenty years of age. European wives were treated with great deference by the population and their status was much higher than it would have been in Britain. They frequently possessed a substantial domestic staff who protected them from any unnecessary effort. Even their young

Tappers on a rubber plantation in Malaya have their buckets of latex weighed at the end of the day's work.

children were handed over to the care of an *amah* for most of the day. Beyond the age of five or six, most children were returned to England to be entrusted to the tender mercies of a boarding school.

Better roads and an increase in the supply of cars diminished the isolation of the individual estates as the century progressed, allowing

Europeans to develop as a much more coherent group which needed less and less social contact with other races. To combat the effect of the climate, hill stations similar to those in northern India were established along a strip about 100 miles north of the capital, Kuala Lumpur. In the 1930s the government even built a golf course and a rest house in the area.

AN IMPERIAL ACADEMY

Throughout the great age of British expansion in the nineteenth century, there was no imperial training centre to compare with the systematic academies set up for imperial officials in Russia, France and Germany.

This amateurish approach to the running of the British Empire began to change in the opening years of the twentieth century. In December 1908 a report, prepared under the Chairmanship of Lord Reay, recommended to the Government the setting up of a School of Oriental Studies as part of the University of London. Shortage of money delayed the start of the School until 23 February 1917 when George V, finally declared it open, to strains of music, both Western and Oriental.

At the outbreak of the Second World War the School was still half-formed, but the war changed its fortunes. A shortage of radio-operators who could interpret Japanese signals; the need for liaison with anti-Japanese groups in the Far East; and the Government Censors' request to translate more than 32,000 letters in 192 Oriental and African languages – all brought in pupils at an unprecedented rate. It paved the way for the post-war expansion of the School of Oriental and African Studies, as it shifted from an imperialist philosophy to one of development, and became a focus of cultural exchange with a decolonizing world.

---

unfavourably with the thriving peasant economy of West Africa, which had survived the Depression with no assistance at all from Whitehall.

One factor that did make an important difference during the inter-war years was the exploitation of copper deposits in Northern Rhodesia. This opportunity arose from technological progress in ore-processing. In 1924 the colony exported only 108 tons of copper; by 1938 she was producing 213,000 tons. However, the consequences were not entirely positive, as the drain on local manpower malignly affected nearby agricultural production.

New Opportunities during the Second World War

The impact of the Second World War on tropical Africa was considerable. From 1938 vegetable oil and minerals – especially copper and industrial diamonds – were in great demand. Japanese conquests in South-East Asia and the Vichy Government's control of parts of French Africa denied the Allies the rich resources of these countries. The resulting rise in commodity prices lifted the menace of bankruptcy from all but the most incompetent farmer. In addition, the preoccupation of Whitehall with the conflict allowed the settlers to acquire even more political power. In Kenya, for example, according to Viscount Cranbourne, the Secretary of State of the time, 'There is ample evidence that the white inhabitants, both official and unofficial, are taking matters into their own hands, and that the Council is taking the form of a Cabinet, arrogating to itself the power to take decisions without any reference home, increasingly intolerant of any guidance from the Colonial Office.' Matters were very different, however, in those colonies dominated by African peasant agriculture, such as Nigeria, Uganda and the Gold Coast.

After decades of struggle, the African farmers could, at last, anticipate a real return for their efforts. However, Africans were no less subject to emergency regulations than the British themselves. They endured rationing and were exhorted to raise productivity. Increasingly, moreover, they found themselves involved in a government-controlled market. There were a series of complex reasons for this. Such restrictions were introduced to ensure that vital goods were distributed in the 'national interest', and as the commodities produced were no less vital to the enemy, it was essential that they were denied to the Axis powers. An additional factor was that the control of producer prices, for the most part computed by reference to prices prevailing in the depressed 1930s, assured Britain of cheap raw materials at a time when her indebtedness to the United States was growing at an alarming rate. Monopoly purchase was also of great importance to the strength of sterling. Government control of significant dollar-earning enterprises contributed directly to national holdings of foreign exchange at a time when British industry was preoccupied with war production.

Differing systems of control were established within individual colonies. By 1942, for example, a West African Produce Control Board had been created, which effectively handled all commodities produced in British West Africa. One justification for such monopolization of purchasing was the establishment of a stabilization fund; this would intervene when prices paid to producers fell on world markets – as they had done in the previous decade. But the creation of such funds, held in London, was tantamount to taxation for, in fact, they strengthened the sterling reserves.

There was no parallel control on agricultural costs. An inflationary spiral became established that caused friction and hardship, particularly after 1944. As the number of people in the wage economy increased but the value of wages was eroded, the growth of unionization was given enormous impetus. In places such as Kenya and the Gold Coast, the unions were in the vanguard of post-war nationalist agitation.

The Post-War World

The era of healthy commodity prices ushered in by the Second World War continued throughout the 1950s, and much of the tropical world enjoyed two decades of unprecedented growth. The boom was fuelled by the momentum of the American economy which absorbed more and more of the world's resources. Europe and Japan were resuscitated by the US loans which increased the demand for raw resources and drove up commodity prices still further.

In Britain the vision of Africa held by the post-war Labour government was wholly different from that of its pre-war predecessors. As we have seen, the country's industrial base had been faltering during the 1930s. Now the economic situation had become very grave. Clement Attlee's Government saw Africa as their lifeline. In the words of Sir Stafford Cripps, the Minister for Economic Affairs in 1947, 'the whole future of the sterling group and its ability to survive depends . . . upon a quick and extensive development of our African resources.'

The immediate potential value of tropical colonies had already been realized during war-time. While British industry proved incapable of a rapid recovery in export markets, colonial production continued to yield small but valuable amounts of foreign exchange. Furthermore, as these colonial commodities were priced in sterling, a range of vital materials was available to domestic industry without the necessity of depleting foreign reserves. This prompted substantial new investment. The critical shortage of edible fats, for example, led to 'the solution' of the ill-fated Ground Nut Scheme in Tanganyika. In a

Native labourers in Tanganyika in 1949 attempt to recover ground-nuts left behind by the combine harvester.

Cabinet memorandum of November 1949, the Minister for Food, John Strachey, pointed out that the scheme had 'become an important symbol in our Colonial Empire'. Unfortunately, this was all too true. A £50 million loan disappeared into the earth of tropical Africa and yielded nothing. No less unfortunate was the disastrous Gambian Egg Scheme in which large numbers of chickens seem to have satisfied the hunger of local animals rather than that of protein-starved Britons.

Ironically, the Labour Party was the first British administration to be actively concerned with getting a real return from its tropical estates. Labour politicians recognized that these colonies needed capital investment if they were to deliver the goods. The Second Colonial Development and Welfare Act of 1940 and the later creation of the Colonial Development Corporation had set the stage for a session of 'pump-priming finance', which completed a large number of investment projects including road building and port modernization. Coupled with this was an investment in the indigenous peoples themselves: more money than ever before was spent on health, welfare and education. With a view to enhancing production, research on Africa was expanded enormously. The colonial administrators turned to technical expertise to stamp out human, animal and plant disease, to prevent soil erosion and to investigate the potential for hydro-electricity, small-scale industrialization and different crops. Development, in the modern sense, was the watchword and Africa played host to legions of technocrats in white coats. These sometimes heavy-handed, frequently disruptive attempts at progress merely stirred the colonial pot. The highly influential agriculturalist Norman Humphrey caused acute concern in Kenya when he predicted that 'unless radical reforms are introduced, the land and the people of South Nyeri face disaster within the next decade'. Needless to say, radical proposals were not implemented and no disaster occurred.

Economic Change and the Roots of Nationalism

These fresh attempts at using Africa intensively provoked active African opposition. For some producers, the new era of profits was accompanied by the interference of an intrusive and conservative administration. Rural radicalism in many parts of Africa was spearheaded not by the poor but by the new rich, who were frustrated by restrictions and by time-consuming demands for inappropriate anti-erosion measures: the theoretical knowledge of the British 'experts' did not match the practical savvy of the locals.

Funding this new era of colonialism was expensive and initial returns were slight. Profits were further depleted by the need to cope with the unrest provoked in part by these novel approaches. By the beginning of the 1950s, however, Britain was starting its economic recovery and the lifeline from the tropics was seen to be less necessary.

The British Caribbean: Prosperity Postponed

By the end of the nineteenth century, the grip of the British West Indies on world sugar production was limp. In a free market, and dependent on a monoculture, the Caribbean colonies were very vulnerable. Furthermore, competition from subsidized sugar beet cultivation in Europe exacerbated matters. Only the Canadian government's enthusiasm for a system of imperial preference saved the British West Indies from complete economic collapse.

As the new century progressed, the islands began to diversify their economies a little. The export of fruit, particularly bananas, became increasingly important now that refrigerated transport was freely available. Bauxite was discovered in British Guiana during the First World War, and later in Jamaica. As the growth of motoring intensified the demand for well-surfaced roads, exports of Trinidadian asphalt grew.

These economic developments did little to protect the British Caribbean against the distress of the 1930s, however. With the model of Gandhi before them, and with a small but growing class of educated citizens, leaders such as Hubert Critchlow sought to channel the anger of the times into the establishment of self-help institutions such as trade unions. After the Second World War, however, large numbers of people emigrated to Britain and later Canada; they chose to leave rather than struggle against the continuing poverty endemic to the Caribbean.

South-East Asia: an Unplanned Bonus

The group of British colonies strung out between mainland Asia and Australia were never more than an afterthought of Empire. Although the inter-war years represented the high point of European influence in the area, British investment there amounted to only three or four per cent of her total overseas financial commitment in 1930. Nevertheless, the area was rich in tin, teak, oil and rubber. Some of the companies exploiting them often achieved returns of over twenty-five per cent.

This world collapsed in the early months of 1942 when the Japanese swept through the area. Not only was the extent of their victory traumatic but its speed was very telling as well. The Europeans were quite obviously 'paper tigers', and although the Japanese were not seen as any improvement by the local citizenry, they were Asian. Thus, once the Second World War was over, and with this example of oriental power fresh in their minds and with India about to achieve independence, it was only a matter of time before British South-East Asia insisted on self-determination. Yet, in the meanwhile, the British – by an unplanned act of serendipity – chanced upon a pot of gold. The reoccupation of Malaya allowed them to use its rubber and tin to help support sterling. These commodities soared in value as they were sold to the booming American economy.

CHAPTER THIRTY-FOUR

NEW WORLDS; THE DOMINIONS: 1914–42

The Empire Premiers' Conference at No. 10 Downing Street: (from left to right) A.J. Balfour, the Maharao of Kutch, W.F. Massey, A. Meighen, Lloyd George, W.M. Hughes, General Jan Smuts, Lord Curzon and Srinavasa Shastri.

Perhaps the most important change in the status of Britain's New World Dominions between the wars was that they ceased to be 'new': the appellation simply dropped out of use. This was partly a reaction to the Great War, in which the Dominions had suffered such grievous losses that any sense of innocent 'newness' in relation to the Old World had been forfeited. Some Dominions, notably Australia and New Zealand, had even set about becoming small imperialists in their own right by acquiring fragments of what used to be the German Pacific Empire. But the main reason for this coming of age was that the Dominions had become increasingly integrated into the conventional system of world affairs, becoming less 'British' in the process. This was more true of some than of others, however: the inter-war period was marked by anxieties which constrained the abilities or even desires of the Dominions to plough an independent furrow.

Towards Constitutional Autonomy

The main theme of Dominion affairs during the 1920s was their attainment of full constitutional autonomy. Political leaders had rallied their electorates with this vision during the First World War; indeed, a 'moral unity', as *The Times* described it, seemed to have strengthened the bonds of Empire as never before. Although these sentiments lost their talismanic power when peace arrived, a constitutional settlement of some kind was recognized to be long overdue. This led to the famous Balfour Declaration on Inter-Imperial Relations at the 1926 Imperial Conference in London which dismantled the legal sovereignty of Parliament at Westminster and recognized the Dominions as 'autonomous communities within the British Empire, equal in status, in no way subordinate to one another . . . though united by a common allegiance to the Crown'. A 'sacramental' British nation was envisaged, in which the Dominions were able to be one and many simultaneously.

After the Statute of Westminster in 1931, the Royal House of Windsor became the main formal link between the Dominions and the United Kingdom. There was a measure of calculation in the ritual that surrounded the monarchy. The crackling radiobroadcasts to the Empire by George V on Christmas Day soon became a cosy legend. This newly heightened loyalty in the overseas Dominions was useful to the old British hierarchy struggling to retain its traditional leadership; it also explained why Dominion views played such a large part in the Abdication Crisis of 1937. In short, these years witnessed the successful transition of a constitutionally defined Commonwealth into one based on looser, but not necessarily less tangible bonds.

Race and Nationhood within the Commonwealth

Race was a cementing factor in the inter-war Commonwealth. The British Government thus helped to deflect criticisms (sometimes from within the Empire) of the Dominions' exclusionist policies on immigration and citizenship. On one occasion, for example, the authorities in London gave advance warning to the

Canadians that the Government of India intended to raise at the League of Nations the question of the domiciliary rights of Indian nationals in British Columbia. The most deviant forms of race discrimination emerged in South Africa, especially after the largely Afrikaner Nationalist Party first entered government in 1924; and by the end of the 1930s the British were expressing concern about the effect of 'beating the white man's drum' in Pretoria on the stability of the African continent. Nevertheless, by 1939, South Africa was only just beginning to be seen as quintessentially a 'problem boy' in the Dominion class.

Whilst jealous of the rights inherent in Dominion Status, these countries were not generally marked by abrasive nationalism. In Australia a local patriotism was evident (as in the cricketing rivalry with Britain which peaked in the Ashes contest of 1932–3) but this did not extend to any desire to separate from the Mother Country. Canada evinced a somewhat more pronounced anti-imperialism in these years. Much of this stemmed from Mackenzie King, Prime Minister for most of the period, who was deeply suspicious that the connection with Britain might involve Canada in another war, and who was very conscious of separatist feeling in Quebec. The desire to emphasize Canada's international, as well as merely local, autonomy led that Dominion to be the first to appoint its own diplomatic representatives in foreign capitals. The result, however, was often mundane: when a Canadian legation was set up in Tokyo, its head had little to do until invited to referee a baseball game between the Japanese Foreign Office and the American embassy. During the 1930s such independent ventures were cut short, since they were likely to increase, not reduce, the dilemmas potentially posed by foreign policy. Furthermore, having the United States as a dominating neighbour had the curious effect of turning the British link into a form of insurance for Canada's own identity. This was true for French as well as English Canadians. Hence of the two possible Anglo-Saxon partners, the English over the ocean were always preferred if only because distance lends enchantment to the view.

In South Africa the elections of 1924 were a more substantial challenge; the pro-British Jan Smuts was defeated by the nationalist J.B.M. Hertzog. However, although Hertzog sometimes pleased the Afrikaner radicals with his republican rhetoric and although he claimed that he had wrenched 'independence'

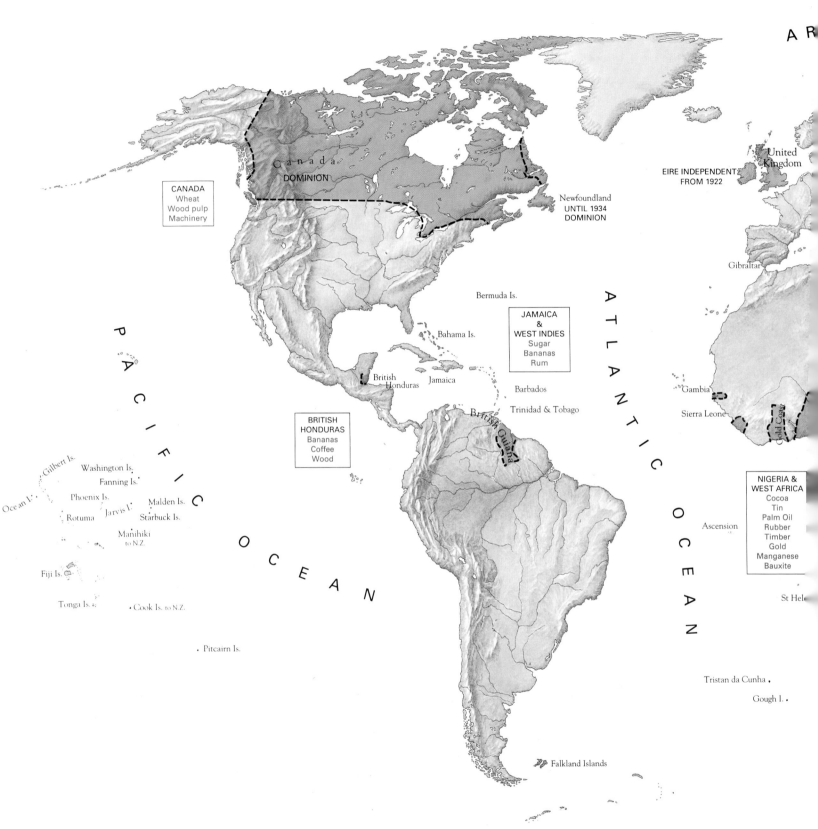

CANADA
Wheat
Wood pulp
Machinery

Canada
DOMINION

Newfoundland
UNTIL 1934
DOMINION

EIRE INDEPENDENT
FROM 1922

United
Kingdom

Gibraltar

Bermuda Is.

Bahama Is.

JAMAICA
&
WEST INDIES
Sugar
Bananas
Rum

British
Honduras

Jamaica

Barbados

Trinidad & Tobago

Gambia

Sierra Leone

Gold Coast

BRITISH
HONDURAS
Bananas
Coffee
Wood

British Guiana

NIGERIA &
WEST AFRICA
Cocoa
Tin
Palm Oil
Rubber
Timber
Gold
Manganese
Bauxite

Ascension

St Hel

Gilbert Is.

Washington Is.

Fanning Is.

Ocean I.

Phoenix Is.

Rotuma

Jarvis I.

Malden Is.

Starbuck Is.

Manihiki
to N.Z.

Fiji Is.

Tonga Is.

Cook Is. to N.Z.

Pitcairn Is.

Tristan da Cunha

Gough I.

Falkland Islands

P A C I F I C   O C E A N

A T L A N T I C   O C E A N

A R

The Empire 1918–42

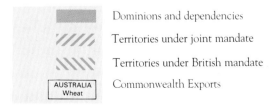

Dominions and dependencies

Territories under joint mandate

Territories under British mandate

AUSTRALIA
Wheat
Commonwealth Exports

CTIC OCEAN

PACIFIC OCEAN

Malta
Cyprus
Palestine
Tr. Jordan
Iraq
Bahrain Qatar
Trucial Oman
Oman

INDIA
Jute
Tea
Rice

BURMA
Teak
Jute
Rubber

MALAYA
Rubber
Tin
Palm Oil
Timber

India
Burma
Hong Kong

Nigeria

Cameroon

Anglo-
Egyptian
Sudan

Aden Prot.
Somaliland

Kuria Muria Is.

Socotra

Laccadive Is

Andaman Is.

Nicobar Is.

British
North Borneo
Brunei
Sarawak

Malaya

Nauru I.

Bismarck Archipelago
Australian Mandate

New Guinea
to Australia

Solomon Is.

New Hebrides

Uganda
Kenya

Tanganyika

Zanzibar

Ceylon

Maldive Is.

Seychelles

Chagos Is.

Christmas Is.

Cocos Is.

INDIAN OCEAN

Australia
1926 DOMINION

Kermadec Is.
to N.Z.

Northern Rhodesia
Nyasaland

Southern Rhodesia

Bechuanaland Prot.

South West Africa

Union of South Africa

DOMINION

Mauritius

RHODESIA
Tobacco
Asbestos
Copper
Meat

SOUTH AFRICA
Gold
Diamonds
Wool
Machinery

AUSTRALIA
Wheat

NEW ZEALAND
Wool
Meat
Dairy Products

New Zealand
DOMINION

Norfolk I.
to Australia

Lord Howe I.
to Australia

Chatham Is. to N.Z.

Auckland Is. to N.Z. Bounty Is. to N.Z.

Antipodes Is.

Campbell I. to N.Z.

Maquarie Is.
to Australia

SOUTHERN OCEAN

205

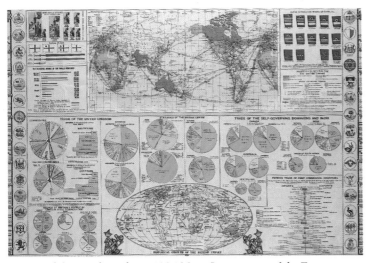

Facts and figures charted in a 1924 Navy League map of the Empire.

from British hands at the 1926 conference, in practice he stayed within the parameters set by Dominion status. It became a Whitehall commonplace to shrug off republican feeling in South Africa. The situation was to become more unstable later, but the immediate 'taming' of Hertzog made for initially easy relations with the most problematical of Britain's overseas Dominions.

The Depression and the Dominions

The crisis of the 1930s was economic at first, rather than diplomatic. Australia was the first to feel the harsh effect of the Depression, because she had borrowed heavily in preceding years in order to finance what would now be called a 'dash for growth'. When receipts from exports plummeted, Australia was unable to service the loans. The Bank of England dispatched Sir Otto Niemeyer to advise the Australian authorities on the merits of austerity, thereby gaining for him a prominent place in the demonology of Australian nationalism. Australia, however, was a rich country, and such adjustments were tolerable. Indeed, the stabilization programme which was implemented proved successful, and therefore established the superiority of the 'central' government of the Commonwealth over the states in the fiscal sphere. Newfoundland, whose legal status was more akin to that of a Dominion, proved less lucky. Not only did the country go bankrupt, but the 'bailiffs' arrived from London in the form of so-called Commissioners of Government. They proceeded to administer the territory from their hotel rooms in the capital, St John's. The financial repercussions of the Depression of the early 1930s threatened thus to complicate relations between imperial partners: one was a great creditor, and the rest

were, as befitted developing societies, habitual debtors.

The most scarring effects of the Depression on the Dominion populations were eventually felt in Canada. The grain-growing provinces of Manitoba, Alberta and Saskatchewan fell victim to the great 'Dust Bowl' which swept over the American plains in 1934–5. Few major agricultural regions of the world were so dependent on a single cash crop, and an often abject poverty ensued. In addition, it was wheat of all the major commodities that suffered the greatest fall in price after 1929. The effects were devastating – especially in the many newly settled localities – amounting to a wholesale reversal of years of pioneering endeavour.

In economic and social terms, the Depression effectively put the clock back in the Dominions, and underlined the fragile basis of their national prosperity. To this there was but one exception: in South Africa the rising price of gold fuelled a steady boom. One consequence of these uncertainties, and the Dominions' loss of markets in a protectionist Europe, was their heightened dependence on Britain. At first the United Kingdom, still faithful to its Free Trade ideals, was unmoved by their pleas for special help, but after the economic and monetary crisis of 1931 the vision of a self-contained imperial trade block temporarily beckoned. This reached its apogee at the Imperial Economic Conference at Ottawa in August 1932.

This conference did not produce entirely satisfactory results, however. The Dominions concluded that Britain was neither able – nor wished – to maintain its role as the fly-wheel of development in other continents. Even in loyal New Zealand, the 1934 Dairy Industry Commission based its suppositions on the principle that the British market was no longer bottomless, and began to look for supplementary markets. Some of this pessimism was exaggerated. As the agriculture of the Dominions diversified, the significance of British custom for their currants, wines, cheeses and similar items was to be considerable. Nevertheless, by the end of the decade, the classic image portraying Britain as the motor of economic growth had become rather faded.

The Approach of War

As the 1930s wore on, the fear of another war became more of a threat than recent economic concerns. This anxiety affected the Dominions strategically and psychologically in different ways. After 1935, Mackenzie King in Canada approached every foreign policy question from the angle of the country's internal cohesion. Such circumspection was natural in a country where there was a large French-speaking population, and where even the English-speaking population harboured suspicions of British

AUGUST 1932: THE IMPERIAL ECONOMIC CONFERENCE

The convening of a great conference in the Canadian capital of Ottawa marked a turning point in the economic direction of the Empire. Faced with the calamity of the Great Depression, the instinctive solidarity of the British Dominions drew them closer together. History and sentiment caused them to look to Britain for leadership, as well as a deal of some sort to bail them out. But the team from London saw the situation very differently. They knew that the citizens of the Dominions enjoyed a higher standard of living than the

electorate in the United Kingdom. Any accommodation would have to be mutual. This fundamental shift in the relationship between London and the governments of the Dominions caused resentment. The discussions became tense and unexpectedly acrimonious. One British participant accused their host, the Canadian Prime Minister Richard Bennett, of having 'the manners of a Chicago policeman and the temperament of a Hollywood film star'.

Not surprisingly, the results of the

conference were modest, having little visible effect on the economic problems of any of the participants. The Dominions resented being told that they had to stand on their own two feet. Bitter accusations were nurtured and published by the press of the aggrieved parties. But, in the end, the various governments did adjust to the realities of the new relationship, even though its consequences took decades to work through. The Ottawa Conference, therefore, marked the high-tide of a vision of an Imperial common market.

BODYLINE: THE ASHES THAT SMOULDERED

In September 1932 the British Test Cricket Team sailed for Australia and a winter contesting 'the Ashes'. The captain, Douglas Jardine, was preoccupied with containing Australia's star batsman Donald Bradman. Jardine's answer was to encourage the aggression of Lancashire's fast bowler Harold Larwood. It was believed that Bradman had flinched when facing Larwood during a Test Match held at the Oval in London in the summer of 1930. That was how 'bodyline' was born. The idea was to attack the man rather than the wicket by bowling short, causing the ball to rear up and threaten the head or body of its intended victim. The batsman would act in self-defence and be inclined to offer a catch as he fended away the ball.

The Australian reaction to the new tactics was summarized by the local journalist who reported that there were two teams on the pitch but only one was playing cricket. Australian fury reached its peak during the 'Battle of Adelaide', in which Larwood's relentless

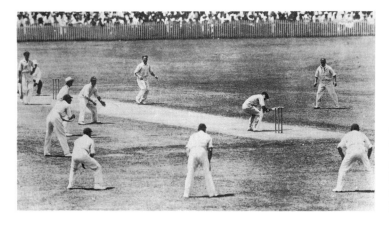

The Australian batsman, Woodfull, ducks under a brutal ball from Larwood in the Fourth Test at Brisbane.

deliveries felled several of the opposition. Jardine's manner did not help matters, for his preoccupation with victory and his diffidence were taken for arrogance by the crowds of spectators. Matters became so heated that the politicians became involved and telegrams raced between London and Canberra. Jardine and his team won the series, largely because

Bradman had been contained. But the inquest back in London left a stain on Jardine's reputation and he only ever captained one other England touring party. His dedication to winning was considered 'bad form' at the time. Today, however, batsmen are protected by crash helmets and body padding and 'bodyline' is almost considered normal.

---

chauvinism. Enforced conscription during the First World War had split the country's loyalties, and the federation was still fragile enough to be pulled apart under similar conditions. Mackenzie King became a warm advocate of the merits of appeasement, even visiting Germany in 1937 and singing Adolf Hitler's praises as a result. Even when the policy of Appeasement began to founder, Mackenzie King still refused to commit Canada to the support of British policy any further than the tentative character of Canadian opinion allowed. Public opinion was, of course, given an emotional boost by the visit of King George VI and Princess Elizabeth in 1939, and British war contracts considerably lubricated the loyalist spirit. Mackenzie King still insisted that the question of whether Canada should stay at peace or go to war was a decision to be made by her own Parliament rather than by someone else. Nevertheless, when hostilities finally broke out, the loyalist adrenalin flowed free and the majority for war was overwhelming.

The strategic preoccupations of Australia and New Zealand were more pressing because their own shores were under threat from Japan. Hence for a while New Zealand, the most loyal of Dominions, doubled up as also the warmest advocate of collective security through the League of Nations. Once the League had collapsed, however, the Antipodean Dominions had to rely entirely on British promises – formally extended at the 1937 Imperial Conference – that, in the event of war, a Royal Navy force would be sent to the Pacific sufficient in strength to keep Japan at bay. In view of the ease with which Singapore fell to the Japanese in 1942, some Australian historians have questioned the good faith of their predecessors in these assurances. Despite the substantial efforts made by Britain to refurbish her naval power in the late 1930s, it had become impossible for her to defend her distant protegés against all eventualities in a troubled and heavily armed region. Politicians and military planners in Australia, as well as in Britain, had to skate over the thin ice of imperial defence so long as no better alternative presented itself. It was fear and loneliness, combined with the affectionate ties of race and history, therefore, which explained why Australia backed Britain in 1939, disdaining even that parliamentary vote which was so important to Canada's self-esteem.

South Africa, of all the white Dominions, came closest at the outset of war to adopting (like Eire) a policy of neutrality. Imperial loyalties among the Union's whites had weakened during the 1930s. In 1931 the Government of South Africa had contemplated making the rand independent of the pound sterling. Three years later it had passed legislation defining local nationality as something different from, and overriding, older conceptions of imperial citizenship. Underlying many of these tensions was the fact that Britain was thought to be 'going soft' on the native question in her own black colonies to the north. Nevertheless, it was the pro-war party that by a tiny majority won the crucial vote in the Union Parliament. The South Africans subsequently played a major part in supplying men and materials to the many Middle Eastern campaigns of the next six years. It is probably true to say that emotional loyalty to Britain, as a consideration which brought about this result, was less important in South Africa's case than in any other Dominion's; above all, the Union was impelled by concern that any defeat of Britain would entail a revolution in the political cartography of Africa – something Pretoria scarcely welcomed.

The Dominions which went to war alongside Britain in 1939, then, only did so after making a rational assessment that it served their interests. Thus the overwhelming majority in the Canadian Parliament for this decision did not prevent Mackenzie King from adding the rider that his country's liability in the present conflict could only be a limited one. All this was natural enough, but it marked a radical change from 1914, when the preponderant attitude had been, in the words of Edmund Barton, one of the founding fathers of the Australian Commonwealth, 'Touch one of us and you touch the lot'. Such blind loyalty, whilst not entirely dissipated over the next twenty-five years, was sufficiently attenuated as to become vulnerable to the bad news which war always brings. It was not, therefore, to be very long before, in the wake of the fall of Singapore, the Australian Prime Minister was to declare that the Dominion would now look to the United States 'free of any pangs as to our traditional links with the United Kingdom'. In the words of General de Gaulle, 'there is nothing so cold as the heart of a state': and by 1939 the Dominions had become states in their own right.

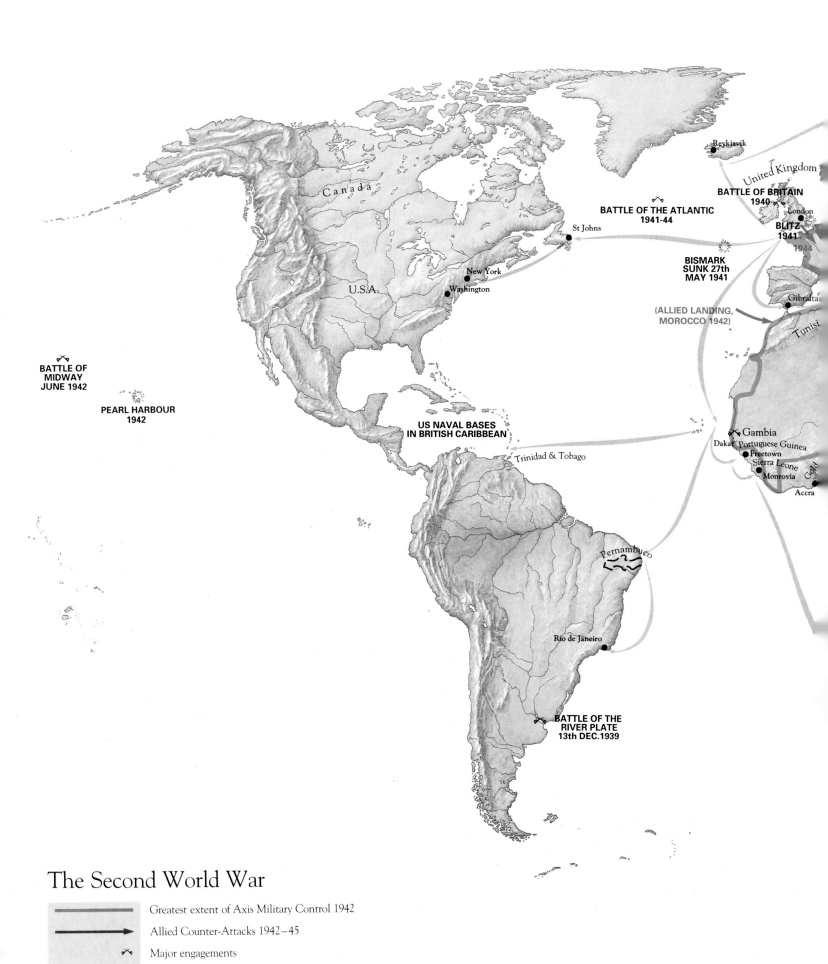

Reykjavik

United Kingdom

BATTLE OF BRITAIN
1940

BATTLE OF THE ATLANTIC
1941-44

London

BLITZ
1941
1944

St Johns

New York

Washington

Canada

U.S.A.

BISMARK
SUNK 27th
MAY 1941

(ALLIED LANDING,
MOROCCO 1942)

Gibraltar

Tunisi

BATTLE OF
MIDWAY
JUNE 1942

PEARL HARBOUR
1942

US NAVAL BASES
IN BRITISH CARIBBEAN

Trinidad & Tobago

Gambia

Dakar Portuguese Guinea

Freetown

Sierra Leone

Monrovia

Accra

Gold

Pernambuco

Rio de Janeiro

BATTLE OF THE
RIVER PLATE
13th DEC.1939

The Second World War

Greatest extent of Axis Military Control 1942

Allied Counter-Attacks 1942–45

Major engagements

Major Bombardments

Allied convoy routes

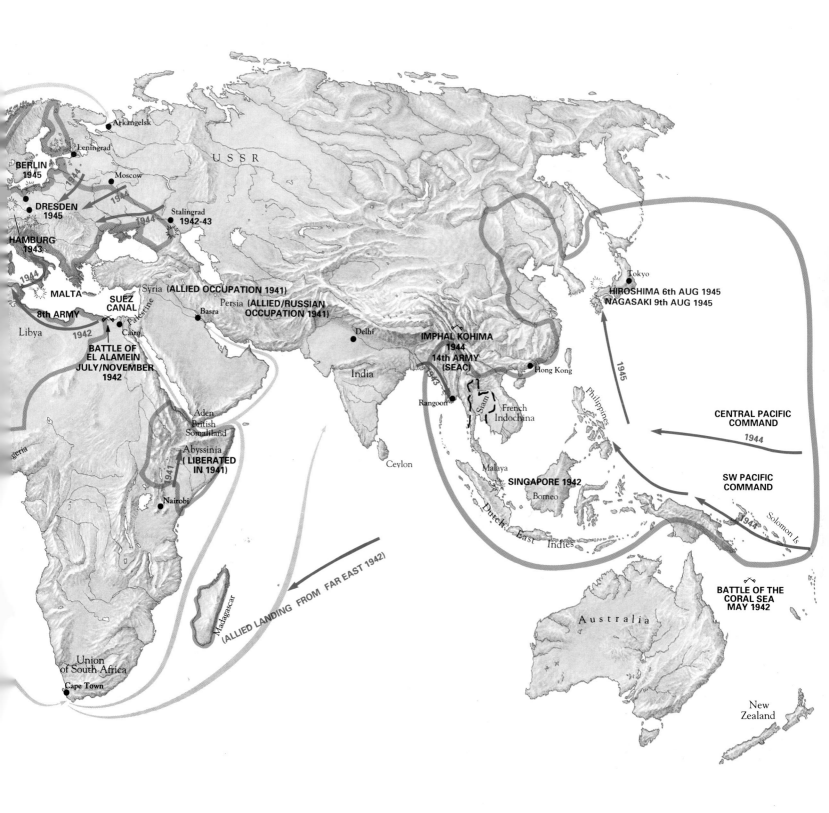

BERLIN
1945

DRESDEN
1945

HAMBURG
1943

1944

MALTA

8th ARMY

Libya

1942

BATTLE OF
EL ALAMEIN
JULY/NOVEMBER
1942

Arkangelsk

Leningrad

Moscow

U S S R

Stalingrad
1942-43

1944

1944

Syria **(ALLIED OCCUPATION 1941)**

SUEZ
CANAL

Palestine

Cairo

Persia **(ALLIED/RUSSIAN
OCCUPATION 1941)**

Basra

Delhi

India

IMPHAL KOHIMA
1944
14th ARMY
(SEAC)

Hong Kong

1945

Rangoon

Siam

French
Indochina

Tokyo

HIROSHIMA 6th AUG 1945
NAGASAKI 9th AUG 1945

1945

Philippines

CENTRAL PACIFIC
COMMAND

1944

SW PACIFIC
COMMAND

Aden
British
Somaliland

Abyssinia
**(LIBERATED
IN 1941)**

1941

Nairobi

Ceylon

Malaya

SINGAPORE 1942

Borneo

Dutch   East   Indies

Solomon Is

1944

geria

Madagascar

(ALLIED LANDING FROM FAR EAST 1942)

Union
of South Africa

Cape Town

Australia

BATTLE OF THE
CORAL SEA
MAY 1942

New
Zealand

CHAPTER THIRTY-FIVE

THE SECOND WORLD WAR

◇

The British Empire proved itself to be as remarkably resilient and coherent during the Second World War as it had been in the First. When France fell in June 1940, however, it had seemed that fragmentation might be a more likely outcome. Imperial problems of the late 1930s had included nationalism in India, riots in the West Indies and white settler demands in Africa. Moreover, the Dominions had already attained independence in the conduct of foreign policy, and the Palestinian mandate had begun to pose an impossible dilemma.

The Imperial War Effort

Despite the international crises of the 1930s, all the 'white' Dominions (except Ireland which remained neutral) decided to follow Britain into war in September 1939. In that month the Anglophile Jan Smuts became Prime Minister of South Africa again; he replaced J.B.M. Hertzog who had been striving to keep his country out of war with Germany. Indeed, as Britain stood alone against the Nazi siege in the autumn of 1940, some in high places considered Smuts, this elder statesman of the Commonwealth, as a possible war leader if anything should happen to Winston Churchill.

As they had in the First World War, white South Africans fought in Africa (this time in the Western Desert), Australians and New Zealanders in the Middle East, and Canadians in Western Europe. Commonwealth forces also fought alongside the British and Americans in the invasion of Italy (1943), the opening of the Second Front (1944) and the liberation of South-East Asia and the South-West Pacific. India, whose economic value had declined as its unreliability had grown during the 1920s and 1930s, once again served as a barrackroom as well as providing war materials and over £1 million in funds; an Indian army swollen to nearly 2½ million soldiers fought in all sectors but particularly in the reoccupation of South-East Asia. The tropical colonies were also put on a wartime footing and while

their peoples were mobilized, their raw materials were called into operation – Malayan rubber and Burma oil, Nigerian tin and Rhodesian copper, West African palm oil and sisal from Tanganyika. A former Colonial Secretary, Malcolm MacDonald, insisting that the colonies went to war voluntarily, explained their response as follows: 'I think it is significant that these sixty million people, scattered over fifty different territories, who are not yet free to govern themselves, who are governed by us, recognised instinctively from that experience that we are the true guardians of the liberties and the happiness of small peoples.'

The centralized machinery of an Imperial War Cabinet that had existed in 1916 was not reactivated in this war. Instead, 'continuous consultation' between Commonwealth members was considered to be the best form of imperial co-ordination. In the dependent Empire, however, Britain's over-rule was more apparent: as in 1914, the Viceroy declared war on behalf of India, without bothering to consult political leaders. The war encouraged centralized direction: ministers were posted to South-East Asia and West Africa, and in Whitehall the previously rather haphazard approach to colonial policy-making was thoroughly overhauled.

The Empire at Bay: 1941–3

The Great War of 1914–18 had been a European civil war with little more than sideshows beyond. By contrast, the activities of both Italy and Japan in 1940–2 had grave implications not only for military strategy but also for the very survival of the Empire. Their campaigns in North Africa and South-East Asia and the Pacific were central to the outcome of the war.

Hitler occupied Europe to the east and west of Germany, launched the Luftwaffe against Britain and invaded Russia; Mussolini, meanwhile, endeavoured to create an empire in North Africa. In August 1940 Italy conquered British Somaliland, and in September she invaded Egypt. British imperial forces counter-attacked under General Wavell, but were forced to retreat when the Italians were reinforced by German divisions under General Rommel. For a while it seemed as if Rommel's onslaught upon Egypt would be successful. Although officially neutral and for decades resentful of the British who were garrisoned there, Egypt had been commandeered for the British war effort. The young King Farouk's lack of enthusiasm for this became so alarming to the British that they gave Farouk a painful choice: forced abdication or acquiescence in the installation of a pro-British government. He chose the latter, and Cairo became, in all essentials, the military capital of the Empire. The stronghold of Cairo having been secured, General Montgomery halted Rommel's Egyptian onslaught at El Alamein in August 1942. He then chased the Germans – by now seriously depleted in fuel and supplies – westwards, linking up with an Anglo-American force in Tunisia in May 1943. The North African campaign had drained the Italo-German Axis of men, aircraft and shipping, providing the Allies at the same time with a base

A Russian war-poster of 1942 shows Hitler being strangled by the Allied forces of Britain, Russia and America.

South African troops leap into action in the Battle of Libya, 1941.

Field Marshal Sir Alan Brooke (1883–1963) (Chief of the Imperial General Staff), Winston Churchill (1874–1965) and General Sir Bernard Montgomery (1887–1976) in Normandy, 1944 (left).

from which to invade Italy. Victory in this theatre of war had saved the lifeline of the British Empire, which ran through Malta and the Suez canal.

British high-handedness in Egypt was not forgotten, however, and national frustrations were to erupt again with humiliating consequences for Britain in the Suez crisis of 1956.

The Struggle in the Pacific

Allied defeats in 1941–2 in South-East Asia and the Pacific were much more damaging. The Japanese ousted the Dutch, French and Americans from their respective colonies in the East Indies, Indo-China and the Philippines, while the British lost Hong Kong, Malaya, Singapore, Borneo, Burma and the Solomon Islands. Although the Anglo-Japanese Treaty of 1902 had, in effect, recognized Britain's inability to police the Far East on her own, Britain had completely underestimated the strength of Japan's military strength and ambitions. 'I trust you'll chase the little men off,' said the Governor of Singapore cheerfully to his General-in-Command as the Japanese landed in Malaya.

After the fall of Singapore in 1942, it became clear that the restoration of any of the European colonies in the region would depend on American power. Australia and New Zealand, the most Anglophile of the Dominions, were forced to turn to the USA for assistance.

America and British Imperialism

The Japanese onslaught brought the Americans into the war. It also assured the Allies of eventual victory: but on whose terms? Americans had no wish to fight for the restoration of European imperialism. The British Empire was especially resented in the USA; it was not only politically distasteful to the great ex-colony, but was economically unacceptable as well because British imperial preferences hampered global free trade. 'One thing for sure we are not fighting for is to hold the British Empire together,' declared *Life* magazine in 1942. Moreover, before America's entry into the war, Churchill and President Roosevelt signed the Atlantic Charter, article 3 of which declared respect for 'the right of all peoples to choose the form of government under which they will live'. Churchill attempted to insert a clause which would exempt the Empire from this right but he was not successful. Churchill subsequently explained away this embarrassing clause by declaring it to apply only to Nazi-occupied Europe. Nevertheless, as the tide turned in the war, so the waves also rolled against the Empire, leaving Churchill as lonely as Canute in his determination not 'to preside over the liquidation of the British Empire.'

It was largely to allay US misgivings about British imperialism that the Chamberlain Government had in 1938 dispatched the Moyne Commission to examine the reasons for unrest in the

BRITISH PROPAGANDA IN BURMA

Attempts to undermine enemy morale by means of propaganda were planned with increasing sophistication during the Second World War. In Europe the strategies of Dr. Goebbels and Lord Haw-Haw were countered by bullish Pathé newsreels. Tactics in the Far East, where the Allied resistance was initially much more dismal, were recorded by Leslie Glass in his book 'The Changing of Kings: Memories of Burma': 'The Head of the Burma section of the Far Eastern Bureau in Delhi later recalled producing a weekly newspaper, Lay Nat Tha ('The Spirit of the Wind') which was

A British aerial propaganda leaflet depicts Dr Ba Maw, the Premier of Japanese-occupied Burma, as a Japanese puppet.

dropped on Burmese villages by the RAF. "In the early days it was difficult to know what to say in Burmese leaflets. We had been beaten by the Japanese, and we were still doing badly in

the war and were very much on the defensive. Promises of early victories might turn out to be hollow. So we concentrated on stirring up the Burmese national spirit against the Japanese." '

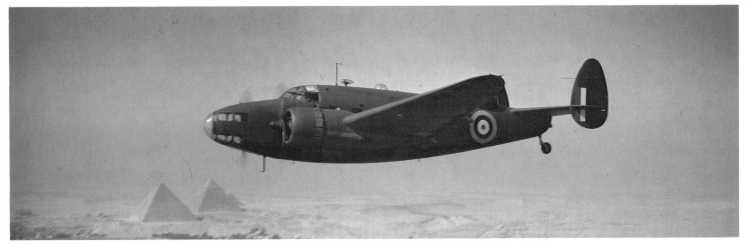

A Lockheed Hudson, the 'workhorse' of the Royal Air Force, flying over the Pyramids in Egypt.

West Indies. British territorial possessions in what America regarded as her backyard – as she had since the Monroe Doctrine of 1823 – were a sensitive issue at the best of times. The Commission's report published in 1940 was consequently a much abbreviated version of the original, which strongly criticized the actions and inertia of colonial government in the Caribbean and contained forthright recommendations for reform. In September 1940, in return for fifty elderly destroyers, the British government leased air and naval bases to the USA in a number of Caribbean islands – including the Bahamas, Jamaica and Trinidad – but, thereafter, Britain was alert to any hint of American interference in the administration of these colonies.

Two years later, as the Japanese threatened the Raj, and with the Anglo-American alliance firmly in mind, Churchill dispatched Stafford Cripps to India. He went with an offer of self-government after the war in exchange for Indian (particularly Congress) co-operation during it, but he returned empty-handed. Indeed Congress launched its 'Quit India' campaign in August 1942. The Prime Minister and Viceroy had, in fact, sabotaged the mission behind Cripps's back. Churchill's attitude towards Gandhi and Indian nationalism had always been dismissive, to say the least.

Nevertheless, the gesture did sweeten the transatlantic 'special relationship', although misgivings lingered: the American General Stilwell complained, for instance, that South-East Asia Command (SEAC) was merely a front to Save England's Asiatic Colonies.

The African Contribution

The loss of Asian possessions meant that Britain leaned more heavily upon Africa. Having failed to establish a Free French régime at Dakar in September 1940, British forces seized Madagascar for General de Gaulle in May 1942. Between 1942 and 1944, five East African brigades and two West African divisions served on the Burma front. In the House of Commons, a Conservative MP warned: 'We shall see after the war a very large number of Africans going home, who are trained or part-trained artisans, with a sense of discipline, with a knowledge of English and educated, in a broad sense, by travel. Now they will be going home to distant villages and remote districts, and to the old life, but seeing it with very different eyes.'

At the same time the production of wartime commodities in Africa was stepped up and the whites reasserted their influence in the settler colonies of Kenya and the Rhodesias. African labourers were conscripted throughout the British dependencies to work down the mines and on the plantations; sometimes they had to suffer conditions quite as appalling as those experienced by African servicemen overseas. Migration to industrial centres, such as Accra and Nairobi, put extra strain on traditional societies. South African power was consolidated, however, because of the region's importance to the Allies.

GEORGE CROSS ISLAND

Because Malta was a vital link in the Allied war effort in the Mediterranean, it was subjected to heavy aerial bombardment from the time when Italy entered the war in 1940 until the liberation of North Africa in 1943. Almost two thousand civilians and garrisoned soldiers were killed; thousands of houses were damaged or destroyed. George VI responded by sending the following message on 15 April 1942: 'To honour her brave people I award the George Cross to the island fortress of Malta to bear witness to a heroism and devotion that will long be famous in history.' This was later inscribed on a marble tablet set in the wall of the Palace of the Grand Masters of the Order of St John of Malta in Valetta.

Maltese stamps depicting the George Cross.

Malta's troubles were not over, however. The Axis naval blockade was pushing the population towards starvation. Many ships of the British Merchant Navy and their crews were lost trying to break the cordon. Even the ships of the Royal Navy on escort duty were not immune. The most serious loss occurred in August 1942 when a submarine sank the aircraft-carrier *Eagle*. Relief only came as the Allies overran the Axis in North Africa.

Malta had done more than survive; she had pinned down Axis forces and contributed to Allied victory. At one point, Germany had over 400 first-class aircraft pounding Malta from Sicily. Almost 700 German and Italian planes were shot down over the island between June 1941 and July 1943, while the RAF stationed on the island destroyed another 190 aircraft on the ground in enemy territory.

Canadian tanks and British infantry rumble through the narrow streets of one of the towns on the River Arno, west of Florence, in 1944.

Sir Stafford Cripps (1889–1952) was remembered for his programme of austerity during 1947–50, when he was Chancellor of the Exchequer.

Churchill advised King George VI that if he, the Prime Minister, ever became a war casualty, Sir Anthony Eden (1897–1977), (left) should become his successor.

Brave New World

It was clear that the Empire would undergo drastic changes after the war. Hitler, like others before him, had already predicted its end: 'The future of the British people is to die of hunger and tuberculosis in their cursed island.'

In 1942–3 there were attempts in London and Washington to draft a joint 'Colonial Charter', but the American version was too riddled with references to independence for British approval. Whitehall was, in turns, impatient with what it felt to be ill-informed criticism of Britain's record overseas, proud of the wisdom acquired through centuries of experience in Africa and Asia, and suspicious of America's motives in insisting on the rights of all countries to determine their political futures. For at least another decade Britain would continue to declare that freedom without security was worthless, and that the 'time was not ripe' to focus upon political change.

It was in these terms that Churchill's Colonial Secretary, Oliver Stanley, addressed the House of Commons in July 1943.

Although the speech was largely unadventurous, the government did commit itself to the eventual achievement of colonial self-government within the Commonwealth. It was less a precise strategy than an idea which had been thrown up by the war, a concept which was to guide and largely justify the colonial policies of both Labour and Conservative parties until 1960. The vague notions of 'partnership' it proposed were in tune with the ideology of the United Nations.

This was the age of master plans and the Colonial Office seized the initiative in preparing for post-war reconstruction. In 1940 and 1945, British taxpayers' money was earmarked for the economic development and social welfare of colonial peoples. Careful thought was also given to updating the time-honoured system of African native administration – via chiefs and other 'traditional leaders'. Furthermore, blueprints were drafted for ways of achieving a closer association between the disparate territories in West, East and Central Africa, the West Indies and South-East Asia.

This 'progressive colonialism' – similar to the 'constructive colonialism' of fifty years earlier – was intended to advance the interests of all concerned. As regards India, however, the wartime coalition continued to face pressure to leave the country altogether. In June 1945 (its last month) Churchill's government struggled to veil the nakedness of its colonial policy in India by adopting the language of trusteeship: the role of the British government was to be one of mediation between competing Indian parties.

Decolonization or a New Imperialism?

When the war ended, and a Labour government had been newly installed in office, it made sense to seek escape from India. The domestic economy was in tatters: Britain was already indebted to the tune of £3.5 billion – mainly to the USA – and the electorate had been promised not only a programme of nationalization but also the creation of a welfare state. On the other hand, however, Britain's overseas commitments beyond the Indian subcontinent were larger than ever, and the Attlee government was in no mind to shed the rich assets of oil and other commodities provided by the Middle East, Africa and South Asia.

Decolonization in South-East Asia was compensated for by a 'new imperialism' elsewhere. Britain saw in her Empire and Commonwealth a means of rehabilitating both sterling and status, and thus prepared to embark upon another chapter of imperial over-rule.

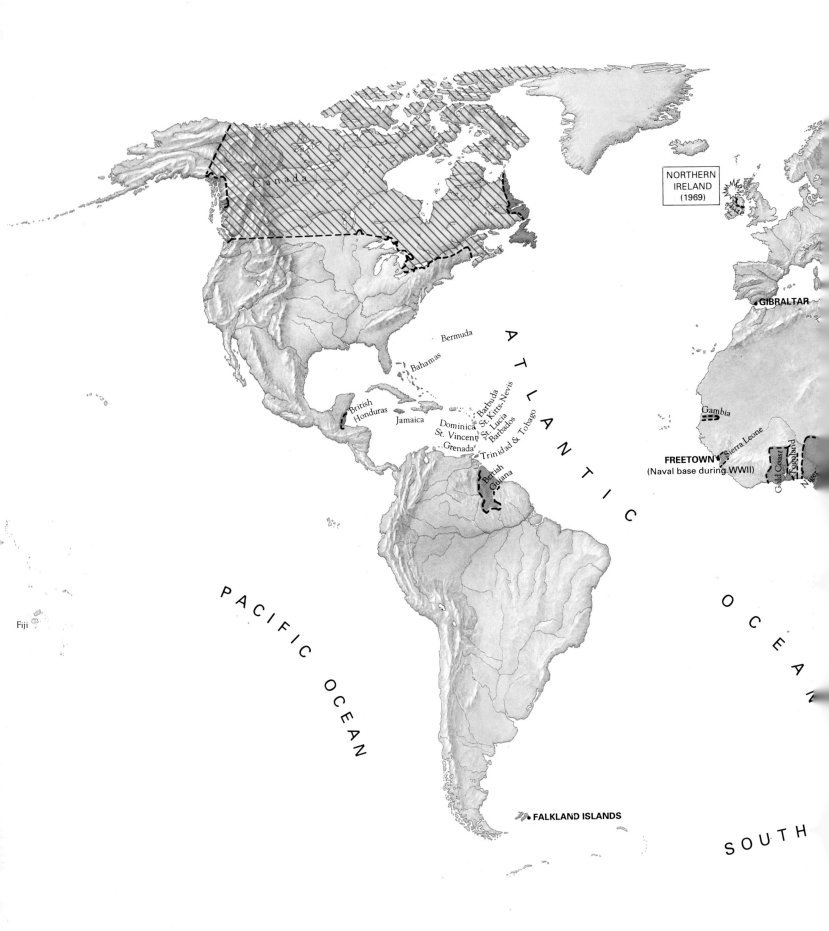

Canada

NORTHERN
IRELAND
(1969)

GIBRALTAR

Bermuda

Bahamas

British
Honduras

Jamaica

A T L A N T I C

Gambia

Barbuda
St. Kitts-Nevis
Dominica
St. Lucia
St. Vincent
Barbados
Grenada
Trinidad & Tobago

Sierra Leone

FREETOWN
(Naval base during WWII)

Gold Coast
Togoland
Niger

British
Guiana

O C E A N

PACIFIC OCEAN

Fiji

FALKLAND ISLANDS

S O U T H

MALTA
(1979)

CYPRUS
(1959)

Cyprus

Palestine

PORT SAID
(1956)

Trans-
Jordan

Kuwait

PROTECTORATES

PERSIAN GULF

Bahrain Quatar
Trucial Oman

India

Burma

HONG KONG
(1997)

ANGLO-
EGYPTIAN
SUDAN

Oman

ADEN
(1967)

Aden
Protectorate

ADEN (1968)

British Somaliland

KENYA
(1952)

Somaliland

Uganda Kenya

TRINCOMALEE
(1957)

Ceylon

British North
Borneo

MALAYA
(1948)

Malaya

Sarawak

SINGAPORE
(1968)

Seychelles

Tanganyika Zanzibar

INDIAN

OCEAN

Solomon
Islands

ZIMBABWE
(1970)

Northern Rhodesia

Southern
Rhodesia

RHODESIA
(1963)

Mauritius

Bechuanaland
Protectorate

Australia

North West Africa

SIMON'S TOWN
(1975)

Swaziland

South
Africa

Basutoland

Cameroon

PACIFIC

OCEAN

New Zealand

N OCEAN

The Empire in Retreat

///// Areas under British Mandate in 1945

■■■ British Dependencies in 1945

\\\\\ British Dominions in 1945

ADEN (1968) • Military Bases and date of British departure

✴ Armed Insurrections

CHAPTER THIRTY-SIX

THE RETREAT FROM EMPIRE

◇

Between 1945 and the late 1960s the greatest empire in the world virtually disappeared; what had taken hundreds of years to assemble took little more than two decades to disintegrate. Such a dramatic event on the world's political stage seems to demand an explanation and many have been supplied that seem to spring from preconceived theories rather than from an examination of the events. The process of dissolution was neither steady nor regular.

Decolonization was concentrated into two great bursts. The first occurred between 1945 and 1948 when Palestine was abandoned, and India, Pakistan, Ceylon and Burma were granted independence. The second flurry of activity came between 1959 and 1965 when Britain quit Africa.

Despite the speed of Britain's imperial retreat, she managed to disentangle herself with remarkably little armed conflict. Although there were exceptions such as Kenya, Malaya, Cyprus and Aden, the disengagement was generally orderly, particularly when compared with Portugal's process of decolonization in Africa, or that of France in Indochina. Perhaps even more remarkable was the way in which this upheaval raised scarcely a ripple in British domestic politics. Yet, as the 1980s have reminded us, the process is not over and there may always be loose ends that cannot be wished away, however much trouble they cause Britain.

A Political Sleight of Hand

Of the many explanations available to account for Britain's imperial retreat, one was particularly popular with the politicians in London during the 1960s. This alleged that the transfer of power had been a carefully planned exercise, long foreseen and managed by Whitehall. Britain's objective had always been, as

Harold Macmillan put it, to share her democratic heritage with the daughter territories.

This exercise in hindsight ignores the surprise experienced by MPs during the 1950s when most politicians were caught off-guard by the pace of change in Britain's colonies. Moreover, the rush to independence left many of the former colonies ill-prepared, a state of affairs incompatible with a vision of an omniscient Whitehall.

The deceptiveness of this later gloss on events is further emphasized when one compares the political speeches of the 1950s with those of the 1970s. In 1951 Winston Churchill was talking about Britain 'gathering her Commonwealth about her' in order to revive her influence in world affairs. In 1952 he was warning the rest of the world that they should not 'underestimate the abiding power of the British Commonwealth and Empire'. By 1971, Edward Heath, the Prime Minister of the day, saw it as a club in which he was 'perfectly prepared to listen now to what members have to say round the table'. His lack of enthusiasm may be judged from the small number of speeches he made on the theme.

The Nationalist Explanation

In the 1980s, hindsight tends to favour the role of nationalism. The post-war fall of the colonial empires is seen as the consequence of an epic struggle between imperialism and nationalism, which created the vast new array of nation states. Such an hypothesis seems to match reality more closely than the conjectures of the 1960s. The last phase of colonial rule did see – almost everywhere – the emergence of some sort of nationalist movement that commanded mass support. The British were confronted with nationalist leaders demanding independence in

Harold Wilson (1916–) became Prime Minister of a Labour Government in 1964 with a majority of only four seats.

BRITAIN HAS LOST AN EMPIRE AND HAS NOT YET FOUND A ROLE "
– MR DEAN ACHESON AN ADVISER OF PRESIDENT KENNEDY

"ER, COULD I BE THE HIND LEGS, PLEASE?"

Harold Macmillan (1894–1987) recognized the end of the imperial idea, but it left him without a portfolio. A cartoon by Vicky in 1962.

short order, and threatening political turbulence if their demands were not met with some speed. It was easy to see such nationalism as an almost inevitable consequence of colonial rule and Western influences. As people in colonial societies acquired Western education, they also absorbed the political ideas that were current in the West, with their emphasis on the right to national self-determination. This educated élite would then demand the rights accorded to their European peers, converting the mass of the population at the same time to this nationalist viewpoint, and precipitating a critical confrontation for control of the country between the imperial administration and the people. This hypothesis allowed many of the political leaders of the new nations the opportunity to present themselves to their electorates in the early days of independence in an heroic light. During periods when economic difficulties and political unrest multiplied, the value of patriotic myths for these inexperienced leaders was immense.

This explanation of decolonization fails, like the first hypothesis, to deal with some embarrassing facts. It seems remarkable that societies with such disparate traditions should develop political movements that were so similar in their aims and abilities at practically the same moment. Almost simultaneously, the equally dissimilar political traditions of their imperial masters, such as France and Britain, are seen to accede to the nationalist demands with little serious resistance. In fact, in many situations in Africa and South-East Asia, collusion between the colonial administration and the would-be rulers – to ensure the continued existence of countries created by the 'paper imperialism' of the 1880s – was more common than confrontation.

Although colonial nationalism was an important element in the process of decolonization, it was only one part. The new leaders were in the right place at the right time to exploit a major shift in the international situation.

A 32,000-ton oil tanker being built at Belfast on the eve of the terminal decline in British ship-building.

Britain Sees the Light

A third hypothesis suggests that Britain realized, during the 1950s, that her future lay in Europe, and immediately took to planning ways of dispensing with her imperial responsibilities. Although their demands were sometimes inconvenient, it was realized that nationalist leaders were necessary partners if the process of disengagement was to be smooth, and if embarrassment at home and abroad was to be minimized. This meant that the victories of the nationalists were hollow, for Britain was merely responding with pragmatic flexibility to the logic of the post-war changes in the world economic and political system.

Again, this version of events fails to take Britain's actual behaviour into account. If London was so intent on consolidat-

ing its relationship with Washington and the European Community, its tenacious commitment to a military and political role east of Suez until the end of the 1960s makes no sense. As late as December 1964 the Prime Minister, Harold Wilson, made a speech to the House of Commons in which he emphasized that 'We cannot afford to relinquish our world role – our role which, for shorthand purposes, is sometimes called our "East of Suez" role.' The idea that Britain was in control also bestows a degree of political purpose and a quality of consistency on British politicians that is belied by the untidiness of the political process.

If one discounts too the hypothesis that the withdrawal of colonial rule was merely a charade to enable Western capitalism to strike a convenient deal with local political bosses, no theory appears to be wholly satisfactory. To understand what really happened one needs to examine the process of decolonization as it unravelled.

The Post-war Reality

At the end of the Second World War the British Empire was still intact and Britain appeared to be one of the three great victorious powers. Appearances, however, were deceptive. The financial cost of the war effort, and the damage sustained by Britain's factories, her shipping and her cities, together with the infrastructure that linked them all, had seriously compromised the country's economic strength.

London realized that timely concessions had to be made to the well-organized nationalists of India and Egypt. In order to retain the goodwill of their former colonial subjects, Britain's departure from both countries had to be prompt. Whitehall wanted a

THE WELFARE STATE

It is an interesting coincidence that as the British Empire was wound up after 1945, the Welfare State emerged in its full glory as the distinctive contribution of post-war British governments. It looked as if Britain had finally turned away from her old imperial preoccupation to the task of social reform at home. The coincidence has sometimes inspired historians to see the Welfare State as the post-imperial phase of British history. Indeed it has been argued that with the rise of the Welfare State, British opinion became

increasingly impatient with the expenditure of resources on an empire widely regarded as remote and redundant.

Paradoxically, the post-war Labour government was no less committed to maintaining British world power than it was to building a welfare state. Moreover, it believed that welfare at home required a vigorous policy of colonial development to produce the food and materials that Britain needed. Far from believing that the voters of the Welfare State had rejected empire, Attlee and his colleagues

thought that they would be outraged at any careless abdication of imperial power.

Later Conservative governments largely shared this attitude. It was not so much the Welfare State that was incompatible with the burdens of empire, as the policies for economic liberalization which emerged in the later 1950s. It was the rapacious consumer, not the idealistic citizen of the Welfare State, who finally proved impatient of the costs and obligations of far-flung empire and clamoured for its abandonment.

united India to remain within the Commonwealth as a close strategic partner. A well-disposed Egypt was necessary too, if a sudden change in the Middle-Eastern situation demanded the return of British troops to their bases along the Suez Canal. In other words, London wanted a post-colonial situation in these two countries in which its influence remained while its troops did not. Concessions could be made to the nationalists as long as Britain's world status was not diminished.

As soon as the Second World War was over, however, Whitehall lost control of events in both India and the Middle East. By the time Mountbatten arrived in India as Viceroy in 1947, inter-communal violence between Hindus and Muslims had reached such terrifying proportions that any solution was preferable to the continual slaughter. Partition destroyed all hope that India would play the international role that London had anticipated. Similarly, Britain's abrupt departure from Palestine both soured relations with the Arab states in the area and made the old lion look very vulnerable. The consequences were to be all too evident in the 1950s.

The Imperial Supermarket

In the aftermath of the first post-war imperial crisis, Whitehall realized that Britain lacked the necessary resources to impose the type of solution that would protect her interests and maintain her influence. Even greater emphasis was placed, therefore, on developing the productive capacity of the African and Asian colonies which remained. In a world driven by the economic engine of the United States, the dollar-earning capacity of Britain's tropical colonies – with their mineral resources of gold, copper and tin, and their agricultural production of sisal, cocoa and rubber – enhanced their value in London's eyes. Such factors bolstered Britain's determination to resist the Communist guerilla movement in Malaya. And these resources also underpinned the transformation of the Commonwealth into an effective trading bloc after the sterling crisis of 1947.

For a time in the early 1950s, this modified version of empire – with its emphasis on the gradual introduction of self-government and the careful preservation of close ties through economic and some strategic co-operation (sustained by the 'special relationship' with the United States) – appeared to be sufficiently resilient to survive in a changing world. Suez wrecked that illusion. Under Harold Macmillan, the Government modified Britain's pursuit of World Power status.

The Imperial Watershed

In retrospect, 1960 appears to be a crucial turning point in

The arrival of the first United Nations troop contingent at Port Said in 1956, when Britain and France were compelled to withdraw from Egypt.

Of all the varied legacies of empire, the one that the British possibly least expected at the end of the Second World War was the appearance in Britain of substantial communities of immigrants from former Empire countries. Originally, however, the arrival of these immigrants was the result of a deliberate policy of recruitment. In the early post-war years there was an acute shortage of labour: the struggle for economic recovery had to compete with the still heavy demands of the Armed Forces for conscript soldiers; and the proportion of the economy still devoted to the manufacture of military equipment remained high. Public services such as London Transport, hard-pressed for staff, looked to the West Indies for labour, attracted perhaps by the fact that in that poverty-stricken region was a large reservoir of unemployed and English-speaking labour. Once established, however, the migratory trend proved stronger than had been expected and was reinforced by new flows from India and Pakistan. Throughout the 1950s, governments in London fretted about the social and political consequences amidst signs of growing racial antagonism. But it was

Porters at London's Waterloo Station reacted to the 'invasion' of their country by British West Indians in 1954 by refusing to handle their baggage.

not until the 1960s that a series of increasingly stringent restrictions was imposed on the free entry of immigrants from Commonwealth countries. In an ironic reversal of roles, the British who once surveyed the racial conflicts

of plural colonial societies with Olympian detachment have learnt at first hand the difficulty of striking a balance between integration and the right of ethnic communities to retain their own identity.

Britain's vision of the role of the Commonwealth. The Soviet Union and the United States dominated the international stage in a manner impossible for London to imitate. The success of the European Economic Community was now obvious for all to see. Britain's economic interests now seemed to require close partnership with the developed industrial nations. In January 1960 the Foreign Secretary Selwyn Lloyd told the consultative assembly of the Council of Europe: 'I want to put to you as simply but as definitely as I can the British position. We regard ourselves as part of Europe, for reasons of sentiment, of history and geography.' But this apparent turn away from the Commonwealth sparked a fierce controversy in British politics.

By the end of 1961, Britain's application to join the EEC had raised questions about how far it would be possible to maintain the system of economic preferences which bound the Commonwealth together. By 1963 this concern had been overtaken by a more fundamental one: how much foreign expenditure could Britain afford, if she was to correct the critical industrial weaknesses in the home economy which seemed to threaten the country's future.

The 1950s had witnessed a great deal of talk about decolonization but few colonies had become independent; in the 1960s, colony after colony was ushered swiftly down the road to independence. Despite London's talk about self-determination and democracy, the weakness that lay behind this accelerated disposal of the imperial assets was cruelly exposed by the Rhodesia fiasco, in which some 200,000 white settlers defied the might of Britain in an attempt to prolong their control of the country.

Full Retreat

Despite the reorientation of Britain's foreign policy and the disentanglement from imperial obligations, London could not bring itself to break the last link with the past. The Indian Ocean had been at the centre of imperial power in the nineteenth century. To abandon the bases at Singapore and Aden, and the aircraft carriers that patrolled the seas between

them, would announce to the world that Britain was just a shrivelled version of its former imperial grandeur. It was not surprising, therefore, that when the economic case for retrenchment became overwhelming, the final drama of the imperial story was buried in a brusque paragraph in a statement made to Parliament by the Prime Minister, Harold Wilson, during the course of a debate on defence in January 1968: 'We have . . . decided to accelerate the withdrawal of our forces from their stations in the Far East which was announced in the Supplementary Statement on defence of July 1967 and to withdraw them by the end of 1971. We have also decided to withdraw our forces from the Persian Gulf by the same date. The broad effect is that, apart from our remaining Dependencies and certain other necessary exceptions, we shall by that date not be maintaining military bases outside Europe and the Mediterranean'.

The course of Britain's retreat from empire was thus unplanned and unintentional. The British were extremely reluctant to relinquish even fragments of the world system they had created in the nineteenth century. It was not until the late 1960s that the final adjustment was made. On the other hand, Whitehall had accepted in principle, as early as the 1940s, that self-government would have to be conceded to the colonies. London had also accepted that in regions such as the Middle East, where it had been the dominant power, it would have to exercise more restraint. These 'reasonable' proposals were forgotten in the chaos of India and Palestine; furthermore, diplomatic pressure inhibited Britain's ability to impose her will by force as she had in India between the wars.

Meanwhile, the long-term relative decline in British economic and military strength ensured that the new post-colonial states would have little incentive to remain closely aligned with London. This meant that independence involved a more complete separation than Britain had envisaged, even as late as 1960. What made this loss of power palatable to British opinion may well have been its gradual nature and the persistent illusion that the Commonwealth was just another name for the Empire.

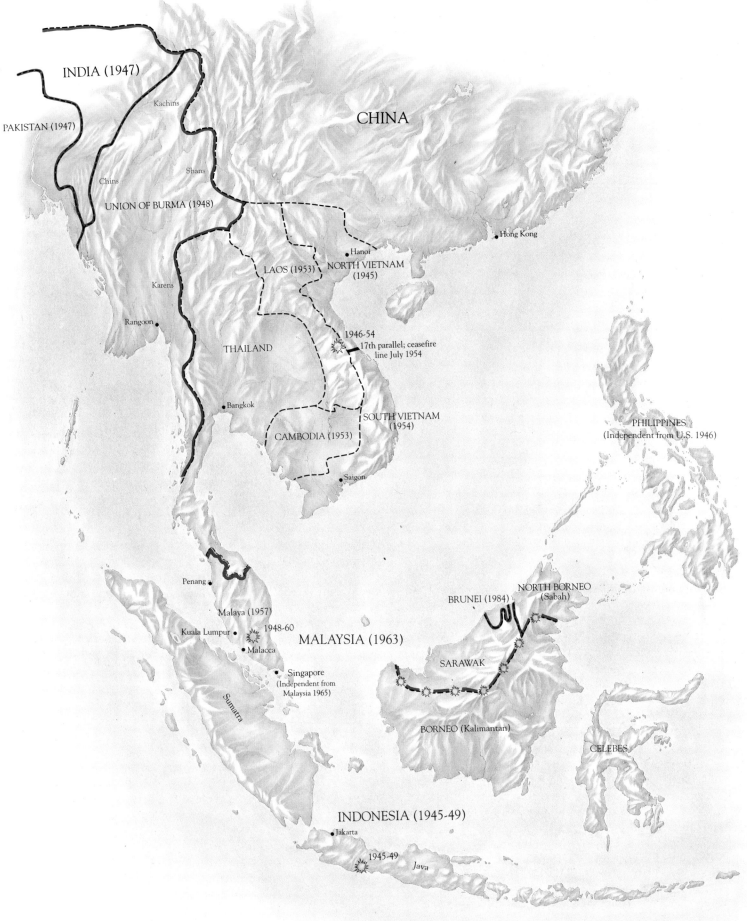

INDIA (1947)

PAKISTAN (1947)

CHINA

Kachins

Chins

Shans

UNION OF BURMA (1948)

Karens

Rangoon

Hanoi

LAOS (1953)

NORTH VIETNAM
(1945)

Hong Kong

THAILAND

1946-54
17th parallel; ceasefire
line July 1954

Bangkok

CAMBODIA (1953)

SOUTH VIETNAM
(1954)

PHILIPPINES
(Independent from U.S. 1946)

Saigon

Penang

Malaya (1957)

BRUNEI (1984)

NORTH BORNEO
(Sabah)

Kuala Lumpur

1948-60

Malacca

MALAYSIA (1963)

SARAWAK

Singapore
(Independent from
Malaysia 1965)

Sumatra

BORNEO (Kalimantan)

CELEBES

INDONESIA (1945-49)

Jakarta

1945-49

Java

Retreat from the Far East

———	Former British dependency and date of independence
- - -	Post-colonial state and date of independence
✴	Colonial conflict
✴- -✴- -	Border Conflict: Malaya–Indonesia Confrontation 1963–66
Karens	Peoples of Burmese frontier areas

CHAPTER THIRTY-SEVEN

THE END OF EMPIRE EAST OF SUEZ

The celebrations in Singapore that greeted Mountbatten when the Japanese surrendered to him on 12 September 1945 could not conceal the fact that an era of Empire had passed. However inspiring the optimism of the moment, the rout of 1942 had badly shaken Britain's imperial self-confidence. No one was ever quite convinced of it again, especially in Asia. What lay ahead for the British government was the grim task of rehabilitation.

Mountbatten's South-East Asia Command shifted its headquarters from Kandy to Singapore and acquired the responsibility of reoccupying not only Britain's lost colonies but also those of France and Holland. Allied resources were stretched to the limit in re-establishing control and reviving the trade in rice. To compound these difficulties, a new spirit of nationalism had, in the words of the Malay proverb, 'emerged from under the coconut shell' during the Japanese occupation. After the war had ended, the colonial dominoes were swiftly toppled, one by one. The Americans retired fairly gracefully from the Philippines in 1946 in contrast to the Dutch and French who were driven from Indonesia and Vietnam in 1949 and 1954 respectively. The immediate post-war period also saw a major transferral of British power in South Asia and Burma.

Struggle for Independence in Burma
With the Raj coming to an end in the Indian subcontinent, an empire east of Calcutta – or even of Suez – no longer seemed appropriate. It was certainly becoming more difficult to control. The Labour Prime Minister Clement Attlee, who had defeated Churchill in the elections of 1945, even began to consider America the strategic centre of British interests, rather than the fragile chain of Empire dominions and dependents that led eastwards from the Mediterranean to Malaysia.

So far as Burma was concerned, withdrawal made sense. Burma's value to Britain had lain in its trade with India and in its strategic position which ensured the security of Bengal. Now that Indian independence was clearly imminent and with the rumbles of nationalism growing louder in Burma itself, there seemed little purpose in hanging on. Moreover, it was reckoned that the task of rehabilitating a country that had twice been fought over would be insupportable. Its economy was shattered and most of its towns had been devastated. All in all, as Chancellor Hugh Dalton remarked trenchantly, 'If you are in a place where you are not wanted, and where you have not got the force to squash those who don't want you, the only thing to do is to come out.'

During the closing stages of the war, Aung San's Anti-Fascist People's Freedom League (AFPFL) had shifted its allegiance from the Japanese to join with Mountbatten in the liberation of Burma. Aung San and his Communist army had then collaborated with Mountbatten in liberating Rangoon from the Japanese in 1945. However, it was quite clear to Mountbatten that the AFPFL would swing from collaboration into armed resistance if the British attempted to reimpose their grip on post-war Burma. A constitution for the post-war period had, in fact, been devised

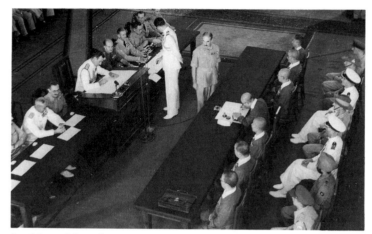

Lord Louis Mountbatten (1900–79), Supreme Commander of the Allied Forces in South-East Asia, and the Japanese General Itagaki sign the surrender documents in Singapore.

by Governor Dorman-Smith (in exile in Simla during the Japanese occupation of Burma), but this did not satisfy the AFPFL. Despite Mountbatten's progressive accord with Aung San in September 1945, the restored Dorman-Smith could not bring himself to negotiate with the AFPFL, and the deadlock was broken only when he was replaced by Sir Hubert Rance in August 1946.

The pace of change quickened: on 20 December 1946 Attlee publicly promised early self-government for Burma, and a Constituent Assembly was elected in the following April. As expected, Aung San's AFPFL party won a resounding victory in the elections. To the dismay of Attlee's Government, however, the Constituent Assembly soon passed a resolution in favour of taking an independent Union of Burma outside the Commonwealth altogether. Three months after the election, Aung San and several members of his government were assassinated. Nevertheless, Burma's advance towards independence scarcely faltered as Thakin Nu, the vice-president of the AFPFL, was asked by Rance to head the government. Under his leadership, the Union of Burma was finally inaugurated at an auspiciously safe hour on 4 January 1948.

It was hard for Britain to come to terms so quickly with the severance of Burma from the Commonwealth. A formula was being devised to accommodate India within the association, and it was hoped that a special relationship with Burma could also be maintained. This was not to be. Burma became racked with both Communist and ethnic insurgency. As the country reverted to its historic isolationism, British influence slowly faded.

The Second Occupation of Malaya
In contrast to Burma, the value of Malaya to Britain grew rather than diminished after the war had ended. Malaya's tin and rubber were in great demand as raw materials for British industry and as major dollar earners. Malaya earned more dollars than any other country in the British Empire, and it became most

A Malay interpreter interrogates one of the 5,000 Communist terrorists belonging to the Malayan People's Anti-British Army in 1951.

important to safeguard this imperial asset. As Hector McNeil, Foreign Office Minister of State, recognized in 1949: 'It would clearly be disastrous if Malaya were ever to meet the same fate as Burma.'

The ease with which Singapore had fallen to the Japanese in 1942 revealed Britain's pre-war strategy in the Far East to have been a thing of shreds and patches. After the Japanese surrender, the Allies reoccupied the region. The British triumphantly hoisted the Union Jack in Singapore once more, determined that their humiliating scuttle from Malaya would never be repeated. They squared up to American anti-imperialism, rapidly rehabilitated the colonial economy, and tried to manipulate the forces of nationalism.

During the war, Britain had devised a radical scheme to consolidate the disparate territories and ethnic communities into one Malayan state. In 1946 the nine Malay states of the peninsula, together with Penang and Malacca, were swept into the Malayan Union. Singapore became a separate colony. Charles Vyner Brooke, who had ruled over Sarawak autocratically, accepting Whitehall's authority only in matters of foreign relations, surrendered his inherited fiefdom to the Crown. North Borneo, which had been administered since the 1880s by a chartered company, also became a crown colony. In this 'second occupation' of South-East Asia, Britain asserted her control more directly than ever before. Her first priority was to pursue her imperial interests with the maximum efficiency; her second was to construct foundations for an eventually self-governing state.

But countries cannot be coerced so simply into nationhood. Intense communal fighting had broken out between Malays and Chinese during the uneasy weeks between the Japanese surrender and the British return. The Malayan Union, by proposing that Chinese and Indians, as well as Malays, would be eligible for citizenship, aggravated this communal bitterness. The indigenous Malays felt betrayed and protested against the Union.

A new communal party, the United Malays National Organisation (UMNO), surprised the British by the popularity of its demonstrations and its campaign of non-cooperation. The government was also nervous that the Chinese-dominated Malayan Communist Party (MCP) might exploit Malay grievances for more revolutionary objectives.

Unwilling to antagonize its traditional Malay collaborators any further, the government swiftly arranged some fresh negotiations. Although the fundamental principles of Britain's policy in creating a strongly governed, multi-racial nation remained unchanged, these negotiations resulted in 1948 in a new constitution – the Federation of Malaya – which replaced the Malayan Union. This endorsed the sovereignty of the Sultans, the hereditary rulers of the Malay states, and the status of the Malays as 'princes of the soil'.

The Malayan Emergency

Shortly after this Anglo-Malay agreement, the Malayan Communist Party launched an unexpected armed insurrection. The MCP had been a wartime ally of the British against the Japanese, controlling the Malayan resistance fighters in the jungles. But the party had always made it clear that the alliance was to be a temporary one against a common foe.

WILSON AND THE WITHDRAWAL FROM SINGAPORE

Britain's dilemma of how to retain an independent world role on a shoestring became more acute in the 1960s. Although America helped Britain finance her base in Singapore, this was, of course, tacitly dependent on British support for America in Vietnam. Any move to withdraw from Singapore would be received with hostility by President Lyndon Johnson, but by 1968 Harold Wilson faced the inevitable. In January 1968 he caused an uproar in the House of Commons by announcing that Britain would abandon her military commitments east of Suez within three years. Richard Crossman in *The Diaries of a Cabinet Minister* described the anxiety:

'Monday January 15th (1968) . . . Cabinet started with George Thomson's report

Lee Kuan Yew, (1923–). First Prime Minister of the Republic of Singapore.

(Thomson, Commonwealth Secretary, had recently visited the Far East) and then with the P.M.'s account of his five hours and his dinner with Harry Lee (Lee Kuan Yew, P.M. of Singapore). After that there was a tremendous effort to get Cabinet to reverse the decision on East of Suez withdrawal we had taken by such a large majority only ten days ago. It was clear after an hour that the weaker brethren of the Cabinet were swinging back. L.B.J. (President Johnson) had certainly stepped up his threats . . . particularly in the economic sphere . . . I knew that the P.M. would have to act. What he did was to nip in very neatly and offer as a compromise that the terminal date for withdrawal . . . should be the end of the calendar year 1971 (instead of March 1971).'

During the closing months of the Japanese occupation, there were outbreaks of bitter fighting between Malays and Chinese. These fearsome clashes arose out of Malaya's communally divided society and from wartime shortages rather than from any Japanese ploy to divide and rule. Malays blamed the Chinese middleman for their problems; the Chinese resented the Malay 'collaborator'. The Malayan Peoples Anti-Japanese Army (MPAJA), which was dominated by Chinese Communists, tried quislings in kangaroo courts and exacted vengeance. It was a time for settling scores.

A Chinese who had been brought up (and regarded himself) as a Malay later recalled how he had been 'turned' by the MPAJA at this time: '. . . when the Japanese surrendered I was working in a Japanese office in Kuala Trengganu. I was only seventeen years old. I was arrested by the communist guerrillas and taken with two others into the jungle. Here we were told that we were Japanese collaborators and had been sentenced to death. We were led

Malaya's High Commissioner, General Sir Gerald Templer, visting slums in Kuala Lumpur.

away from the camp and told to dig our own graves. The other two were shot and I, very much shaken, was led back to the camp. There I was told that I had been spared and that if I studied hard and cooperated I would be let off, if I refused I would be shot. I was kept in the jungle from September 1945 until January 1947 when I was led out of the jungle and given a job

in the General Labour Union offices.

The violence subsided with the restoration of British rule as Templer systematically starved the MPAJA out of the jungles. However, the spectre of communal conflict was to hang over the Malayan Union of 1948 and the ensuing period of Communist insurgency and decolonization.

Sure enough, after the war had ended, not all the arms that had been parachuted into jungle hide-outs by the British were returned. Between 1945 and 1947, Communists successfully infiltrated other political parties and mounted strikes. The aim was to paralyse the tin and rubber industries and to bring the country to a halt. These two industries offered the most vulnerable targets.

On 16 June 1948, three planters on a rubber estate were murdered. The British government failed at first to appreciate the extent of the danger to unprotected plantation owners; a state of emergency was declared and the High Commissioner was recalled, to be replaced by Henry Gurney. Although Gurney prepared the ground for peaceful decolonization and for the eventual defeat of the Communists (stubbornly referred to as 'bandits' in government propaganda), British policy appeared to drift.

Many men were lost as random patrols were sent into the jungles to search for guerilla fighters. As General Templer later recalled: 'The terrorist in the jungle had become as sensitive as a wild animal. He could smell cigarette smoke half a mile away and if you used brilliantine on your hair or too much toothpaste he could detect that too . . .'

British-owned rubber plantations were turned into armed camps, as the situation became more desperate. In October 1951 Gurney was ambushed in his car and killed. The British Conservative government, returned in the general election later that month, was goaded into more positive action. General Sir Gerald Templer was appointed High Commissioner and Director of Operations, 'with more powers than any soldier since Cromwell', as one bemused plantation owner observed.

Templer lost no time in implementing fully the Briggs Plan, which had been adopted only half-heartedly before. This involved the resettling of half a million Chinese squatters in new villages away from the edges of the jungles, where they had previously been well-placed to provide food and information to the Communists.

In September 1953 the first 'White Area' – Malacca – was declared. Here, improved security allowed the relaxation of

emergency restrictions and food rationing. Templer recognized the psychological importance of establishing these 'white areas', in order to encourage the rural population to ally with the government against the Communists. Lines of communication between guerillas in the north and south of the country were cut as the 'white areas' spread, and the guerillas were slowly starved out of the jungles. By the time Templer left Malaya in June 1954, Chin Peng and his Communist guerillas had retreated north to the Thai border.

National Politics on the Path to Independence

At the same time as Malayans were becoming increasingly involved in local elections and were being appointed to the Executive Council, the government in Whitehall was persuaded that self-government for Malaya should follow sooner rather than later.

In their campaign against the insurgents, the government had benefited from the fact that the Malayan Communist Party was drawn almost exclusively from the minority Chinese community. This tactical advantage was only short-term, however,

Chin Peng, leader of the Communist guerillas, on his way to the Baling conference.

On 31 August 1957, the Instrument of the Transfer of Power is handed over in the Merdeka Stadium, Kuala Lumpur, by the Duke of Gloucester.

for it posed a threat to race relations in the future and to the political stability of any self-governing state. Malayan politics were founded on separate racial blocks; popular enthusiasm never adopted British ideals of inter-racial collaboration. In the early 1950s three racially exclusive parties emerged: the United Malays National Organisation (UMNO), the Malayan Chinese Association and the Malayan Indian Congress. In an alliance, leaders of the MCA and MIC accepted the political dominance of UMNO in the hope that Chinese and Indian economic interests would be safe-guarded and that Malay political privileges would be gradually eroded after independence.

The British at first distrusted the Alliance Party, but when it demonstrated its popular support by winning fifty-one out of fifty-two seats at the first federal elections in July 1955, there seemed little to gain by obstructing it. Tunku Abdul Rahman was appointed Malayan Chief Minister, and on 31 August 1957, Malaya achieved independence. The emergency officially ended three years later without major concessions to Chin Peng. Malaya was to remain a staunch ally of the West in the containment of Communism in South-East Asia.

Indonesian President Sukarno, Philippine President Diosdado Macapagal and Malayan Prime Minister Tunku Abdul Rahman.

The New State of Malaysia

In 1957 Britain also signed an Anglo-Malayan Defence Agreement by which she shouldered the burden of regional defence and continued to govern the colonies of Singapore, Sarawak and North Borneo (later Sabah). Britain was also responsible for the oil-rich 'protected state' of Brunei. Still, this was an expensive Asian commitment and, when Tunku Abdul Rahman revived a British plan to create a Federation of Malaysia including Singapore and the non-Chinese territories of British Borneo, Britain backed it enthusiastically. It would allow her to retreat from the rump of her South-East Asian commitments while salvaging her strategic influence in the area. The new state of Malaysia was inaugurated in September 1963.

Sukarno, the charismatic President of Indonesia, which included the larger part of Borneo, was not at all enthusiastic about the new state, which he immediately condemned as a 'neo-colonial' conspiracy. He launched an armed 'policy of confrontation' against Malaysia and, for three years, war was waged in the jungles of Borneo between Sukarno's troops and joint Malaysian, British and Commonwealth forces. In 1965 the one million Chinese of Singapore proved too much for the Malays to accommodate politically within the Federation, and Singapore became an independent city-state. In the following year, a peace agreement was reached with Suharto, the new President of Indonesia, who had ousted Sukarno in a coup.

The British Empire Weighs Anchor

During the sterling crisis of July 1967, Britain's Labour government realized that the cost of maintaining a military presence in South-East Asia could no longer be borne. The Anglo-Malaysian Defence Agreement was replaced by the Five Power Treaty, which spread the defence burden more evenly between Australia, Malaysia, New Zealand, Singapore and Britain. In 1971 the British finally weighed anchor, and the naval base in Singapore was abandoned. Britain's commitment to the Protectorate of Brunei came to an end in January 1984 when the Sultanate achieved full independence within the Commonwealth.

CHAPTER THIRTY-EIGHT

THE MEDITERRANEAN AND THE MIDDLE EAST AFTER 1947

◇

Britain did not find it hard to maintain her position as the dominant power in the Middle East during the inter-war years. With a garrison on the Suez Canal, air bases in Iraq, naval supremacy in the Persian Gulf, a mandate over Jordan, direct administrative control of Palestine and a string of Mediterranean redoubts, Britain looked unshakeable. Furthermore, with Moscow preoccupied with the struggle for economic progress, Britain's old rival in the region seemed to have abandoned her old expansionist plans, at least for the time being.

The Second World War changed all this. The British discovered that it was possible to win the war but lose the peace. Whitehall knew that it could no longer afford the military muscle necessary to sustain its position in the eastern Mediterranean. Yet, given the enhanced strategic and economic importance of the area, neither could Britain withdraw. It was the protection of the Empire's lines of communication to India that had initially drawn Britain into the Middle East but, with the end of the Raj in 1947, this rationale seemed increasingly irrelevant. At first, Whitehall tried to resist the logic of the new situation. For a number of years politicians persuaded themselves that an independent India would be ready to continue its old colonial role as Britain's great strategic partner in the East, even if under new management.

Much more critical was the renewed international involvement of the Soviet Union. Its aggressive expansion through Eastern Europe, and the blockade of Berlin before the NATO alliance was founded in 1949, caused considerable anxiety in London. Ernest Bevin, the British Foreign Secretary, told his opposite number in Washington, General Marshall, that the Soviets were up to 'every devilment' and wanted to 'cause us the greatest political embarrassment everywhere'. In this context, the vulnerability of the Soviet oilfields in the Caucasus to attack from Middle Eastern airfields was seen as a crucial counter-thrust to any strike by the Red Army across central Europe. Thus, far from being redundant, the Middle East was cast as Britain's first line of defence against Communist aggression.

The Withdrawal from Palestine

These strategic criteria were paramount in the minds of those trying to negotiate a British disengagement from Palestine and Egypt. The British were determined to retain their influence in both countries. This was no easy matter, however, for the tide of nationalism was running high. British difficulties were particularly acute in the case of Palestine where a commitment to promote the country as a 'national home' for the Jews and Arabs had been made in the 1917 Balfour Declaration. It is doubtful whether the Foreign Office realized how vociferous the 'existing non-Jewish communities' and their allies in neighbouring countries would be in the coming decades. Caught between the two opposing lobbies, London had tried to limit the numbers of Jewish immigrants to Palestine prior to 1939. After the war, the pressure became too great, and Britain lost control of the immigration problem.

In May 1948 British troops finally left Palestine, the country which they had administered for thirty years.

Yet, even in the post-war turmoil, Whitehall still entertained a fantasy wherein the Arabs and the Jews would be confined to different districts with the British army 'holding the ring'. Such plans were impossible to realize without American backing, and the likelihood of President Truman condoning any move that might be criticized as anti-Jewish was remote, given his electoral vulnerability. Meanwhile, leaders of the Jewish community encouraged the flow of immigrants, refugees from war-torn Europe and the concentration camps, while Jewish terrorist groups intensified their efforts against the British administration. The situation reached its climax when two British army sergeants were kidnapped by the Irgun, one of the leading terrorist groups. The British authorities were warned that if three Jewish prisoners who had just been convicted were hanged, the sergeants would die. Major Charleston, the superintendent of Acre, refused to execute the Jews and was sent back to Britain. The three men were led singing to the gallows in Acre prison. The sergeants were hanged from the rafters of a factory, then taken to an orange grove and strung up. Worldwide expression of horror at the incident was intense. The growing failure of the administration to contain the civil unrest drew increasingly fierce criticism from the Palestinian Arabs and their sympathizers abroad; these neighbouring states were vital if the Middle East was to be retained as a strategic bastion in the Cold War against the Soviet Union.

In the end, the British will to stay in Palestine collapsed, since every alternative open to them seemed to culminate in the alienation of a friendly power. Rather than be held responsible for decisions for which they had little sympathy, or preside over a

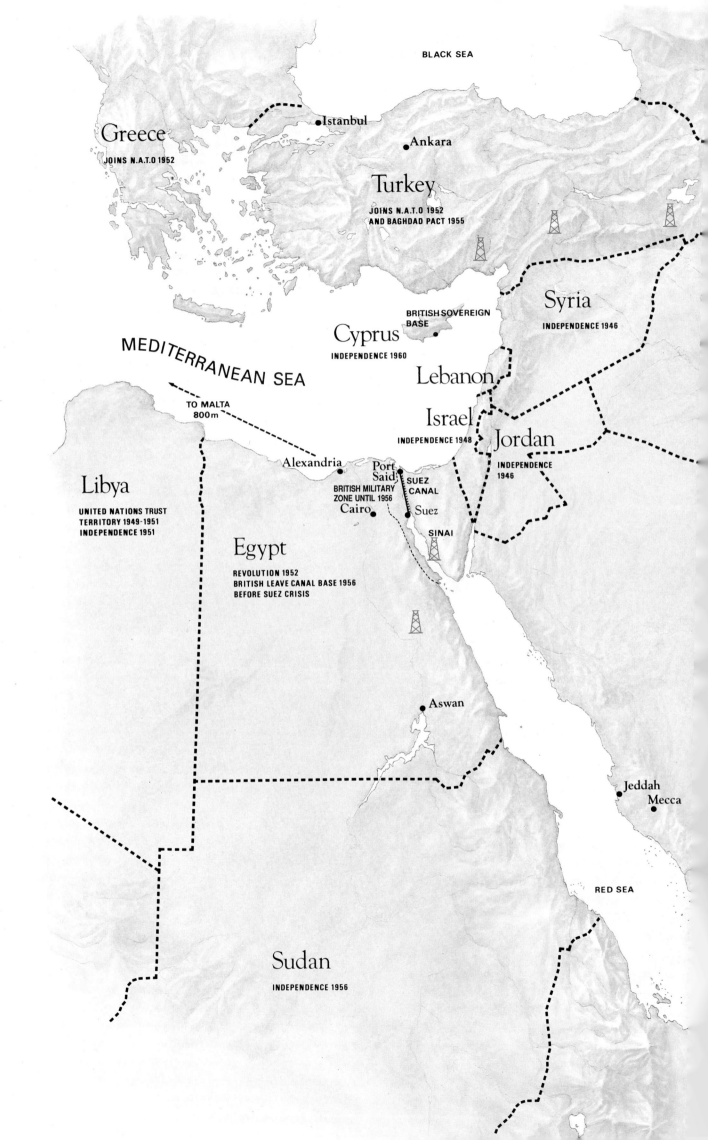

BLACK SEA

Greece

JOINS N.A.T.O 1952

Istanbul

Ankara

Turkey

**JOINS N.A.T.O 1952
AND BAGHDAD PACT 1955**

Syria

INDEPENDENCE 1946

MEDITERRANEAN SEA

**BRITISH SOVEREIGN
BASE**

Cyprus

INDEPENDENCE 1960

Lebanon

Israel

INDEPENDENCE 1948

Jordan

**INDEPENDENCE
1946**

TO MALTA
800m

Alexandria

Port
Said

**SUEZ
CANAL**

Libya

**UNITED NATIONS TRUST
TERRITORY 1949-1951
INDEPENDENCE 1951**

**BRITISH MILITARY
ZONE UNTIL 1956**

Cairo

Suez

SINAI

Egypt

**REVOLUTION 1952
BRITISH LEAVE CANAL BASE 1956
BEFORE SUEZ CRISIS**

Aswan

Jeddah
Mecca

RED SEA

Sudan

INDEPENDENCE 1956

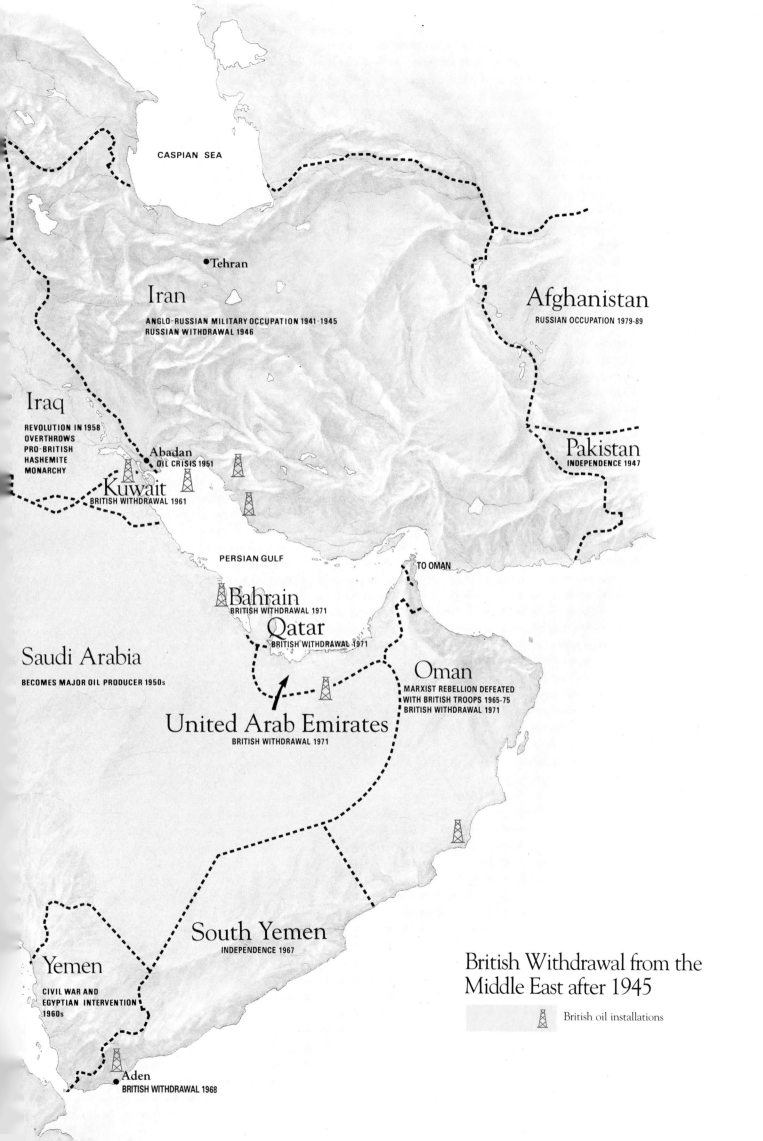

CASPIAN SEA

•Tehran

Iran

ANGLO-RUSSIAN MILITARY OCCUPATION 1941-1945
RUSSIAN WITHDRAWAL 1946

Afghanistan

RUSSIAN OCCUPATION 1979-89

Iraq

REVOLUTION IN 1958
OVERTHROWS
PRO-BRITISH
HASHEMITE
MONARCHY

Pakistan

INDEPENDENCE 1947

Abadan
OIL CRISIS 1951

Kuwait
BRITISH WITHDRAWAL 1961

PERSIAN GULF

TO OMAN

Bahrain
BRITISH WITHDRAWAL 1971

Qatar
BRITISH WITHDRAWAL 1971

Saudi Arabia

BECOMES MAJOR OIL PRODUCER 1950s

Oman

MARXIST REBELLION DEFEATED
WITH BRITISH TROOPS 1965-75
BRITISH WITHDRAWAL 1971

United Arab Emirates

BRITISH WITHDRAWAL 1971

South Yemen

INDEPENDENCE 1967

Yemen

CIVIL WAR AND
EGYPTIAN INTERVENTION
1960s

British Withdrawal from the
Middle East after 1945

⛏ British oil installations

Aden
BRITISH WITHDRAWAL 1968

THE ABADAN CRISIS

The great British-owned oil refinery at Abadan was one of the symbols of British power and influence in the Middle East. Up to and even after the Second World War, this most important centre of oil production in the Middle East was to be found at the head of the Persian Gulf in south-west Persia (Iran). The oilfields had first been opened up by British interests soon after 1900 and a large and valuable company, known first as the Anglo-Persian Oil Company, had emerged to exploit the rapidly growing market for oil as transport of all kinds converted to oil-fuelled engines. In 1914, the British government, at Churchill's urging, took a share in the company as a way of guaranteeing oil supplied to the Royal Navy. But after the Second World War, relations between the company and the Teheran government plummeted. There were tensions over the size of the royalty payment. Then the nationalist leader Mossadeq came to power determined to free Iran from all foreign interference, both British and Russian. In a swift coup he nationalised the oilfields and the refinery in 1951. Fearing American

An aerial view of the Anglo-Iranian Oil Company's refinery at Abadan, in 1951, when nationalization had brought work to a standstill.

disapproval, the British dared not intervene militarily. Instead they tried to bring pressure to bear by withdrawing all the Company's staff from the refinery and using legal means to prevent the Iranian government from selling the oil abroad. In 1953 a military coup backed and aided by the British and Americans, restored the Shah to power and ended Mossadeq's experiment. But the British never recovered their old share of Iranian oil and the crisis symbolised the fragility of their power in the Middle East even before Suez.

---

partition which the Arabs would regard as a betrayal, London decided to resign its mandate and to withdraw by June 1948, leaving both sides to fight it out. This decision led to the foundation of the state of Israel in 1949.

The British lost more than prestige when they abandoned their Palestinian mandate. Withdrawal raised hopes elsewhere in the Arab world that British influence could be driven out. Worse still, the humiliating defeat of the Arab states in the first Arab-Jewish War of 1948–9 intensified the bitterness of the Arab nationalists towards Britain, whose 'betrayal' of the Palestinians made her a convenient scapegoat for the embarrassing failure of those who had fought and lost. Guilt by association also tarnished the prestige of the monarchies in the region – Egypt, Iraq and Jordan – who had been London's closest allies. The demands of radicals for new internal policies and a much fiercer anti-Western stance gained increasing credibility. In this dismal context, it was never likely that Anglo-Egyptian relations would improve.

The Rise of Egyptian Nationalism
Britain had intended to adopt a lower profile in Egypt after the Second World War. In the abortive negotiations for a new treaty in 1946, an offer was made to withdraw all troops from Egypt in exchange for the right to return in the event of an international crisis. However, a disagreement over the future of the Sudan and the disintegrating situation in Palestine sabotaged the talks, which meant that the Canal Zone garrison had to remain.

By the early 1950s the strain was beginning to tell. The force had risen to eighty thousand men – more than twelve times the number resident in pre-war days – since all local labour had been withdrawn from the British bases. On 25 January 1952, an incident on the Canal between the British army and the Egyptian police triggered an explosion of anti-British feeling that engulfed Cairo in riots. By the end of the following day, 750

establishments had been burned or destroyed, 30 people were dead and the cost of the damage estimated at £50 million, as the British Embassy reported: 'The British Club was surrounded by a savage mob under organized leadership which broke into the premises. . . . In all ten British . . . were killed. Elsewhere gangs of fire raisers deliberately and wantonly attacked British commercial premises.' When the Egyptian monarchy collapsed in the revolution of July 1952, which soon brought Nasser to power, the British quickly tried again to negotiate a new treaty.

Problems in Iran
As the pressure mounted in Egypt, Britain's influence in the Middle East suffered another humiliating blow. The Persian Gulf had long been regarded as a British lake. Likewise, the southern regions of Iran which bordered the sea were taken to be a British sphere of influence. There was also an economic stake in the neighbourhood; the Anglo-Iranian Oil Company (now known as British Petroleum) was well established, with a refinery at Abadan. With a stake in the company of over 50 per cent, profitability was of particular interest to the British government, especially at a time when there was considerable pressure on sterling.

At the end of hostilities in 1945, London had been anxious about Russian intentions, since the Soviet Union occupied parts of northern Iran. These fears were allayed for a time when Stalin called his army home. However, nationalism was as much in the ascendant in this part of the region as elsewhere and the oil concession was viewed with suspicion and deep misgivings. Certainly, the locals had some cause for complaint about the modest royalties paid to the Tehran government when compared with the deals struck since 1945 between the oil companies and Venezuela and Mexico.

All these tensions came to a head in 1951 when Mossadeq became the country's Prime Minister. His solution was simple but radical: he nationalized the Oil Company's installations and concessions. All attempts at compromise failed. Nervous of American and Soviet reaction to military intervention in such a sensitive area, London pulled out all British personnel in an attempt to embarrass the company's operations. When this failed, the British government made moves to block the company's sales on the grounds that the oil did not actually belong to the National Iranian Oil Company. In the event, Mossadeq's triumph was short-lived. In 1953, in a move that symbolized the shifting balance of power in the Western alliance, the CIA intervened, promoting a coup by the Iranian army and restoring the Shah to power. The refinery and other production facilities were placed under the control of a consortium of Western oil companies, of which a significant number were American. These developments were symptomatic of the real decline of British influence in the Middle East, but the next phase of that decline was to be far more violent.

The Suez Crisis

With the Suez Agreement made with Colonel Nasser in 1954, the British hoped that they had at last healed the breach with Egypt which had been widening since 1945. Under the terms of the document, the British were to leave their bases by the middle of 1956, retaining the right of re-entry in the event of an external threat. In the minds of those who drafted the Agreement, this could only mean the Soviet Union. The withdrawal was made easier by the knowledge that the nuclear deterrent had changed the strategic equation, reducing the value of the Middle Eastern bases.

Another implication of the Agreement was that Egypt would be drawn into the Western sphere of influence. Perhaps an organization equivalent to NATO could be created. Nasser, though, had other ideas. His position inside Egypt was far from secure and to be labelled a Western lackey would have been counter-productive. Indeed, he regarded Britain's influence in the region as malign, particularly as she was a prop to the monarchies of Iraq and Jordan, whom he saw as rival powers. The creation of the Baghdad Pact, in which Turkey, Iraq and Pakistan joined Britain in a defensive alliance, made the threat even greater. As a result, Nasser clearly believed that he needed to make a move before he was totally isolated. He began to buy arms from the Eastern bloc, seeing this as an important step on the road to independence. He described its effect a month after the deal was signed in March 1955: 'The greatest thing the arms deal has done is to give our people a feeling of pride in themselves and pride in their country.' He intensified the dissemination of nationalist propaganda through daily broadcasts on Cairo's 'Voice of the Arabs' radio. The State Department in

Washington then withdrew its support for American funding of the Aswan Dam, upon which so many Egyptian hopes had been pinned. Nasser seized the one convenient, alternative source of finance as compensation; he nationalized the Suez Canal Company, previously in Anglo-French hands.

Britain now faced a dilemma. She still had extensive interests east of Suez, to which the Canal provided a swift but vulnerable sea route. Furthermore, her prestige was at stake. It was soon discovered, however, that the United States, whose change of mind had largely precipitated the crisis in the first place, was opposed to military intervention. In addition, much non-aligned opinion around the world was sympathetic to Nasser's action. Nevertheless, Eden, the Prime Minister, thought Nasser was unlikely to compromise and took the military option. The plan was prepared in collusion with the French and the Israelis, the idea being that Israel would appear to be the aggressor, with the Europeans playing the role of peace-keepers, occupying the Canal in order to protect it. From the very start, in October 1956, the collusion was obvious. The American administration made its displeasure at the deception very clear. Britain and France were humiliatingly forced to withdraw. Almost at a stroke, Britain's claim to be the dominant power in the Middle East collapsed. All that remained was the control of the Aden base, the treaties with the petty states of the Persian Gulf and a fragile friendship with Jordan. On the Western side, the United States was, henceforth, to play the leading role.

Prime Minister Gamal Abdel Nasser of Egypt (1918–70) is carried on the shoulders of cheering crowds at Port Said, after the British evacuation in 1956.

EGYPTIAN NATIONALISM

By the early 1950s Britain and Egypt had been locked in a close and often uncomfortable embrace for seventy years – ever since the British had occupied the country in 1882 to prevent the nationalist leader Colonel 'Urabi from endangering (as the British saw it) the security of their great strategic route to the East through the Suez Canal. For convenience (since they did not want to keep a large garrison in Egypt), the British had always tried to reach an understanding with Egyptian leaders that

would guarantee their access to the Canal and allow them to intervene if Egypt seemed likely to fall under the influence of another power. But there had always been a strong current of anti-British nationalism that tended to rise to the surface from time to time in violent opposition to any form of subservience to British influence. This had happened in 1919 and it revived strongly after the Second World War. The failure to negotiate a new treaty for the reduction of Britain's military presence,

the post-war social and economic instability, and the fiasco of Egypt's defeat in the first Arab–Israeli war of 1948–49 all intensified the anti-British feeling. In the Canal Zone, strikes and terrorist incidents created a dangerous atmosphere that culminated in a shoot-out between British troops and Egyptian police: fierce anti-foreign riots swept through Cairo, and the ensuing political turbulence eventually brought Gamal Abdel Nasser to power in 1952.

THE DIVISION OF CYPRUS

It was the peculiarity of Cyprus that nationalist opposition to British colonial rule did not take the form of a demand for independence. The majority Greek population, forming some four fifths of the population (the remainder being Muslim Turkish–Cypriots), favoured *enosis* or union with mainland Greece. A political campaign to this end had been waged intermittently long before the Second World War, and this flared up again after 1950. Archbishop Makarios was head of the Greek Orthodox Church on the island and an extremely skilful politician. He developed wide international contacts, and was able to attract the support of the Greek government in Athens. On the other side there was a small, but tightly organized opposition terrorist movement (known as EOKA) led by Colonel George Grivas. A terror campaign broke out in 1955. But despite a bloody struggle that petered out in 1958, Cyprus did not join Greece. Under the treaty of 1960, Britain, Greece and Turkey jointly agreed that Cyprus would

A scene near Famagusta in 1955, following one of Archbishop Makarios's (1913–77) fiery speeches demanding passive resistance.

become independent (although Britain retained two 'sovereign base areas'). Makarios, facing the threat of civil war between Greek and Turkish Cypriots, reluctantly accepted the fait accompli. But the situation in Cyprus remained unstable: extremist groups among the Greek Cypriots sought to overthrow the power-sharing constitution. On the first occasion, in 1964, British troops intervened to prevent fighting between the two communities. But ten years later in 1974, a new round of political upheaval led to the overthrow of the 1960 constitution as Turkey occupied and then partitioned the island.

Cyprus

Suez was not the end of British troubles in the Mediterranean and the Middle East. A storm was already brewing in Cyprus. Here, the problem was not a nationalist campaign for independence, but a demand from the Greek majority on the island for *enosis*, or union with mainland Greece – an ambition that received considerable encouragement from Athens. Britain resisted this demand because she was in the process of relocating her Middle Eastern forces on the island. It was also evident that while Ankara would accept British control of the Turkish-Cypriot community, *enosis* was out of the question; Turkey's situation on the Soviet southern flank made her arguments much more persuasive than those of Athens.

But if the British hoped that *enosis* would die a quick death, they were mistaken. The Orthodox Church, led by Archbishop Makarios, was the most powerful force in Greek-Cypriot life. Deeply committed to union with Greece, it provided the means to mobilize Greek-Cypriot feeling. In the spring of 1955 the EOKA terrorist campaign began. The right-wing group, led by Georgios Grivas, was small, tightly organized and difficult to penetrate. Yet, this time, the British did not give in. Instead, they skilfully turned the tables on the Greek-Cypriots, making any solution conditional on the agreement of both Greece and Turkey. Makarios was confronted with a choice between partition or complete independence from the mainland and, fearful of Turkish intervention, he gave way.

Under the 1959 treaty, Cyprus became an independent republic within the Commonwealth, while Britain retained the two 'sovereign base areas' in perpetuity. Unfortunately for the islanders, their leaders had not learned their lesson. When, in 1974, the Greeks revived their earlier ambitions, the Turkish army intervened and a *de facto* partition was established.

The Remaining Outposts

Nostalgia and necessity coloured Britain's view of Malta, which was also affected by the international tide of political change.

Yet such was the strength of feeling that lingered from the close association of the war years that, at one point, the leaders of both Britain and Malta proposed that 'there should be not less than three Maltese representatives in the House of Commons'. An agreement was never signed, however, partly because the question of economic aid was never settled. Meanwhile, until the early 1960s, the War Office kept insisting that a base on the islands was essential to defend Britain's interests. By 1964, when Malta achieved independence, the Chiefs of Staff had changed their minds and such strategic concepts were felt to be 'anachronistic'.

Reducing their military presence in the Mediterranean did not mean that the British had lost interest in what was happening east of Suez. One of the most striking features of the last phase of Britain's imperial career was the increased strategic importance attached to Aden and Singapore and to Britain's ability to maintain her influence in the Indian Ocean. To ensure that Aden would remain a safe and loyal base, the British embarked on a bold experiment to solder together a South Arabian federation.

This was to include the semi-feudal princely states of the hinterland and the urban cauldron that was Aden proper. Having set up this unstable structure, they proposed to guarantee its internal and external security. The experiment did not last long. The unstable politics of the federation, the rapid growth of urban terrorism in Aden and, after 1964, the intensifying pressure at home to achieve far-reaching defence economies made the burden of Aden's defence appear less and less worthwhile. In 1967 Britain formally declared that she would withdraw from her bases in Singapore and Aden, and give up her guarantees for the security of the tiny but rich Arab states which fringed the southern rim of the Persian Gulf.

By 1971, all but a few fragments of the extraordinary power that Britain had exercised in the Middle East since the early nineteenth century had vanished. Only a few loose ends remained to be unravelled.

CHAPTER THIRTY-NINE

AFRICA: THE WIND OF CHANGE

◇

With the exception of the Union of South Africa, which had been self-governing since 1910, Africa had failed to live up to the enthusiastic predictions of imperialists which had developed towards the end of the nineteenth century. Expectations of huge profits from Africa had been honed by the kind of salesmanship which had created the South Sea Bubble in the early eighteenth century. John Verschoyle, editor of *Fortnightly Review* at the end of the nineteenth century, had foreseen a 'vast empire administered by as great or a greater company than the old East India Company'. Similarly, Cecil Rhodes, in an interview, described parts of what later became Southern Rhodesia as 'simply full of gold reefs'. Unfortunately, the very limited amount of private and public capital which individual colonies had attracted produced disappointing dividends. Africa's potential remained, but the size of the continent demanded massive investment and the financial markets were more attracted to those more familiar areas that gave a quicker yield.

The Second World War changed Africa's economic situation completely. British colonies in general, and the African colonies in particular, were essential suppliers of raw materials to the Allies. Furthermore, when the bulk of Britain's manufacturing industry was diverted to non-export activities, the colonies continued to sell their raw materials outside the Empire. This role was enhanced after 1945. Until at least 1949, African resources were regarded by the Labour government as a crucial element in the battle to save foreign exchange. The same commodities – cocoa, palm oil, sisal, cotton, groundnuts, gold, copper and tin – would also attract foreign exchange into the sterling area, a very great consideration in light of the massive indebtedness of Britain to the United States during the 1940s.

In 1889 the Kikuyu chief, Kamari, was persuaded to sign a treaty establishing British administration in Kenya, where the occupation proved far from peaceful.

The Roots of Change

The heightened importance of Britain's African possessions seems an unlikely context for the development of policies that were to lead to the independence of that part of the Empire. However, this enhanced economic potential posed a problem for Britain. In relation to the size of their populations and the territories administered, the African colonies had been run by very small groups of civil servants. This was necessary because the cost of colonial administration was borne by local taxation – in particular customs and excise revenue – and the money yielded hitherto by the African colonies had been very limited. On the other hand, the increased demand for African commodities entailed further investment and development. In the straitened economic circumstances in which Britain found herself between 1939 and the early 1950s, direct investment from either the government or the private sector was severely restricted. Furthermore, the growth of colonial production would have meant that the infrastructure of each territory, the training and dissemination of new skills, would all have to be given higher priority. The administrative mechanisms Britain had imposed on Africa were, however, ill-adapted to the promotion of rapid economic change. In the West African colonies, Nigeria or the Gold Coast, a sparse British presence relied upon a structure of local government dominated by 'traditional' chiefs – a devolved system which was called 'indirect rule'. In the settler enclaves of Kenya or the Rhodesias, on the other hand, colonial rule had come to be dominated by the Europeans. Both kinds of government were conservative, slow to react to change and unpromising prosecutors of radical policies. One prominent Rhodesian politician, Roy Welensky, envisaged the likely pattern of development in 1946: 'I say that for 50 or possibly 100 years the African has an important part to play here, but he has to play that part as a junior partner.'

The imposition of more closely supervised administrations on the African colonies would have posed the immediate problem of manpower costs and resources. Consequently, a more co-operative strategy was conceived. This involved the gradual concession of more representative central institutions, the recognition and nurturing of non-political trade unions and a more open attitude towards educated and thus, it was believed, more economically progressive and productive Africans. The Secretary of State for the Colonies in the post-war Labour government, Arthur Creech Jones, declared in a public statement in 1948 that 'our conception of African development is based on Western political philosophy, and as far as I can see at present, that of the African leaders is based on the same idea.' He also believed that the Africans would benefit from their experience of local government. These preconceptions failed to recognize the changes that had taken place since the 1920s.

The Rise of African Nationalism

Early expressions of the desire for self-rule had been limited to a circumscribed, educated African élite. The increased pace of

Morocco

Algeria

Tunisia

Libya
INDEPENDENT 1951

Egypt

• CAIRO

Spanish Sahara
RENAMED WESTERN
SAHARA AFTER 1958

Mauritania

Mali

Niger

Chad

Anglo-Egyptian Sudan
INDEPENDENT 1956 AS SUDAN

Eritrea
MERGED WITH ETHIOPIA 1962

Senegal

Upper
Volta
INDEPENDENT 1984
AS BURKINA FASO

Gambia
INDEPENDENT 1965

Port.Guinea
FREETOWN

Guinea

Dahomey
INDEPENDENT 1960
AS BENIN

Djibouti

Sierra Leone
INDEPENDENT 1961

Ivory
Coast

Nigeria
INDEPENDENT 1960

Ethiopia

Liberia

Gold Coast
INDEPENDENT 1957 AS
GHANA

ACCRA •

Togo

Togo
BRITISH MANDATE
INDEPENDENT 1957
MERGED WITH
GHANA

LAGOS •
NORTH SECTOR OF
BRITISH MANDATED
CAMEROON
INDEPENDENT 1960
MERGED WITH NIGERIA

Cameroon
INDEPENDENT 1960

Central African
Republic

Kenya
INDEPENDENT 1963

Uganda
INDEPENDENT 1962

Somaliland

British
Somaliland
INDEPENDENT 1960
MERGED WITH SOMALI
AS SOMALIA

Cameroon
BRITISH MANDATE
INDEPENDENT 1960 AND
MERGED WITH FRENCH
MANDATE CAMEROON

Equatorial Guinea

Gabon

Congo

Rwanda

Belgian Congo
INDEPENDENT 1971 AS ZAIRE

Burundi

• MOMBASA
Zanzibar
INDEPENDENT 1963

Cabinda
(ANGOLA)

Tanganyika
INDEPENDENT 1961

MERGED IN 1963 WITH ZANZIBAR
TO FORM TANZANIA

Angola

Northern
Rhodesia
INDEPENDENT 1964
AS ZAMBIA

Moçambique

Southern
Rhodesia
INDEPENDENT 1980 AS
ZIMBABWE

Nyasaland
INDEPENDENT 1964
AS MALAWI

Namibia
INDEPENDENT 1990's

Bechuanaland
INDEPENDENT 1966
AS BOTSWANA

Madagascar

Union of South
Africa

• DURBAN

Swaziland
INDEPENDENT 1967

Basutoland
INDEPENDENT 1966 AS LESOTHO

CAPE TOWN •

Africa: Towards Independence

///// Territories placed by U.N. under British trusteeship in 1946

▬ British Commonwealth States and dates of independence

SOUTH AFRICA LEAVES THE COMMONWEALTH

After the war, the Union of South Africa became a strident opponent of Britain's policy of decolonization. At the same time, the white supremacist National Party rose to power in Pretoria. Throughout the 1950s the policies of Britain and South Africa diverged more and more, and by 1960 a crisis was imminent.

Early in 1960 Harold Macmillan toured Africa. His journey culminated in a speech in Cape Town which emphasized the changes that had come about in the rest of the continent during the preceding few years. Just over a month later, 67 unarmed black demonstrators were shot dead by police in the Transvaal township of Sharpeville. That killed any chance of an accommodation between

Pretoria and the newly independent states to the north. On 5 October 1960 white South Africans voted on their constitutional future. By choosing a republic they ensured that

Pretoria had to reapply for Commonwealth membership. South Africa found that she had few friends in the new Commonwealth and on 15 March her application was withdrawn.

---

economic change in the hothouse conditions of the 1940s, however, had paved the way for the emergence of political movements that were led by the intelligentsia but supported by large numbers of ordinary Africans. Thus, the gradualism of British policy was immediately challenged by a new and forceful African political style which demanded independence, not in a matter of decades but at once – 'Self Government Now' was the rallying cry of the Convention People's Party in the Gold Coast. The party leader, Kwame Nkrumah, declared in a pamphlet: 'We have talked too much and pined too long over our disabilities – political, social and economic – and it is now time that we embarked on constitutional positive steps to achieve positive results.' This new political style was evident in active press campaigns, in pressure on Parliament by sympathetic MPs, in strikes and in street demonstrations.

Nationalists could be checked by shows of force, yet this opened up the possibility of numerous colonial wars, which could be costly operations. Such a violent reaction was not, in any case, on the Labour Party agenda, given its record of anti-colonial protest before the Second World War. The military option was also extremely risky in diplomatic terms.

International Pressure

By 1945 the international environment was one of anti-colonialism. The two superpowers, the Soviet Union and the United States, both opposed colonial rule, albeit for different reasons. At the height of its own expansionist triumph, Moscow saw the colonial world as a fertile seedbed for Communism. The United States (by 1945 the world's dominant economic power) demanded free trade in the free world and an end to preferential treatment for any state. Washington was also anxious about the possibility of frustrated nationalists turning towards Moscow for support. The United Nations too now contained powerful anti-colonial voices, most notably that of India, an independent member state after 1947. A Britain compromised by economic weakness no longer had the power to outface the critics of colonial rule as she had done in the inter-war years.

If force was an unlikely option, so was that of buying off the nationalist cause with liberal concessions. By the late 1940s, the nationalist leaders in Africa would have been satisfied with nothing short of the form of socialized political economy then being introduced into Britain by the Labour government. Free health care, free and universal education and a large government stake in the economy was, however, beyond the means of an already over-taxed and financially austere Britain. Despite the increase in export prices since 1942, local revenues in Africa remained limited and incapable of supporting welfare policies on

such a scale without external assistance. To supply such aid would have been completely unacceptable to the British electorate. Thus, the two options that might have sustained British rule had to be abandoned because of their cost. Whitehall had little alternative but to adapt to the prevailing situation in each of the colonies individually.

West Africa takes the Lead

Radical nationalism was most developed in West Africa, notably in Nigeria and the Gold Coast. These states were judged to have economically sound futures and a large, educated élite capable of filling the roles previously allocated to expatriate officers. Accordingly, vigorous nationalist protests were eventually accommodated to some extent by the introduction of increasingly representative central institutions. The first stage involved short periods of relatively successful 'diarchy', in which British officials and elected African politicians managed the colonial states in tandem. Such cooperation often resulted in a very active partnership, particularly on the Gold Coast where the Governor at the time of the 1951 election, Sir Charles Arden-Clarke, had Nkrumah, the leader of the victorious political party released from jail. As the Governor later recalled, 'My choice was fairly simple: if I did not release him we would not even make a start with working the Constitution; and if I did release him he would find it very difficult to refuse to work the Constitution or give it a trial.' Consequently, the Gold Coast became independent as Ghana in 1957, while Nigeria followed her lead and claimed indpendence in 1960.

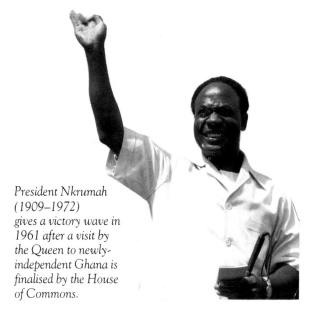

President Nkrumah (1909–1972) gives a victory wave in 1961 after a visit by the Queen to newly-independent Ghana is finalised by the House of Commons.

Britain accepted the quickening pace of decolonization because she no longer saw Africa as a potential economic support. The growing strength of the British economy meant that the African colonies were increasingly considered to be dispensable. Nevertheless, during the 1950s, the Conservative government had to contend with a strong pro-imperial lobby in its ranks, who regarded the retreat from what it saw as imperial glory as sacrilege. The Conservative leadership did not try to put back the clock in West Africa, however, for it was clear that any attempt to abandon or slow down the process of decolonization would have provoked massive, hostile and therefore costly protests in the affected colonies.

East and Central Africa

Unfortunately for the rest of the African colonies, the states of Nigeria and Ghana were seen as exceptional. They had powerful, mass nationalist movements, successful economies that had weathered the Depression of the 1930s without assistance from London, and high rates of literacy and skilled labour. Most other areas of Africa, because of their mixture of African peoples or the presence of white settlers, were seen as being too small, too poor, or too complicated politically to warrant similar treatment to Ghana, Nigeria and, less successfully, Sierra Leone. In the early 1950s, gradualism was still the order of the day in the rest of Africa, where London regarded nationalism as being less sophisticated than in West Africa. A large-scale peasants' revolt amongst the Kikuyu of Kenya (known as the Mau Mau) was treated as a primitive tribal movement by the British, who tried to suppress it with military force. Philip Mitchell, Governor of Kenya from 1944 to 1952, made the official view all too clear at the end of his term of office: 'The great mass of the people in this region are still in a state of ignorance and backwardness, uncivilised, superstitious, economically weak to the point of near helplessness, and quite unable to construct a civilised future for themselves.'

The nationalist movements in the remaining colonies had not yet reached the heights of organized strength which had forced Whitehall to reconsider its approach in West Africa. This encouraged London to think that time was on its side. Whitehall thought that the inherent problems of the smaller, poorer states could be coped with in a federal context. The Central African Federation, which linked the three colonies of Southern and Northern Rhodesia and Nyasaland, was established in 1953. A similar kind of federation was strongly advocated for the three East African territories of Kenya, Uganda and Tanganyika. These amalgamations were seen by the nationalists as an attempt to extend settler power in both regions and did much to stimulate their growth as a political force.

It rapidly became clear that the presence of settler-dominated Southern Rhodesia in the Central African Federation would have a formative effect on its future. Economic policy was shaped by the perceptions of the local white politicians who dominated the Federal legislature. Development expenditure tended to be most prominent in Southern Rhodesia, the area with the largest white population. At the same time, the locals in the other two colonies objected, in increasingly vehement fashion, to being turned into a pool of cheap labour for their southern neighbours. Fired with this example, the nationalists in Kenya, Uganda and Tanganyika were galvanized into political action. Their reaction was so vigorous that Whitehall had to abandon its notion of a second federation. As a political activist in Tanganyika put it, 'National freedom – *uhuru* – was an uncomplicated principle, and it needed no justification.'

The Last Push

The Conservative government accepted the basic tenets of the Labour colonial policy laid down by Creech Jones and his successor, James Griffiths, but was in no hurry to decolonize, despite the rising nationalist tide. The Suez fiasco was to change everything. Both the British and the French were reminded by the mid-1950s of the importance of the United States within the North Atlantic Alliance. But, as far as active decolonization was concerned, the palace revolution within the Conservative Party which followed the resignation of Prime Minister Anthony Eden was of greater significance to Whitehall.

Those who came to power in Harold Macmillan's Government

WHITE SETTLERS AND KENYA

The colonization of Kenya began only during the opening years of the twentieth century. Settlement was tentative at first and it was not until African land was appropriated and offered on long leases that colonization really took off after 1915. Films and novels have portrayed white Kenyans as an idle, dissolute bunch but few of the 12,000 who were established by 1926 were able to do more than eke out a marginal existence. Their enterprises were rarely successful and their plight was compounded when commodity prices fell during the 1930s. Throughout the colonial period the native Africans remained the most enterprising and successful exploiters of the land. By the time that Whitehall realized that this was so, the white minority had appropriated a disproportionate amount of political power. The *Mau Mau* Emergency of the early 1950s forced London to face the facts and to decide eventually that the white settlers were too much of a liability. Their strenuous

Time seems to have stood still for the members of the Nairobi Jockey Club, still secure behind the white fence of their enclosure at the Ngong Races more than twenty years after Kenya's independence.

objections to full democracy for the entire population were shrugged off and, in the end, they had to choose whether to remain and accept black majority rule or leave. Ironically, those who stay have led a charmed existence in the new export-orientated Kenya.

Jomo Kenyatta (1894–1978) held responsible by Britain for the Mau Mau rebellion, became the first Prime Minister, and later President, of independent Kenya.

Marshal Idi Amin Dada of Uganda (1925–) staged a successful military coup in 1971, and became President in 1976. He fled into exile after a nationalist insurrection in 1979.

turned their backs on the once-powerful imperial lobby in both Parliament and the country at large. Britain's strategic future was seen to lie within NATO in a strong alliance with the United States, whilst her economic future appeared to rest with the developed world, in particular in association with the increasingly affluent Europeans. When Harold Macmillan visited Africa in 1959, he made a speech in Cape Town that encapsulated London's new vision of Africa: 'the most striking of all the impressions I have formed since I left London a month ago is of the strength of this African national consciousness. In different places it takes different forms, but it is happening everywhere. The wind of change is blowing through this continent, and, whether we like it or not, this growth of national consciousness is a political fact. We must all accept it as a fact, and our national policies must take account of it.' These new directions meant that what remained of the Empire was surplus to requirements, whatever the die-hards of the Conservative Party might say and however vocal they might be.

Many of the African colonies were still poor, small or plagued with the political problems that arose from intransigent groups of settlers or from rival factions within the African population. On the other hand, the boom in world commodity prices continued throughout the 1950s. Even though this economic growth appeared to have reached a plateau by the late 1950s, colonial revenue had improved and, accompanied by selective development grants from a variety of sources including the Colonial Development Corporation, it encouraged increased levels of investment in building programmes, health schemes and projects that developed the infrastructure. In addition, the colonial education system had expanded. Thus, by the end of the 1950s, local university colleges were producing a stream of graduates able to take the jobs once earmarked for expatriates.

The success of African colonial progress was relative. Although temporarily flushed with enhanced revenues, many states remained poor. But, in the rush to decolonize, Whitehall tended to gloss over these problems. The British government was more concerned with the political difficulties raised by the enclaves of European settlers in Central and East Africa.

The Settlers' Rearguard Action

Initially, London attempted to cajole the white politicians into accepting multi-racialism but the settlers resisted, insisting that this was merely a recipe for drowning slowly rather than suddenly. Africans, understandably, clamoured for 'one man one vote'. In those colonies where the number of settlers was small, Whitehall lost no time in granting independence. Tanganyika

was the first to go in 1961. It was followed a year later by Uganda, despite the ethnic conflicts that bedevilled the country both before and after independence. In Kenya, Britain washed her hands of the settlers, in effect, by granting independence in 1963 to a government elected on the basis of manhood suffrage. That left London with just one major problem.

The Central African Federation, wracked by the opposition of the indigenous peoples of Northern Rhodesia and Nyasaland, finally faltered and crumbled in the early 1960s. In July 1964, Nyasaland was transformed into the independent state of Malawi. In October, Northern Rhodesia followed to become Zambia. This left just the one white outpost in the south.

In Southern Rhodesia millions of blacks were dominated by just over 20,000 whites who controlled all the levers of power. Deeply entrenched, the settlers could withstand anything Britain might try – except invasion. Any attempt to widen the franchise was opposed. In 1965 the Minister of Information in the Rhodesian government pointed out the dangers of democracy in a speech: 'The British Government has sold out to an ideology that sterilizes creative political thinking. To satisfy an abstract principle that political power must be exercised on the basis of a counting of heads no matter what may be in them. They are prepared to destroy civilization itself.'

Oblivious to Macmillan's 'wind of change' speech in Cape Town, the white Rhodesians finally broke away from London late in 1965 and unilaterally declared themselves independent. The Salisbury government, however, proved vulnerable in the end to its own black guerillas. After a war of attrition which lasted until the late 1970s, the reins of power were finally handed over to the black majority in 1980, when the country was renamed Zimbabwe.

Meanwhile, even the most problematic of loose ends had been dealt with in Britain's eagerness to be rid of its colonial responsibilities south of the Sahara. The British Mandate in Togo was joined to Ghana in 1957. British Somaliland was given to Somalia in June 1960. The following year, the British Mandate in Cameroon was divided between Nigeria and the French ex-colony of Cameroon. More dramatically, in February 1965, the minute strip of the Gambia attained full 'nation' status. Bechuanaland, which changed its name to Botswana, followed in September 1966, with Basutoland taking the name 'Lesotho' and becoming independent the following month. Swaziland was next in September 1968.

Thus, in a period of less than ten years, the whole of Britain's African empire, with the exception of Rhodesia, was released from imperial control.

NORTHERN IRELAND
Catholics
Protestants

Gibraltar

Britain

Canada

ATLANTIC

·Bermuda

Bahamas

Turks
& Caicos Islands

British Virgin
Islands

Cayman Islands

Anguilla

Belize

Antigua & Barbuda

Jamaica

St Kitts
Nevis

Montserrat

St Lucia

St Vincent

Barbados

Grenada

PACIFIC

OCEAN

Ascension Island

O

C

E

A

N

St. Helena

FIJI
(1987)
Indians
Fijians

·Pitcairn Island

Tristan da Cunha

Falkland Islands

South Georgia

SOUTH

British Antarctic Territory

Legacies of Conflict and Uncertainty

Areas of ethnic conflict

Grenada   Areas of strategic uncertainty

Commonwealth countries with the Queen as Head of State

Remaining British dependencies

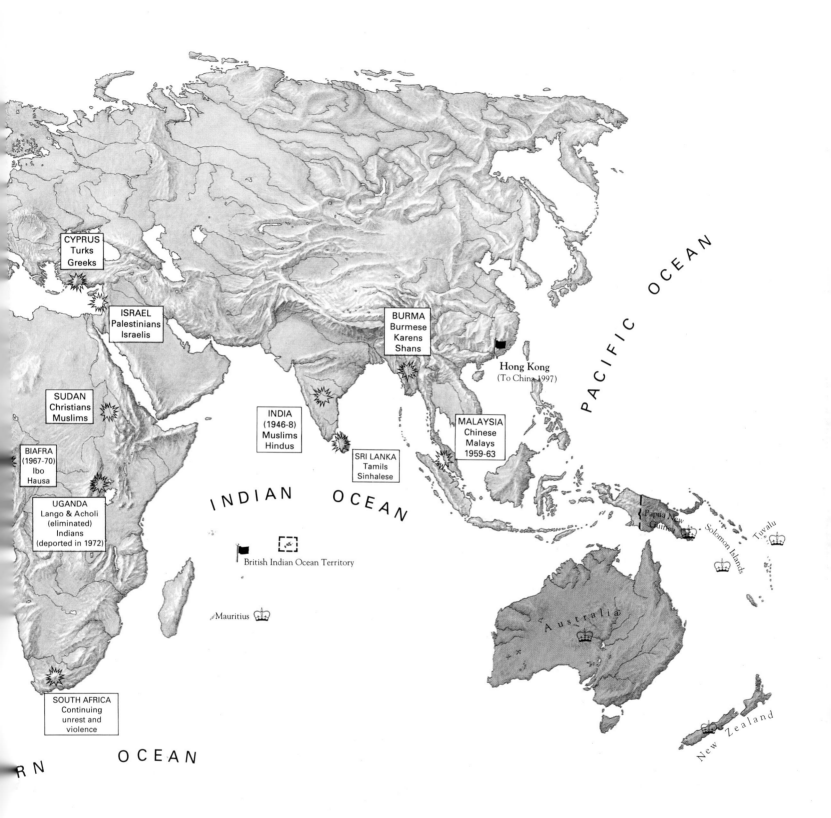

CYPRUS
Turks
Greeks

ISRAEL
Palestinians
Israelis

BURMA
Burmese
Karens
Shans

Hong Kong
(To China 1997)

PACIFIC OCEAN

SUDAN
Christians
Muslims

INDIA
(1946-8)
Muslims
Hindus

MALAYSIA
Chinese
Malays
1959-63

BIAFRA
(1967-70)
Ibo
Hausa

SRI LANKA
Tamils
Sinhalese

UGANDA
Lango & Acholi
(eliminated)
Indians
(deported in 1972)

INDIAN   OCEAN

Papua New
Guinea

Solomon Islands

Tuvalu

British Indian Ocean Territory

Mauritius

Australia

SOUTH AFRICA
Continuing
unrest and
violence

New Zealand

RN   OCEAN

CHAPTER FORTY

THE LAST OUTPOSTS

◇

Winding up an empire can be an untidy business, as was the case with the British Empire. In the early stages, during the 1940s and 1950s, progress towards independence by colonial aspirants was relatively slow, but in the 1960s the pace accelerated dramatically and, by the middle of the decade, it had become clear that any territory which sought independence would promptly be given it. Indeed, the remaining colonial territories were seen more and more as an embarrassment to the British government for which they might be called to account at the United Nations at any time. Worse still, colonial unrest might have required the engagement of the British army, a prospect that was increasingly dreaded by Whitehall. It was in this context that many small colonies were launched as independent states, with barely the resources to survive. Many of these vulnerable ex-colonies have found the Commonwealth an attractive club whose membership protects them from some of the harsher realities of international politics. However, these residual attachments are not the only loose ends to which Britain has to attend.

Political Ambiguities

Of the 48 members of the Commonwealth, the Queen is Head of State in 16, as well as being the British monarch. Her constitutional role in each of these 16 is performed by a governor general, appointed on the recommendation of the government of the country concerned. By constitutional convention, these governors general are under no obligation to consult the Queen about the daily conduct of affairs. Nor, by the same convention, can the Queen be advised by the British Government on her relations with these particular countries; she is legally as much the Queen of Canada as she is of Britain. On paper these various interests remain distinct; in practice they can turn into a political quagmire, as was clearly demonstrated by the Grenadan crisis of 1983.

Grenada is an independent Commonwealth country which

Cuban prisoners guarded by one of the 6,000 US troops who landed in Grenada on 26 October 1983.

has retained the Queen as Head of State. Following the murder of the Prime Minister, Maurice Bishop, in a coup d'état, the Governor General appealed to the United States and neighbouring Caribbean states to intervene. The consequent imbroglio had many of the elements of high farce. Reportedly, messages from the Governor General to the British Foreign Office were sent in error to a plastic-bag factory in east London which was unable to arouse Whitehall's interest in them. Many observers saw American intervention as an insult to the Queen, including, according to rumour, the Monarch herself. However, much political speculation was conducted in ignorance of the constitutional position. If the Governor General had consulted the Queen before appealing to Washington, the role of the Crown in independent Commonwealth countries would have become a subject of discussion or even controversy. More seriously, particularly in American eyes, the receptiveness of the 'Queen of Grenada' to the views known to be held by the British government might have prompted suggestions that London was using the constitutional link to exert a backstage influence. Yet, despite these constitutional niceties, the Grenada incident was also a case of America assuming the role of policeman in what Washington saw as its own backyard, with President Reagan stigmatizing the island as 'a Marxist virus' as early as spring 1982. Grenada proved to be a very minor storm in the Anglo-American teacup, but it does serve as one example of how practical complications can arise from problems hitherto addressed only on paper.

The Residual Colonies

More serious problems, of a recurring nature, are created by those remnants of empire that Britain wishes to retain (frequently for defence purposes), or that have declined decolonization. The 'sovereign base areas' of Akrotiri and Dhekelia in Cyprus are two examples of the former. Apart from their usefulness as refuelling stations, they are also important as 'listening posts', incorporating an array of sophisticated electronic monitoring devices that cover the Middle East, an area of vital interest to the West. A similar function is more modestly performed on the island of Ascension, in the middle of the South Atlantic, where Britain maintains a communications centre and provides facilities for a missile-tracking station used by the United States. A third, unique region to which Britain is unwilling to relinquish its claim is the British Antarctic Territory which, although an inhospitable environment lacking an indigenous population, retains tantalizing potential in respect of economic resources.

The second group of colonies that remain dependent on Britain are those that have resisted decolonization. Most prominent among these is Bermuda, which thrives on tourism and offshore banking and is more prosperous than many of the micro-states that have become fully independent members of the Commonwealth. Indeed, by the end of the 1970s, the islands' citizens enjoyed an average income that ranked among

THE INDEPENDENCE OF GUYANA

The Duke of Kent hands over the formal instruments of independence to Guyana's Prime Minister, Forbes Burnham, in 1966.

Guyana, formerly British Guiana, was the only British colony on the South American mainland. Conquered at the beginning of the nineteenth century from the Dutch, it developed as a plantation colony specializing in the production of sugar. This fact is the key to its politics. Like many plantation colonies, Guyana became a complex plural society. Negro slaves brought from West Africa made up the bulk of the population until the late nineteenth century. Then they were gradually outnumbered by the inflow of workers brought as 'indentured' labour from India in a system that lasted until 1917. By 1960 these 'East Indians' were the largest group in a total population of under half a million. Perhaps inevitably, the advent of greater political participation after 1945 accentuated racial divisions. At first, however, the two charismatic political leaders, Cheddi Jagan an Indian dentist, and Forbes Burnham, a lawyer of Afro-Caribbean descent, cooperated in the campaign for independence. But after 1953, when Jagan's open Marxist sympathies led the British to suspend the constitution, they moved into open rivalry. By the time of independence in 1966, Burnham was able to exploit Afro-Caribbean hostility to the East Indians and the fears of richer East Indians at Jagan's radicalism, in order to outmanoeuvre his old ally and form the first independence government. Burnham remained in power, becoming increasingly autocratic, until his death in 1985. As with most colonies, the transfer of sovereignty was peaceful and dignified, with a member of the royal family in attendance at the ceremony. But this was no guarantee that the ex-colony would wish to keep the Queen as head of state. Like most Afro-Asian members of the Commonwealth, Guyana became a republic within a few years of independence.

---

the highest in the world. Less successful are those Caribbean islands with tiny populations, such as Montserrat, the Caymans, Anguilla, the Turks and Caicos and the British Virgin Islands. Their limited resources, the uncertainties of going it alone and the enjoyment of full self-government in local affairs make independence an unattractive option. For the even smaller British territories scattered around the world, such as St Helena, Tristan da Cunha and Pitcairn Island, a similar judgement applies even more emphatically. This situation is unlikely to change in the foreseeable future.

It is the third group of remaining colonies, however, that has caused the greatest difficulties. In each case, the problem has been how to devise a political future for a colony without jeopardizing its right to self-determination, and without antagonizing any neighbouring state that has been asserting a claim to sovereignty over the territory. Only one of the four situations confronted by the British government since 1960 has, so far, been satisfactorily resolved. This involved Belize, formerly the colony of British Honduras, whose territory was claimed by the neighbouring republic of Guatemala. The latter prosecuted its case by portraying Britain as a colonial power, even in the late 1970s. In the words of the Guatemalan Vice President, Britain was 'deliberately obstructing the understanding between the people of Belize and Guatemala. And the United Kingdom government is in the meantime pursuing not only a colonialistic attitude, but at the same time is in more than one way placing – wishing to place – Guatemala on its knees.' Such aggression meant that, before independence, a detachment of British troops was deployed to deter Guatemalan hostility, since the prospect of a change in the colony's status seemed likely to provoke an unfriendly act. Consequently, independence was postponed until 1981, when discreet pressure appears to have been placed upon Guatemala by the United States to forego its claim. Even so, Belize has continued to rely upon the presence of a small British military contingent to deter any change of heart by her neighbour.

The Rock
The situation of Gibraltar has created a much more intractable problem. First conquered in 1704, it was ceded in perpetuity to Britain by Spain in 1713, a concession which has never ceased to rankle with Madrid. In the 1960s, Spain tried to exploit

the international hostility to colonialism by enlisting United Nations support for the recovery of Gibraltar. At the same time, London's commitment to the colony's role as a naval base was diminishing and British concessions appeared a possibility. Very few of Gibraltar's citizens were Spanish and the prospect of being ruled by General Franco did not appeal to them, particularly as the colony exercised a degree of self-government that had been established as early as 1921. As the Chief Minister was to point out in 1981: 'The "Englishman" does not lord it over the Gibraltarian. We live in mutual respect: so too does Catholic and Jew, Jew with Protestant, Protestant with Catholic, Catholic with Hindu, Hindu with non-conformist or agnostic.' It may well have been the possibility of what Madrid scornfully called 'this artificially constituted human group' achieving complete independence that spurred the Spanish government to its denunciation of British colonialism. Ironically, there was no doubt that the people of Gibraltar preferred their colonial status to 'freedom' with Spain. No British government could hope to smuggle past the House of Commons proposals that would have forced Gibraltar into the arms of Spain. The emotive power of 'the Rock's' long association with Britain would have raised a storm of opposition, especially while Spain lacked even the semblance of a democracy. To counter Spain's anti-colonial rhetoric, Britain declared in 1969 that Gibraltar was a city and not a colony. Furthermore, it outmanoeuvred Spain by conducting a referendum in which 12,138 voters chose British rule and only 44 Spanish. Madrid's riposte was one of pique. Too late, and without any great effect, she decided to impose an economic siege.

Since Franco's death in 1975, democracy has been restored to Spain and she has entered both NATO and the EEC. Although there have been diplomatic moves to reduce friction over the issue of Gibraltar, the only success to date has been the re-opening of the border; the fundamental issue of sovereignty remains frozen.

The Hong Kong Connection
In the early 1980s, on the other side of the world, Hong Kong's prospects raised questions that were at the very heart of the political and economic stability of much of the Far East. The British has acquired the island by the Treaty of Nanking in 1842, intending to use it as a commercial springboard from

which to penetrate the hitherto inaccessible and rule-bound markets of Manchu China. Hong Kong was subsequently developed as a naval base for the patrolling of China's coasts and rivers in an attempt to stamp out, or at least curb, piracy. However, until the Second World War, its importance was strictly limited.

The return of peace to Far Eastern waters saw a transformation in Hong Kong. The Communist takeover of mainland China in 1949 initiated a flood of refugees whose first port of call was the British colony. As a centre of capitalist enterprise enjoying cheap labour, a high level of managerial expertise and a hugh regional market, the island's economy boomed, growing at an annual rate of 10 per cent for over twenty years. Thus, by the 1980s, its government could claim that Hong Kong was the world's third most important financial centre. The consequences of this unique pattern of development were to have a profound effect on the colony's future and on the future of the rest of the region.

Hong Kong had become a bizarre kind of colony – far richer than many independent countries, yet lacking the most rudimentary forms of self-government. This state of affairs seemed scarcely to worry the native population and even a senior member of the administration could say, at an important public occasion, 'We proceed by consensus rather than debate', without embarrassment. The island remained a colony by collusion. Had the Peking government chosen to invade, British resistance would have been purely formal. However, Peking chose not to do so for a number of reasons. First, it could not tell how the United States would react; fear of an aggressive American response had prevented China's invasion of Taiwan. Secondly, China had become increasingly reliant upon Hong Kong as an economic window on the capitalist world – perhaps 25 per cent of China's trade passed through the colony. As a result, Peking acquired a large stake in the stability and efficiency of Hong Kong's financial markets. Thirdly, with improvements in Sino-American relations, Chinese hopes of recovering Taiwan through diplomatic subtlety increased and the fate of Hong Kong became the acid test of Peking's good intentions. Although China's rulers were prepared to bide their time, they were adamant that Hong Kong should not be allowed to develop self-governing institutions that might complicate a future handover.

In Chinese eyes, the original loss of Hong Kong by the first 'unequal treaty' was an injustice, a 'loss of face' that had to be rectified. The colony was a reminder of the time when Westerners had shamelessly exploited their temporary military superiority by imposing on China agreements that were indefensible in the post-colonial world. These agreements did, however, contain some clauses that worked in China's favour. Part of the colony had been ceded in perpetuity, but the larger area, the New Territories, without which Hong Kong was not viable as a community, had been leased in 1898 for 99 years. Thus, 1997 became the year around which Hong Kong's fate turned. Britain was in theory bound to hand back only the leased territory, but in practice the entire colony would have to be returned. From Britain's point of view, it was essential that she made an effort to safeguard the way of life of Hong Kong's population.

With a new and less insular regime in Peking, the British found this objective far less difficult to achieve than they might have feared. Negotiations were successfully timed to take advantage of a favourable mood in Peking and to settle the colony's future well in advance. The outcome was the Anglo-Chinese Hong Kong Agreement of 1984. By its terms, Hong Kong was to revert to mainland control in 1997, but was to enjoy extensive autonomy. In the most significant clause, the

The Union Jack is raised triumphantly as the Falkland Islands are returned to British rule after the 1982 war. This consolidated Mrs Thatcher's position as national leader.

HONG KONG

Since the 1960s Hong Kong has remained an astonishing anachronism in the post-colonial world, a bizarre colony perched on the edge of China, indefensible, rich, an industrial and financial centre of vast importance. First acquired by the British in 1842, Hong Kong's significance for the next century rested on its value as a naval base for the British fleet in the Far East which watched over British commercial interests on the Chinese mainland, and as a centre of British trading activity on the China coast – Hong Kong had once been a key distribution point for the opium the British brought to China. But as long as China remained accessible to Western commerce, Hong Kong's economic importance remained limited. The great city of Shanghai was a much larger commercial

A Hong Kong tram carries an advertisement for one of the most lasting of all British brands.

centre. In 1949, however, the triumph of Chinese Communism closed China to the West and, with the great outflow of often talented refugees to assist it, Hong Kong's phenomenal rise began. Remarkably, despite periodic crises in relations with China, especially during the 'cultural revolution' of the 1960s, there was no concerted effort by Peking to recover control of the colony. The 1984 Hong Kong agreement between Britain and China reflects Peking's acceptance of the vital importance of continuity after the handback in 1997: Hong Kong's capitalist system and way of life is assured a further fifty years of freedom after 1997. But whether it will really be possible to secure Hong Kong's long-standing autonomy from mainland China in this way is as uncertain as China's own future.

At the 28th Summit Conference of British Commonwealth Nations in Vancouver in 1987, members voted to oust Fiji from the group, following the coup of that year.

Chinese government agreed that Hong Kong would be allowed to keep its existing character as a capitalist society and economy for fifty years after the handover. The agreement was greeted with relief in Britain, but it remains to be seen how the complex interim arrangements will be managed in the run-up to 1997 and how secure will be the arrangements scheduled for the following fifty years.

The Falklands Crisis

Each of the three colonies already described – Belize, Gibraltar and Hong Kong – presents difficulties, but the problems are not insoluble. No one in Whitehall can be as hopeful about the most intractable of all the remnants of the Empire: the Falkland Islands. The Islands were acquired at much the same time as Hong Kong, but there the similarity ends. The tiny population, which stood at less than 2,000 in the 1970s, was of British descent. Like Malta or Gibraltar, the place was basically a redundant naval base whose economy depended – precariously – on wool exports. Only its use as a staging post on the way to Antarctica seemed relevant to the future. The local population enjoyed partial self-government and left no doubt in the minds of Whitehall that it wished to remain British. Nevertheless, by the 1960s, London had come to regard this remote outpost as an inconvenience. It was also the cause of considerable friction with Argentina, who regarded the Islands as Argentine territory, stolen by a colonial aggressor. The Falklands depended, however, on the tolerance of Argentina and Uruguay for their air and sea links with the outside world. In the end, pragmatic reflection suggested that an arrangement with Argentina was the inevitable price of economic viability for the islanders.

This was the background to the ill-fated proposal to return the islands' sovereignty to Argentina, in exchange for a 'lease-back' agreement in which Britain would continue to administer the islands while the Falklanders maintained their autonomy. This 'solution' never won any political credibility in Britain, where the skilfull Falklands lobby aroused British opinion against the brutal military dictatorship then running Argentina. The proposal was unceremoniously discarded by the House of Commons and negotiations foundered. Unfortunately, circumstances ensured that matters did not rest there.

By 1982, the Argentine dictatorship was desperate for some form of patriotic triumph in order to revive its flagging fortunes at home. At the same time, for reasons of economy, Britain chose to reduce even further its already minimal maritime presence in the area. This move almost certainly encouraged the regime in Buenos Aires to think that an act of force would not be resisted. At the beginning of April 1982, Argentine forces occupied the Falkland Islands and South Georgia and declared an end to British rule.

British reaction was fierce. A large naval task force was immediately dispatched to the South Atlantic and, while it sailed towards its destination, negotiations were conducted between the two protagonists, with the United States acting as peace-broker. However, the British government was shrewd enough not to temporize for too long, for a lack of action might confuse home opinion. The torpedoing of the battleship *General Belgrano* marked the start of the shooting war in which the vulnerability of the British ships to attack from Argentine aircraft became a key factor. In the event, the successful landing of British troops at San Carlos Bay proved to be the turning point in the struggle. Within four weeks, the Argentine garrison in Port Stanley had surrendered and the British forces sailed home to a rapturous welcome.

In retrospect, the most remarkable aspect of the Falkland Islands episode might seem to be the strong reaction of the British government and the fact that public opinion remained so firmly behind it. However, this is not so surprising as it first appears. For all their renunciation of empire, British governments had never disavowed their aspirations to the status of a major power. Therefore, if Britain had not reacted vigorously, such claims would never have been seriously entertained by other, competing nations in the future. Again, opinion in Parliament was particularly sensitive to the aggressive absorption of British subjects into an alien state. For all that, the great risks and difficulties of the enterprise are evidence that, in certain cases, the loose ends of empire retain the same power to make or break governments as the much grander colonial commitments of the imperial era. Although Britain's eyes were increasingly focused on Europe, it did not relinquish old responsibilities lightly. In a complex world of balance and counterbalance, the ties of empire still counted, and in the 'realpolitik' of the 1980s they could constitute a useful counterweight to Brussels or Washington.

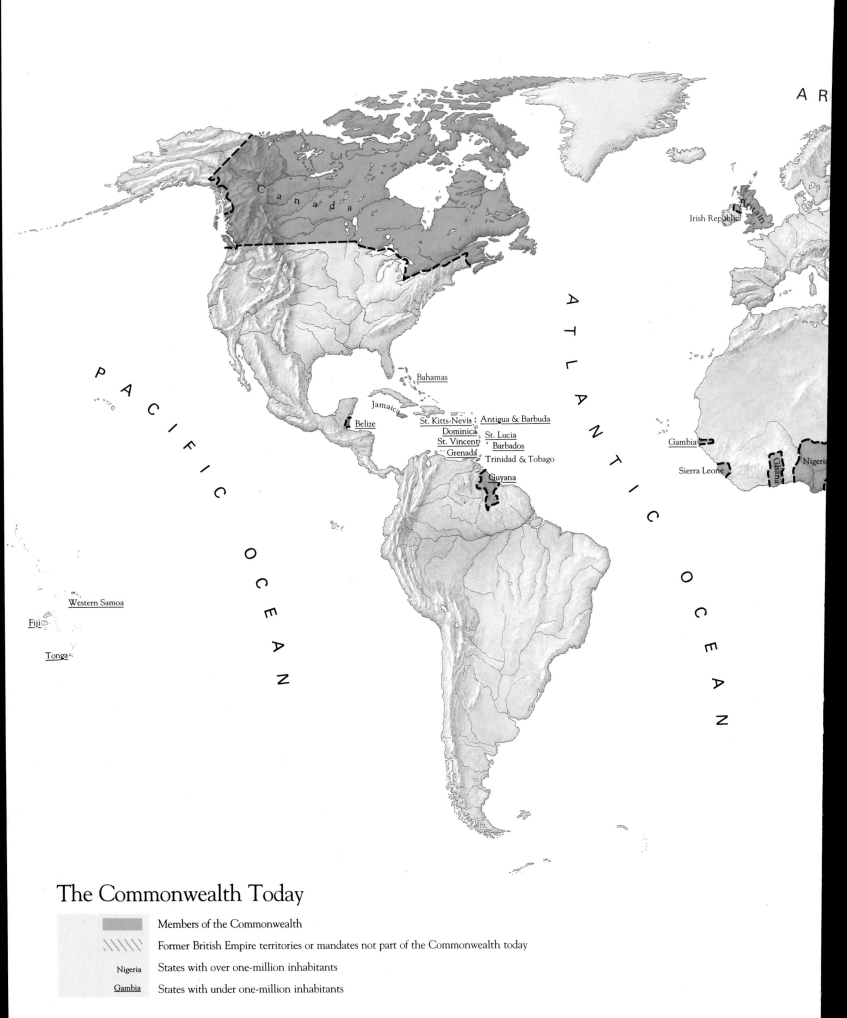

A R
Irish Republic
Britain
Canada
ATLANTIC OCEAN
PACIFIC OCEAN
Bahamas
Jamaica
Belize
St. Kitts-Nevis
Dominica
St. Vincent
Grenada
Antigua & Barbuda
St. Lucia
Barbados
Trinidad & Tobago
Guyana
Gambia
Sierra Leone
Ghana
Nigeria
PACIFIC OCEAN
Western Samoa
Fiji
Tonga

The Commonwealth Today

ARCTIC OCEAN

PACIFIC OCEAN

INDIAN OCEAN

SOUTHERN OCEAN

Malta
Cyprus
Palestine/Israel
Jordan
Iraq
Pakistan
India
Bangladesh
Burma
Sudan
Uganda
Kenya
Tanzania
Malawi
Zambia
Zimbabwe
Botswana
Swaziland
South Africa
Lesotho
Sri Lanka
Maldives
Seychelles
Mauritius
Malaysia
Singapore
Brunei
Nauru
Tuvalu
Kiribati
Solomon Islands
Vanuatu
Papua New Guinea
Australia
New Zealand

CHAPTER FORTY-ONE

THE COMMONWEALTH TODAY

◇

The modern Commonwealth is an enigma. As an international organization, its composition and structure, or lack of it, make it appear loose-knit and decentralized to the point of imminent disintegration. It has no financial, economic or judicial unity, and no institutions of the kind found in the European Community to harmonize its divergent interests. No treaty holds its members together; nor does it have any express international purposes, such as those laid down in the Charter of the United Nations. There is no machinery to take collective decisions and members are bound only by those commitments into which they have entered freely. Moreover there are no common regional interests, although some countries are allied to other such groups, like NATO. In fact, the only qualification for membership is one of historical accident, that of once having been a British colony. Yet, despite all that and even within the tense context of modern international relations, the Commonwealth still exists. An historical accident has become a practical, if loose association of common interests.

The Process of Decolonization

The roots of today's Commonwealth can be found in the constitutional relationship that developed before 1914 between Britain and the self-governing colonies – the so-called 'white dominions'. Although they were responsible for their own internal policies, Britain took care of defence and external relations. After 1900, a tradition grew up whereby the Prime Ministers of each colony met periodically in London to discuss matters of common interest, and to be briefed on foreign affairs and defence. However, although loyal to the Empire, they valued their independence and could not be cajoled into any more formal association. After the First World War, this inclination towards independence grew, as the Australian Prime Minister made clear: 'Unless Dominion status is quickly solved in a way that will satisfy the aspirations of these rising nations, separatist movements are to be expected.' At a crucial meeting in London in 1926 it was agreed that Canada, Australia, South Africa, New Zealand and the Irish Free State should have the right to manage their own foreign relations. This was embodied in the Statute of Westminster in 1931, which also conferred a constitutional status upon them that was equal to Britain's.

The decolonization of India was brought about by economic change and a strident non-white nationalism. Yet it became the model of a sovereign republic within the Commonwealth for many of the countries that followed. As India's leaders drew up their plans for a new constitution, they made it clear that becoming a republic was an indispensable part of the country's future status and national identity. Sooner than give up a republican constitution, they would leave the Commonwealth. So, after anxious consultations, the British reluctantly agreed. The London Declaration of 1949 laid down a new formula – theoretically limited to India as a special case but in practice made available to other colonies as they followed the path to independence. In return for this concession, the Indians recog-

An Illustrated Atlas of the British Commonwealth of Nations

The optimistic foundation of the British Commonwealth as shown in this 1937 illustration from an early 'Atlas of Empire'.

nized the British monarch as the 'Head of Commonwealth', an honorific role without constitutional functions. Once the break had been made, however, the Indian Prime Minister, Pandit Nehru, was keen to retain a special link with Britain, as he made clear: 'In the world as it is today it is not desirable to break contacts and links and seek isolation.'

The truth of the matter was that an India alone was vulnerable. To the north she faced three powerful potential enemies: Muslim Pakistan, with its Middle Eastern sympathizers, China and the Soviet Union. For their part, the British were equally keen to maintain the impression of an Anglo-Indian strategic partnership in the Indian Ocean which massaged their somewhat faded prestige. The arrangement was also expected to diminish the danger that India might become fiercely anti-colonial and anti-western. Both sides gained something.

The same was true of those colonies that achieved independence in the 1950s and early 1960s. Britain could maintain the illusion that she was still a power with worldwide influence while, for the newly emergent countries, membership of the Commonwealth imposed no formal obligations. Membership carried with it the assumption of close and regular diplomatic contact which enhanced the prestige of fledgling politicians; it gave them experience of a broader international context. And, up until the 1960s, it also encouraged the traditions and practices of parliamentary democracy. The careful emphasis placed both on equality and on the voluntary basis of membership eased the passage of the new states into an acceptable

The Imperial State Crown is a reminder of how dramatic has been the change in the role of the British monarchy. Until the 1940s, whoever sat on the British throne was also ruler of the British dominions and colonies overseas, as well as 'King-Emperor' of India. But from 1949 onwards, these exalted titles were steadily modified. India led the way in demanding that the old obligation to recognize the British monarch as head of state in all Commonwealth countries should be relaxed. The British government reluctantly agreed. Thereafter, many of the Afro–Asian territories that attained independence exercised the 'Indian' option and declared themselves republics, while requesting that they be admitted to membership of the Commonwealth. Even so, of the 48 countries in the Commonwealth, 16 still prefer to keep a royal head of state, and the Queen is as much Queen of these countries as she is of the United Kingdom. That the

The St Edward's Crown incorporates the Koh-i-noor diamond, confiscated by the British on the annexation of the Punjab in 1849. It was added to the crown jewels of Queen Victoria. The Royal Sceptre boasts the Great Star of Africa, cut from the famous Cullinan diamond .

Queen should be the monarch of so many independent states makes the British Crown unique among the monarchies of the world. And that the republican Commonwealth countries have recognized the Queen in this role rather than demanding a rotating chairmanship is a testimony to her international prestige.

perpetuation of their links with Britain. In return, Commonwealth members could expect military and technical assistance, the implied promise of support if attacked, and privileged access to British markets.

A Changing World Context

This cosy afterglow of post-imperial complacency received a sharp jolt during the Suez Crisis of 1956, for the Indian Prime Minister was not slow to voice his criticism: 'Neither peace nor freedom can come if strong nations, trusting to their armed power, seek to compel weaker countries to obey their will.' That the former 'Jewel in the Crown' should criticize the 'mother-country' was a major shock. Policy-makers realized that an association which included an independent-minded India could not automatically be counted on in times of trouble. The mandarins of Whitehall began looking elsewhere.

As the 1960s dawned, the success of the European Economic Community began to seem increasingly attractive to Britain. Despite having her application for membership rejected in 1963 and 1967, a series of economic crises at home made the six community countries more and more alluring. Disenchantment with the Commonwealth was not diminished by Rhodesia's secession in 1965. The tension that this induced between Britain and the Afro-Asian members was a running sore that would not heal. That Britain sought to 'keep the majority of

people in Aden down by force' while allowing 'a band of unprincipled and racially minded men to get away with it' in Rhodesia, became a common theme. And the way in which leaders, whose own democratic support was doubtful, berated Britain for her reluctance to take action against a country governed by 'kith and kin', did much to destroy pro-Commonwealth sentiment in the Conservative Party during this time.

Other changes were also afoot. The core of the former colonies, Canada, Australia and New Zealand were, albeit reluctantly, moving closer to America in diplomacy and culture. By the 1960s, the importance of their defence arrangements with the United States far exceeded the importance of those with Britain. In fact, it began to look as though the Commonwealth was about to disintegrate.

Yet it did not. And whatever might be said in the rhetoric of after-dinner speeches, its survival cannot be attributed to either idealism or sentiment. It was hard-nosed self-interest that won the day.

The Realities of Independence

Of the forty-eight members, only four – Britain, Canada, Australia and New Zealand – are developed countries. Almost all the rest, though varying enormously in wealth, size, population and potential, belong to (or see themselves as part of) the Third World. Consequently, they have very little say in the key institutions with which the western industrial powers seek to regulate the world economy: the International Monetary Fund, the World Bank and the General Agreement on Tariffs and Trade (GATT). The Commonwealth's primary significance for many of its members is that, however unsatisfactorily, it does allow a large number of less-developed countries to discuss and air their problems at meetings attended by industrial countries – especially Britain and Canada – who have great influence in the inner councils of the pre-eminent economic organizations.

Secondly, many Commonwealth member-states are so small that they can be defined as 'microstates', with populations of a million or less and with resources to match. They are acutely vulnerable, not only to external aggression, but also to the more insidious operations of organized crime. With minimal resources, they have difficulty in maintaining the scale of diplomatic representation required to ensure that their needs and interests are heeded by larger powers. They are often dependent on the

"I'M SURE YOU CHILDREN WON'T OBJECT IF MOTHER HAS A LATCHKEY, TOO."

David Low, on the Commonwealth Prime Ministers' Conference of 1948.

MOTHER OF PARLIAMENTS

It was once a fashionable notion that the great legacy of British rule in the independent states of the Commonwealth would be the existence of representative institutions all over the world modelled on the Mother of Parliaments at Westminster. Like many of the vanities in the last age of imperial grandeur, this turned out to be an empty dream.

In the nineteenth century, however, it had seemed quite plausible as the colonies of white settlement acquired self-government. Even here it was easy to overlook the differences in colonial politics. These included the absence of anything like the House of Lords and the quite different way in which the Parliaments of Canada or Australia had to operate in a federal system. The United Kingdom after all was a unitary state with one parliament only.

Nevertheless, as they set about extending self-government in their non-white colonies, it was natural for the British to adapt their own system of government for local use. One of the main reasons for this was the strong belief that if it was properly managed it would not only be the most efficient form of government but also that it would offer the best chance of preserving British influence as self-government gradually became more complete.

In the final rush to transfer sovereignty, care was taken to implant at least the forms of Westminster-style government in the independence constitutions, with careful provision for ministers to be answerable to members of parliament. In many parts of the Commonwealth, these have survived and flourished, with necessary modifications. But in parts of the Afro–Asian Commonwealth, political conditions have not allowed more than the hollowest of these forms to continue.

sale of a single commodity or service, constantly exposed to sudden changes in the market, and they lack the 'weight' to exert pressure on their more powerful clients. Even forming an association amongst themselves would do little to reinforce their individual positions. The Commonwealth at least provides a context in which their viewpoint will receive a hearing.

Even for considerably larger Afro-Asian countries, the advantages of membership are not to be scorned. For the 'frontline states' in central and southern Africa, membership is a lever through which to obtain more economic aid, by emphasizing the threat to their independence from South Africa. It is also their best available platform from which to try to mobilize international pressure against that country. As one East African Foreign Minister put it: 'When the chips are down, we know that few around this table will come to our aid when we face the consequences of the armed struggle.'

Viewed more cynically, the Commonwealth offers a glamorous stage on which régimes threatened with domestic discontent can perform heroic feats of international diplomacy. Even for a large country like India, membership serves a significant purpose. She has few natural friends in world politics; relations with both Pakistan and China have, at different times, erupted into violence; those with the United States have been poor; and friendship with the Soviet Union, although important, has been of limited value, certainly in the economic field. Moreover,

India's relations with many Afro-Asian states are complicated by the status of Indian immigrant communities within their boundaries. The Commonwealth, therefore, in which her size and historic situation as the first Afro-Asian member guarantee her status, is recognized by India – for all these reasons – as too valuable to be given up lightly.

The attractions of the Commonwealth might seem minimal for the more developed countries. Yet, even for Canada, Australia and New Zealand, it helps to counterbalance their necessary closeness to the United States. Furthermore, it helps all three expand their contacts with the Third World and, when necessary, distance themselves from the major Western powers by displaying 'small-power' sympathies and attitudes.

Britain herself has been grateful on more than one occasion for the presence of the Afro-Asian members, who have moderated Third World opinion in critical situations. The resolution of the Rhodesian conflict was made acceptable by the presence of a range of Commonwealth observers at the handover. In the early stages of the Falklands crisis in 1982, it was essential to prevent Argentina's Latin American sympathizers from presenting the issue of sovereignty as a colonial issue, with Argentina cast as the liberator, rallying Third World countries against Britain at the United Nations. The support of Commonwealth countries ensured that there would be no bloc vote by the Third World behind Argentina.

Two little girls display a dutiful Union Jack on the Queen's visit to the British West Indies in 1985, which was celebrated by traditional parades and speeches.

The Queen and the Duke of Edinburgh are presented to the Chiefs of the Central Region on the Royal tour of Ghana in 1961.

Commonwealth Infrastructure

The stage on which most of these roles are played is the Commonwealth Heads of Government Meeting. Formerly held in London once every two years, the venue now varies. Meetings are held to discuss matters of common interest. No resolutions are passed and there is no attempt to formulate common policies. Given the highly publicized acrimony of many of the discussions over the years, it is hardly surprising that an agreed end-of-meeting communiqué is all that most gatherings have been able to manage, and even this has frequently been seen as an heroic achievement.

To get that agreement, the language used tends to the vacuous, as can be seen in just one example: 'We believe that at this historic moment our world society should take stock of its considerable achievements as well as its failures, and allow hope and encouragement from the former to strengthen resolve in redressing the latter.' It is no wonder that the association's early demise is frequently predicted. Yet, as we have seen, it is the opportunity to display acrimony in public that helps hold the Commonwealth together.

A more practical institution to sustain the same purpose was organized in 1968. The Commonwealth Secretariat was set up to service the heads of government meeting, assuming a function previously undertaken by the Commonwealth Relations Department in Whitehall. In keeping with the devolutionary process that has continued throughout the twentieth century, it should provide all associated governments with a mechanism for monitoring and advising on matters of concern. Yet, in practice, especially under the present Secretary-General, Sir Sonny Ramphal, it has been less a self-effacing and deferential bureaucracy than a pressure group promoting a 'Commonwealth point of view' – something which has irritated some politicians.

Another medium of adhesion is the role of the 'Head of the Commonwealth' herself. Although the Queen has no authority over many member countries (being constitutional head of state in only seventeen out of forty-eight), her personal dignity and prestige, as well as her unparalleled experience on the international scene, give her an authority within the organization that is peerless.

The Sporting and Cultural Legacy

So far, we have seen the Commonwealth only in a political context. Yet, one of Britain's strongest legacies to her former colonies is in the promotion of cultural and sporting links. The latter provide more regular and intimate contacts between the developed and the Third World than exist anywhere else. By contrast with the Commonwealth Games, for example, the Olympic Games serve only to emphasize the overwhelming sporting dominance of the Superpowers and the other countries of the industrial world, where vast resources can be requisitioned in the cause of athletic prowess. For many of the small and microstates of the Commonwealth, its sporting occasions are their only opportunity to shine.

In the arts too, Commonwealth access to English language institutions gives many writers the entrée to a wider patronage than they might otherwise have hoped for. The Booker Prize, the most prestigious literary prize for fiction in Britain, has in recent years been the forum for much Commonwealth success. Recent winners include the South African J.M. Coetzee, the New Zealander Kevi Hulme and the Australian Thomas Keneally.

Yet, culture consists of more than the arts. In the field of jurisprudence, models inherited from Britain remain pervasive. Professional associations and the social models they provide are another legacy that prospers. The Commonwealth Press Union, for example, by bringing together a number of journalists every year, seeks to promote a greater knowledge and understanding not merely of Britain but also between the visitors themselves.

Set against a background of world-threatening political and strategic alignments, these contacts and achievements may seem meagre. But they epitomize the modern character of the Commonwealth as a network of practical links, whose overall effect is to modify the brute force of political or economic calculation among the member states and those that surround them.

More than a generation has passed since Britannia ruled the waves and since the journey began that led her away from world domination. It is perhaps ironic that what was once the great British Empire is now a Commonwealth of the meek and vociferous, drawn together by mutual anxiety.

POSTSCRIPT

———◇———

The Captains and the Kings Depart

Books on Empire sometimes conclude with 'balance sheets'. To construct one for the British Empire is an impossible task. As the preceding chapters show, the intentions of empire-builders ranged across the whole spectrum of human imperatives, from pure greed to dedicated self-sacrifice. Many, particularly in the early days, were little more than looters. In the centuries that followed, others regarded a dedication to the poor in the colonies as part of their Christian duty or even, like Lord Palmerston in 1845, as the moral imperative of the 'enlightened' state: 'Our duty – our vocation – is not to enslave but to set free; and I may say without any vainglorious boast . . . that we stand at the head of moral, social and political civilization. Our task is to lead the way and direct the march of other nations.'

By the early twentieth century, the cynicism of English radicals such as the publicist J.A. Hobson began to erode this imperial vision: 'Imperialism in practice . . . is mainly the expression of two dominant human instincts, self-assertion and acquisitiveness.'

It is easy to frame judgements in hindsight. There were practices, such as the slave and opium trades, that were abhorrent even to large sections of contemporary opinion. But it is much more difficult, for instance, to take a moral stance on Britain's low level of investment in the colonies during the nineteenth century. At that time there was hardly a government in the world which considered heavy financial outlays to be part of its economic duty. The creation of stability and the 'rule of law', rather than economic development, were considered the highest ideals of the state.

The British Empire was a vast and complex series of processes, linked in ambiguous ways to the growth of a world-capitalist economy. It was not, despite the cartographers' convention of 'red on the map', a territorial state, and was certainly never centrally planned or directed. It was, instead, a rather haphazard network that was cast around the world, made up of forced treaties, parochial flows of money, land-hungry emigrations, punitive expeditions and exhausted compromises with indigenous rebels. The formal boundaries of British rule were pushed forward for different reasons: to secure new profits, to check the fierce resistance which often ensued, and above all, to pre-empt local and European enemies.

In a relatively short time by world-historical standards, the penumbra of British rule retreated. The cost to the metropolis had become too great and the attendant panoply of governors, district officers and imperial assemblies was gradually considered a moral and economic anachronism. By the 1960s the advanced economies had fashioned other ways of perpetuating their domination over the poorer and divided societies. It was also a time when the privileged native élites which had inherited the colonies were able to dominate their people by using subtler methods than those of their forefathers, who had collaborated directly with the white 'bwanas' and 'sahibs'. The new governments often maintained informal links with former colonial powers to ease the passage of financial and military aid, and were also able to exploit the rallying calls of religion, nationalism and ethnicity when the occasion arose. In some ways, nationalism is simply empire-building carried on by other hands.

What remains from the supernova of the 'expansion of England' is a myriad of scattered institutions, mythologies and struggles set in a transformed landscape. Ethnic conflicts in Sri Lanka, Fiji or New Zealand will wax and wane; the English language will continue to spread around the world, though changing its forms and accents; British governmental and parliamentary traditions will continue to be bent and buckled under the stresses of local political conflict. Most of all, the changes in a country's resources, pioneered in the days of the British Empire, will persist far into the future. The transformation of the ecology of the Antipodes, the forestation programmes or the intricate irrigation works in northern India and the patterns of urban settlement in North America are all among the many legacies of the imperial age. For better or for worse, they will persist for centuries to come.

PICTURE CREDITS

Abbreviations
t = top, tl = top left, tr = top right, c = centre,
b = bottom, etc.

For the pictures on pages 25t, 226b Associated Press Ltd;
114, 117t, 160b, 161 Australian High Commission
Photographic Library, London; 3, 19tr, 21, 22,
118–119, 247t The Bridgeman Art Library, London; 12b
British Airways/RAF Museum, Hendon; 20t, 33, 50b,
67, 103tr British Library, London; 214–215 Camera
Press Ltd, London; 156b Canada House, London; 196
Colorific; 193 Curtis Brown Ltd on behalf of the
Broadwater Collection; 147b De Beers Consolidated
Mines; 49 English Heritage, The Iveagh Bequest,
Kenwood; 27b, 28b, 31t, 32, 37b, 42, 48b, 51, 54b, 55t,
56, 57, 60b, 61, 65t, 73, 94, 95, 98br, 99, 101, 108b,
109, 122, 125, 149, 155tl, 155tr, 172, 173b, 165 E.T.
Archive; 25b, 27t, 29, 45, 79br, 83t, 105 Fotomas Index,
London; 168, 237tl, 237tr, 240, 252t, 242b, 243, 248
Frank Spooner Pictures; 156t Glenbow Archives,
Calgary, Canada (NA-504-3); 186 The Hugh Lane
Municipal Gallery of Modern Art, Dublin; 20b, 31b, 60t,

104t, 134bl, 147t, 151, 182, 187b, 192t, 194t, 200, 202,
203, 211tr, 213tl, 213tr, 213bl, 230, 232 Hulton
Deutsch; 50t, 74b, 82, 83b, 90, 93, 104b, 117b, 133b,
135tr, 141tl, 145b Ikon; 173t Ikon/The National Trust,
Trevelyan Collection; 176–177, 180, 181, 183, 199b,
211tl, 212 Imperial War Museum, London; 98bl
Inchcape Group PLC/Godfrey New Photographics; 124
Institute of Mechanical Engineers; 123 Liverino, Naples;
198c, 218br, 235t, 247b London Express News and
Features Services; 14–15, 36, 37t, 39, 59b, 68–69, 79bl,
80, 89tr, 89tr, 89b, 100tl, 100tr, 107, 111bl, 115, 116,
160t, 163, 166, 167b, 169 Macdonald/Aldus Archives;
236 Magnum, London; 54t, 55b, 74t, 97, 108t, 128,
134br, 138, 139t, 139b, 140, 141tr, 187t, 199t Mansell
Collection, London; 43t, 53, 65b, 66t, 84b, 87, 133tl,
133tr, 137, 145t, 155b, 174 Mary Evans Picture Library;
28 National Gallery of Ireland, Dublin; 162t National
Gallery of Victoria, Melbourne; 43b National Maritime
Museum, London; 12tl, 12tc, 12tr, 18, 19tl, 25t, 26b, 44,
48t, 64, 75, 84t, 91, 103tl, 111br, 127 National Portrait
Gallery, London; 66b, 130, 210 Picturepoint 135tl, 185,
192b, 195tl, 195tr, 197, 198t, 198b, 218bl, 220, 221,

223, 224t, 224b, 225b, 227, 231, 235b, 249 Popperfoto,
London; 110 Reproduced by Gracious Permission of Her
Majesty The Queen; 150, 233 Royal Commonwealth
Institute, London; 23 Staatliche Museen Preussicher
Kulturbesitz, Berlin; 129 The Tate Gallery, London; 157
University of Washington Libraries, Seattle; 19b, 59t
Wellcome Institute for the History of Medicine, The
Library; 241 West India Committee, London.

The editors are grateful to Hamish Hamilton Ltd. for
permission to quote from *Diaries of a Cabinet Minister,
Vol. II* by Richard Crossman.
© By the estate of R.H.S. Crossman 1976